Disney

DONALD DUCK & UNCLE $CROOGE

World of the Dragonlords

by Byron Erickson and Giorgio Cavazzano

Publisher | **GARY GROTH**
Editor | **DAVID GERSTEIN**
Design | **KEELI McCARTHY**
Production | **PAUL BARESH**
Associate Publisher| **ERIC REYNOLDS**

Fantagraphics Books, Inc. | 7563 Lake City Way NE | Seattle WA 98115 | (800) 657-1100

Visit us at *fantagraphics.com*. Follow us on Twitter at @fantagraphics
and on Facebook at facebook.com/fantagraphics

Cover art by Giorgio Cavazzano, color by Hachette
Title page art by Giorgio Cavazzano, color by Sanoma

First printing: November 2021 | ISBN 978-168396-483-4
Printed in China | Library of Congress Control Number: 2021937430

Special thanks to Maya Åstrup, Giorgio Cavazzano, John Clark, Byron Erickson,
Kevin Pearl, and Sabina Scarpa

**The stories in this volume were originally created in English in Denmark,
and were first published in Germany in the following magazines:**

"A Door Opens... And Closes!" in *Die tollsten Geschichten von Donald Duck Sonderheft* #189, February 11, 2003 (D/D 99001)

"Slaves of the Morg" in *Die tollsten Geschichten von Donald Duck Sonderheft* #190, March 11, 2003 (D/D 99002)

"Jute" in *Die tollsten Geschichten von Donald Duck Sonderheft* #191, April 8, 2003 (D/D 99003).

"Three for Three" in *Die tollsten Geschichten von Donald Duck Sonderheft* #192, May 13, 2003 (D/D 99004)

"Escape from the Morg" in *Die tollsten Geschichten von Donald Duck Sonderheft* #193, June 10, 2003 (D/D 2000-001)

"Mama" in *Die tollsten Geschichten von Donald Duck Sonderheft* #194, July 8, 2003 (D/D 2000-002)

"Freedom Marsh" in *Die tollsten Geschichten von Donald Duck Sonderheft* #195, August 12, 2003 (D/D 2000-003)

"Brendon" in *Die tollsten Geschichten von Donald Duck Sonderheft* #196, September 9, 2003 (D/D 2000-004)

"Toom Raiders" in *Die tollsten Geschichten von Donald Duck Sonderheft* #197, October 7, 2003 (D/D 2000-005)

"Family Matters" in *Die tollsten Geschichten von Donald Duck Sonderheft* #198, November 11, 2003 (D/D 2000-006)

"Sniffles" in *Die tollsten Geschichten von Donald Duck Sonderheft* #199, December 9, 2003 (D/D 2000-007)

"Home" in *Die tollsten Geschichten von Donald Duck Sonderheft* #200, January 13, 2004 (D/D 2000-008).

ALSO AVAILABLE
Donald Duck: The Forgetful Hero (Giorgio Cavazzano) (*Disney Masters* Vol. 12)
Uncle Scrooge: Pie in the Sky (William Van Horn) (*Disney Masters* Vol. 18)
The Complete Life and Times of Scrooge McDuck Deluxe Edition (Don Rosa)
Walt Disney's Donald Duck: Balloonatics (Carl Barks)
Walt Disney's Uncle Scrooge: Island in the Sky (Carl Barks)

FROM OUR NON-DISNEY CATALOG
Nuft and the Last Dragons: The Great Technowhiz (Freddy Milton)

Contents

All story chapters written by Byron Erickson, drawn by Giorgio Cavazzano, inked by Sandro Zemolin, and lettered by Jon Babcock. Other credits as noted below. Character portraits on this page: art by Marco Rota, color by Disney Italia.

Foreword by Byron Erickson 4

Illustration 6
Art by Marco Rota, Color by Disney Italia

Chapter 1: "A Door Opens... and Closes!" . . . 7
Color by Scott Rockwell

Chapter 2: "Slaves of the Morg" 23
Color by Susan Daigle-Leach

Illustrations 35
Art by Marco Rota, Color by Disney Italia

Chapter 3: "Jute" 37
Color by Marie Javins

Chapter 4: "Three for Three" 49
Color by Marie Javins

Illustrations 65
Art by Marco Rota, Color by Disney Italia

Chapter 5: "Escape From the Morg" 67
Color by Scott Rockwell

Chapter 6: "Mama" 83
Color by Barry Anglin Grossman

Sketches 95
Art by Giorgio Cavazzano

Chapter 7: "Freedom Marsh" 97
Color by Marie Javins

Chapter 8: "Brendon" 109
Color by Marie Javins

Sketches 125
Art by Giorgio Cavazzano

Chapter 9: "Toom Raiders" 127
Color by Susan Daigle-Leach

Chapter 10: "Family Matters" 139
Color by Susan Daigle-Leach

Sketches 151
Art by Giorgio Cavazzano

Chapter 11: "Sniffles" 153
Color by Scott Rockwell

Chapter 12: "Home" 169
Color by Scott Rockwell

Sketches 181
Art by Giorgio Cavazzano

Byron Erickson 183
John Clark and David Gerstein

Giorgio Cavazzano 184
Francesco Stajano

A Three-Year Dragon Quest 185
Interview with Giorgio Cavazzano by Luca Boschi

The stories and illustrations in this volume have been reprinted in their entirety as first created in 1999-2011.

BYRON ERICKSON

Foreword

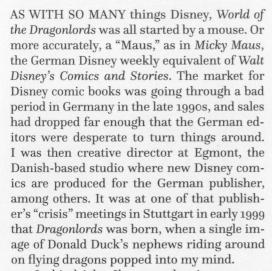

AS WITH SO MANY things Disney, *World of the Dragonlords* was all started by a mouse. Or more accurately, a "Maus," as in *Micky Maus*, the German Disney weekly equivalent of *Walt Disney's Comics and Stories*. The market for Disney comic books was going through a bad period in Germany in the late 1990s, and sales had dropped far enough that the German editors were desperate to turn things around. I was then creative director at Egmont, the Danish-based studio where new Disney comics are produced for the German publisher, among others. It was at one of that publisher's "crisis" meetings in Stuttgart in early 1999 that *Dragonlords* was born, when a single image of Donald Duck's nephews riding around on flying dragons popped into my mind.

In hindsight, I'm sure that image came to mind as a result of what the Germans were willing to try—a long story told in serial form (they wanted something that would hook the readers into coming back issue after issue). They asked that it feature Huey, Dewey, and Louie in a major role (their market research indicated that their readers identified most with the nephews), and that it be a fantasy adventure, which would attract more interest than a mundane treasure hunt. And oh, yeah—it would be nice if I could get a "star" artist to draw it.

The details came later. Working off that single inspirational image, I spent the next couple of months outlining a plot, characters, and a fantasy world complex enough to justify all the pages I'd been handed, but also a story *visual* enough to tell in comics form. I also worked hard to make sure that I still had a *Disney* story, one that was grounded in Duckburg and the Ducks' personalities, one that moved and was motivated by who they are and how they relate to one another.

At some point in the plotting process, I realized that what I had here was a story about the Duck *family*: thrown into and separated by a war in a fantasy world, but always struggling to come together again. This family theme is mirrored by other characters—most specifically the baby dragons and their mother—and maybe something is learned about families along the way, or maybe it's something we all already know but sometimes forget to remember. What that is I'll leave to the readers to figure out for themselves.

I still needed a "star artist" to draw the story, and I always had only one man in mind for *Dragonlords*—Giorgio Cavazzano, star artist among star artists and Italian Disney artist supreme. Giorgio and I had collaborated before in 1997 on "Secret of the Incas" (*Uncle Scrooge Adventures* 53-54), a long story we did to celebrate Uncle Scrooge's 50th anniversary. Since Giorgio generally works as a freelance artist for Disney Italy, all contact between us was filtered through them. Although ultimately successful, the experience was frustrating for both of us because we couldn't communicate directly.

This frustration was finally addressed in June 1999 when I traveled to Cavazzano's home in Merano, Italy (near Venice) to pitch the *Dragonlords* plot to him. During the course of my pitch, Giorgio added a number of improvements and enhancements to the story, and a lot of good gag ideas, and the visit ended with him agreeing to draw the entire series with the proviso that we worked directly, a condition I was only too willing to accept. It should be mentioned here that because I don't speak Italian, "directly" meant using the translation skills of Teresa Zemolin, the wife of Alessandro Zemolin, Cavazzano's longtime inker. I'll be forever grateful for her help and assistance (and guilty that she had to translate so many pages of my long-winded manuscripts).

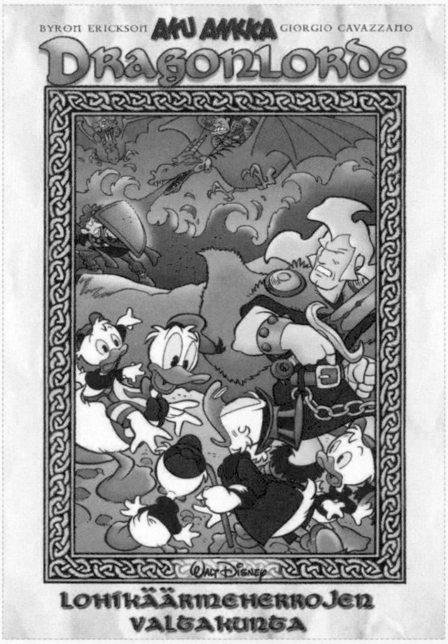
BYRON ERICKSON
AKU ANKKA
GIORGIO CAVAZZANO
Dragonlords
LOHIKÄÄRMEHERROJEN
VALTAKUNTA

Shortly after our meeting, Giorgio drew up a series of character sketches that completely influenced the course of the series. They were so "spot on" that every time I needed help getting back into a character's personality, I had only to look at those sketches to remember whom I was writing about. And as the chapters rolled along, I only had to look at Giorgio's marvelous finished artwork to inspire me anew to do a third or even a fourth rewrite; I was determined that my scripts would be worthy of his talents. As you can tell, I'm certainly happy with what Giorgio drew—his artwork is so much more than lively, stunning, and emotional, but it would take ten more pages to describe how and why. Your time would be better spent just looking at the pictures.

Dragonlords took a little over two years to write and draw, and by the time it was finished, the situation in Germany had changed. Sales were back up (the comics business has always been cyclical), editors had changed, and the people in charge were no longer willing to publish such a "radical" series in *Micky Maus*. To be fair, no publisher in the Nordic countries was willing, either (12 chapters and 164 pages seemed to be the deal-killer here). The story languished in a file drawer until 2003, when the Germans finally began to serialize *Dragonlords* in *Donald Duck Sonderheft*, a monthly comic aimed at fans and collectors. Shortly thereafter, Italy followed suit with publication in *Zio Paperone*, again a monthly aimed at older fans.

Ah, but then those wonderful people at Sanoma—the Disney publisher in Finland—collected all 12 chapters into a book, complete with a brand-new cover by Giorgio Cavazzano drawn especially for the Finnish edition. And they even put my name on the cover! Seriously, this edition was a dream come true. Despite the fact that I consciously wrote a story I knew would be serialized, I'd hoped even from the beginning that someday it would be published complete in one book. "If only," I thought, "I could convince Sanoma to publish an English edition just for me..."

Of course, several years later in 2005, the American publisher Gemstone—and its excellent editor John Clark—did exactly that. But the resulting book, while very nice, had a low press run and didn't make it into many hands. Flash forward to today: Fantagraphics is here with a brand new mass-market edition. And they've topped off the adventure with a Cavazzano interview and Italian cover drawings—by another comics legend, Marco Rota—that are making their *first* American appearance in this book.

So thanks to David Gerstein, Gary Groth, Keeli McCarthy, and everyone else at Fantagraphics—and John Clark—for their faith in the story; and especially thanks to you, the discerning American readers, for daring to dive into our tale of Ducks and dragons!

OPPOSITE: In 2011, artist Marco Gervasio created this image of the nephews riding their dragons for the first Italian collected edition of *World of the Dragonlords*. Color by Stefano Intini.

ABOVE: This 2004 Finnish *Dragonlords* anthology, featuring Giorgio Cavazzano's original version of our cover illustration, was the first collected edition in the world.

Cover drawing for Italian *Zio Paperone* 165 (2003), illustrating "A Door Opens... and Closes!"
Art by Marco Rota, color by Disney Italia.

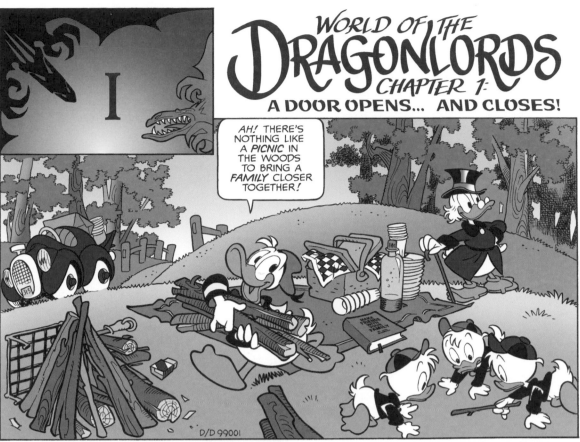

WORLD OF THE DRAGONLORDS
CHAPTER 1:
A DOOR OPENS... AND CLOSES!

AH! THERE'S NOTHING LIKE A *PICNIC* IN THE WOODS TO BRING A *FAMILY* CLOSER TOGETHER!

D/D 99001

OR AS DOC SCHMOCK SO *WISELY* WRITES, "THE FAMILY THAT *PICNICS* TOGETHER, *BONDS* TOGETHER!"

GOSH, I CAN'T WAIT UNTIL THE *HIGHLIGHT* OF THE GOOD DOCTOR'S TOGETHERNESS PICNIC PROGRAM— THE *"BONDING BONFIRE"!*

MAKE FRIENDS WITH YOUR FAMILY BY DOC SCHMOCK

WE'LL ALL HOLD HANDS WHILE WE *DANCE* AROUND THE BONFIRE AND SING THE *"BONDING SONG"!* THE BOYS WILL *LOVE* IT!

OKAY, WE'RE AGREED! WE'LL MAKE OUR *BREAK* AS SOON AS UNCA DONALD IS BUSY LIGHTING THAT *STUPID* BONFIRE!

WE'LL *SCATTER,* MEET UP AT THE TRUCK STOP ON ROUTE 101, AND *HITCH A RIDE* BACK TO *DUCKBURG!*

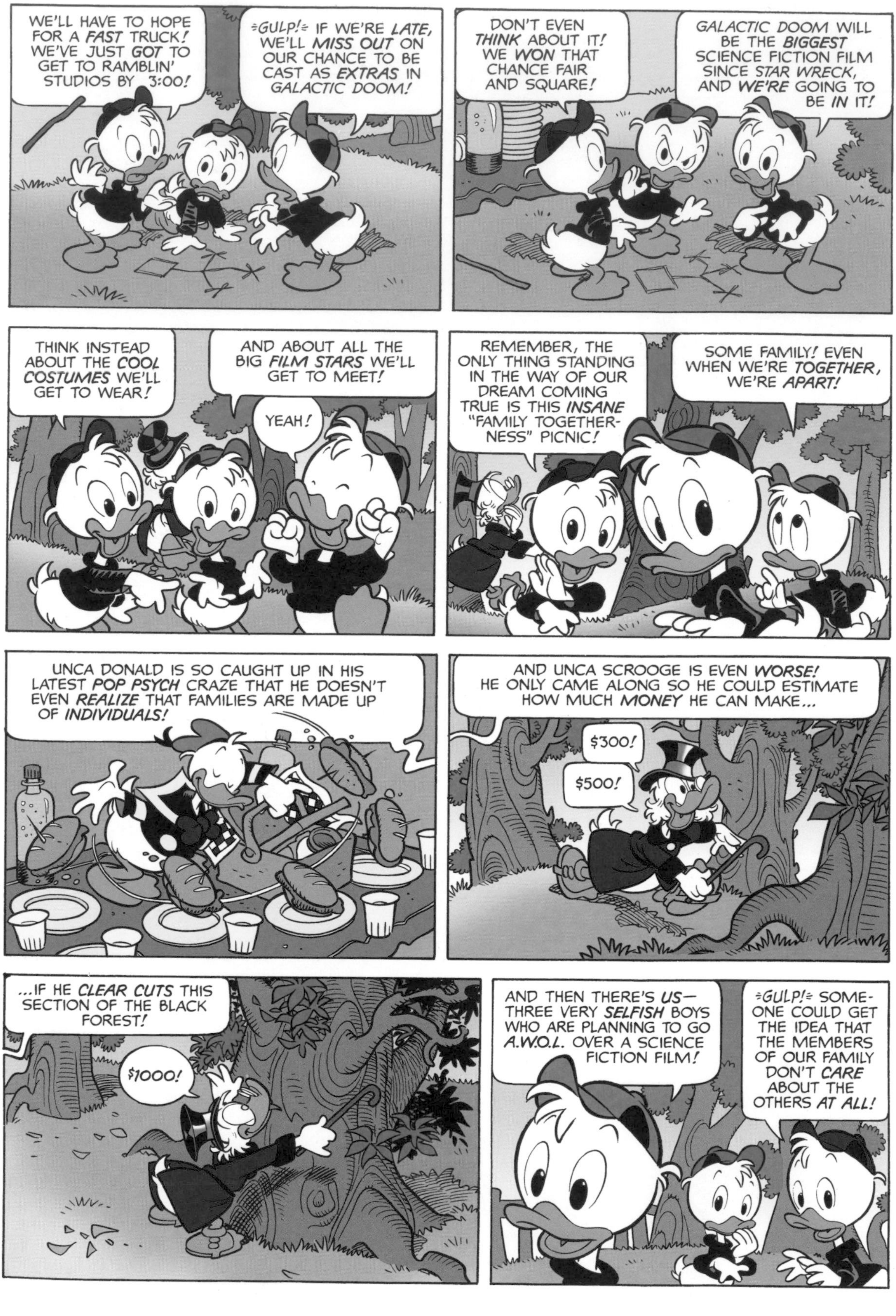
WE'LL HAVE TO HOPE FOR A *FAST* TRUCK! WE'VE JUST *GOT* TO GET TO RAMBLIN' STUDIOS BY 3:00!
=GULP!= IF WE'RE *LATE*, WE'LL *MISS OUT* ON OUR CHANCE TO BE CAST AS *EXTRAS* IN *GALACTIC DOOM!*
DON'T EVEN *THINK* ABOUT IT! WE *WON* THAT CHANCE FAIR AND SQUARE!
GALACTIC DOOM WILL BE THE *BIGGEST* SCIENCE FICTION FILM SINCE *STAR WRECK*, AND *WE'RE* GOING TO BE *IN* IT!
THINK INSTEAD ABOUT THE *COOL COSTUMES* WE'LL GET TO WEAR!
AND ABOUT ALL THE BIG *FILM STARS* WE'LL GET TO MEET!
YEAH!
REMEMBER, THE ONLY THING STANDING IN THE WAY OF OUR DREAM COMING TRUE IS THIS *INSANE* "FAMILY TOGETHER-NESS" PICNIC!
SOME FAMILY! EVEN WHEN WE'RE *TOGETHER*, WE'RE *APART!*
UNCA DONALD IS SO CAUGHT UP IN HIS LATEST *POP PSYCH* CRAZE THAT HE DOESN'T EVEN *REALIZE* THAT FAMILIES ARE MADE UP OF *INDIVIDUALS!*
AND UNCA SCROOGE IS EVEN *WORSE!* HE ONLY CAME ALONG SO HE COULD ESTIMATE HOW MUCH *MONEY* HE CAN MAKE...
$300!
$500!
...IF HE *CLEAR CUTS* THIS SECTION OF THE BLACK FOREST!
$1000!
AND THEN THERE'S *US*— THREE VERY *SELFISH* BOYS WHO ARE PLANNING TO GO *A.W.O.L.* OVER A SCIENCE FICTION FILM!
=GULP!= SOME-ONE COULD GET THE IDEA THAT THE MEMBERS OF OUR FAMILY DON'T *CARE* ABOUT THE OTHERS *AT ALL!*

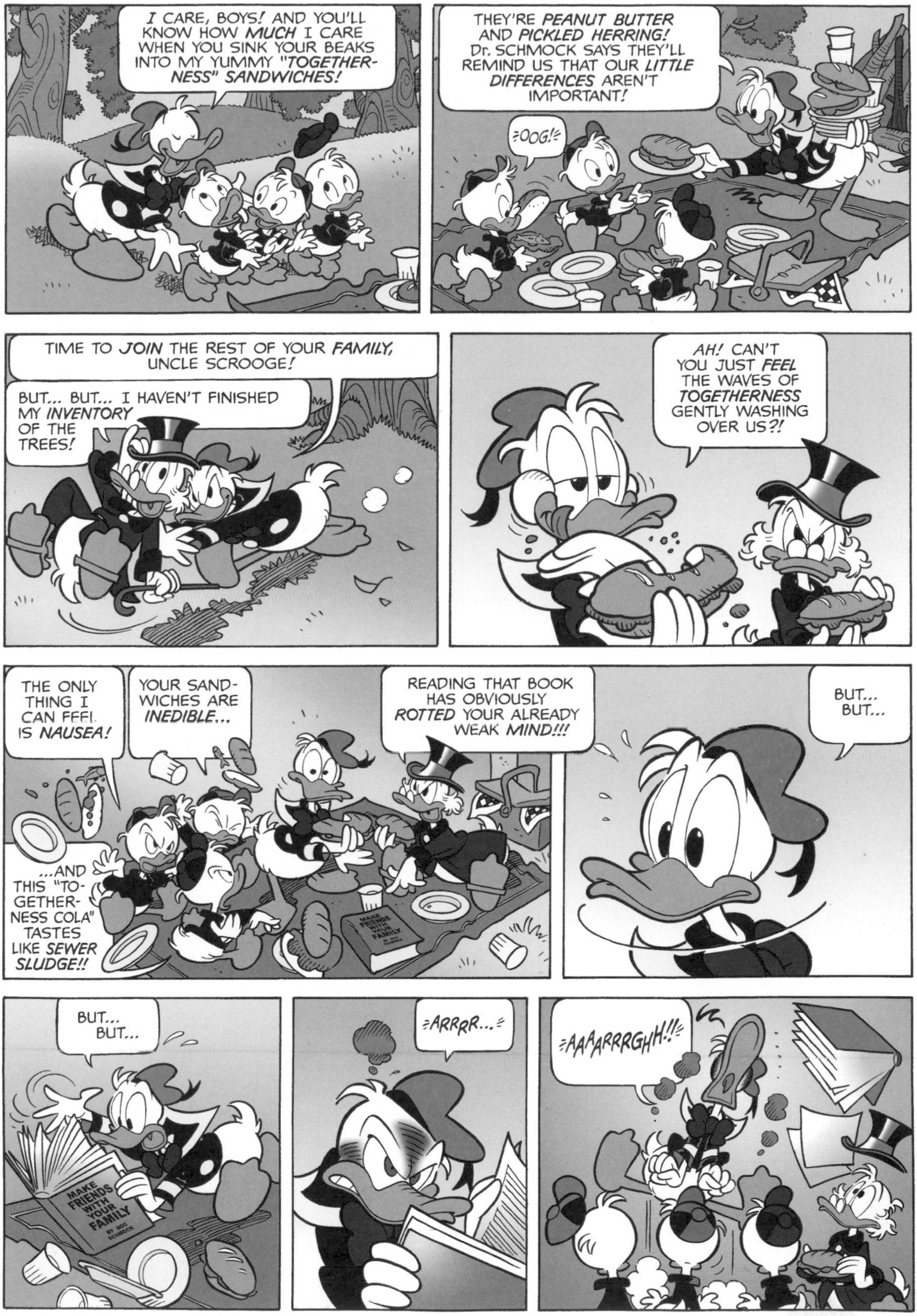
I CARE, BOYS! AND YOU'LL KNOW HOW MUCH I CARE WHEN YOU SINK YOUR BEAKS INTO MY YUMMY "TOGETHERNESS" SANDWICHES!
THEY'RE PEANUT BUTTER AND PICKLED HERRING! Dr. SCHMOCK SAYS THEY'LL REMIND US THAT OUR LITTLE DIFFERENCES AREN'T IMPORTANT!
OOG!
TIME TO JOIN THE REST OF YOUR FAMILY, UNCLE SCROOGE!
BUT... BUT... I HAVEN'T FINISHED MY INVENTORY OF THE TREES!
AH! CAN'T YOU JUST FEEL THE WAVES OF TOGETHERNESS GENTLY WASHING OVER US?!
THE ONLY THING I CAN FEEL IS NAUSEA!
YOUR SANDWICHES ARE INEDIBLE...
...AND THIS "TOGETHERNESS COLA" TASTES LIKE SEWER SLUDGE!!
READING THAT BOOK HAS OBVIOUSLY ROTTED YOUR ALREADY WEAK MIND!!!
MAKE FRIENDS WITH YOUR FAMILY
BUT... BUT...
BUT... BUT...
MAKE FRIENDS WITH YOUR FAMILY
BY DOC SCHMOCK
ARRRR...
AAAARRRGHH!!

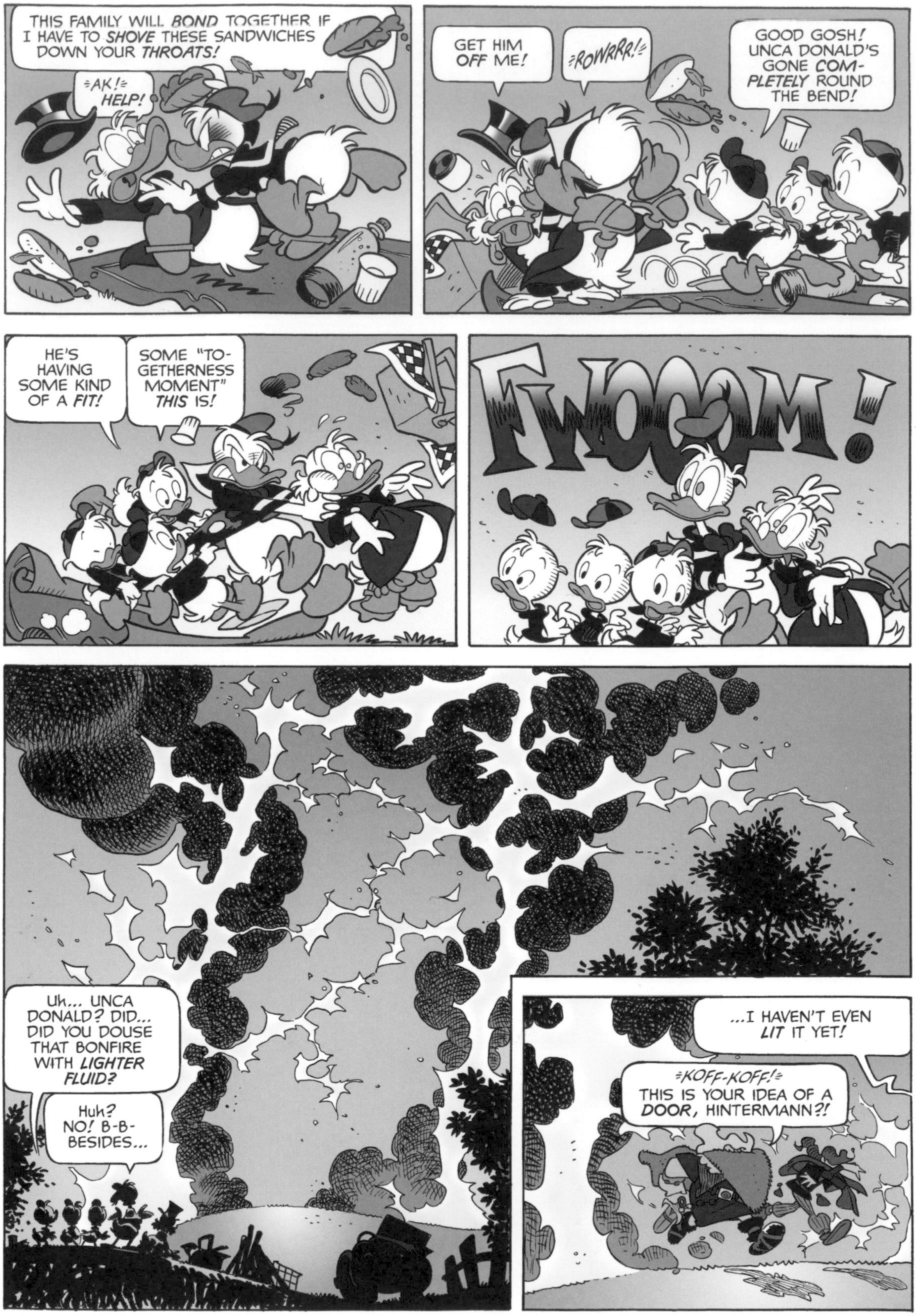
THIS FAMILY WILL BOND TOGETHER IF I HAVE TO SHOVE THESE SANDWICHES DOWN YOUR THROATS!
AK! HELP!
GET HIM OFF ME!
ROWRRR!
GOOD GOSH! UNCA DONALD'S GONE COM-PLETELY ROUND THE BEND!
HE'S HAVING SOME KIND OF A FIT!
SOME "TO-GETHERNESS MOMENT" THIS IS!
FWOOOM!
Uh... UNCA DONALD? DID... DID YOU DOUSE THAT BONFIRE WITH LIGHTER FLUID?
Huh? NO! B-B-BESIDES...
...I HAVEN'T EVEN LIT IT YET!
KOFF-KOFF! THIS IS YOUR IDEA OF A DOOR, HINTERMANN?!

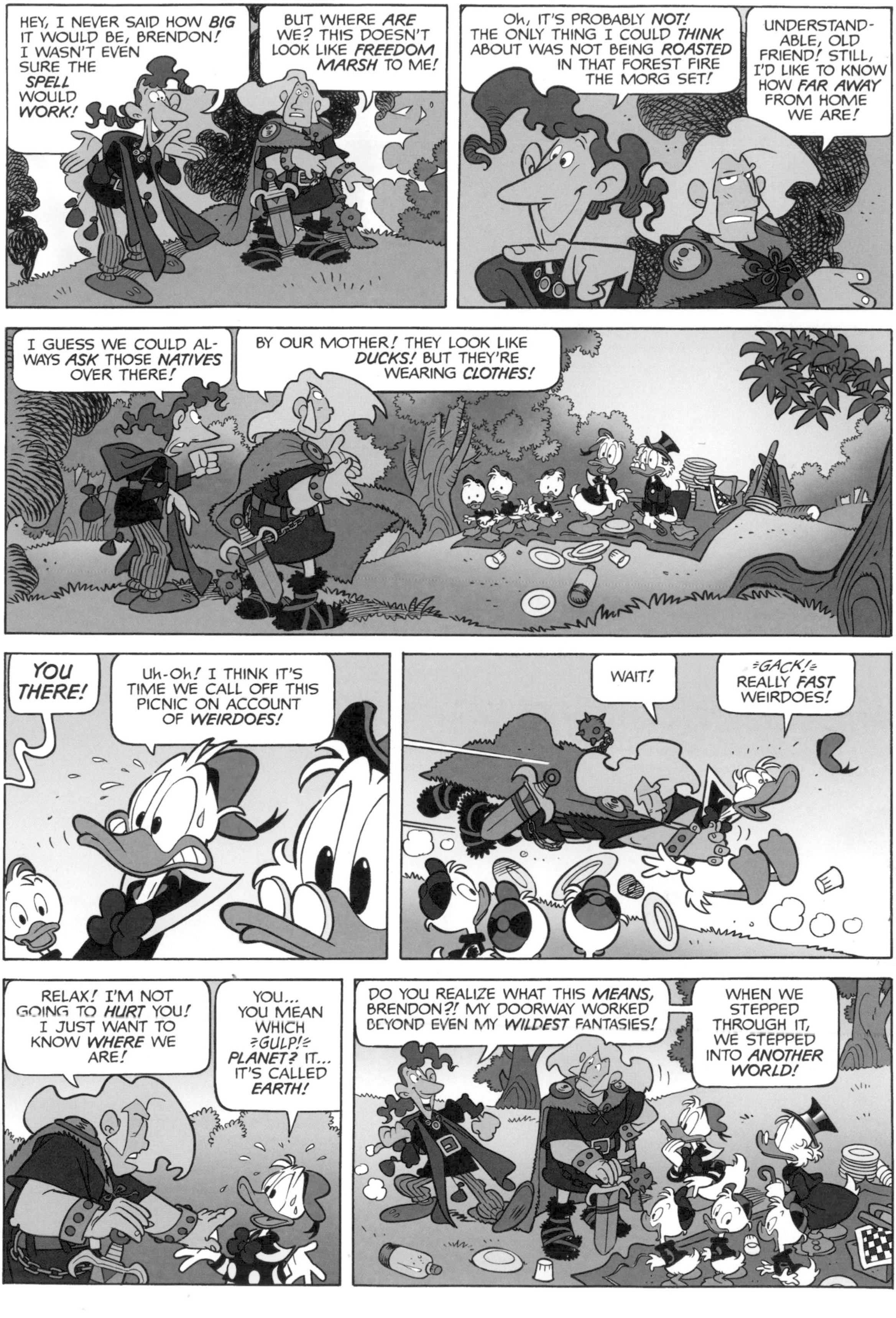
HEY, I NEVER SAID HOW BIG IT WOULD BE, BRENDON! I WASN'T EVEN SURE THE SPELL WOULD WORK!
BUT WHERE ARE WE? THIS DOESN'T LOOK LIKE FREEDOM MARSH TO ME!
Oh, IT'S PROBABLY NOT! THE ONLY THING I COULD THINK ABOUT WAS NOT BEING ROASTED IN THAT FOREST FIRE THE MORG SET!
UNDERSTAND-ABLE, OLD FRIEND! STILL, I'D LIKE TO KNOW HOW FAR AWAY FROM HOME WE ARE!
I GUESS WE COULD AL-WAYS ASK THOSE NATIVES OVER THERE!
BY OUR MOTHER! THEY LOOK LIKE DUCKS! BUT THEY'RE WEARING CLOTHES!
YOU THERE!
Uh-Oh! I THINK IT'S TIME WE CALL OFF THIS PICNIC ON ACCOUNT OF WEIRDOES!
WAIT!
GACK! REALLY FAST WEIRDOES!
RELAX! I'M NOT GOING TO HURT YOU! I JUST WANT TO KNOW WHERE WE ARE!
YOU... YOU MEAN WHICH GULP! PLANET? IT... IT'S CALLED EARTH!
DO YOU REALIZE WHAT THIS MEANS, BRENDON?! MY DOORWAY WORKED BEYOND EVEN MY WILDEST FANTASIES!
WHEN WE STEPPED THROUGH IT, WE STEPPED INTO ANOTHER WORLD!

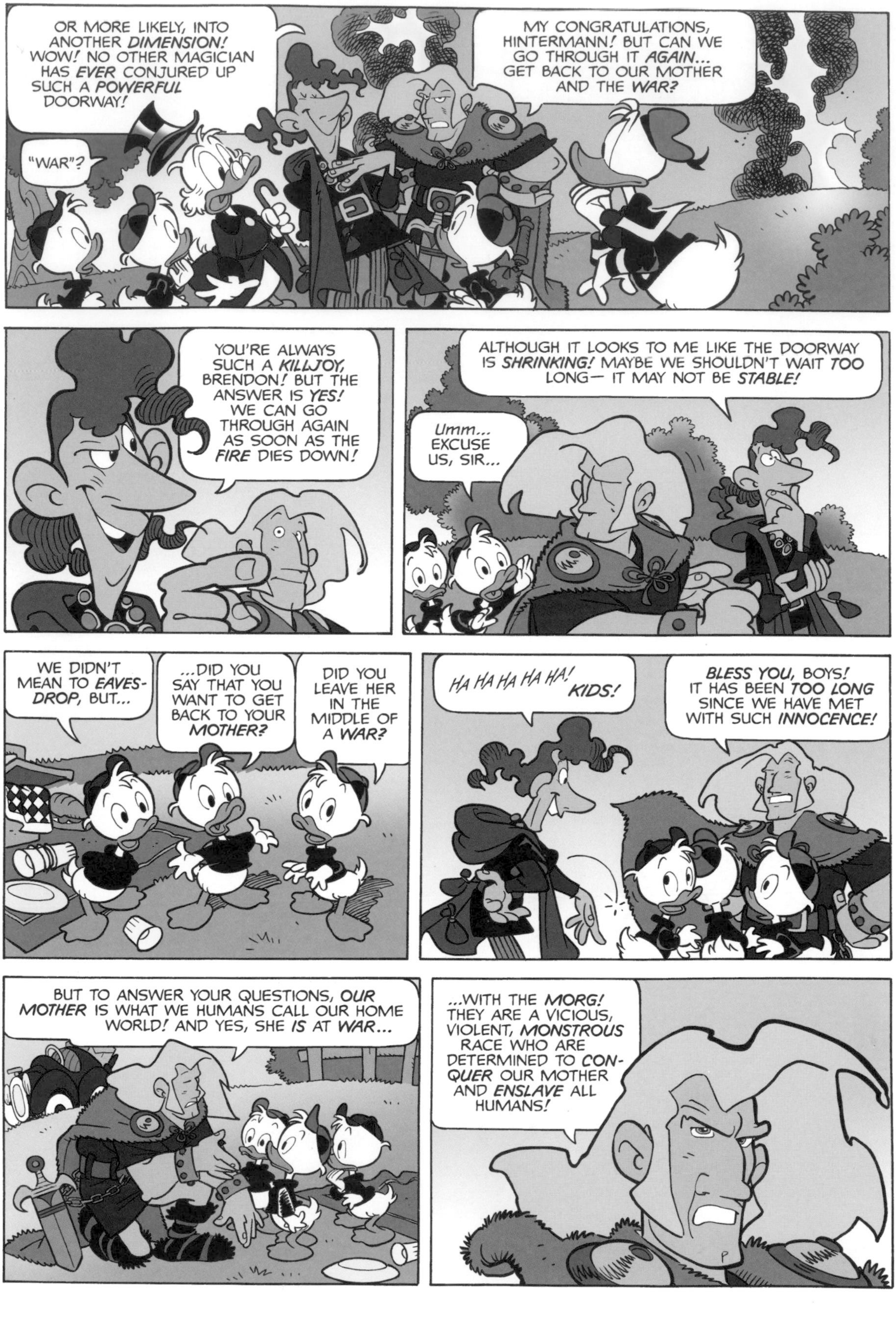
OR MORE LIKELY, INTO ANOTHER DIMENSION! WOW! NO OTHER MAGICIAN HAS EVER CONJURED UP SUCH A POWERFUL DOORWAY!
"WAR"?
MY CONGRATULATIONS, HINTERMANN! BUT CAN WE GO THROUGH IT AGAIN... GET BACK TO OUR MOTHER AND THE WAR?
YOU'RE ALWAYS SUCH A KILLJOY, BRENDON! BUT THE ANSWER IS YES! WE CAN GO THROUGH AGAIN AS SOON AS THE FIRE DIES DOWN!
ALTHOUGH IT LOOKS TO ME LIKE THE DOORWAY IS SHRINKING! MAYBE WE SHOULDN'T WAIT TOO LONG— IT MAY NOT BE STABLE!
Umm... EXCUSE US, SIR...
WE DIDN'T MEAN TO EAVES-DROP, BUT...
...DID YOU SAY THAT YOU WANT TO GET BACK TO YOUR MOTHER?
DID YOU LEAVE HER IN THE MIDDLE OF A WAR?
HA HA HA HA HA HA! KIDS!
BLESS YOU, BOYS! IT HAS BEEN TOO LONG SINCE WE HAVE MET WITH SUCH INNOCENCE!
BUT TO ANSWER YOUR QUESTIONS, OUR MOTHER IS WHAT WE HUMANS CALL OUR HOME WORLD! AND YES, SHE IS AT WAR...
...WITH THE MORG! THEY ARE A VICIOUS, VIOLENT, MONSTROUS RACE WHO ARE DETERMINED TO CON-QUER OUR MOTHER AND ENSLAVE ALL HUMANS!

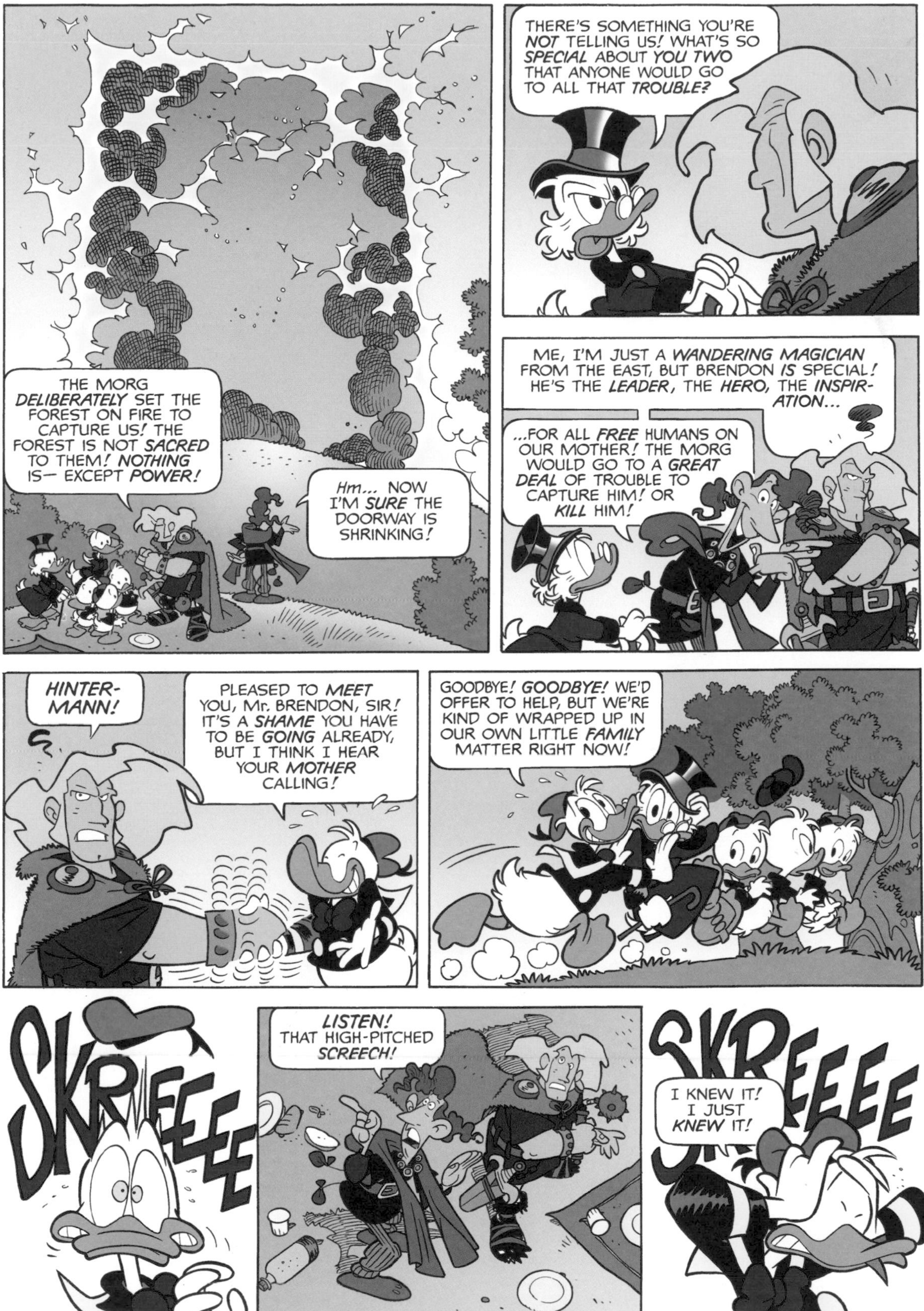
THE MORG DELIBERATELY SET THE FOREST ON FIRE TO CAPTURE US! THE FOREST IS NOT SACRED TO THEM! NOTHING IS— EXCEPT POWER!
Hm... NOW I'M SURE THE DOORWAY IS SHRINKING!
THERE'S SOMETHING YOU'RE NOT TELLING US! WHAT'S SO SPECIAL ABOUT YOU TWO THAT ANYONE WOULD GO TO ALL THAT TROUBLE?
ME, I'M JUST A WANDERING MAGICIAN FROM THE EAST, BUT BRENDON IS SPECIAL! HE'S THE LEADER, THE HERO, THE INSPIRATION...
...FOR ALL FREE HUMANS ON OUR MOTHER! THE MORG WOULD GO TO A GREAT DEAL OF TROUBLE TO CAPTURE HIM! OR KILL HIM!
HINTER-MANN!
PLEASED TO MEET YOU, Mr. BRENDON, SIR! IT'S A SHAME YOU HAVE TO BE GOING ALREADY, BUT I THINK I HEAR YOUR MOTHER CALLING!
GOODBYE! GOODBYE! WE'D OFFER TO HELP, BUT WE'RE KIND OF WRAPPED UP IN OUR OWN LITTLE FAMILY MATTER RIGHT NOW!
SKREEEEE
LISTEN! THAT HIGH-PITCHED SCREECH!
SKREEEEE
I KNEW IT! I JUST KNEW IT!

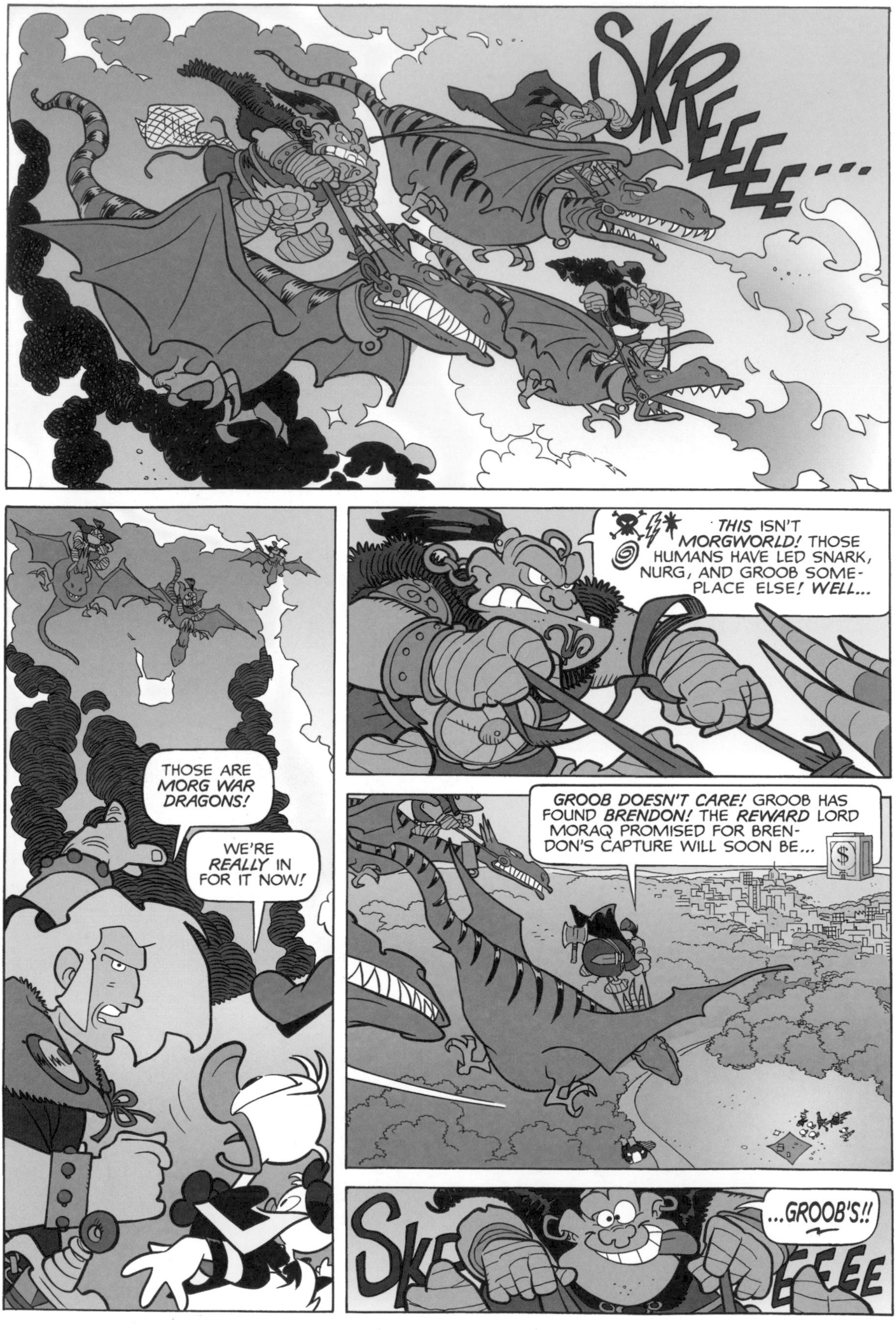
SKREEEEE...
THOSE ARE MORG WAR DRAGONS!
WE'RE REALLY IN FOR IT NOW!
THIS ISN'T MORGWORLD! THOSE HUMANS HAVE LED SNARK, NURG, AND GROOB SOME-PLACE ELSE! WELL...
GROOB DOESN'T CARE! GROOB HAS FOUND BRENDON! THE REWARD LORD MORAQ PROMISED FOR BREN-DON'S CAPTURE WILL SOON BE...
...GROOB'S!!
SKEEEEE

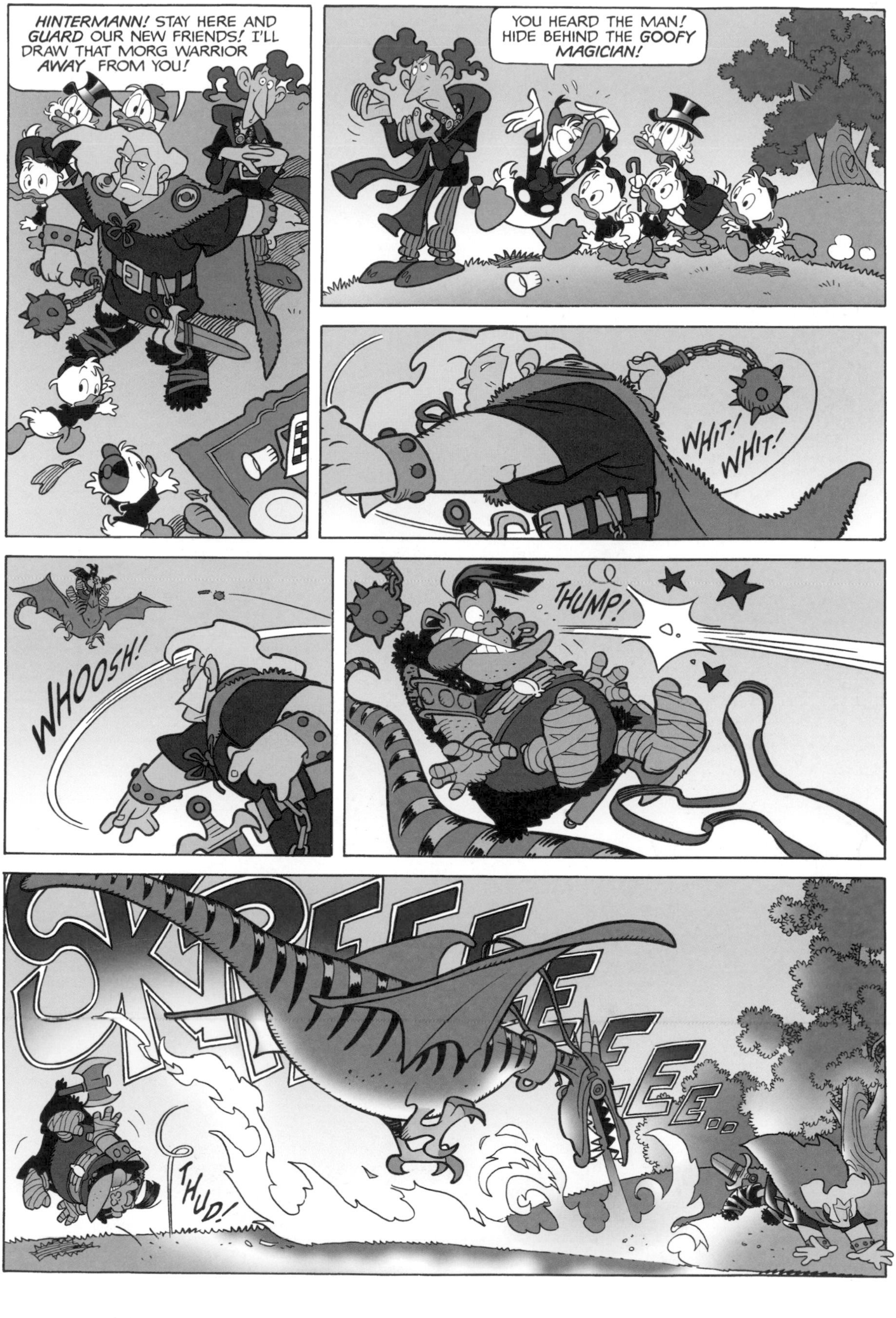
HINTERMANN! STAY HERE AND GUARD OUR NEW FRIENDS! I'LL DRAW THAT MORG WARRIOR AWAY FROM YOU!
YOU HEARD THE MAN! HIDE BEHIND THE GOOFY MAGICIAN!
WHIT! WHIT!
WHOOSH!
THUMP!
THUD!

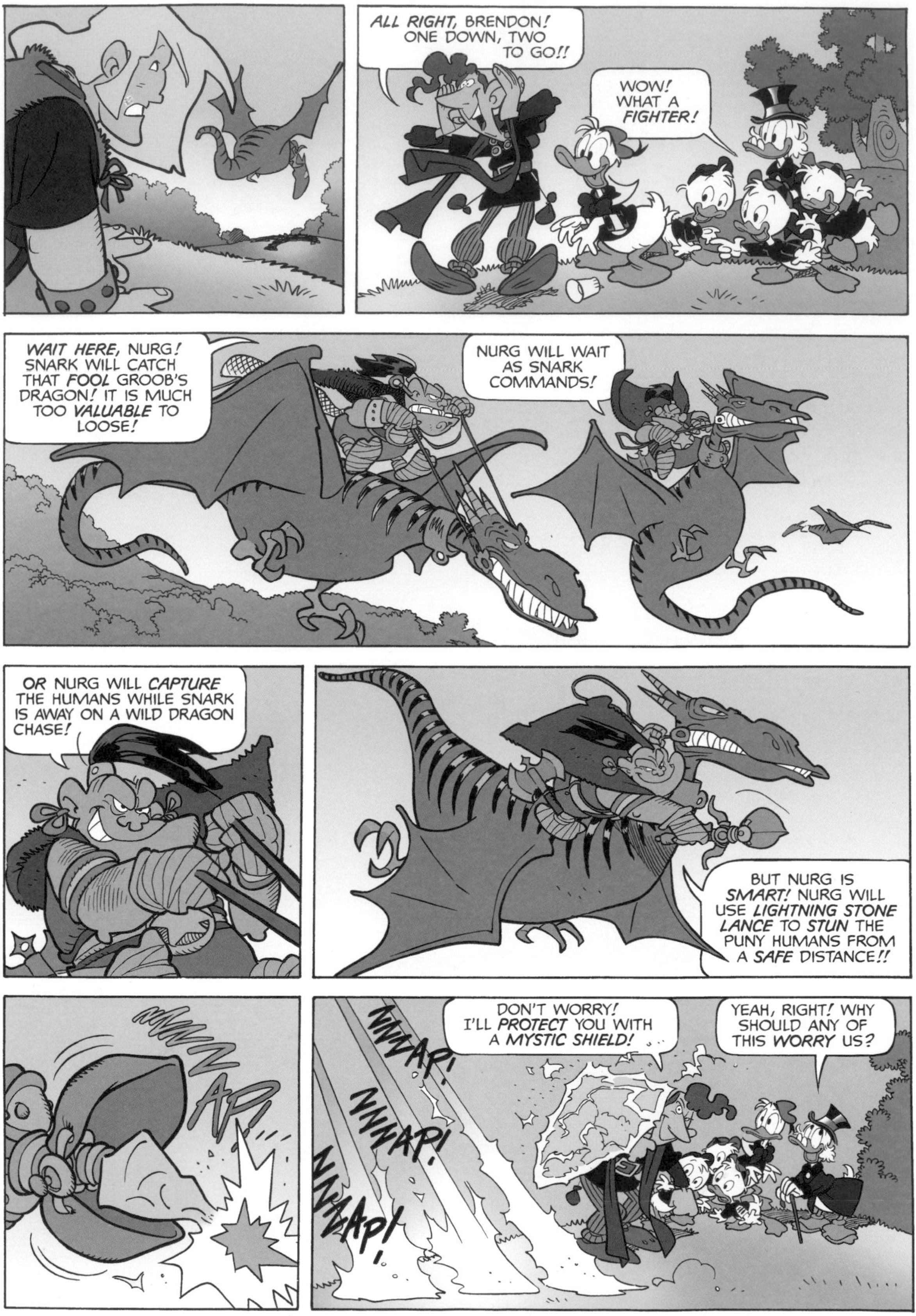
ALL RIGHT, BRENDON! ONE DOWN, TWO TO GO!!
WOW! WHAT A FIGHTER!
WAIT HERE, NURG! SNARK WILL CATCH THAT FOOL GROOB'S DRAGON! IT IS MUCH TOO VALUABLE TO LOOSE!
NURG WILL WAIT AS SNARK COMMANDS!
OR NURG WILL CAPTURE THE HUMANS WHILE SNARK IS AWAY ON A WILD DRAGON CHASE!
BUT NURG IS SMART! NURG WILL USE LIGHTNING STONE LANCE TO STUN THE PUNY HUMANS FROM A SAFE DISTANCE!!
NNNZAP!
NNNZAP!
NNNZAP!
NNNZAP!
DON'T WORRY! I'LL PROTECT YOU WITH A MYSTIC SHIELD!
YEAH, RIGHT! WHY SHOULD ANY OF THIS WORRY US?

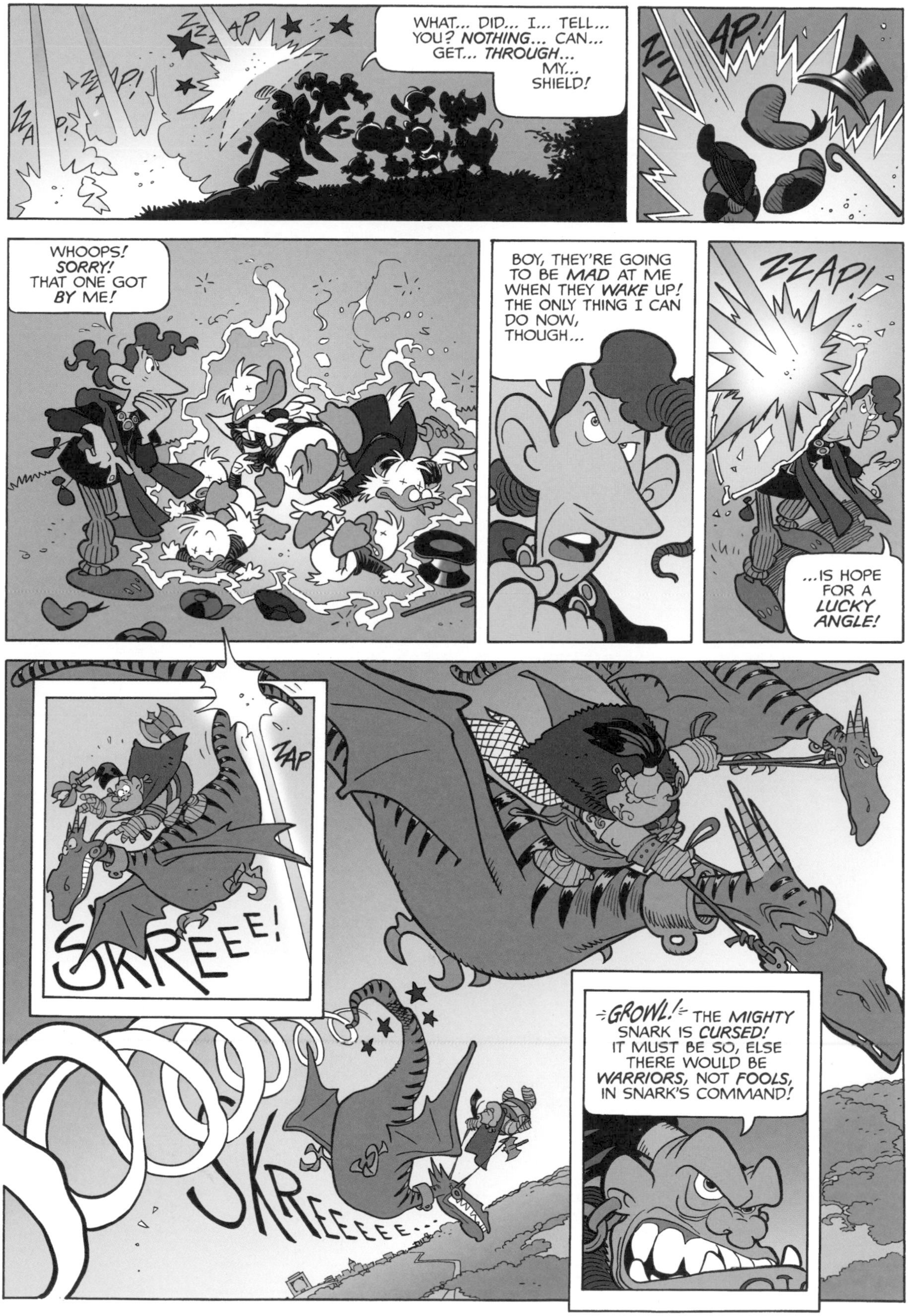
ZZZAP
ZZZAP!
ZAP!
WHAT... DID... I... TELL... YOU? NOTHING... CAN... GET... THROUGH... MY... SHIELD!
ZZAP!
WHOOPS! SORRY! THAT ONE GOT BY ME!
BOY, THEY'RE GOING TO BE MAD AT ME WHEN THEY WAKE UP! THE ONLY THING I CAN DO NOW, THOUGH...
ZZAP!
...IS HOPE FOR A LUCKY ANGLE!
ZAP
SKREEE!
SKREEEEE...
GROWL! THE MIGHTY SNARK IS CURSED! IT MUST BE SO, ELSE THERE WOULD BE WARRIORS, NOT FOOLS, IN SNARK'S COMMAND!

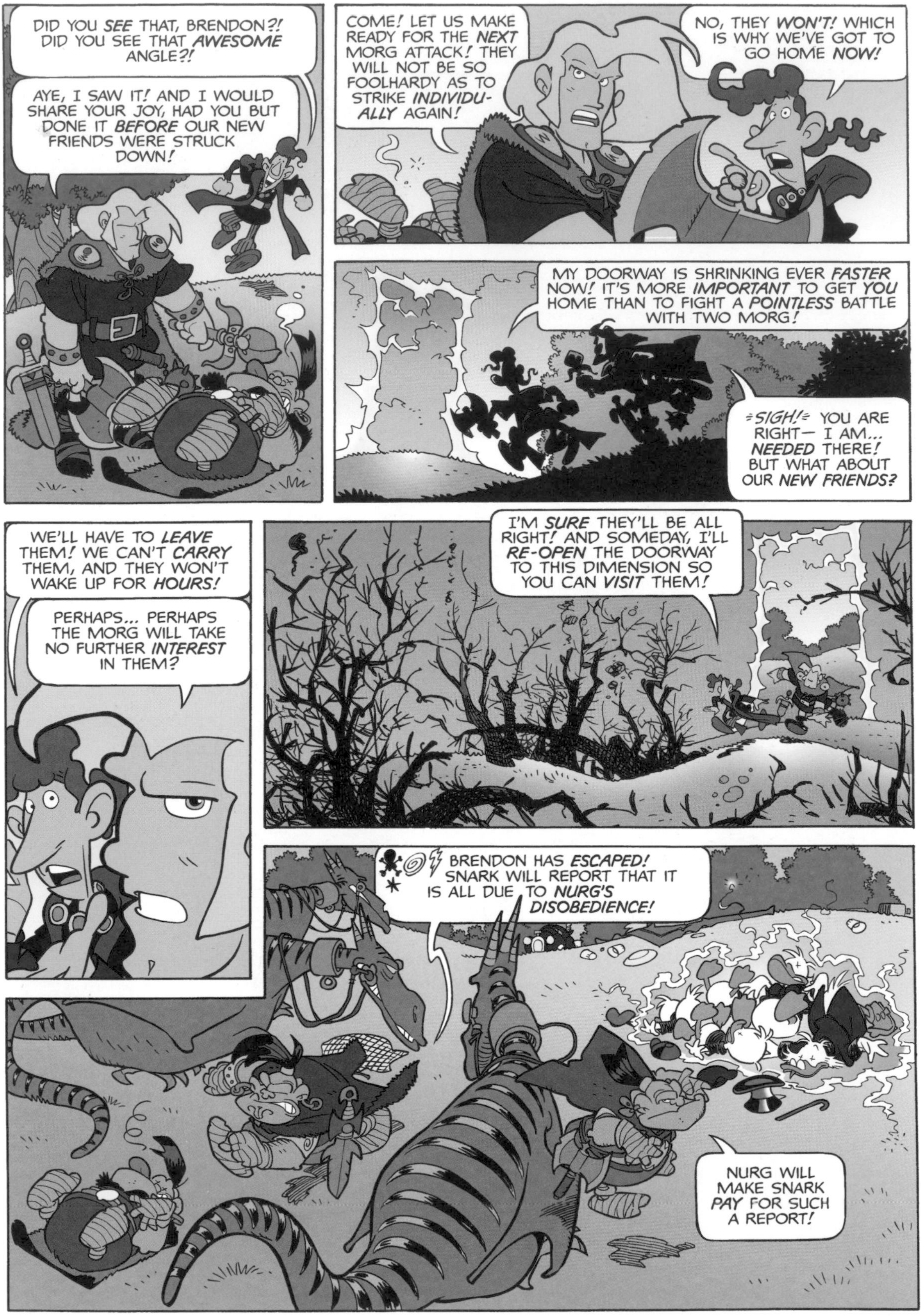
DID YOU SEE THAT, BRENDON?! DID YOU SEE THAT AWESOME ANGLE?!
AYE, I SAW IT! AND I WOULD SHARE YOUR JOY, HAD YOU BUT DONE IT BEFORE OUR NEW FRIENDS WERE STRUCK DOWN!
COME! LET US MAKE READY FOR THE NEXT MORG ATTACK! THEY WILL NOT BE SO FOOLHARDY AS TO STRIKE INDIVIDU-ALLY AGAIN!
NO, THEY WON'T! WHICH IS WHY WE'VE GOT TO GO HOME NOW!
MY DOORWAY IS SHRINKING EVER FASTER NOW! IT'S MORE IMPORTANT TO GET YOU HOME THAN TO FIGHT A POINTLESS BATTLE WITH TWO MORG!
SIGH! YOU ARE RIGHT— I AM... NEEDED THERE! BUT WHAT ABOUT OUR NEW FRIENDS?
WE'LL HAVE TO LEAVE THEM! WE CAN'T CARRY THEM, AND THEY WON'T WAKE UP FOR HOURS!
PERHAPS... PERHAPS THE MORG WILL TAKE NO FURTHER INTEREST IN THEM?
I'M SURE THEY'LL BE ALL RIGHT! AND SOMEDAY, I'LL RE-OPEN THE DOORWAY TO THIS DIMENSION SO YOU CAN VISIT THEM!
BRENDON HAS ESCAPED! SNARK WILL REPORT THAT IT IS ALL DUE TO NURG'S DISOBEDIENCE!
NURG WILL MAKE SNARK PAY FOR SUCH A REPORT!

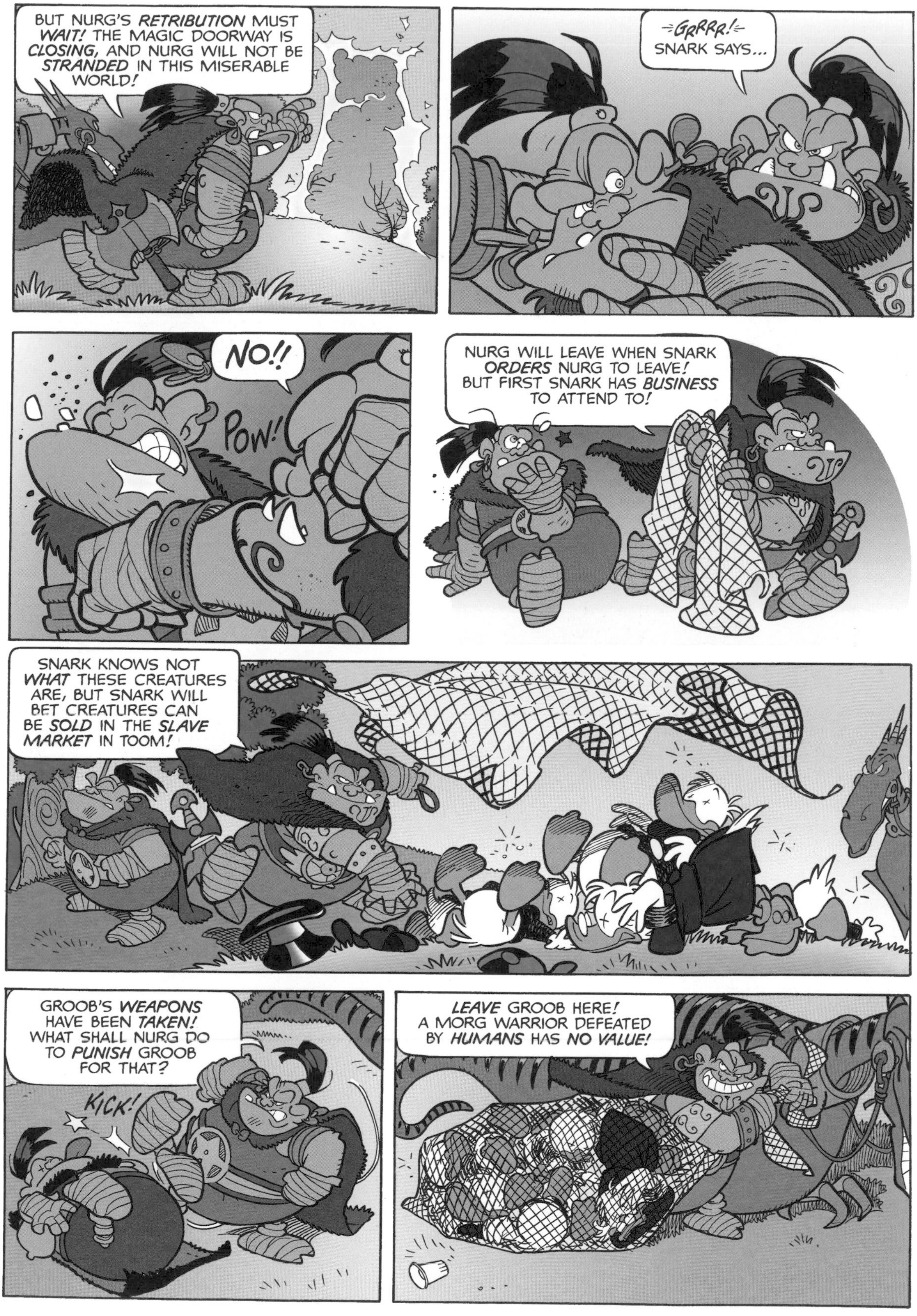
BUT NURG'S RETRIBUTION MUST WAIT! THE MAGIC DOORWAY IS CLOSING, AND NURG WILL NOT BE STRANDED IN THIS MISERABLE WORLD!
GRRRR! SNARK SAYS...
NO!!
POW!
NURG WILL LEAVE WHEN SNARK ORDERS NURG TO LEAVE! BUT FIRST SNARK HAS BUSINESS TO ATTEND TO!
SNARK KNOWS NOT WHAT THESE CREATURES ARE, BUT SNARK WILL BET CREATURES CAN BE SOLD IN THE SLAVE MARKET IN TOOM!
GROOB'S WEAPONS HAVE BEEN TAKEN! WHAT SHALL NURG DO TO PUNISH GROOB FOR THAT?
KICK!
LEAVE GROOB HERE! A MORG WARRIOR DEFEATED BY HUMANS HAS NO VALUE!

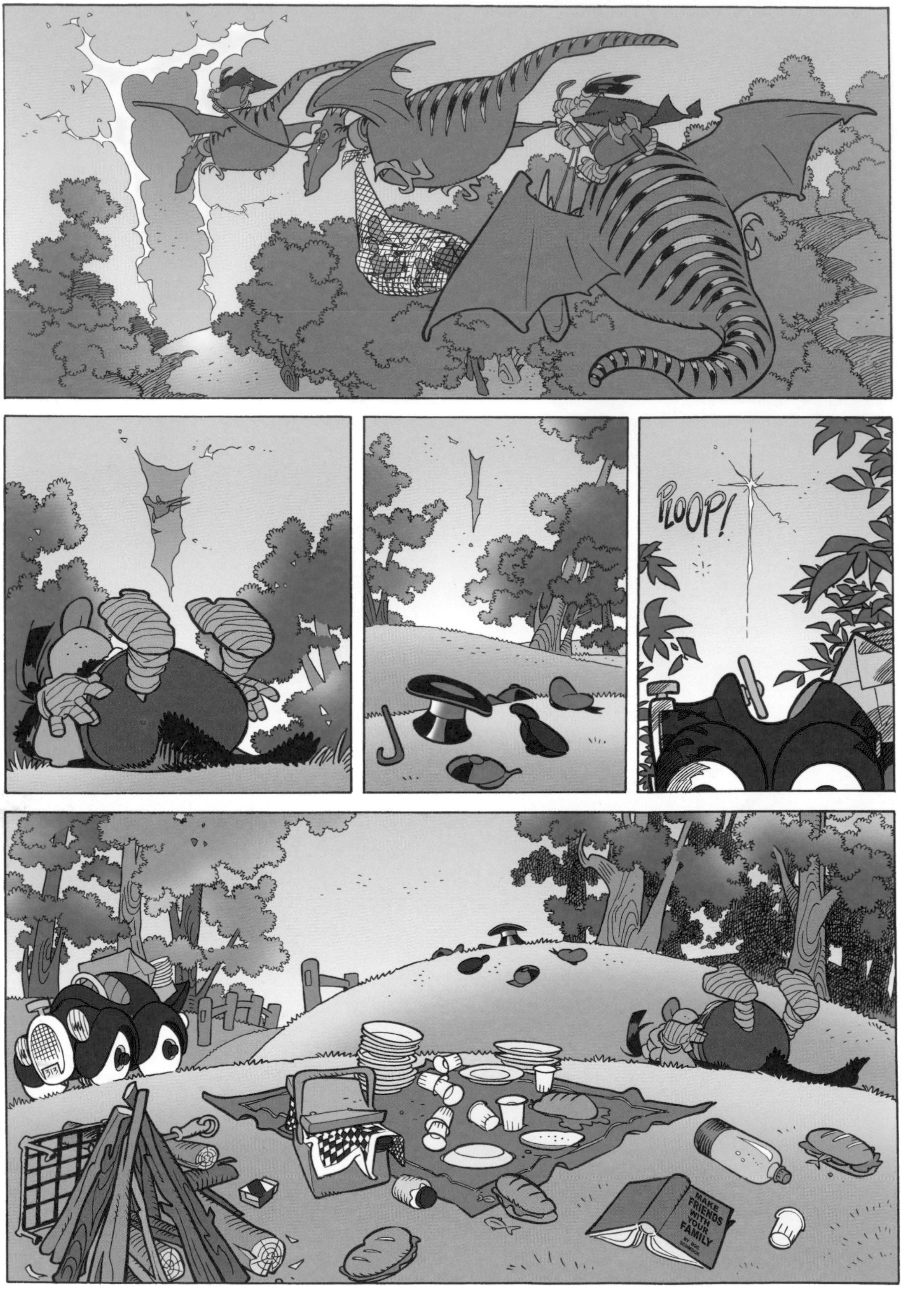
PLOOP!
MAKE FRIENDS WITH YOUR FAMILY
BY DOC SCHMOCK

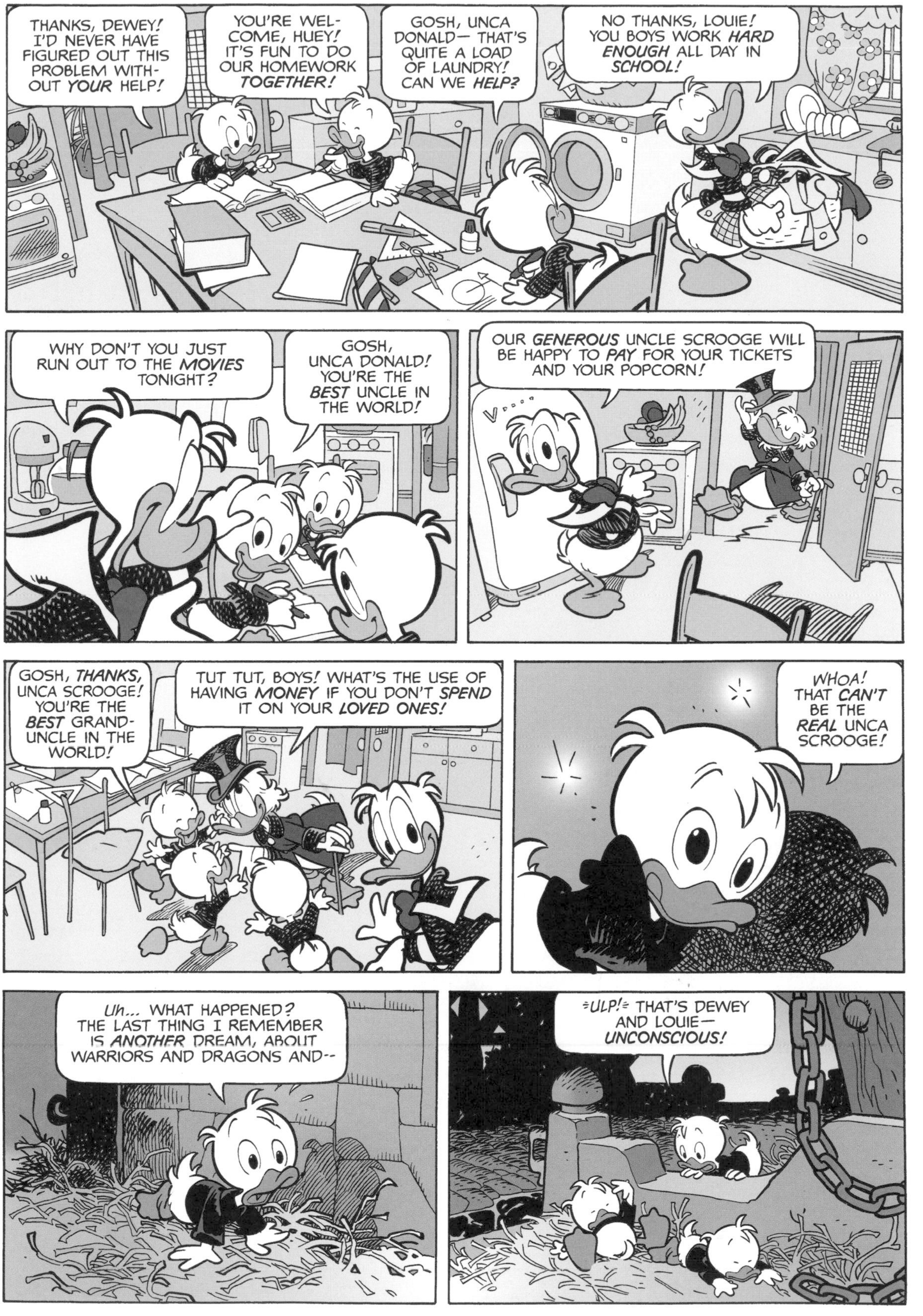
THANKS, DEWEY! I'D NEVER HAVE FIGURED OUT THIS PROBLEM WITH- OUT YOUR HELP!
YOU'RE WEL- COME, HUEY! IT'S FUN TO DO OUR HOMEWORK TOGETHER!
GOSH, UNCA DONALD— THAT'S QUITE A LOAD OF LAUNDRY! CAN WE HELP?
NO THANKS, LOUIE! YOU BOYS WORK HARD ENOUGH ALL DAY IN SCHOOL!
WHY DON'T YOU JUST RUN OUT TO THE MOVIES TONIGHT?
GOSH, UNCA DONALD! YOU'RE THE BEST UNCLE IN THE WORLD!
OUR GENEROUS UNCLE SCROOGE WILL BE HAPPY TO PAY FOR YOUR TICKETS AND YOUR POPCORN!
GOSH, THANKS, UNCA SCROOGE! YOU'RE THE BEST GRAND- UNCLE IN THE WORLD!
TUT TUT, BOYS! WHAT'S THE USE OF HAVING MONEY IF YOU DON'T SPEND IT ON YOUR LOVED ONES!
WHOA! THAT CAN'T BE THE REAL UNCA SCROOGE!
Uh... WHAT HAPPENED? THE LAST THING I REMEMBER IS ANOTHER DREAM, ABOUT WARRIORS AND DRAGONS AND--
≈ULP!≈ THAT'S DEWEY AND LOUIE— UNCONSCIOUS!

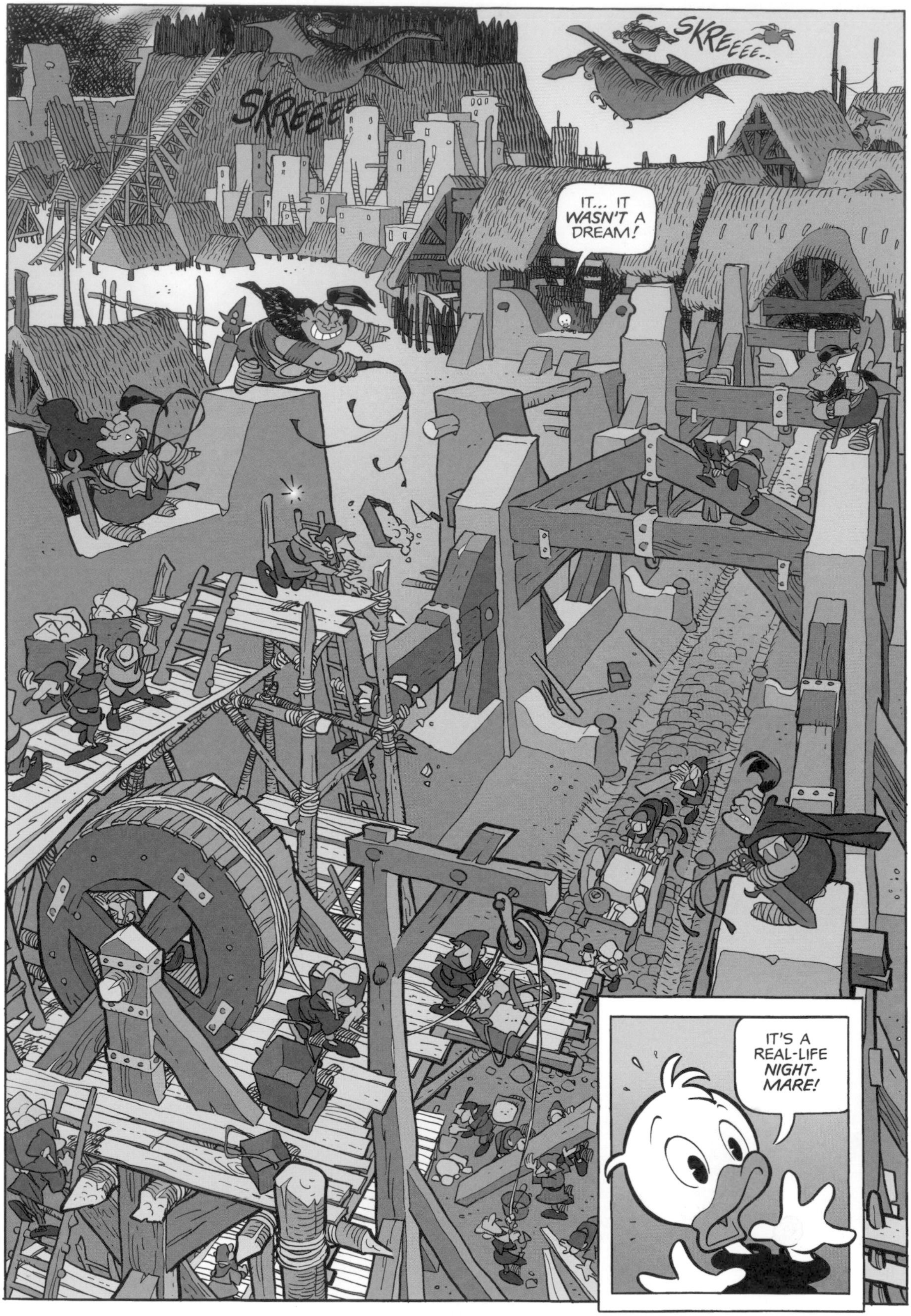
SKREEEE
SKREEEE...
IT... IT WASN'T A DREAM!
IT'S A REAL-LIFE NIGHT-MARE!

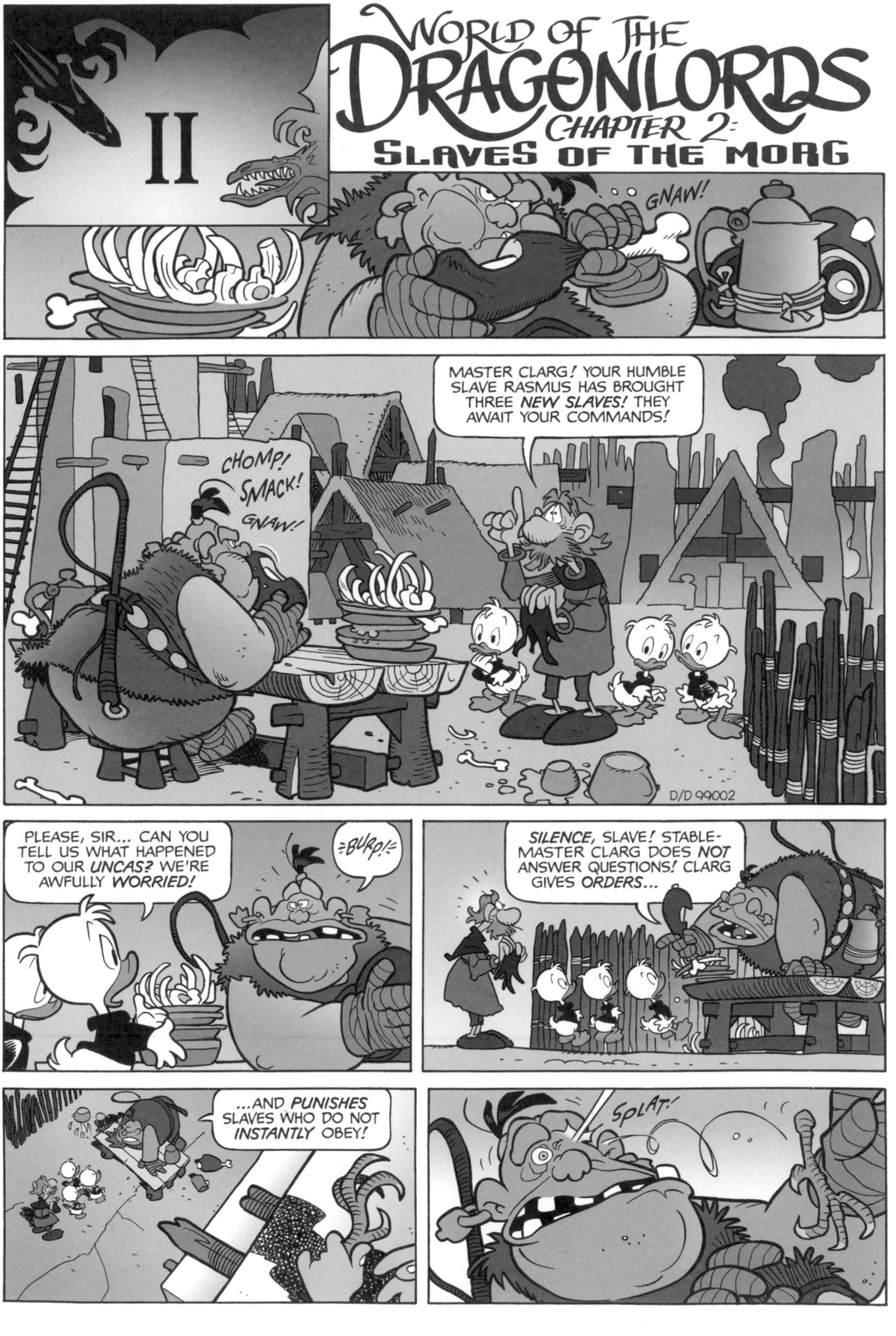
WORLD OF THE DRAGONLORDS
II
CHAPTER 2:
SLAVES OF THE MORG
GNAW!
MASTER CLARG! YOUR HUMBLE SLAVE RASMUS HAS BROUGHT THREE NEW SLAVES! THEY AWAIT YOUR COMMANDS!
CHOMP!
SMACK!
GNAW!
D/D 99002
PLEASE, SIR... CAN YOU TELL US WHAT HAPPENED TO OUR UNCAS? WE'RE AWFULLY WORRIED!
BURP!
SILENCE, SLAVE! STABLE-MASTER CLARG DOES NOT ANSWER QUESTIONS! CLARG GIVES ORDERS...
...AND PUNISHES SLAVES WHO DO NOT INSTANTLY OBEY!
SPLAT!

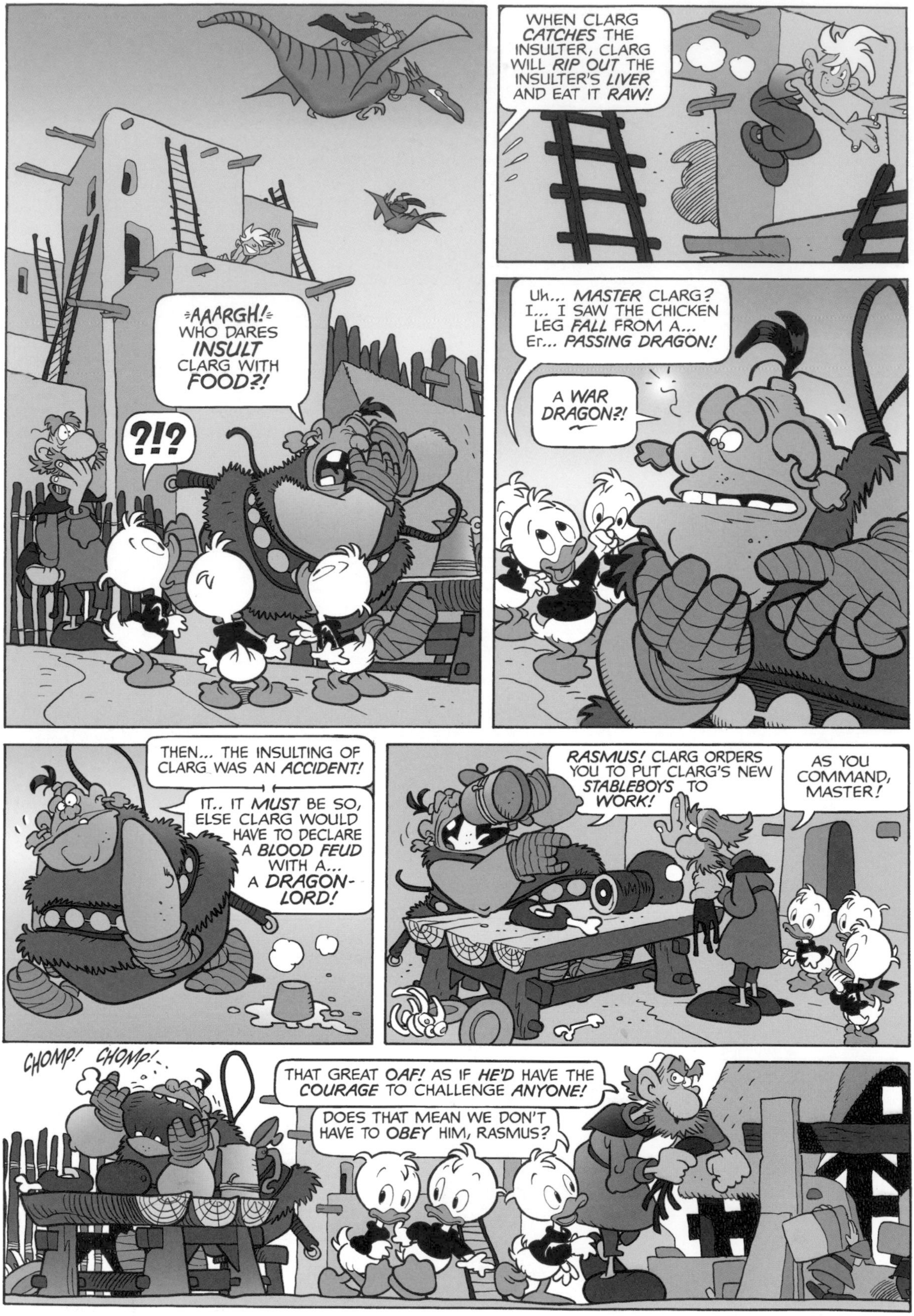

=AAARGH!= WHO DARES INSULT CLARG WITH FOOD?!
?!?
WHEN CLARG CATCHES THE INSULTER, CLARG WILL RIP OUT THE INSULTER'S LIVER AND EAT IT RAW!
Uh... MASTER CLARG? I... I SAW THE CHICKEN LEG FALL FROM A... Er... PASSING DRAGON!
A WAR DRAGON?!
THEN... THE INSULTING OF CLARG WAS AN ACCIDENT!
IT.. IT MUST BE SO, ELSE CLARG WOULD HAVE TO DECLARE A BLOOD FEUD WITH A... A DRAGON-LORD!
RASMUS! CLARG ORDERS YOU TO PUT CLARG'S NEW STABLEBOYS TO WORK!
AS YOU COMMAND, MASTER!
CHOMP! CHOMP!
THAT GREAT OAF! AS IF HE'D HAVE THE COURAGE TO CHALLENGE ANYONE!
DOES THAT MEAN WE DON'T HAVE TO OBEY HIM, RASMUS?

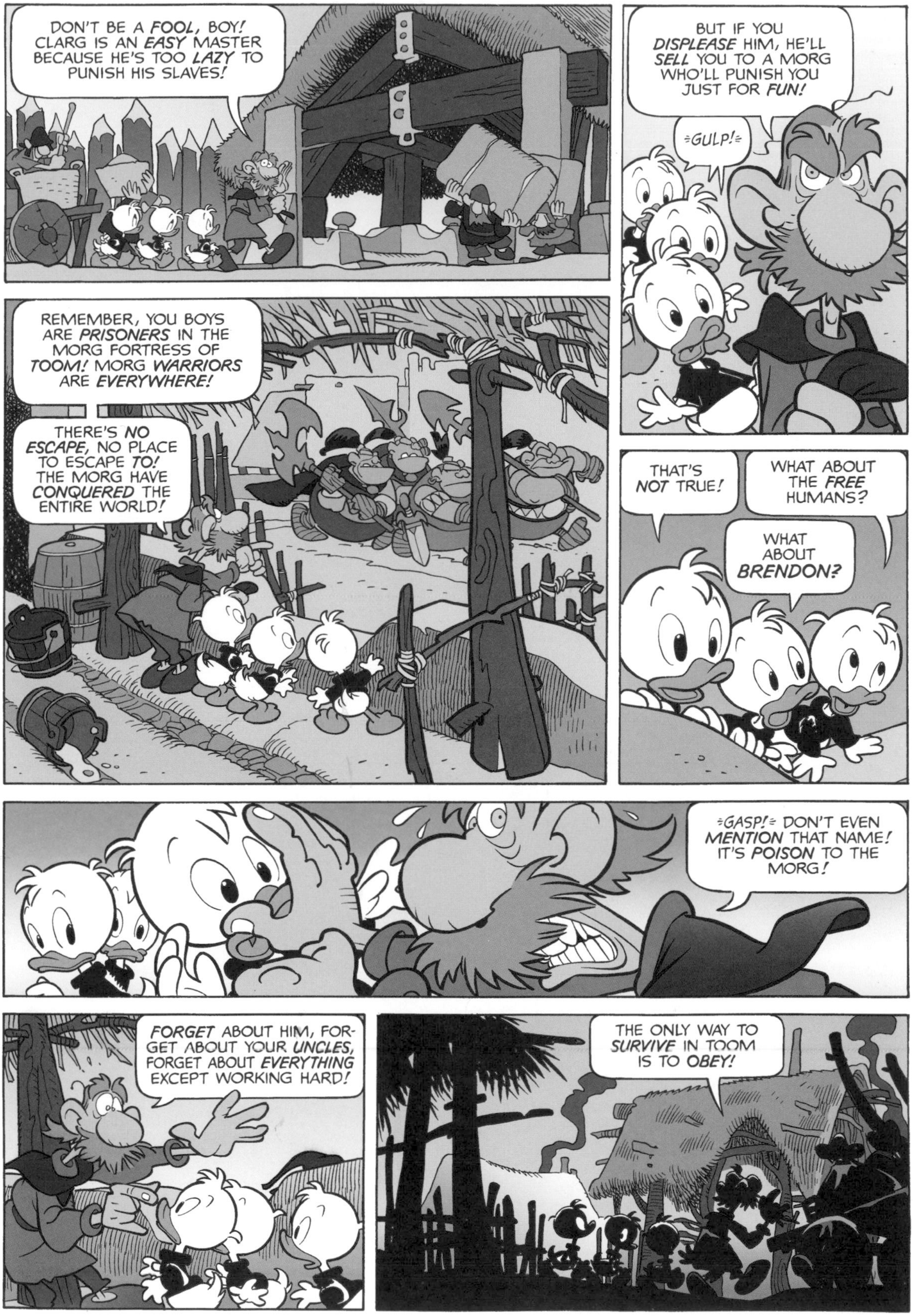
DON'T BE A FOOL, BOY! CLARG IS AN EASY MASTER BECAUSE HE'S TOO LAZY TO PUNISH HIS SLAVES!
BUT IF YOU DISPLEASE HIM, HE'LL SELL YOU TO A MORG WHO'LL PUNISH YOU JUST FOR FUN!
=GULP!=
REMEMBER, YOU BOYS ARE PRISONERS IN THE MORG FORTRESS OF TOOM! MORG WARRIORS ARE EVERYWHERE!
THERE'S NO ESCAPE, NO PLACE TO ESCAPE TO! THE MORG HAVE CONQUERED THE ENTIRE WORLD!
THAT'S NOT TRUE!
WHAT ABOUT THE FREE HUMANS?
WHAT ABOUT BRENDON?
=GASP!= DON'T EVEN MENTION THAT NAME! IT'S POISON TO THE MORG!
FORGET ABOUT HIM, FORGET ABOUT YOUR UNCLES, FORGET ABOUT EVERYTHING EXCEPT WORKING HARD!
THE ONLY WAY TO SURVIVE IN TOOM IS TO OBEY!

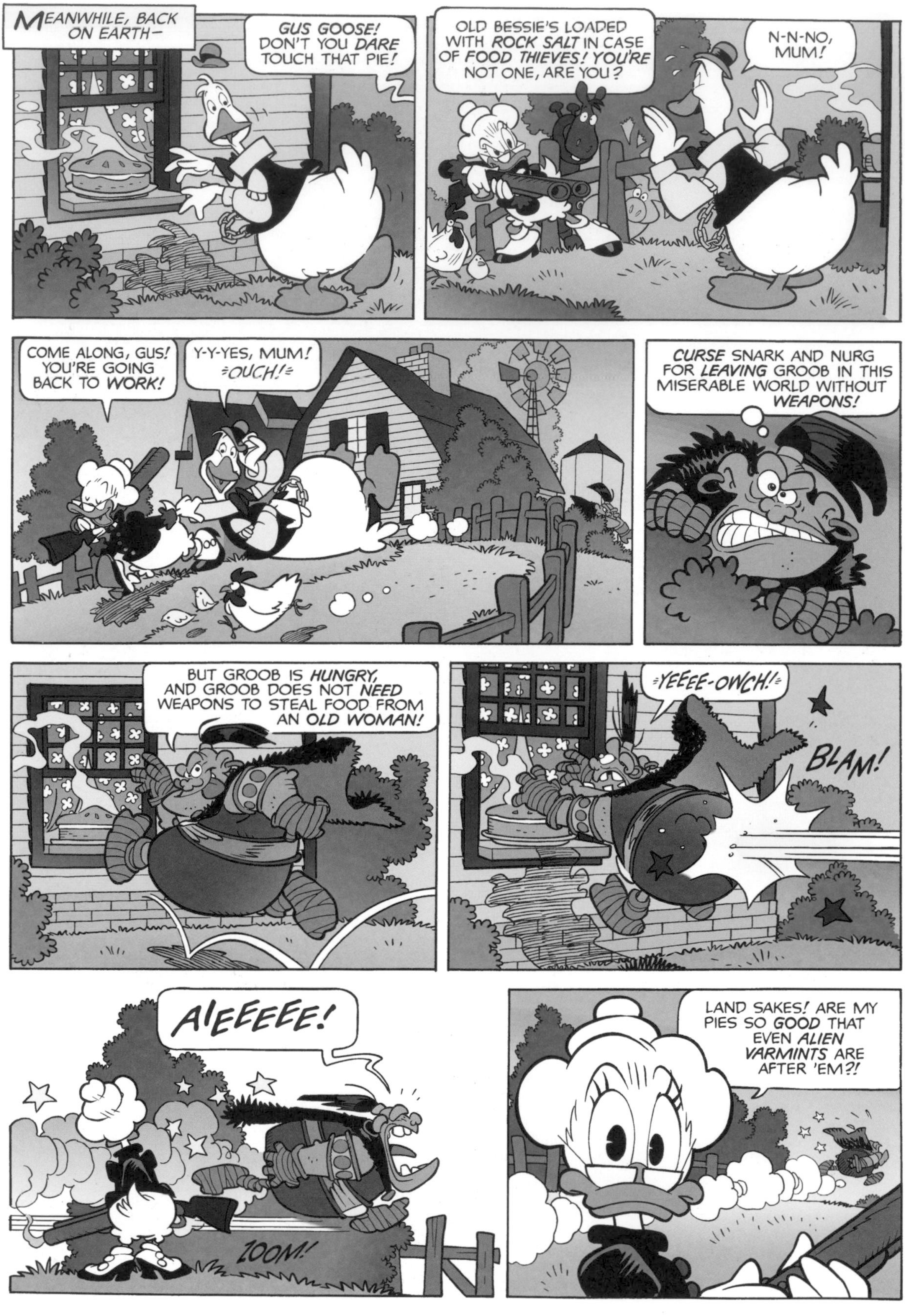
MEANWHILE, BACK ON EARTH—
GUS GOOSE! DON'T YOU DARE TOUCH THAT PIE!
OLD BESSIE'S LOADED WITH ROCK SALT IN CASE OF FOOD THIEVES! YOU'RE NOT ONE, ARE YOU?
N-N-NO, MUM!
COME ALONG, GUS! YOU'RE GOING BACK TO WORK!
Y-Y-YES, MUM! OUCH!
CURSE SNARK AND NURG FOR LEAVING GROOB IN THIS MISERABLE WORLD WITHOUT WEAPONS!
BUT GROOB IS HUNGRY, AND GROOB DOES NOT NEED WEAPONS TO STEAL FOOD FROM AN OLD WOMAN!
YEEEE-OWCH!
BLAM!
AIEEEEE!
ZOOM!
LAND SAKES! ARE MY PIES SO GOOD THAT EVEN ALIEN VARMINTS ARE AFTER 'EM?!

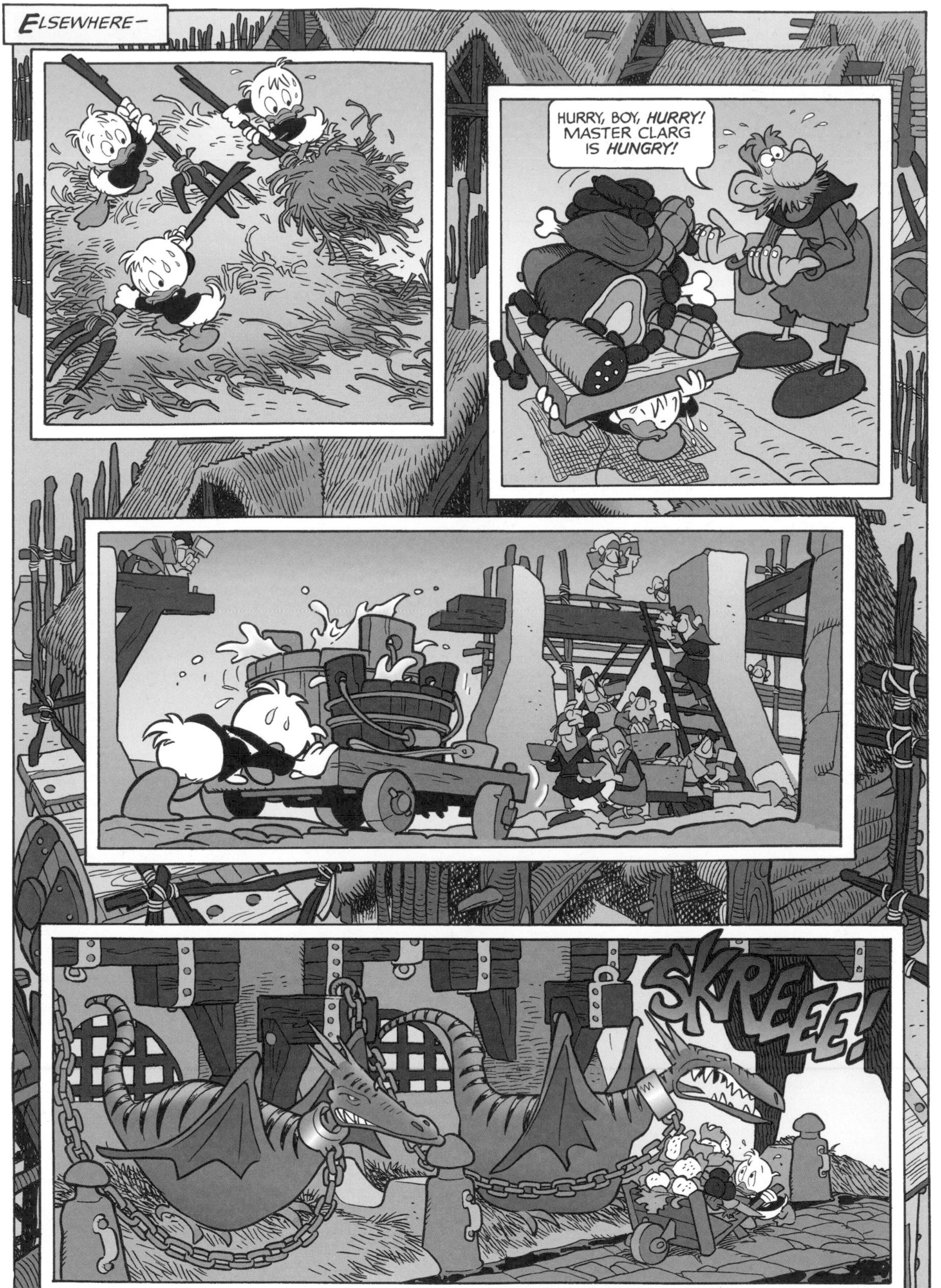
ELSEWHERE—
HURRY, BOY, HURRY! MASTER CLARG IS HUNGRY!
SKREEE!

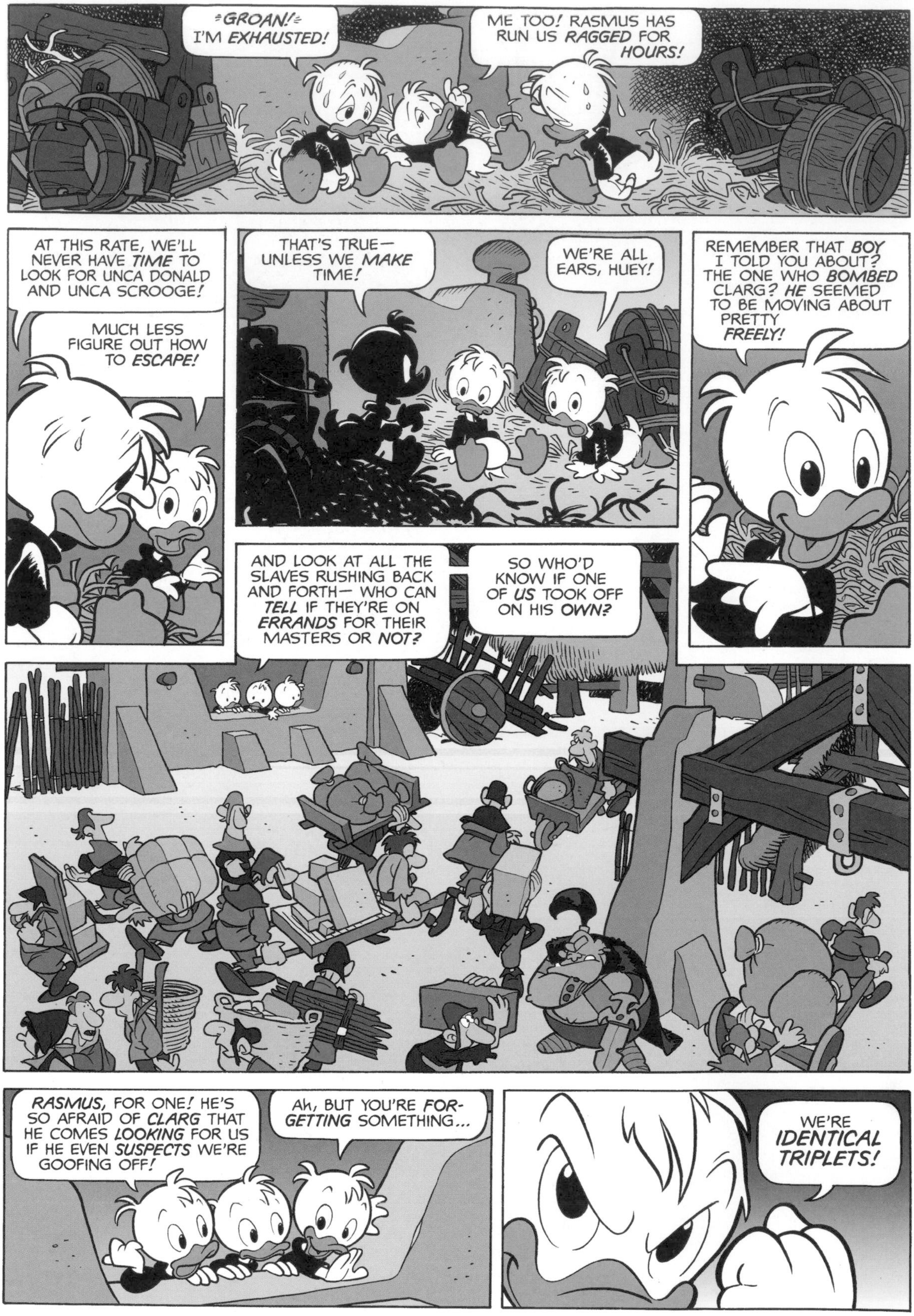
≈GROAN!≈ I'M EXHAUSTED!
ME TOO! RASMUS HAS RUN US RAGGED FOR HOURS!
AT THIS RATE, WE'LL NEVER HAVE TIME TO LOOK FOR UNCA DONALD AND UNCA SCROOGE!
MUCH LESS FIGURE OUT HOW TO ESCAPE!
THAT'S TRUE— UNLESS WE MAKE TIME!
WE'RE ALL EARS, HUEY!
REMEMBER THAT BOY I TOLD YOU ABOUT? THE ONE WHO BOMBED CLARG? HE SEEMED TO BE MOVING ABOUT PRETTY FREELY!
AND LOOK AT ALL THE SLAVES RUSHING BACK AND FORTH— WHO CAN TELL IF THEY'RE ON ERRANDS FOR THEIR MASTERS OR NOT?
SO WHO'D KNOW IF ONE OF US TOOK OFF ON HIS OWN?
RASMUS, FOR ONE! HE'S SO AFRAID OF CLARG THAT HE COMES LOOKING FOR US IF HE EVEN SUSPECTS WE'RE GOOFING OFF!
Ah, BUT YOU'RE FORGETTING SOMETHING...
WE'RE IDENTICAL TRIPLETS!

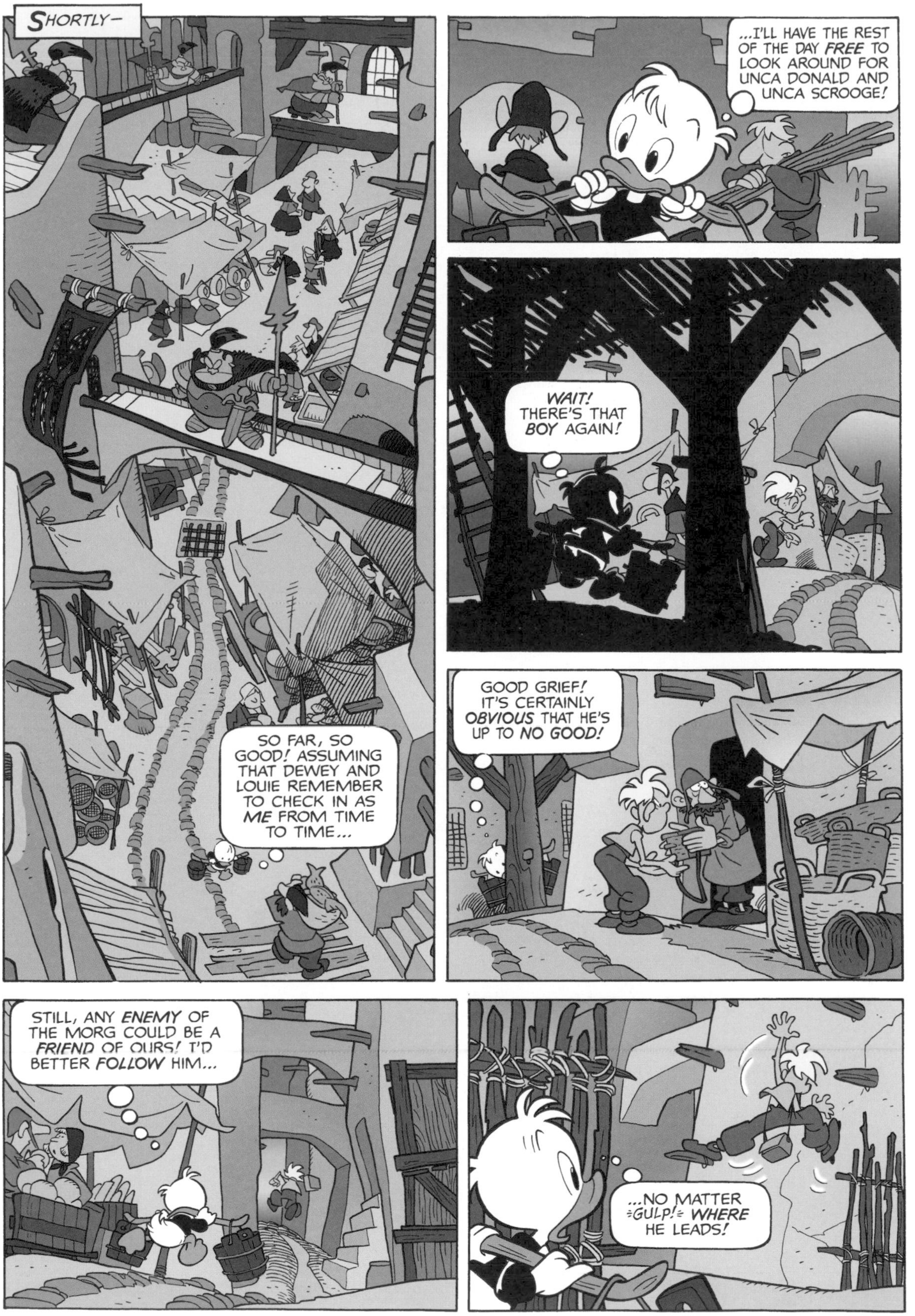
SHORTLY—
SO FAR, SO GOOD! ASSUMING THAT DEWEY AND LOUIE REMEMBER TO CHECK IN AS ME FROM TIME TO TIME...
...I'LL HAVE THE REST OF THE DAY FREE TO LOOK AROUND FOR UNCA DONALD AND UNCA SCROOGE!
WAIT! THERE'S THAT BOY AGAIN!
GOOD GRIEF! IT'S CERTAINLY OBVIOUS THAT HE'S UP TO NO GOOD!
STILL, ANY ENEMY OF THE MORG COULD BE A FRIEND OF OURS! I'D BETTER FOLLOW HIM...
...NO MATTER GULP! WHERE HE LEADS!

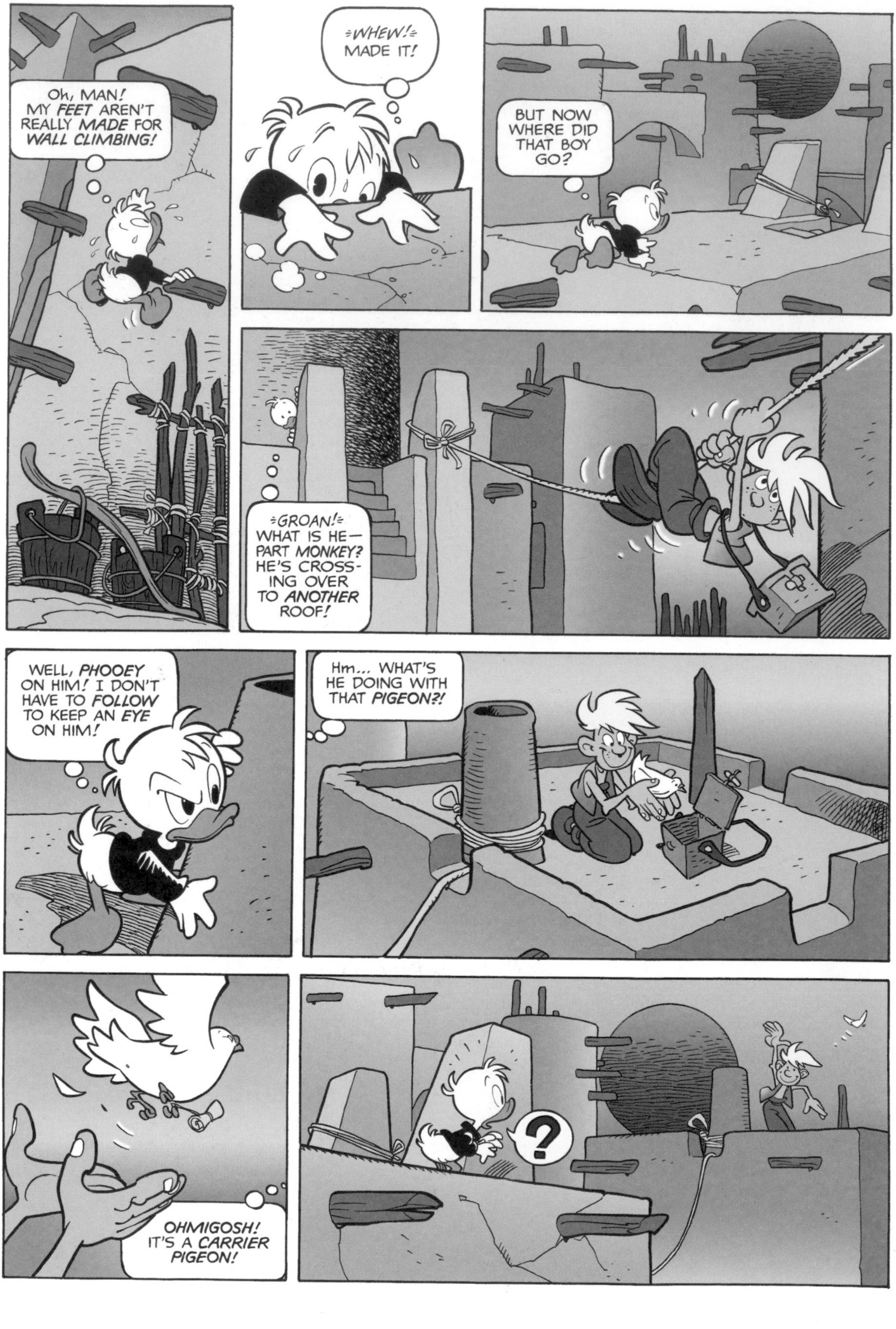

Oh, MAN! MY FEET AREN'T REALLY MADE FOR WALL CLIMBING!
WHEW! MADE IT!
BUT NOW WHERE DID THAT BOY GO?
GROAN! WHAT IS HE— PART MONKEY? HE'S CROSSING OVER TO ANOTHER ROOF!
WELL, PHOOEY ON HIM! I DON'T HAVE TO FOLLOW TO KEEP AN EYE ON HIM!
Hm... WHAT'S HE DOING WITH THAT PIGEON?!
OHMIGOSH! IT'S A CARRIER PIGEON!
?

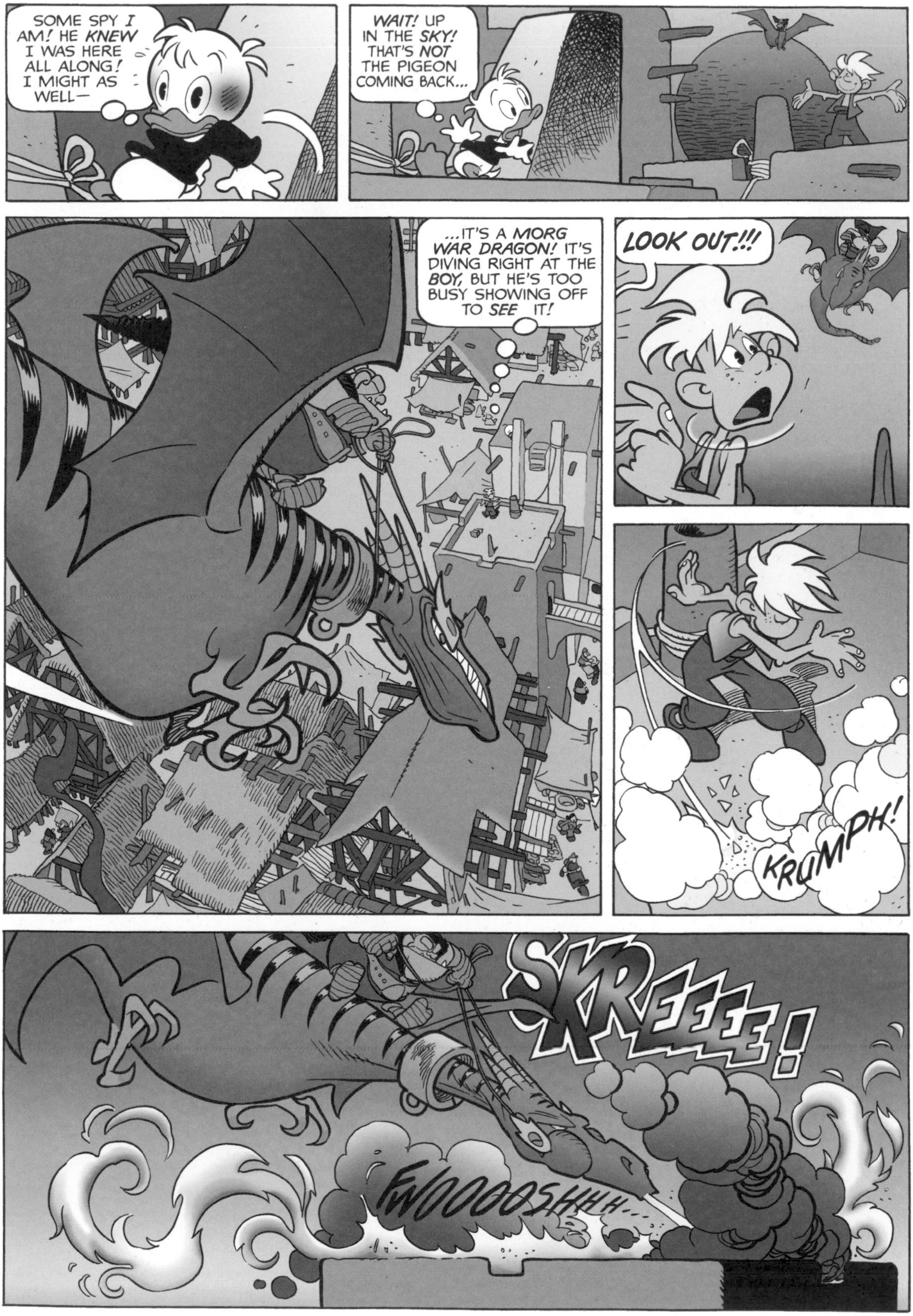
SOME SPY I AM! HE KNEW I WAS HERE ALL ALONG! I MIGHT AS WELL—
WAIT! UP IN THE SKY! THAT'S NOT THE PIGEON COMING BACK...
...IT'S A MORG WAR DRAGON! IT'S DIVING RIGHT AT THE BOY, BUT HE'S TOO BUSY SHOWING OFF TO SEE IT!
LOOK OUT!!!
KRUMPH!
SKREEEE!
FWOOOOSHHH

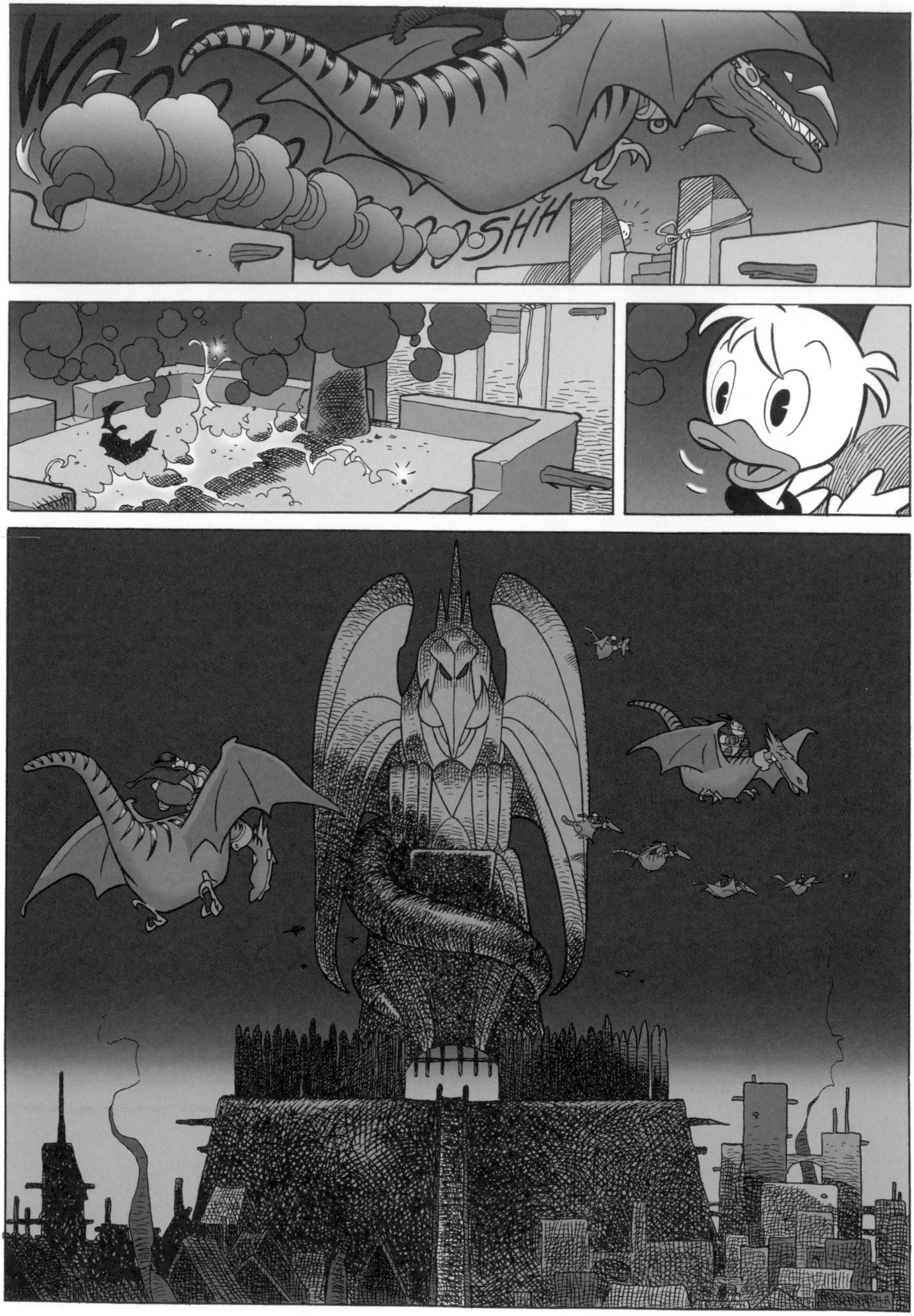
WOOOOOSHH

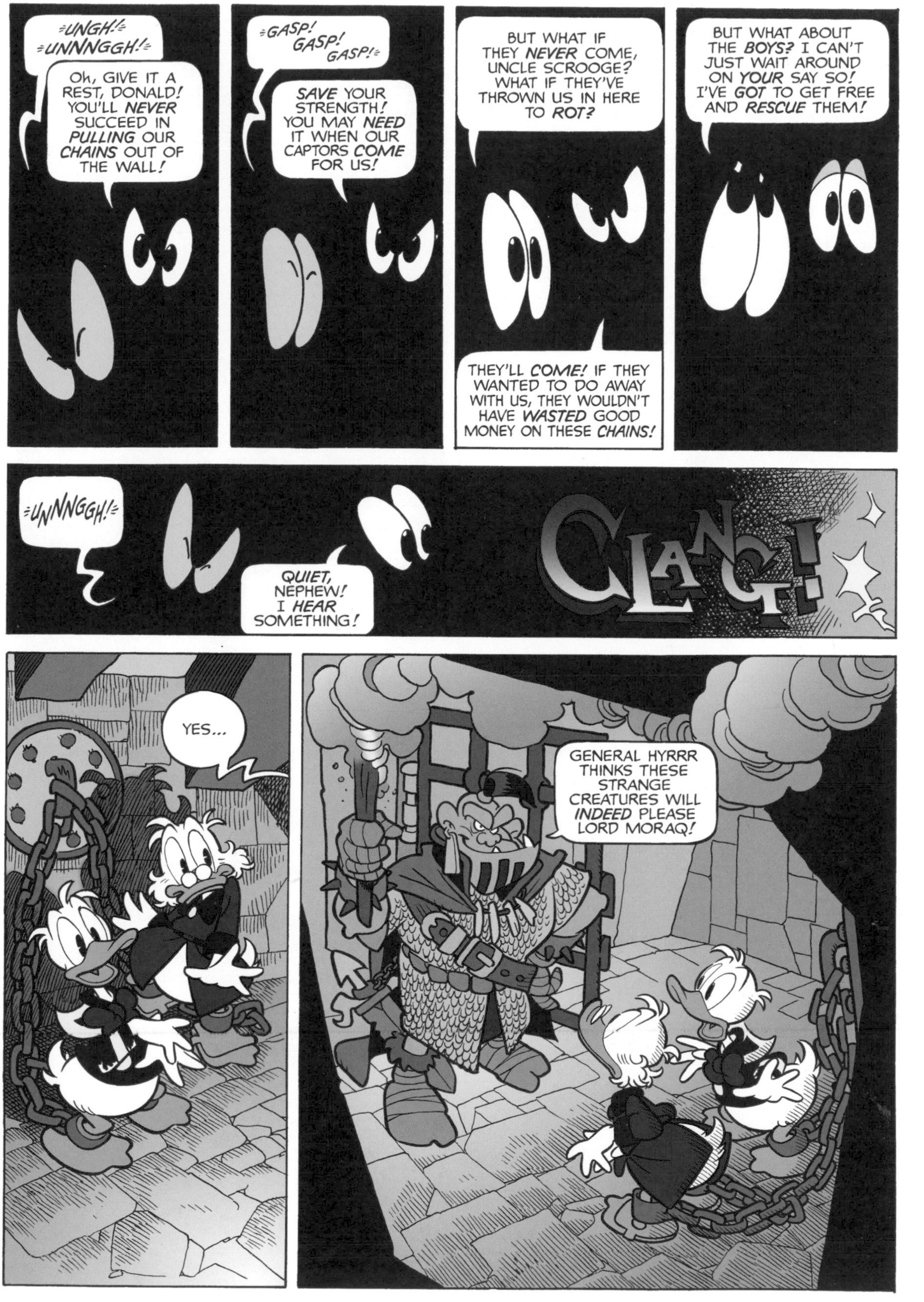
UNGH! UNNNGGH!
Oh, GIVE IT A REST, DONALD! YOU'LL NEVER SUCCEED IN PULLING OUR CHAINS OUT OF THE WALL!
GASP! GASP! GASP!
SAVE YOUR STRENGTH! YOU MAY NEED IT WHEN OUR CAPTORS COME FOR US!
BUT WHAT IF THEY NEVER COME, UNCLE SCROOGE? WHAT IF THEY'VE THROWN US IN HERE TO ROT?
THEY'LL COME! IF THEY WANTED TO DO AWAY WITH US, THEY WOULDN'T HAVE WASTED GOOD MONEY ON THESE CHAINS!
BUT WHAT ABOUT THE BOYS? I CAN'T JUST WAIT AROUND ON YOUR SAY SO! I'VE GOT TO GET FREE AND RESCUE THEM!
UNNNGGH!
QUIET, NEPHEW! I HEAR SOMETHING!
CLANG!
YES...
GENERAL HYRRR THINKS THESE STRANGE CREATURES WILL INDEED PLEASE LORD MORAQ!

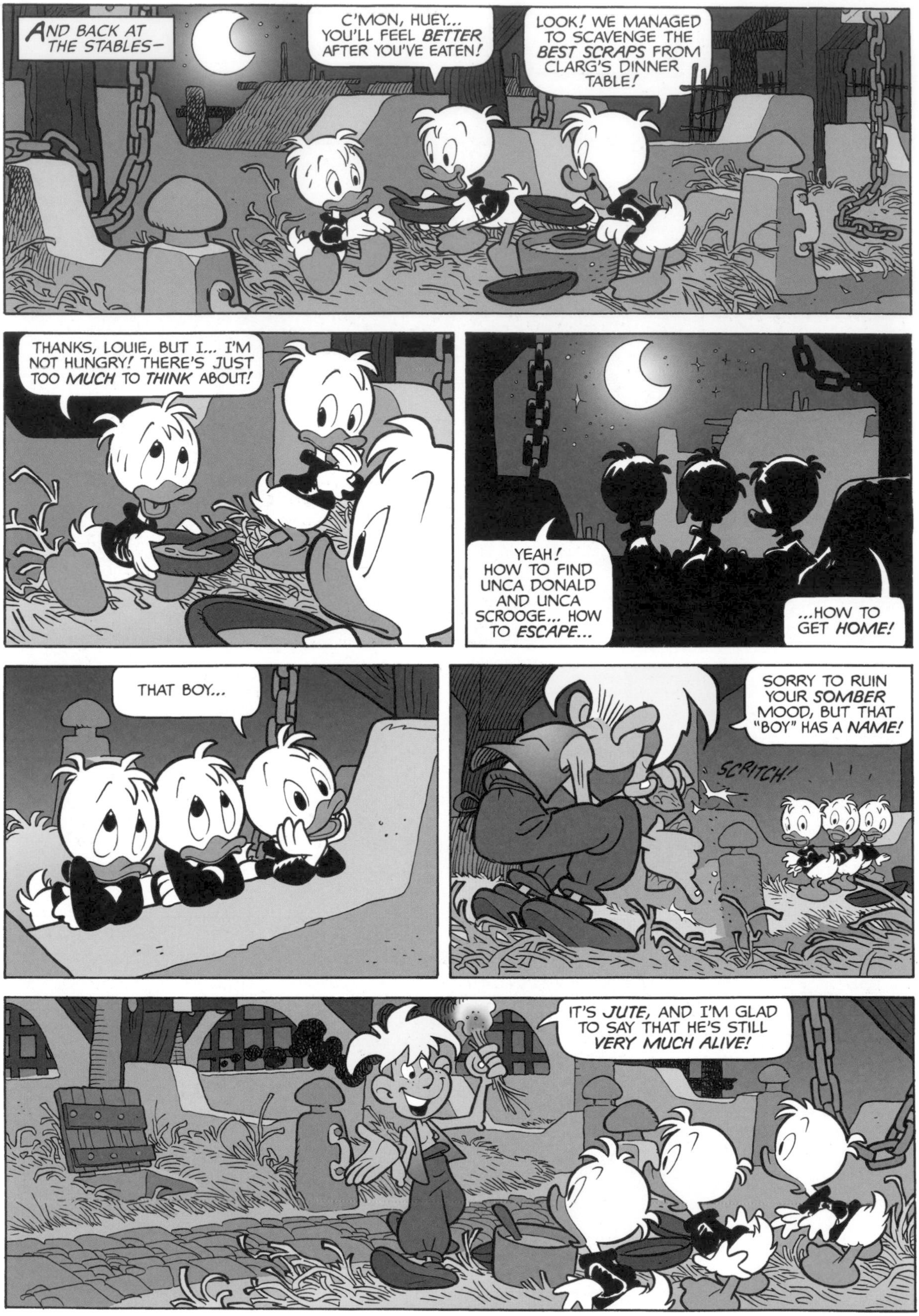
AND BACK AT THE STABLES—
C'MON, HUEY... YOU'LL FEEL BETTER AFTER YOU'VE EATEN!
LOOK! WE MANAGED TO SCAVENGE THE BEST SCRAPS FROM CLARG'S DINNER TABLE!
THANKS, LOUIE, BUT I... I'M NOT HUNGRY! THERE'S JUST TOO MUCH TO THINK ABOUT!
YEAH! HOW TO FIND UNCA DONALD AND UNCA SCROOGE... HOW TO ESCAPE...
...HOW TO GET HOME!
THAT BOY...
SORRY TO RUIN YOUR SOMBER MOOD, BUT THAT "BOY" HAS A NAME!
SCRITCH!
IT'S JUTE, AND I'M GLAD TO SAY THAT HE'S STILL VERY MUCH ALIVE!
CONTINUED...

Cover drawing for Italian *Zio Paperone* 166 (2003), illustrating "Slaves of the Morg."
Art by Marco Rota, color by Disney Italia.

Cover drawing for Italian *Zio Paperone* 167 (2003), illustrating "Jute." Art by Marco Rota, color by Disney Italia.

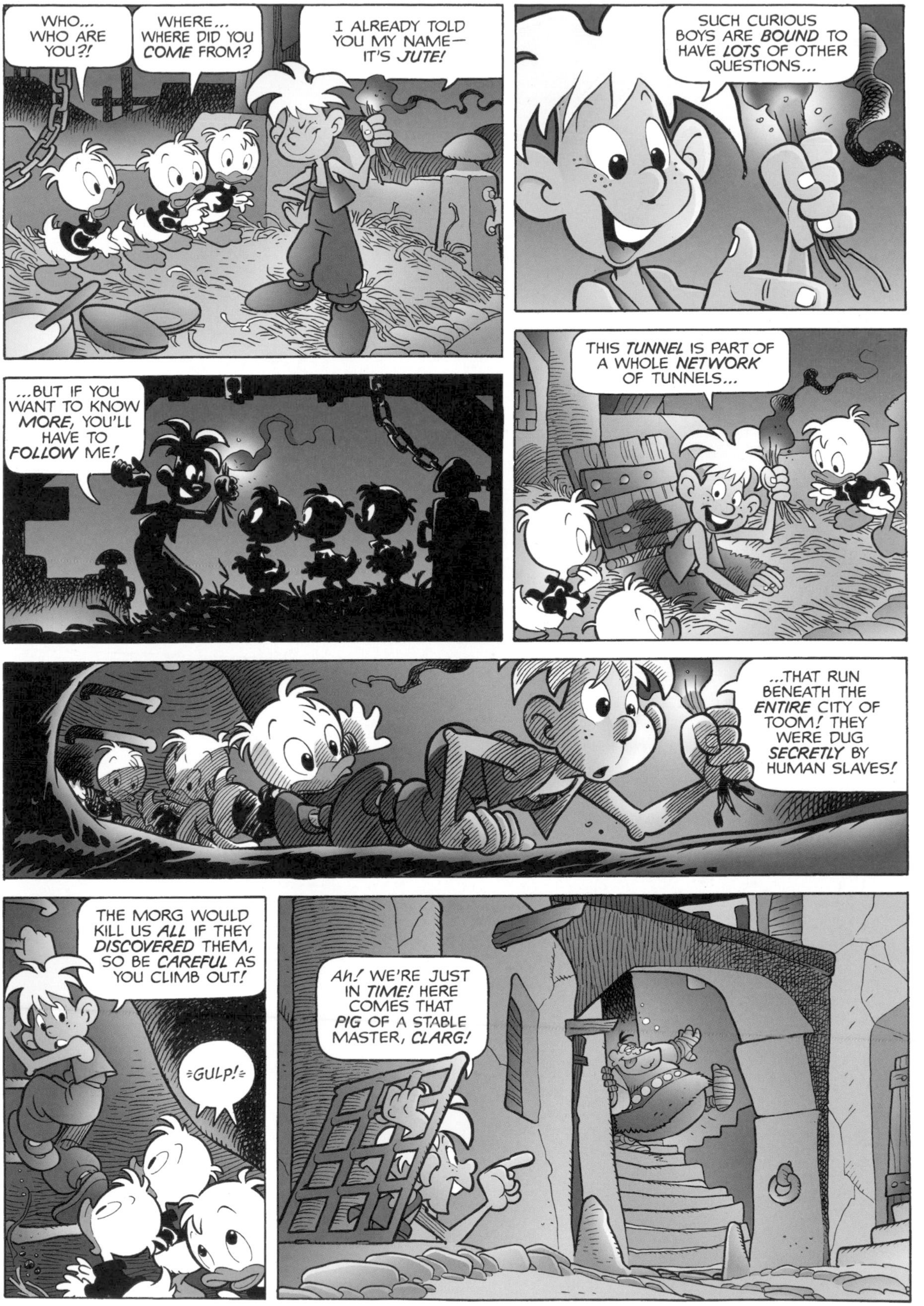
WHO... WHO ARE YOU?!
WHERE... WHERE DID YOU COME FROM?
I ALREADY TOLD YOU MY NAME— IT'S JUTE!
SUCH CURIOUS BOYS ARE BOUND TO HAVE LOTS OF OTHER QUESTIONS...
...BUT IF YOU WANT TO KNOW MORE, YOU'LL HAVE TO FOLLOW ME!
THIS TUNNEL IS PART OF A WHOLE NETWORK OF TUNNELS...
...THAT RUN BENEATH THE ENTIRE CITY OF TOOM! THEY WERE DUG SECRETLY BY HUMAN SLAVES!
THE MORG WOULD KILL US ALL IF THEY DISCOVERED THEM, SO BE CAREFUL AS YOU CLIMB OUT!
GULP!
Ah! WE'RE JUST IN TIME! HERE COMES THAT PIG OF A STABLE MASTER, CLARG!

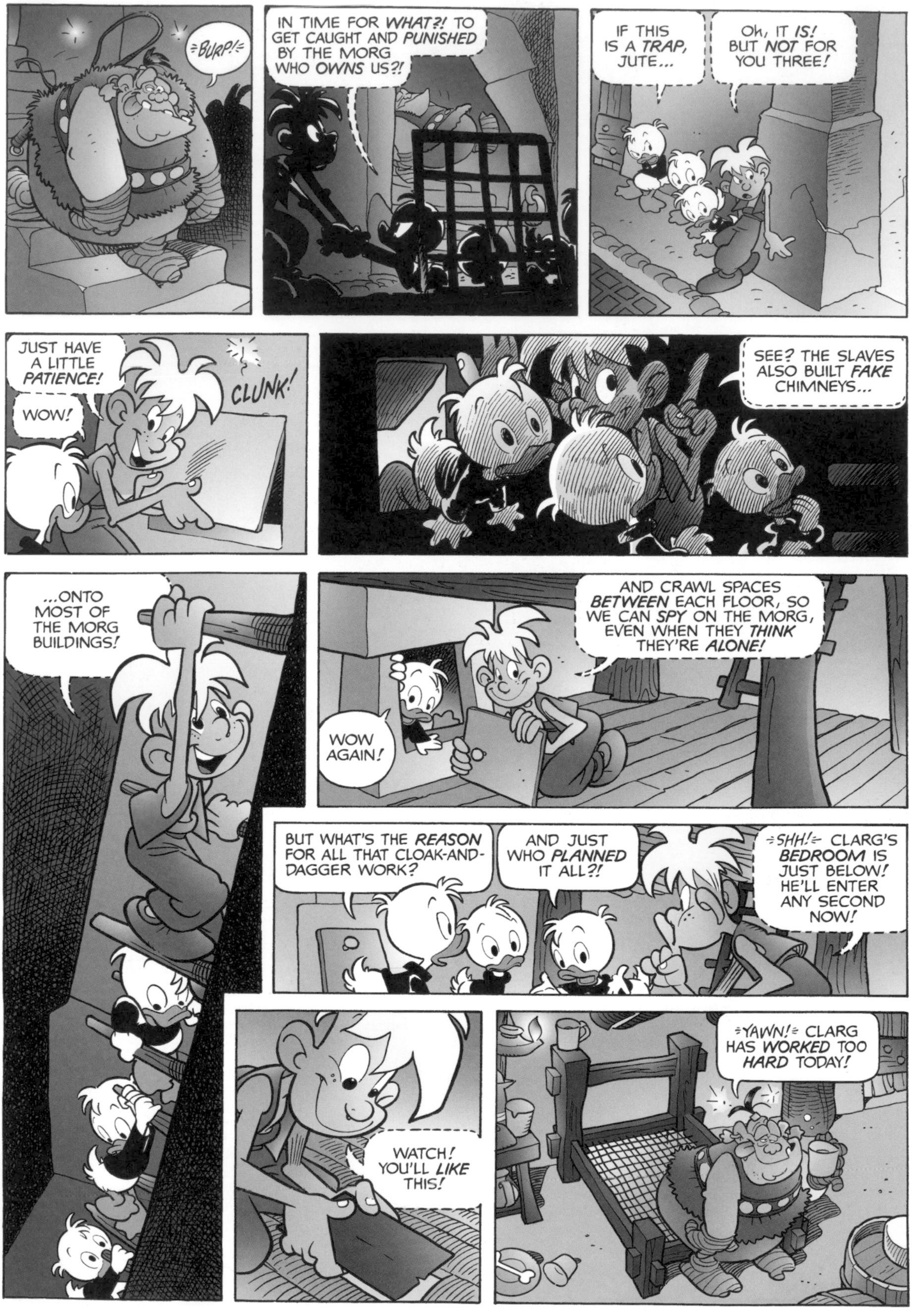

BURP!
IN TIME FOR WHAT?! TO GET CAUGHT AND PUNISHED BY THE MORG WHO OWNS US?!
IF THIS IS A TRAP, JUTE...
Oh, IT IS! BUT NOT FOR YOU THREE!
JUST HAVE A LITTLE PATIENCE!
CLUNK!
WOW!
SEE? THE SLAVES ALSO BUILT FAKE CHIMNEYS...
...ONTO MOST OF THE MORG BUILDINGS!
AND CRAWL SPACES BETWEEN EACH FLOOR, SO WE CAN SPY ON THE MORG, EVEN WHEN THEY THINK THEY'RE ALONE!
WOW AGAIN!
BUT WHAT'S THE REASON FOR ALL THAT CLOAK-AND-DAGGER WORK?
AND JUST WHO PLANNED IT ALL?!
SHH! CLARG'S BEDROOM IS JUST BELOW! HE'LL ENTER ANY SECOND NOW!
WATCH! YOU'LL LIKE THIS!
YAWN! CLARG HAS WORKED TOO HARD TODAY!

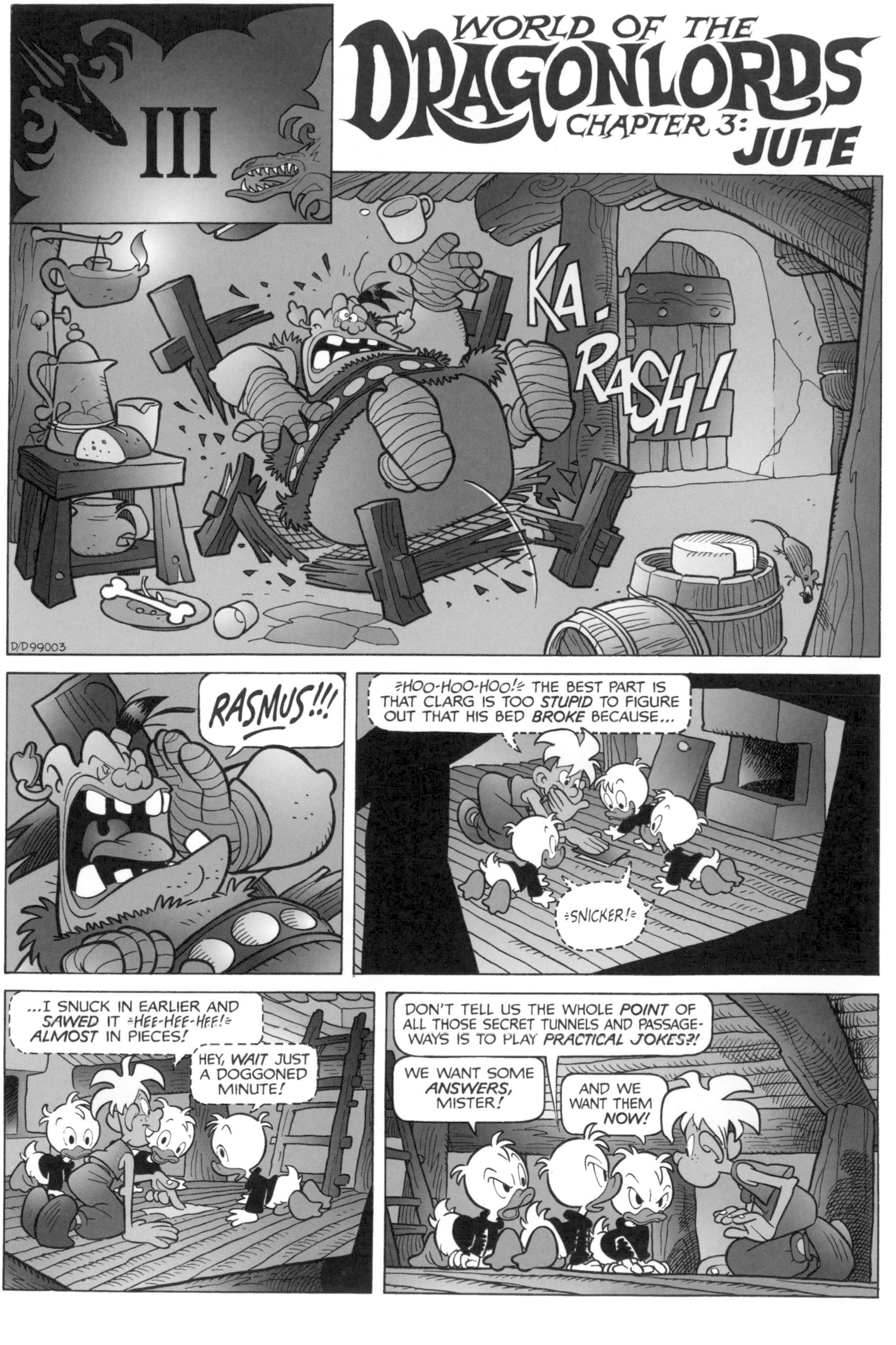
III
WORLD OF THE DRAGONLORDS
CHAPTER 3: JUTE
KA-RASH!
D/D99003
RASMUS!!!
HOO-HOO-HOO! THE BEST PART IS THAT CLARG IS TOO STUPID TO FIGURE OUT THAT HIS BED BROKE BECAUSE...
SNICKER!
...I SNUCK IN EARLIER AND SAWED IT HEE-HEE-HEE! ALMOST IN PIECES!
HEY, WAIT JUST A DOGGONED MINUTE!
DON'T TELL US THE WHOLE POINT OF ALL THOSE SECRET TUNNELS AND PASSAGEWAYS IS TO PLAY PRACTICAL JOKES?!
WE WANT SOME ANSWERS, MISTER!
AND WE WANT THEM NOW!

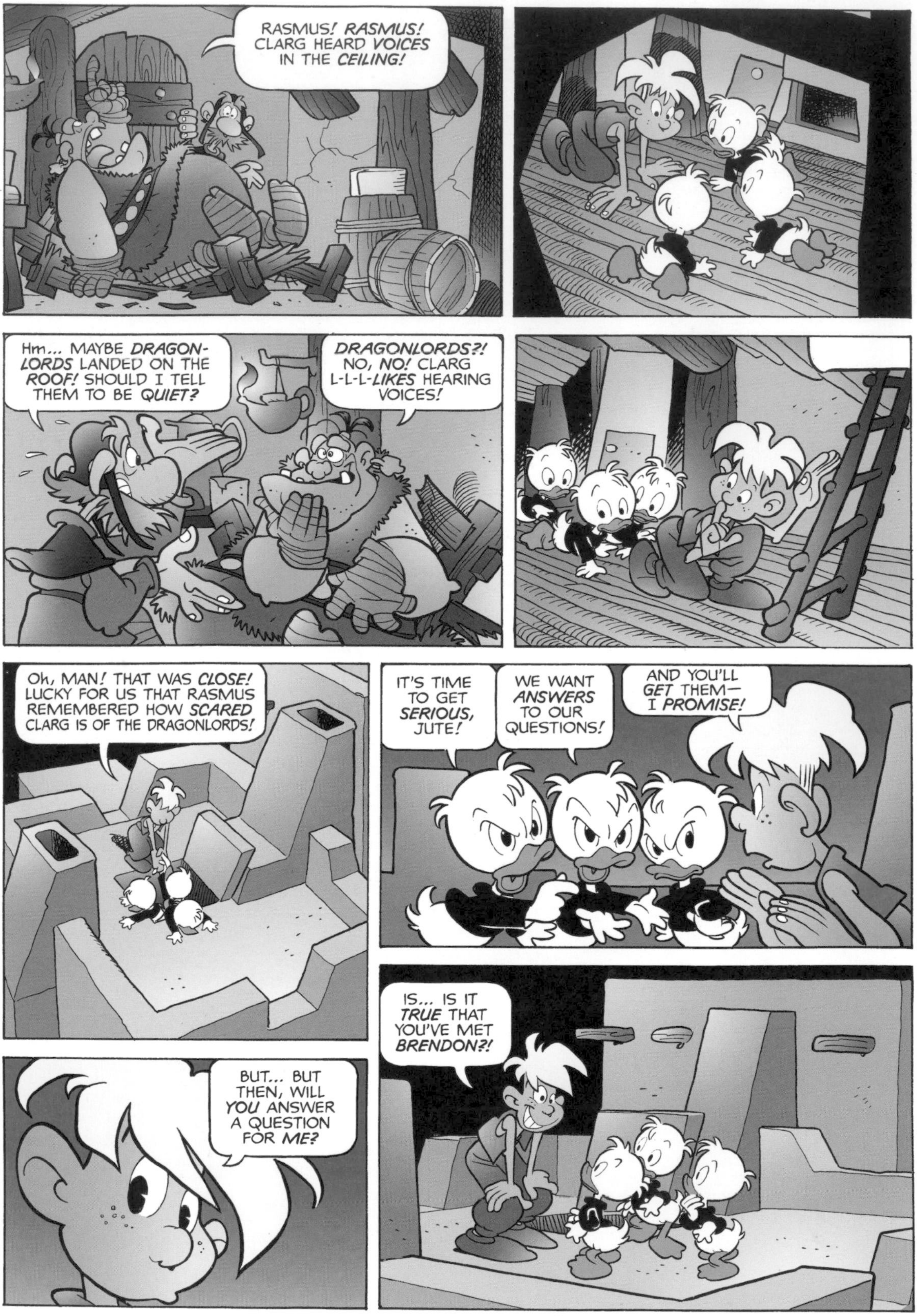
RASMUS! RASMUS! CLARG HEARD VOICES IN THE CEILING!
Hm... MAYBE DRAGON-LORDS LANDED ON THE ROOF! SHOULD I TELL THEM TO BE QUIET?
DRAGONLORDS?! NO, NO! CLARG L-L-L-LIKES HEARING VOICES!
Oh, MAN! THAT WAS CLOSE! LUCKY FOR US THAT RASMUS REMEMBERED HOW SCARED CLARG IS OF THE DRAGONLORDS!
IT'S TIME TO GET SERIOUS, JUTE!
WE WANT ANSWERS TO OUR QUESTIONS!
AND YOU'LL GET THEM— I PROMISE!
BUT... BUT THEN, WILL YOU ANSWER A QUESTION FOR ME?
IS... IS IT TRUE THAT YOU'VE MET BRENDON?!

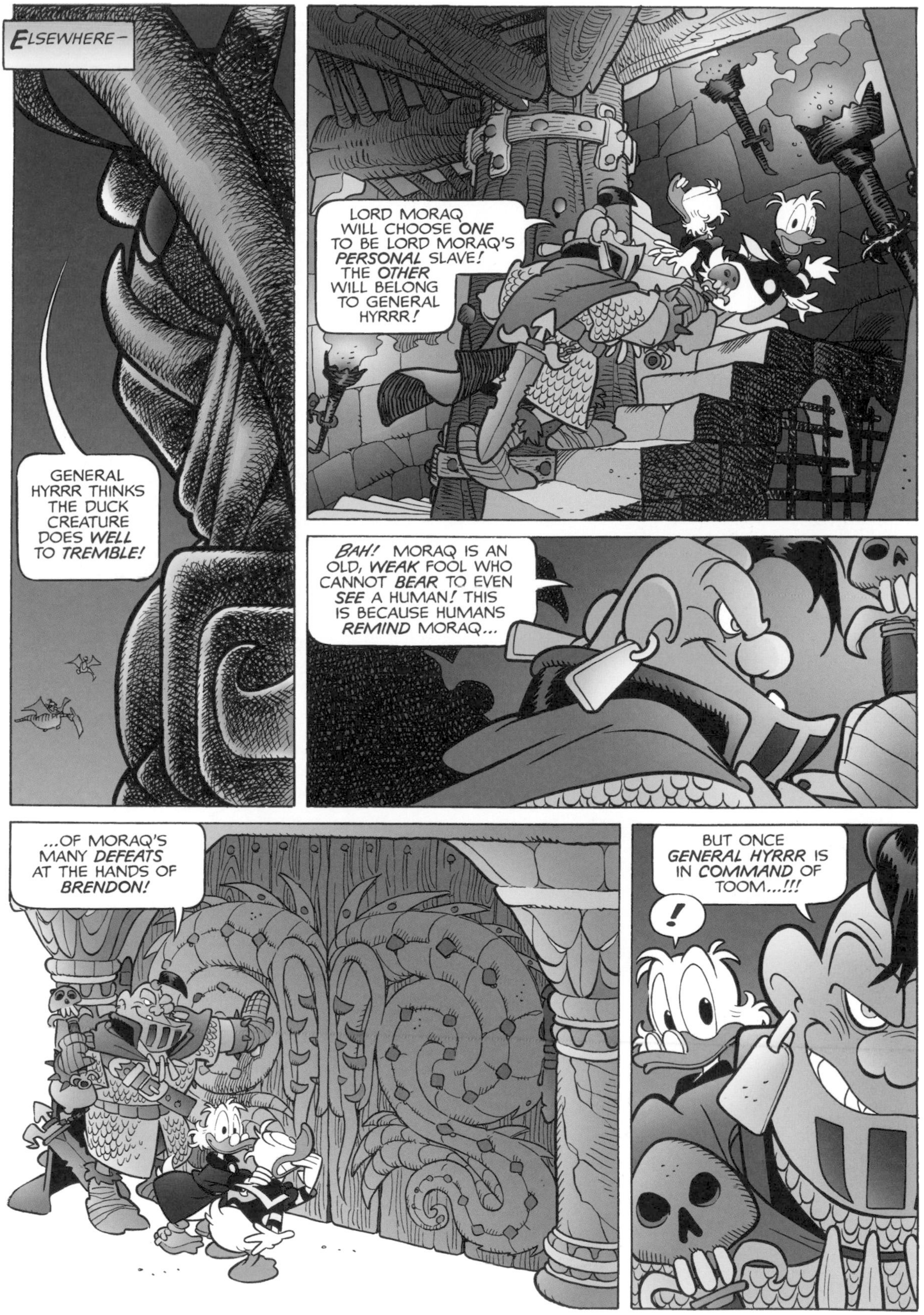
ELSEWHERE—
LORD MORAQ WILL CHOOSE ONE TO BE LORD MORAQ'S PERSONAL SLAVE! THE OTHER WILL BELONG TO GENERAL HYRRR!
GENERAL HYRRR THINKS THE DUCK CREATURE DOES WELL TO TREMBLE!
BAH! MORAQ IS AN OLD, WEAK FOOL WHO CANNOT BEAR TO EVEN SEE A HUMAN! THIS IS BECAUSE HUMANS REMIND MORAQ...
...OF MORAQ'S MANY DEFEATS AT THE HANDS OF BRENDON!
BUT ONCE GENERAL HYRRR IS IN COMMAND OF TOOM...!!!
!

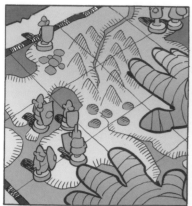

LORD MORAQ? GENERAL HYRRR HAS BROUGHT THE DUCK CREATURES!

IT MAKES LITTLE DIFFERENCE, BUT LORD MORAQ CHOOSES *THAT* ONE! TAKE THE OTHER AND *GO!*

LORD MORAQ IS IN THE MIDST OF PLANNING A *STRATEGY* TO DEFEAT BRE—

≈GRR!≈ THE *HUMAN!*

WHAP!

FIFTY ADDITIONAL DRAGONLORDS WILL ARRIVE SOON! THEN THE MORG WILL *ENCIRCLE* THE FREE HUMANS AND—

BAH! "STRATEGIES" ARE *NOT* THE *MORG* WAY! THE MORG ATTACK *HEAD*-ON AND *CRUSH* THE HUMANS' SKULLS!

WHAT?! DOES GENERAL HYRRR DARE *CHALLENGE* LORD MORAQ'S COMMAND?!

NOT... YET...

LORD MORAQ *THOUGHT* NOT!

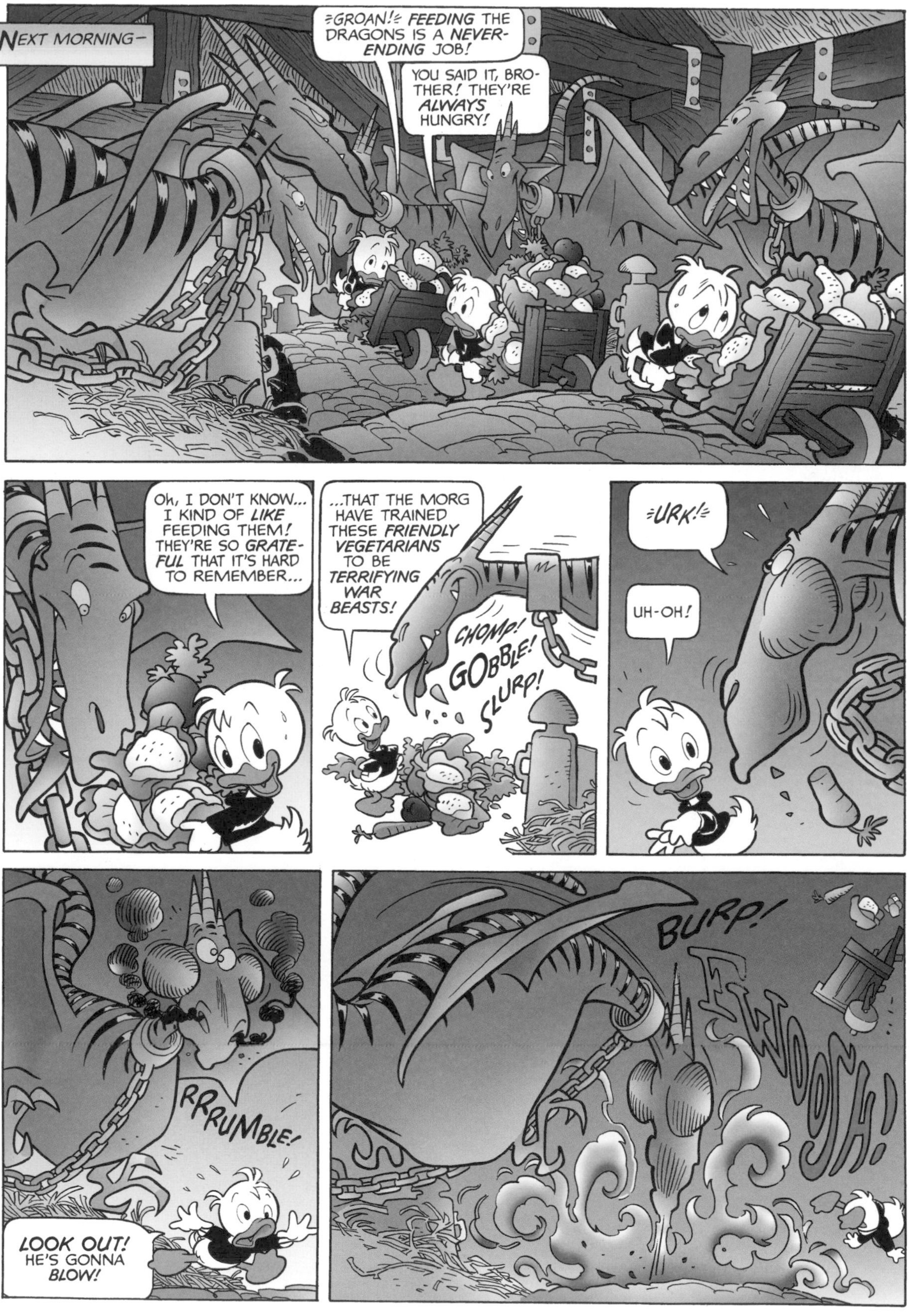
NEXT MORNING—
≈GROAN!≈ FEEDING THE DRAGONS IS A NEVER-ENDING JOB!
YOU SAID IT, BROTHER! THEY'RE ALWAYS HUNGRY!
Oh, I DON'T KNOW... I KIND OF LIKE FEEDING THEM! THEY'RE SO GRATEFUL THAT IT'S HARD TO REMEMBER...
...THAT THE MORG HAVE TRAINED THESE FRIENDLY VEGETARIANS TO BE TERRIFYING WAR BEASTS!
CHOMP! GOBBLE! SLURP!
≈URK!≈
UH-OH!
RRRUMBLE!
LOOK OUT! HE'S GONNA BLOW!
BURP!
FWOOSH!

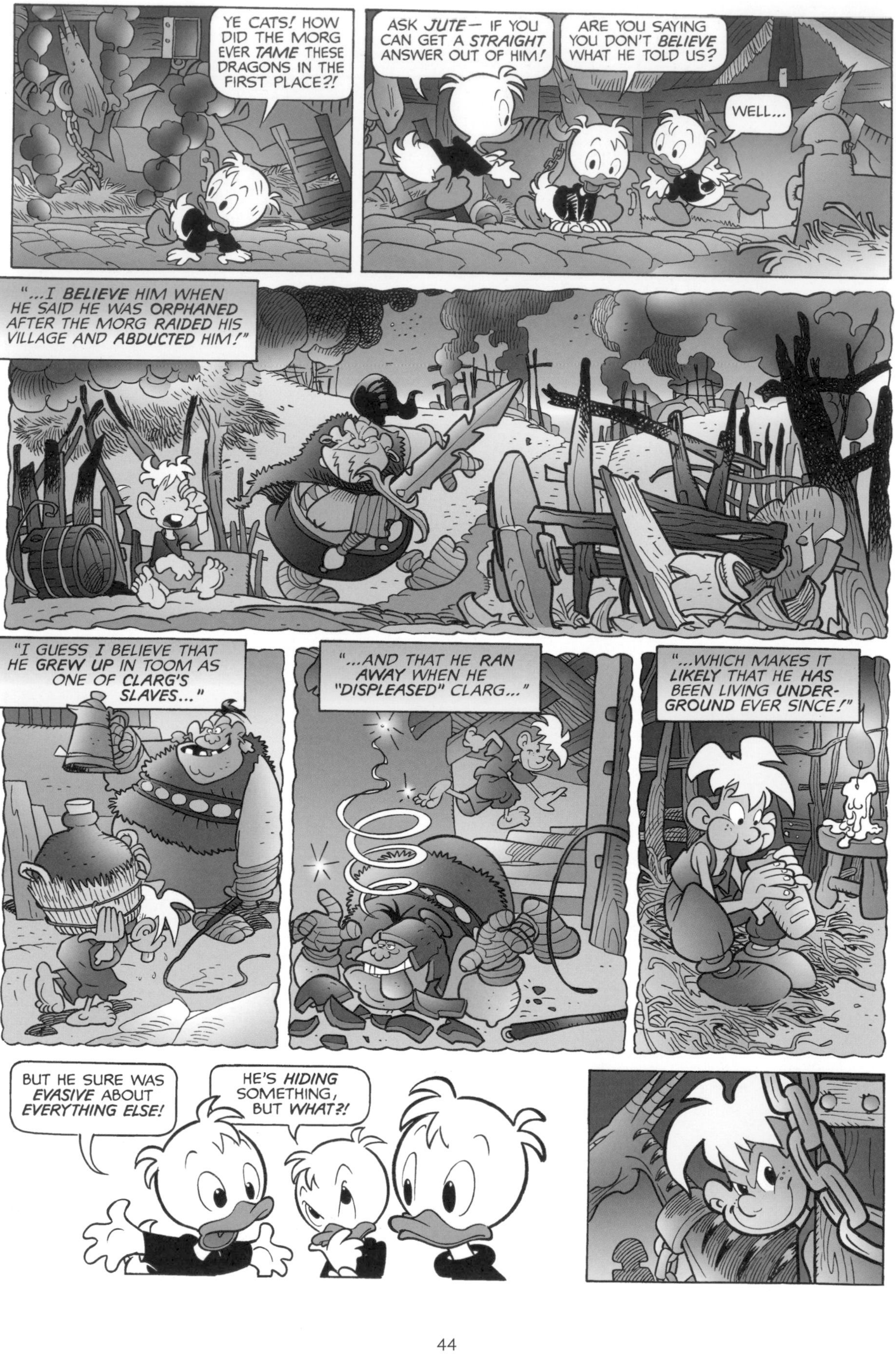

YE CATS! HOW DID THE MORG EVER TAME THESE DRAGONS IN THE FIRST PLACE?!
ASK JUTE— IF YOU CAN GET A STRAIGHT ANSWER OUT OF HIM!
ARE YOU SAYING YOU DON'T BELIEVE WHAT HE TOLD US?
WELL...
"...I BELIEVE HIM WHEN HE SAID HE WAS ORPHANED AFTER THE MORG RAIDED HIS VILLAGE AND ABDUCTED HIM!"
"I GUESS I BELIEVE THAT HE GREW UP IN TOOM AS ONE OF CLARG'S SLAVES..."
"...AND THAT HE RAN AWAY WHEN HE "DISPLEASED" CLARG..."
"...WHICH MAKES IT LIKELY THAT HE HAS BEEN LIVING UNDER-GROUND EVER SINCE!"
BUT HE SURE WAS EVASIVE ABOUT EVERYTHING ELSE!
HE'S HIDING SOMETHING, BUT WHAT?!

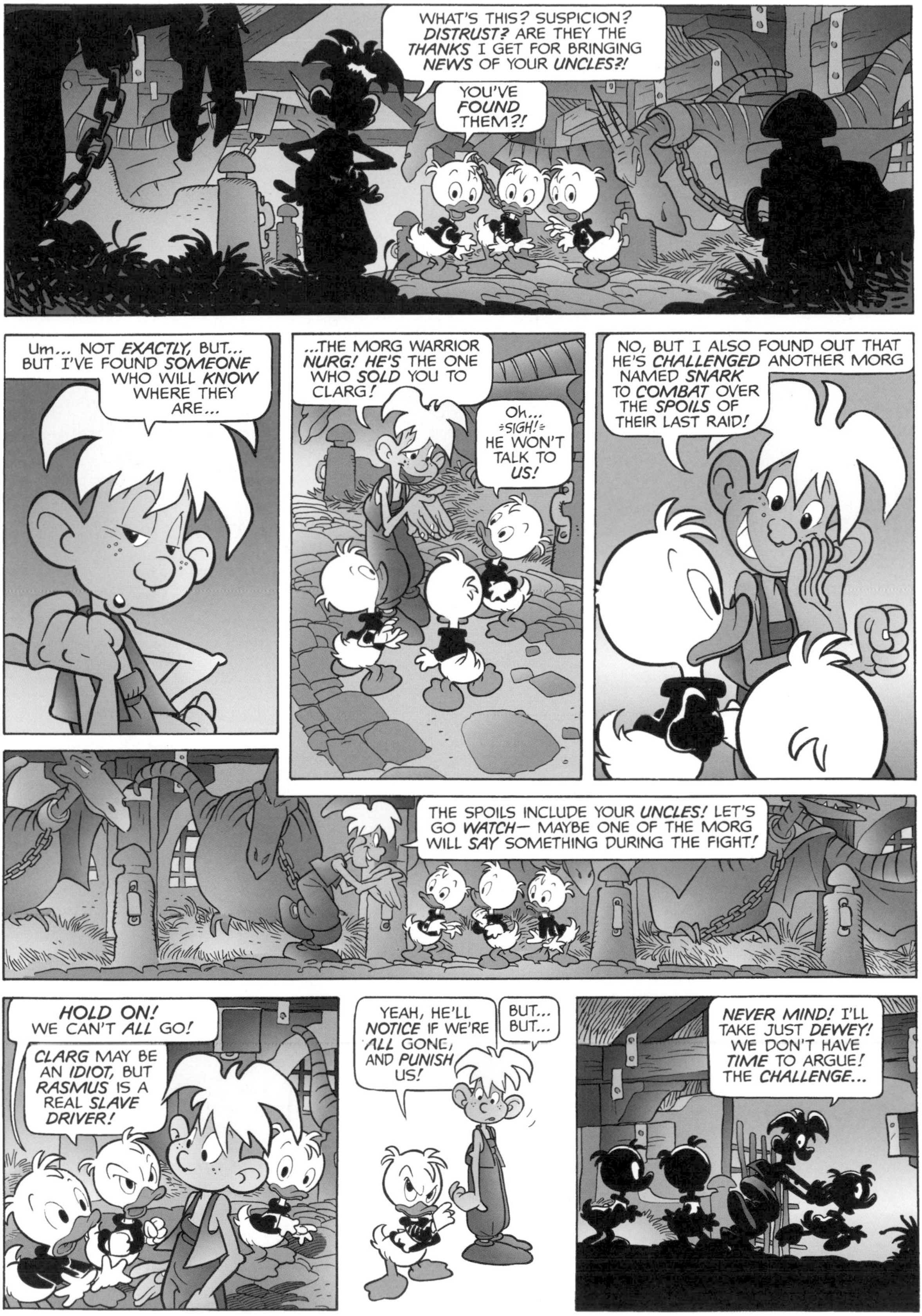
WHAT'S THIS? SUSPICION? DISTRUST? ARE THEY THE THANKS I GET FOR BRINGING NEWS OF YOUR UNCLES?!
YOU'VE FOUND THEM?!
Um... NOT EXACTLY, BUT... BUT I'VE FOUND SOMEONE WHO WILL KNOW WHERE THEY ARE...
...THE MORG WARRIOR NURG! HE'S THE ONE WHO SOLD YOU TO CLARG!
Oh... SIGH! HE WON'T TALK TO US!
NO, BUT I ALSO FOUND OUT THAT HE'S CHALLENGED ANOTHER MORG NAMED SNARK TO COMBAT OVER THE SPOILS OF THEIR LAST RAID!
THE SPOILS INCLUDE YOUR UNCLES! LET'S GO WATCH— MAYBE ONE OF THE MORG WILL SAY SOMETHING DURING THE FIGHT!
HOLD ON! WE CAN'T ALL GO!
CLARG MAY BE AN IDIOT, BUT RASMUS IS A REAL SLAVE DRIVER!
YEAH, HE'LL NOTICE IF WE'RE ALL GONE, AND PUNISH US!
BUT... BUT...
NEVER MIND! I'LL TAKE JUST DEWEY! WE DON'T HAVE TIME TO ARGUE! THE CHALLENGE...

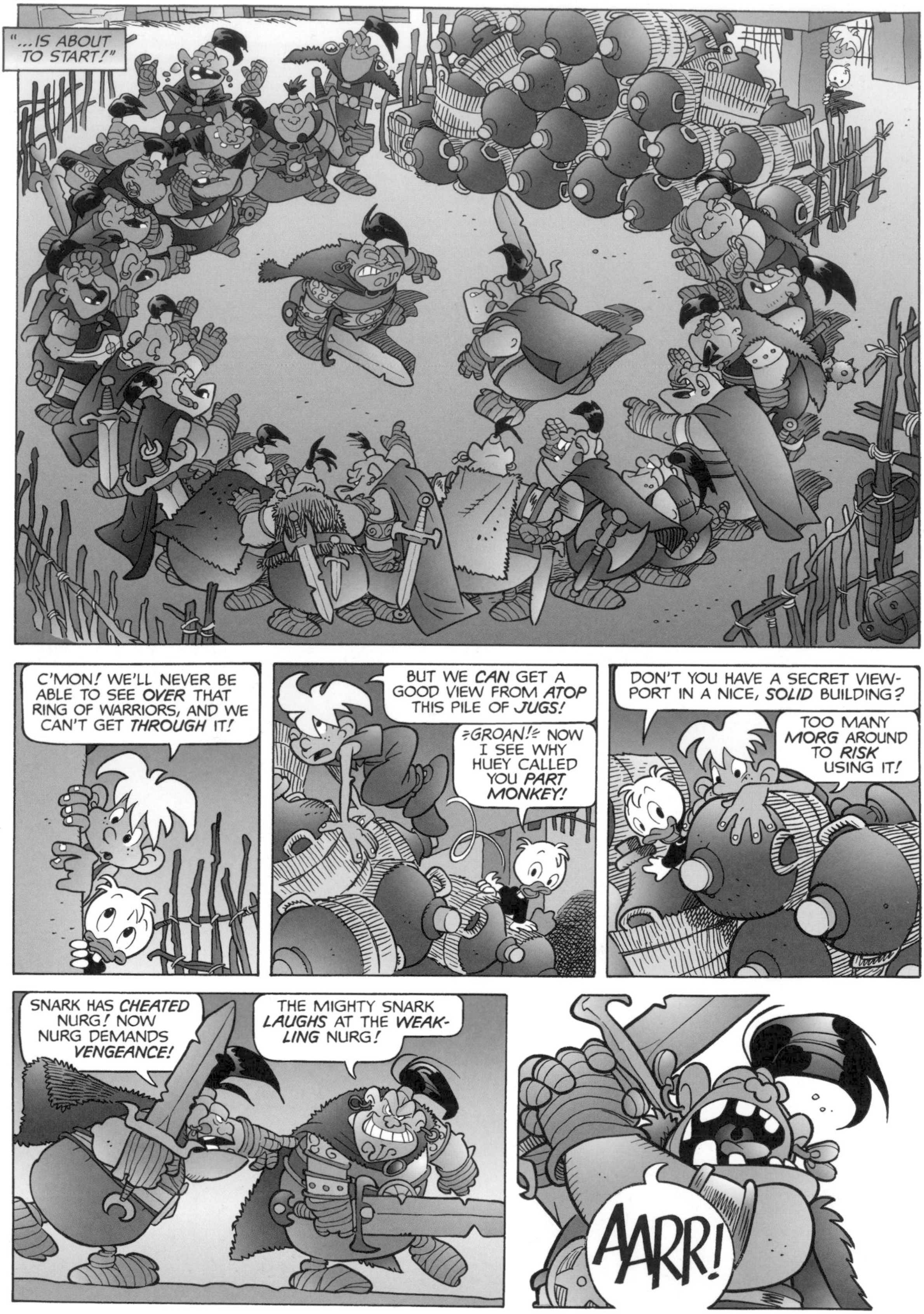

"...IS ABOUT TO START!"
C'MON! WE'LL NEVER BE ABLE TO SEE OVER THAT RING OF WARRIORS, AND WE CAN'T GET THROUGH IT!
BUT WE CAN GET A GOOD VIEW FROM ATOP THIS PILE OF JUGS!
GROAN! NOW I SEE WHY HUEY CALLED YOU PART MONKEY!
DON'T YOU HAVE A SECRET VIEW-PORT IN A NICE, SOLID BUILDING?
TOO MANY MORG AROUND TO RISK USING IT!
SNARK HAS CHEATED NURG! NOW NURG DEMANDS VENGEANCE!
THE MIGHTY SNARK LAUGHS AT THE WEAK-LING NURG!
AARR!

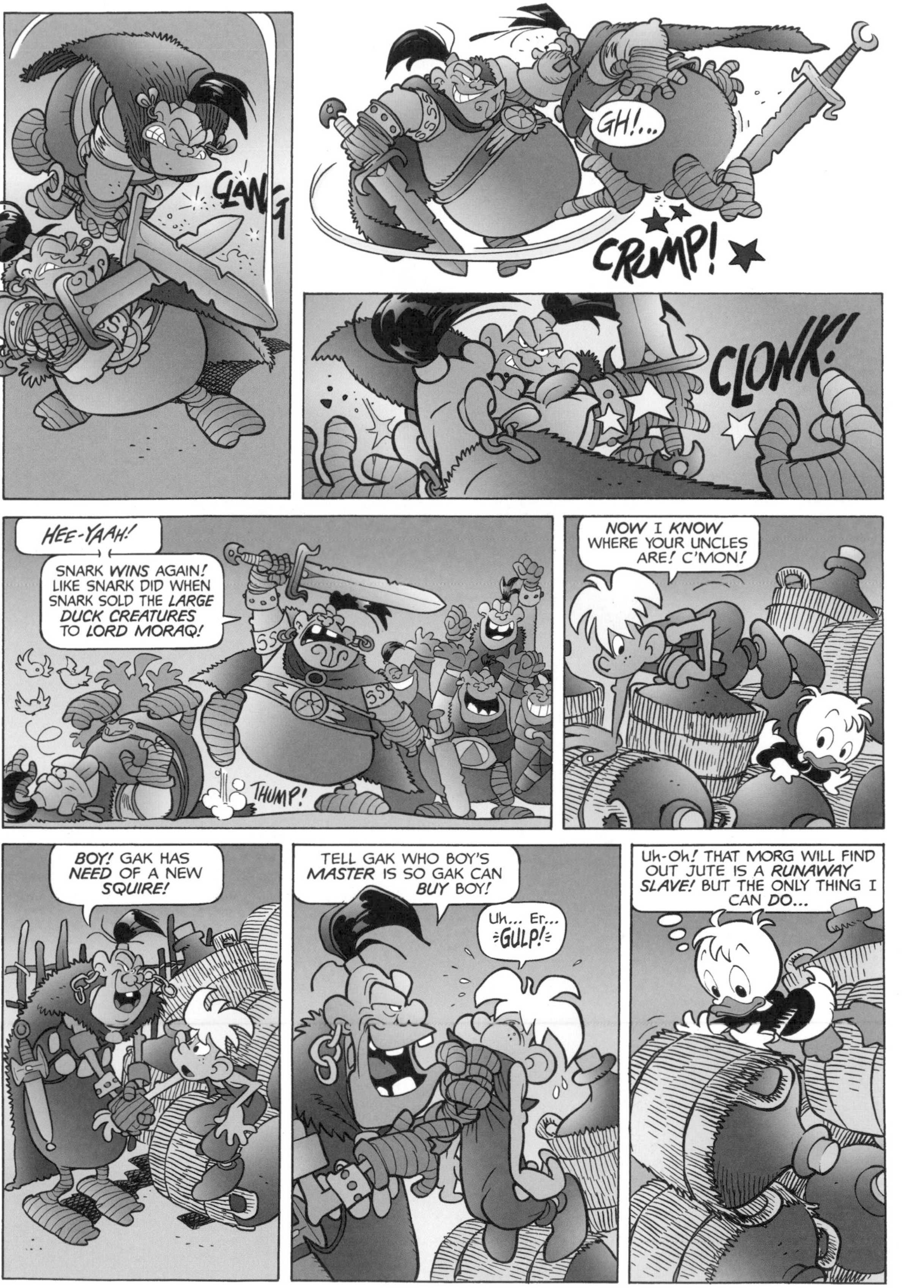
CLANG
GH!...
CRUMP!
CLONK!
HEE-YAAH!
SNARK WINS AGAIN! LIKE SNARK DID WHEN SNARK SOLD THE LARGE DUCK CREATURES TO LORD MORAQ!
THUMP!
NOW I KNOW WHERE YOUR UNCLES ARE! C'MON!
BOY! GAK HAS NEED OF A NEW SQUIRE!
TELL GAK WHO BOY'S MASTER IS SO GAK CAN BUY BOY!
Uh... Er... GULP!
Uh-Oh! THAT MORG WILL FIND OUT JUTE IS A RUNAWAY SLAVE! BUT THE ONLY THING I CAN DO...

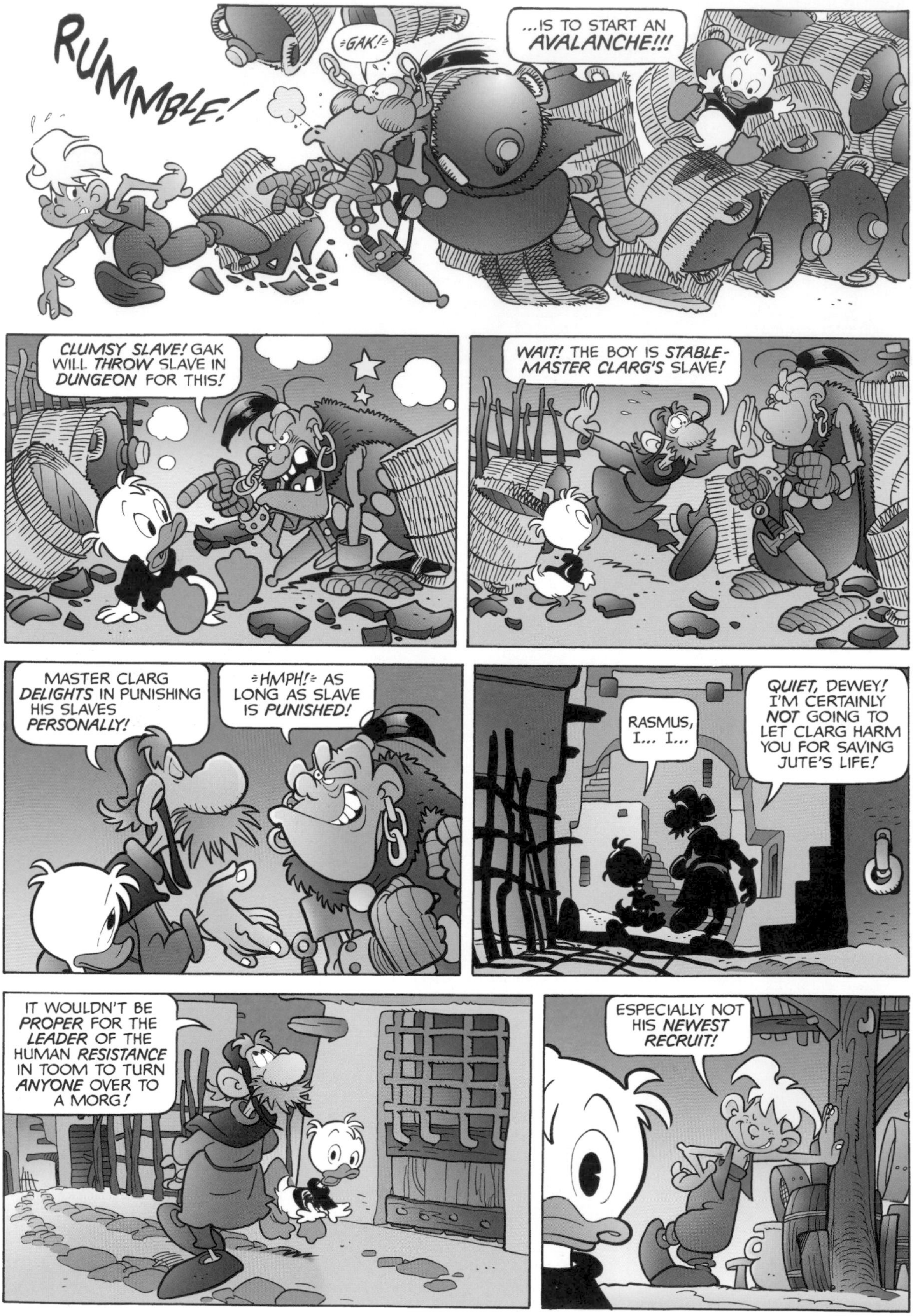
RUMMBLE!
=GAK!=
...IS TO START AN AVALANCHE!!!
CLUMSY SLAVE! GAK WILL THROW SLAVE IN DUNGEON FOR THIS!
WAIT! THE BOY IS STABLE-MASTER CLARG'S SLAVE!
MASTER CLARG DELIGHTS IN PUNISHING HIS SLAVES PERSONALLY!
=HMPH!= AS LONG AS SLAVE IS PUNISHED!
RASMUS, I... I...
QUIET, DEWEY! I'M CERTAINLY NOT GOING TO LET CLARG HARM YOU FOR SAVING JUTE'S LIFE!
IT WOULDN'T BE PROPER FOR THE LEADER OF THE HUMAN RESISTANCE IN TOOM TO TURN ANYONE OVER TO A MORG!
ESPECIALLY NOT HIS NEWEST RECRUIT!

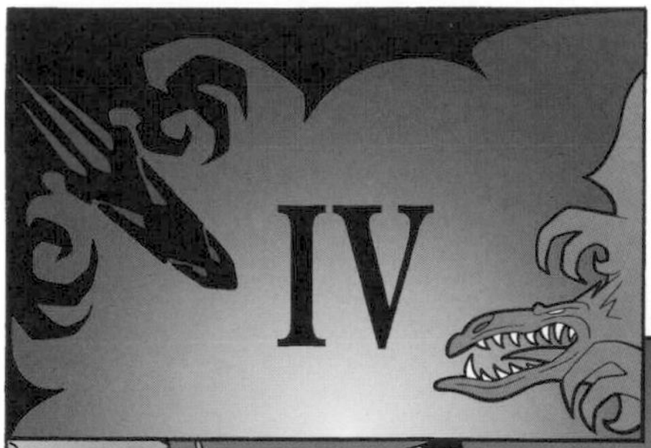
IV

WORLD OF THE DRAGONLORDS
CHAPTER 4: THREE FOR THREE

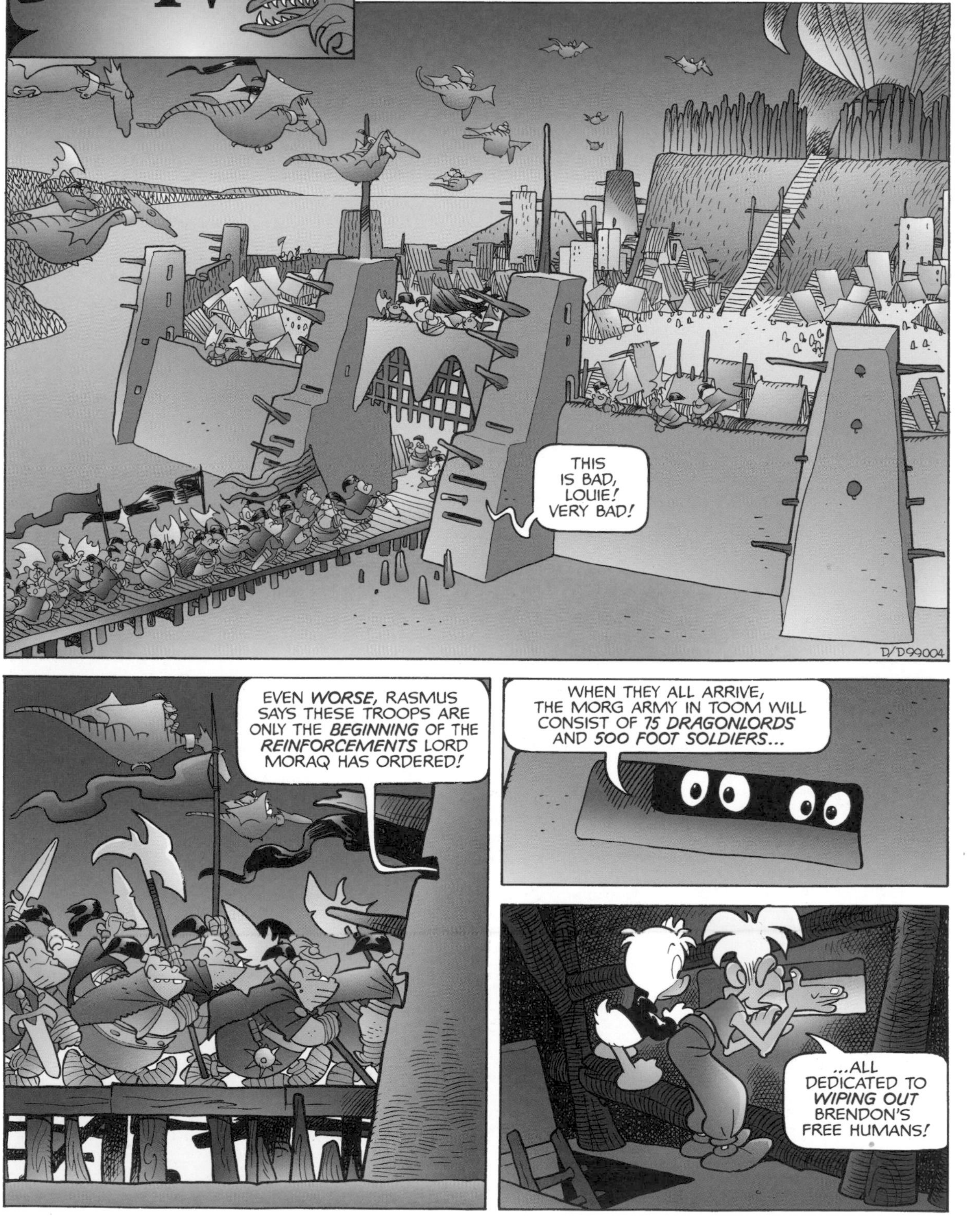
THIS IS BAD, LOUIE! VERY BAD!
D/D99004
EVEN WORSE, RASMUS SAYS THESE TROOPS ARE ONLY THE BEGINNING OF THE REINFORCEMENTS LORD MORAQ HAS ORDERED!
WHEN THEY ALL ARRIVE, THE MORG ARMY IN TOOM WILL CONSIST OF 75 DRAGONLORDS AND 500 FOOT SOLDIERS...
...ALL DEDICATED TO WIPING OUT BRENDON'S FREE HUMANS!

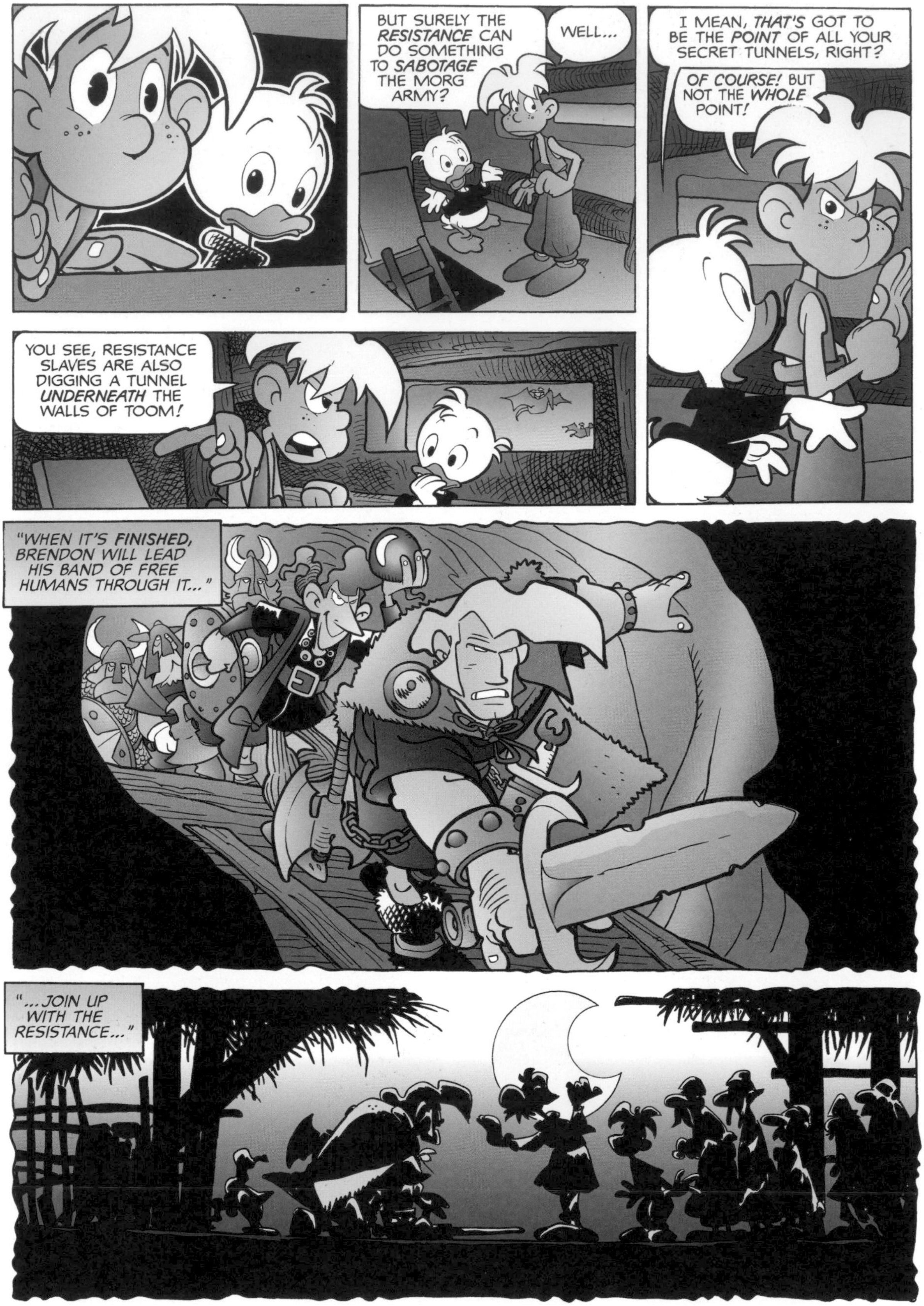
BUT SURELY THE RESISTANCE CAN DO SOMETHING TO SABOTAGE THE MORG ARMY?
WELL...
I MEAN, THAT'S GOT TO BE THE POINT OF ALL YOUR SECRET TUNNELS, RIGHT?
OF COURSE! BUT NOT THE WHOLE POINT!
YOU SEE, RESISTANCE SLAVES ARE ALSO DIGGING A TUNNEL UNDERNEATH THE WALLS OF TOOM!
"WHEN IT'S FINISHED, BRENDON WILL LEAD HIS BAND OF FREE HUMANS THROUGH IT..."
"...JOIN UP WITH THE RESISTANCE..."

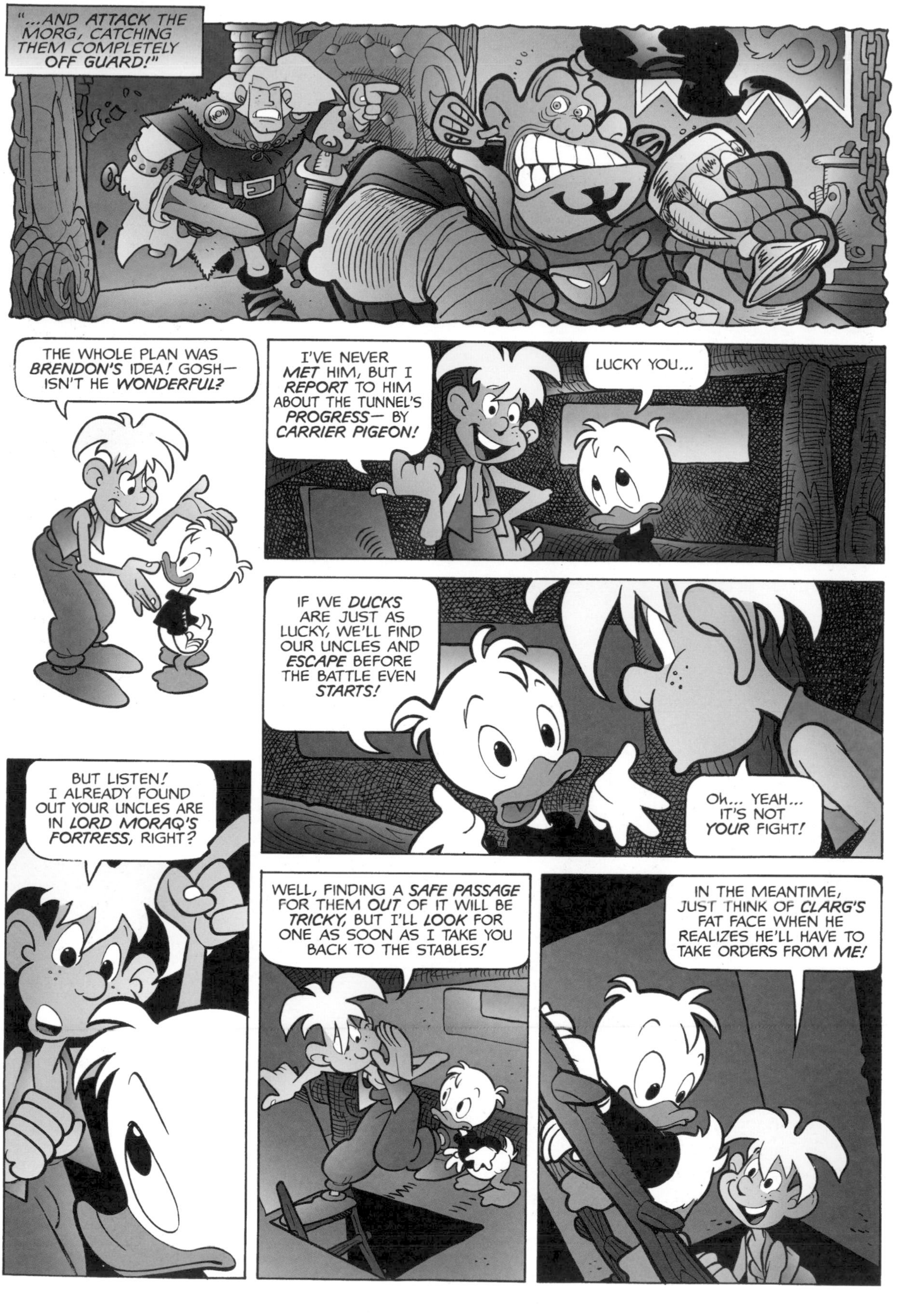

"...AND ATTACK THE MORG, CATCHING THEM COMPLETELY OFF GUARD!"
THE WHOLE PLAN WAS BRENDON'S IDEA! GOSH— ISN'T HE WONDERFUL?
I'VE NEVER MET HIM, BUT I REPORT TO HIM ABOUT THE TUNNEL'S PROGRESS— BY CARRIER PIGEON!
LUCKY YOU...
IF WE DUCKS ARE JUST AS LUCKY, WE'LL FIND OUR UNCLES AND ESCAPE BEFORE THE BATTLE EVEN STARTS!
Oh... YEAH... IT'S NOT YOUR FIGHT!
BUT LISTEN! I ALREADY FOUND OUT YOUR UNCLES ARE IN LORD MORAQ'S FORTRESS, RIGHT?
WELL, FINDING A SAFE PASSAGE FOR THEM OUT OF IT WILL BE TRICKY, BUT I'LL LOOK FOR ONE AS SOON AS I TAKE YOU BACK TO THE STABLES!
IN THE MEANTIME, JUST THINK OF CLARG'S FAT FACE WHEN HE REALIZES HE'LL HAVE TO TAKE ORDERS FROM ME!

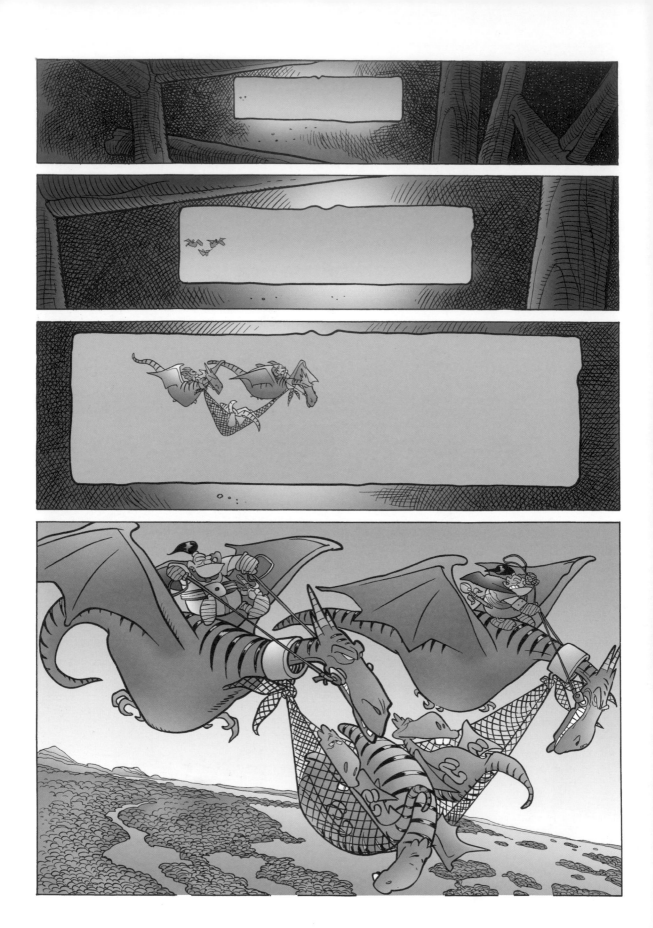

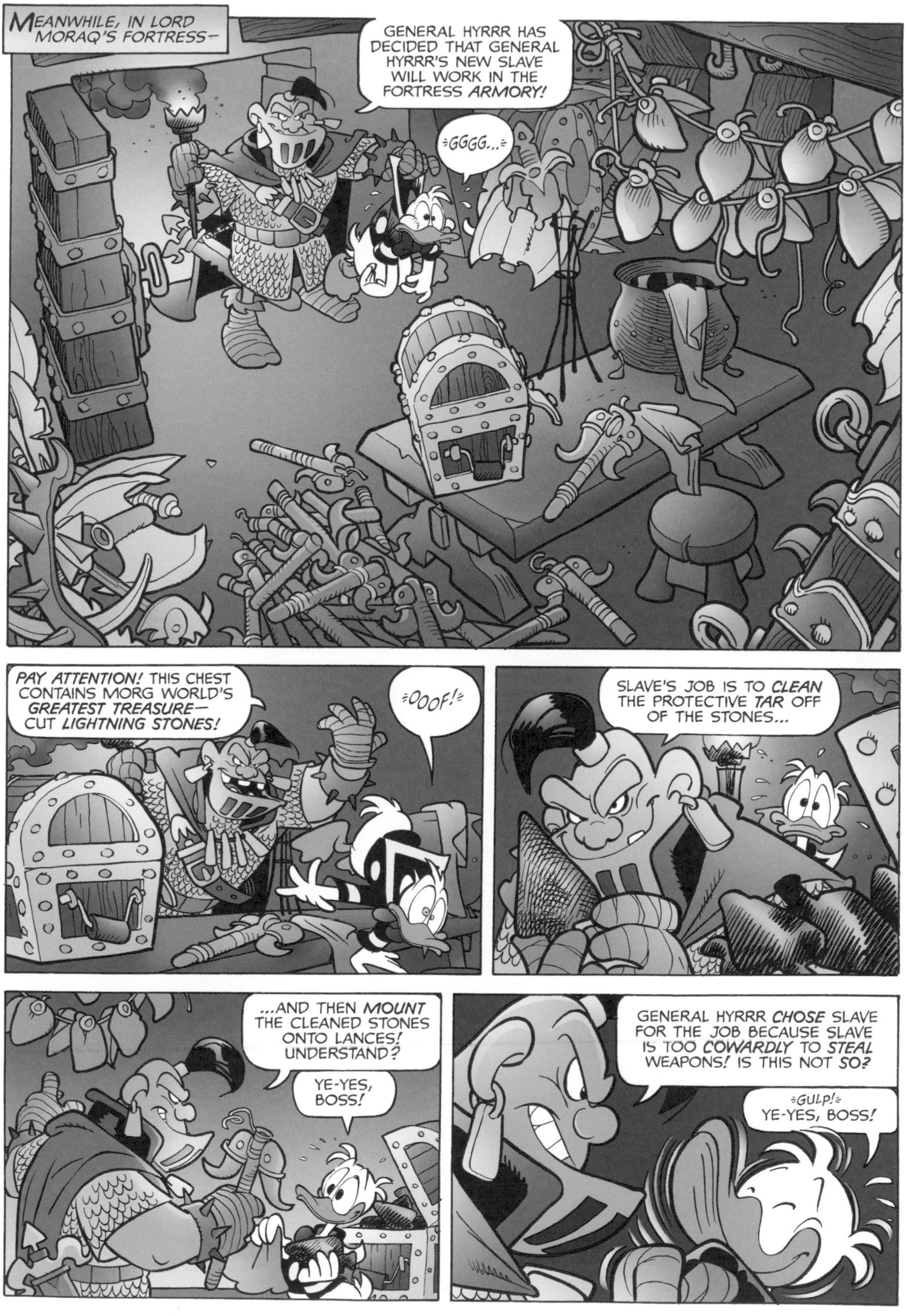
MEANWHILE, IN LORD MORAQ'S FORTRESS—
GENERAL HYRRR HAS DECIDED THAT GENERAL HYRRR'S NEW SLAVE WILL WORK IN THE FORTRESS ARMORY!
GGGG...
PAY ATTENTION! THIS CHEST CONTAINS MORG WORLD'S GREATEST TREASURE— CUT LIGHTNING STONES!
OOOF!
SLAVE'S JOB IS TO CLEAN THE PROTECTIVE TAR OFF OF THE STONES...
...AND THEN MOUNT THE CLEANED STONES ONTO LANCES! UNDERSTAND?
YE-YES, BOSS!
GENERAL HYRRR CHOSE SLAVE FOR THE JOB BECAUSE SLAVE IS TOO COWARDLY TO STEAL WEAPONS! IS THIS NOT SO?
GULP!
YE-YES, BOSS!

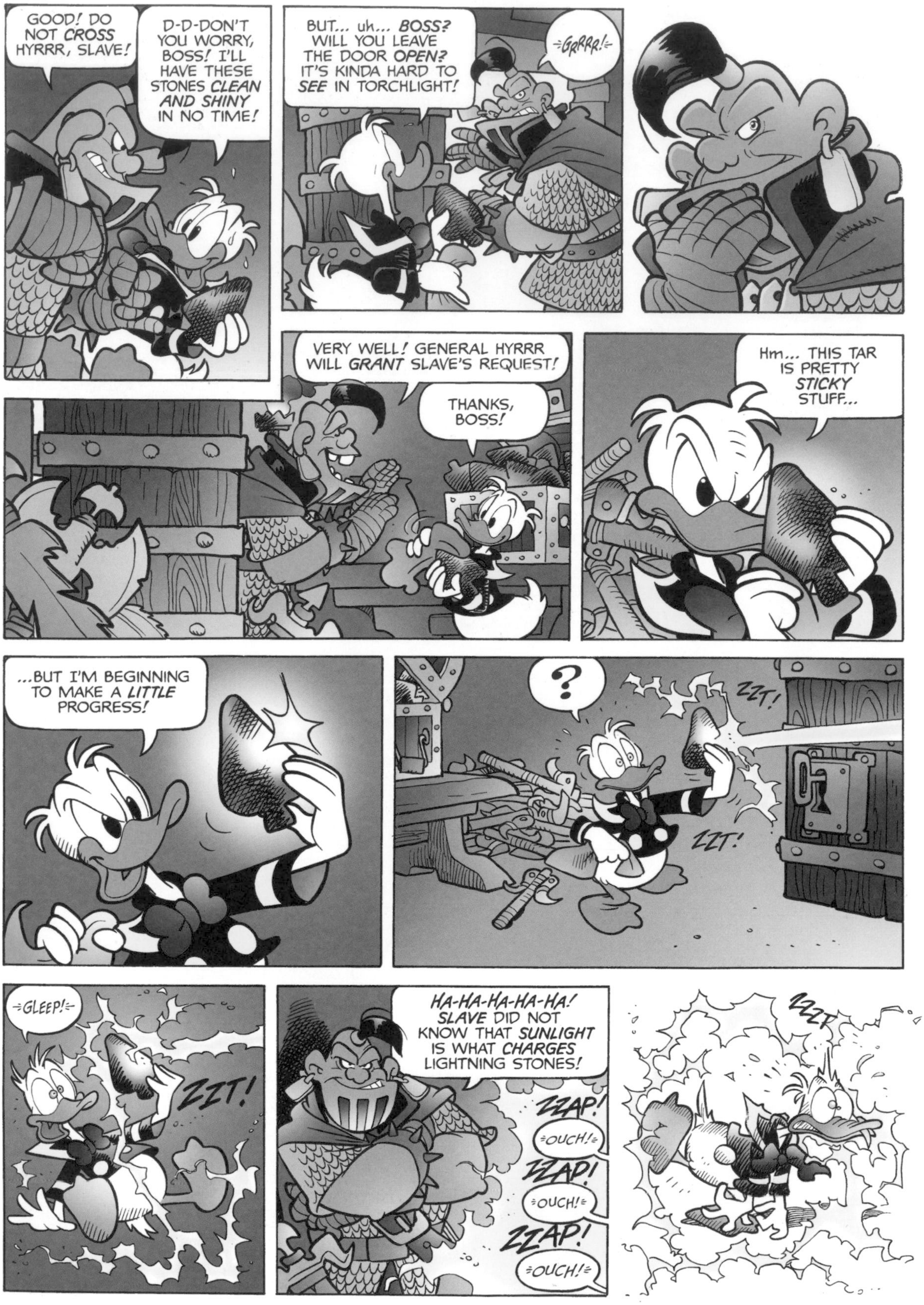

GOOD! DO NOT CROSS HYRRR, SLAVE!
D-D-DON'T YOU WORRY, BOSS! I'LL HAVE THESE STONES CLEAN AND SHINY IN NO TIME!
BUT... uh... BOSS? WILL YOU LEAVE THE DOOR OPEN? IT'S KINDA HARD TO SEE IN TORCHLIGHT!
GRRRR!
VERY WELL! GENERAL HYRRR WILL GRANT SLAVE'S REQUEST!
THANKS, BOSS!
Hm... THIS TAR IS PRETTY STICKY STUFF...
...BUT I'M BEGINNING TO MAKE A LITTLE PROGRESS!
?
ZZT!
ZZT!
GLEEP!
ZZT!
HA-HA-HA-HA-HA! SLAVE DID NOT KNOW THAT SUNLIGHT IS WHAT CHARGES LIGHTNING STONES!
ZZAP!
OUCH!
ZZAP!
OUCH!
ZZAP!
OUCH!
ZZZT

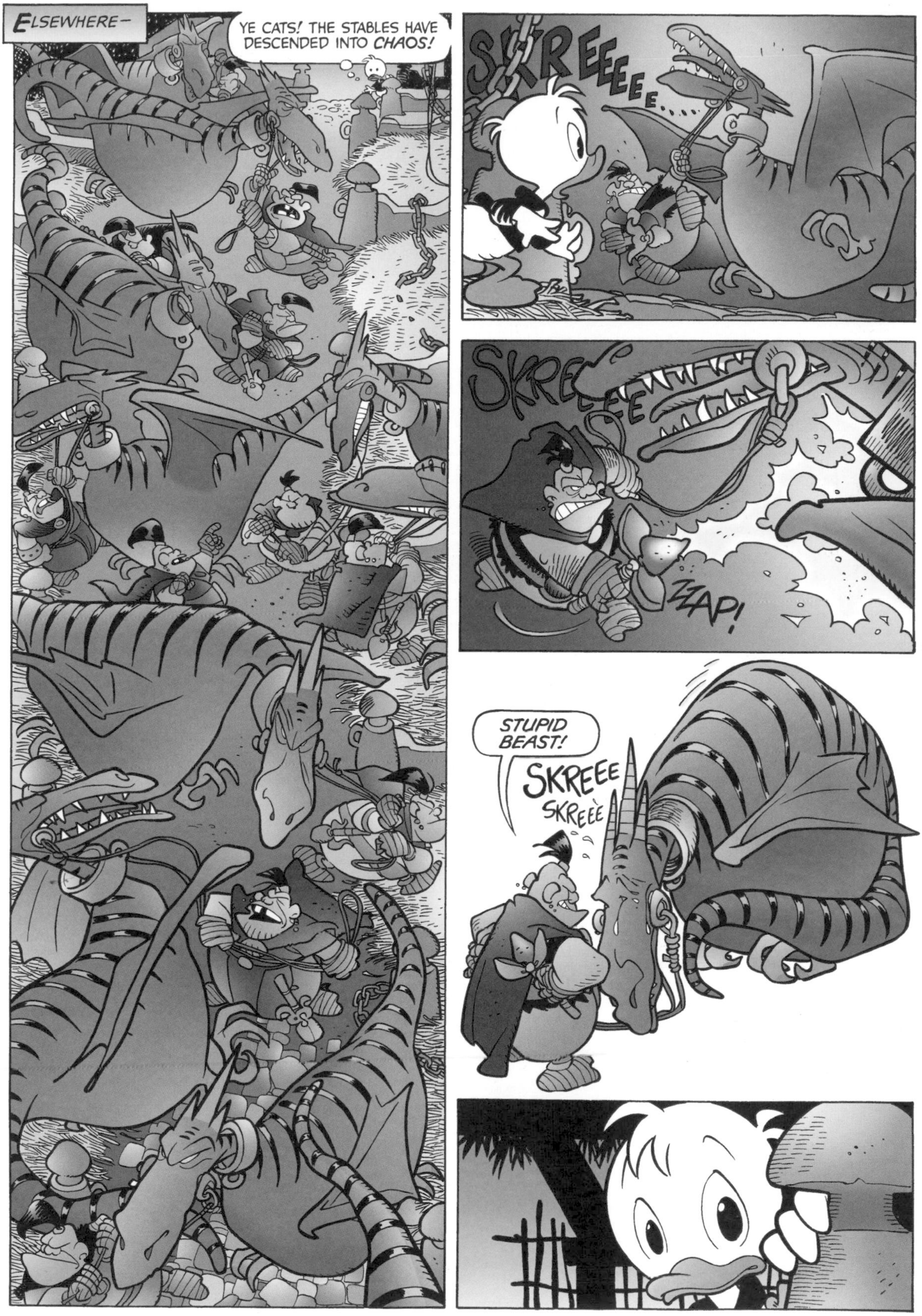
ELSEWHERE—
YE CATS! THE STABLES HAVE DESCENDED INTO CHAOS!
SKREEEEEEE...
SKREEEE
ZZAP!
STUPID BEAST!
SKREEE
SKREEE

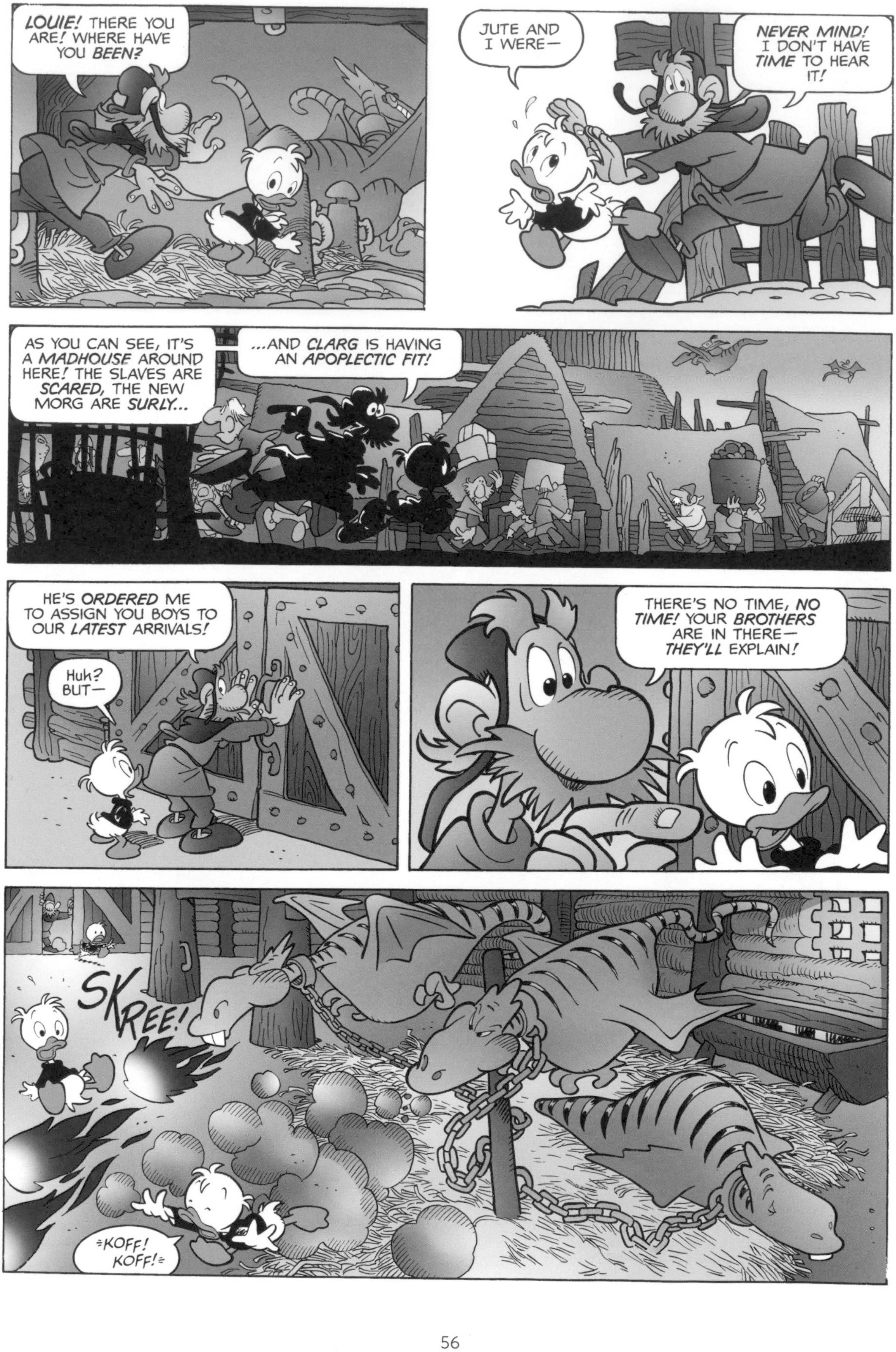
LOUIE! THERE YOU ARE! WHERE HAVE YOU BEEN?
JUTE AND I WERE—
NEVER MIND! I DON'T HAVE TIME TO HEAR IT!
AS YOU CAN SEE, IT'S A MADHOUSE AROUND HERE! THE SLAVES ARE SCARED, THE NEW MORG ARE SURLY...
...AND CLARG IS HAVING AN APOPLECTIC FIT!
HE'S ORDERED ME TO ASSIGN YOU BOYS TO OUR LATEST ARRIVALS!
Huh? BUT—
THERE'S NO TIME, NO TIME! YOUR BROTHERS ARE IN THERE— THEY'LL EXPLAIN!
SKREE!
KOFF! KOFF!

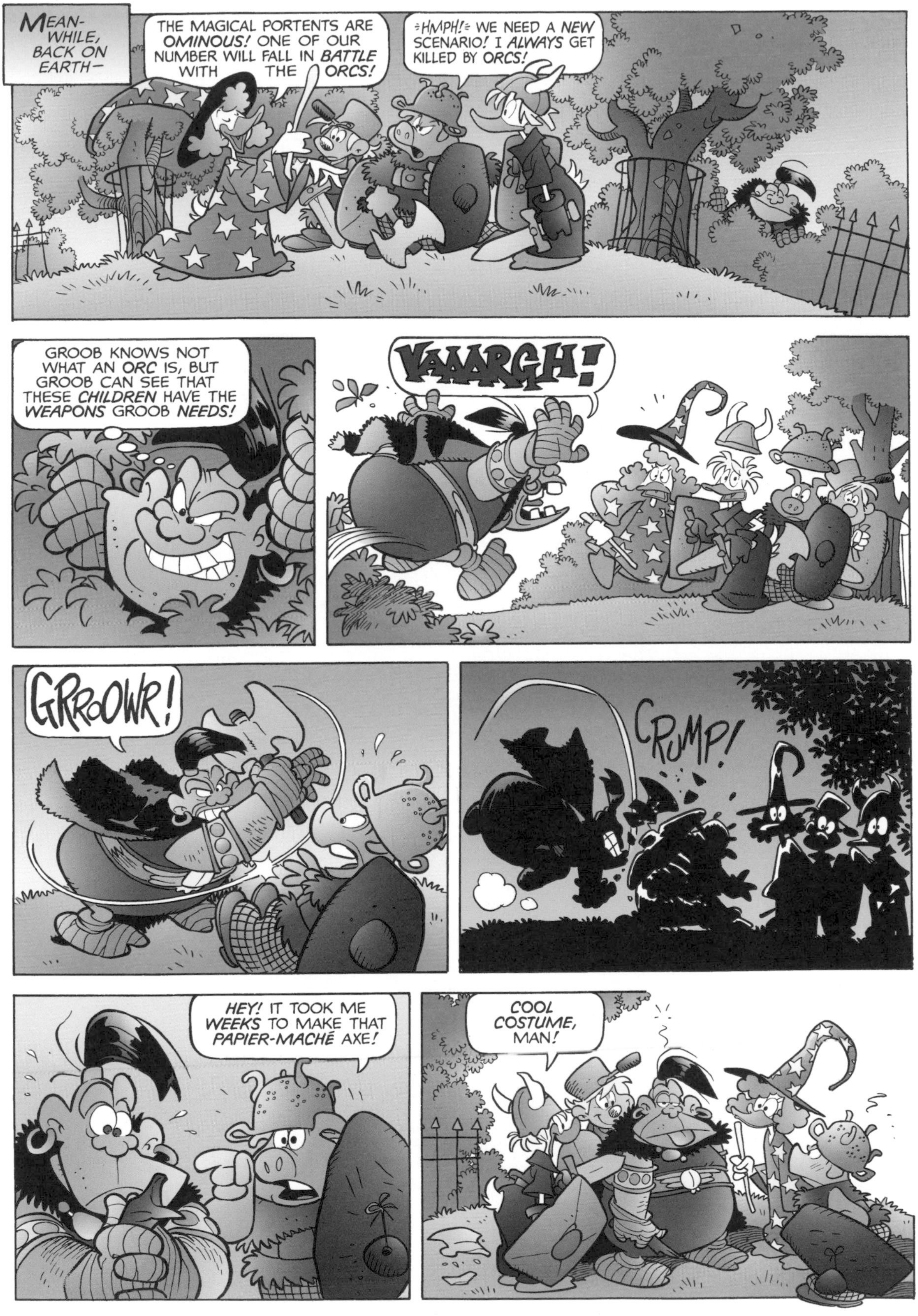
MEAN-WHILE, BACK ON EARTH—
THE MAGICAL PORTENTS ARE OMINOUS! ONE OF OUR NUMBER WILL FALL IN BATTLE WITH THE ORCS!
=HMPH!= WE NEED A NEW SCENARIO! I ALWAYS GET KILLED BY ORCS!
GROOB KNOWS NOT WHAT AN ORC IS, BUT GROOB CAN SEE THAT THESE CHILDREN HAVE THE WEAPONS GROOB NEEDS!
YAAARGH!
GRROOWR!
CRUMP!
HEY! IT TOOK ME WEEKS TO MAKE THAT PAPIER-MACHÉ AXE!
COOL COSTUME, MAN!

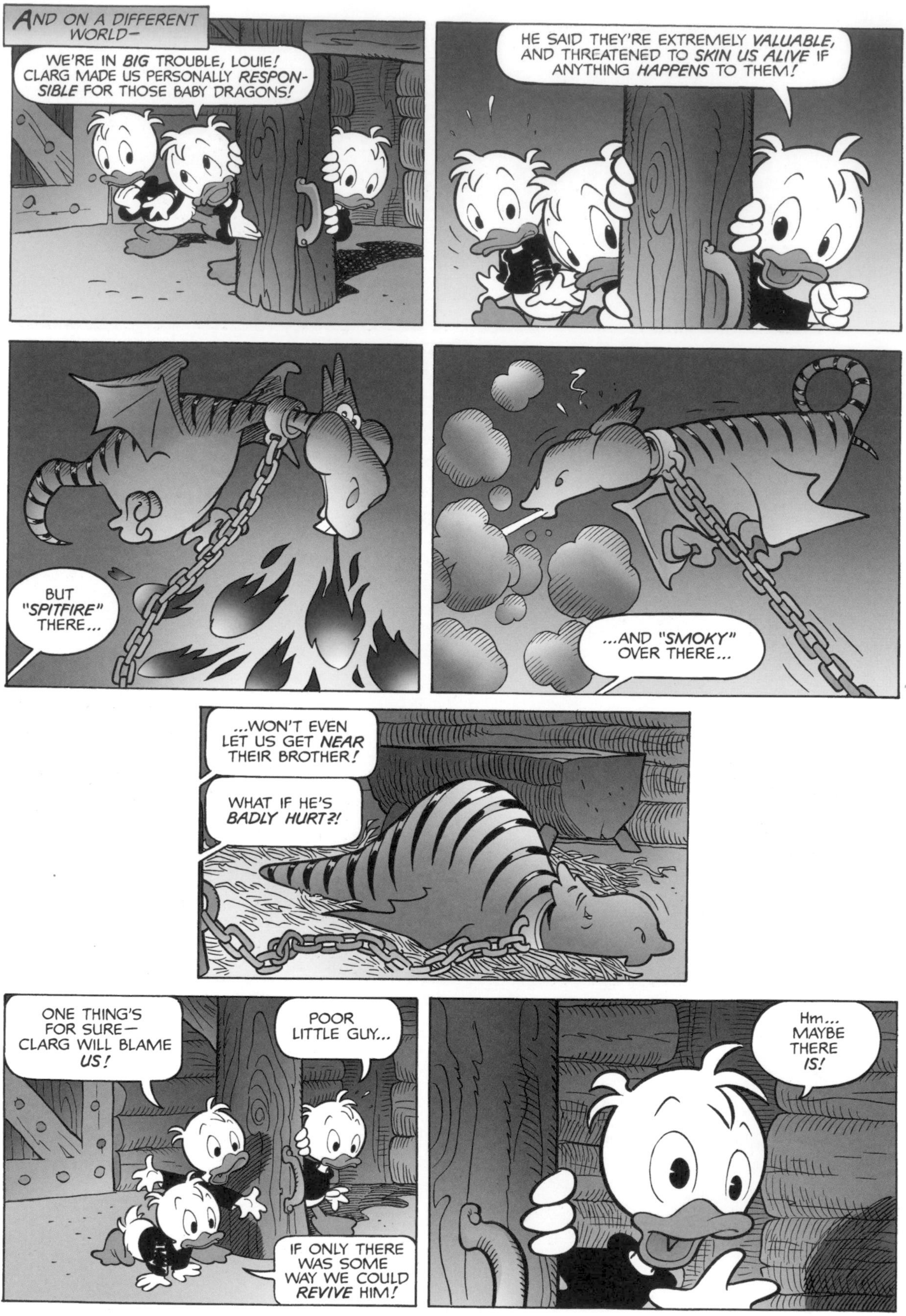
AND ON A DIFFERENT WORLD—
WE'RE IN BIG TROUBLE, LOUIE! CLARG MADE US PERSONALLY RESPONSIBLE FOR THOSE BABY DRAGONS!
HE SAID THEY'RE EXTREMELY VALUABLE, AND THREATENED TO SKIN US ALIVE IF ANYTHING HAPPENS TO THEM!
BUT "SPITFIRE" THERE...
...AND "SMOKY" OVER THERE...
...WON'T EVEN LET US GET NEAR THEIR BROTHER!
WHAT IF HE'S BADLY HURT?!
ONE THING'S FOR SURE— CLARG WILL BLAME US!
POOR LITTLE GUY...
IF ONLY THERE WAS SOME WAY WE COULD REVIVE HIM!
Hm... MAYBE THERE IS!

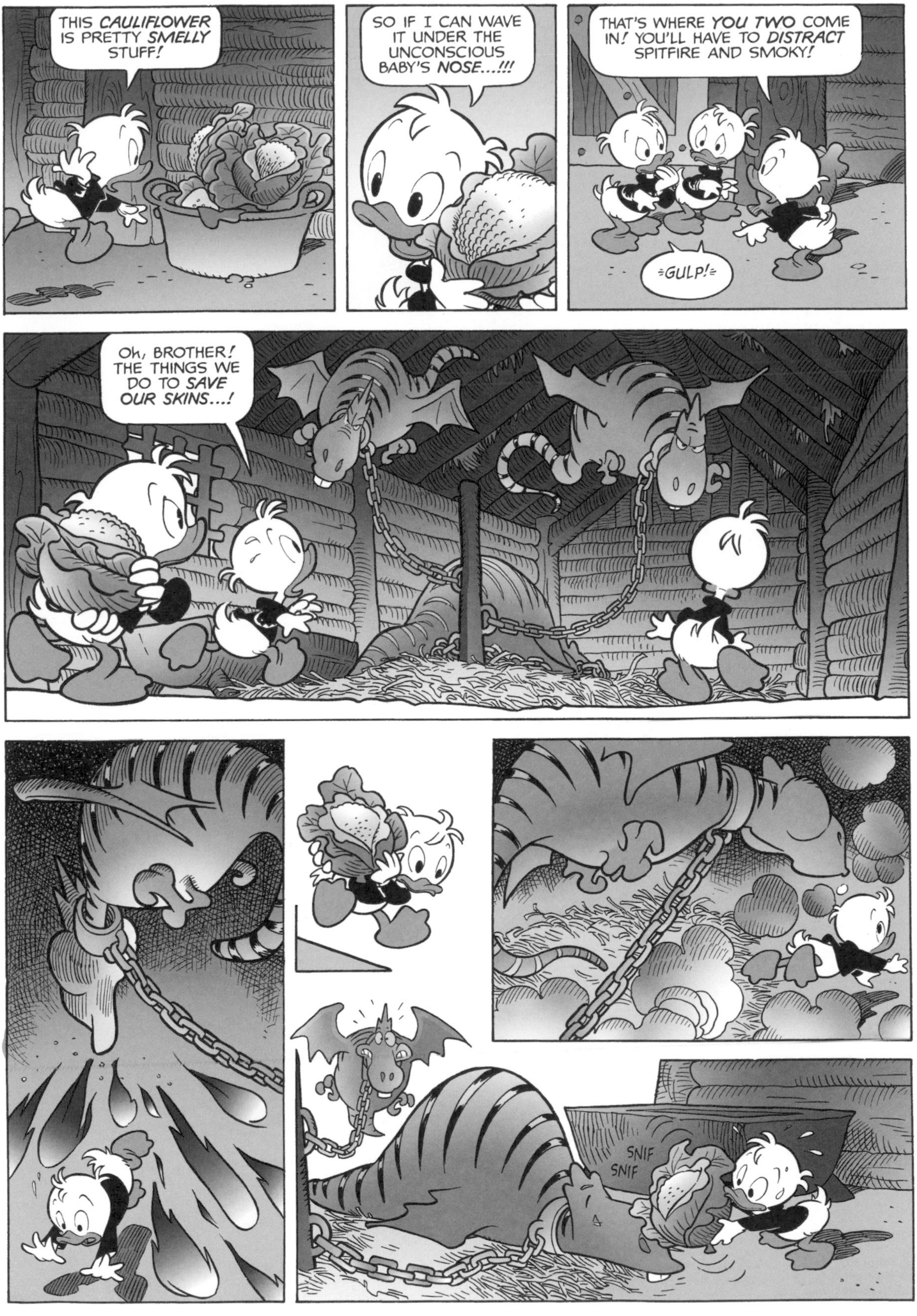
THIS CAULIFLOWER IS PRETTY SMELLY STUFF!
SO IF I CAN WAVE IT UNDER THE UNCONSCIOUS BABY'S NOSE...!!!
THAT'S WHERE YOU TWO COME IN! YOU'LL HAVE TO DISTRACT SPITFIRE AND SMOKY!
GULP!
Oh, BROTHER! THE THINGS WE DO TO SAVE OUR SKINS...!
SNIF SNIF

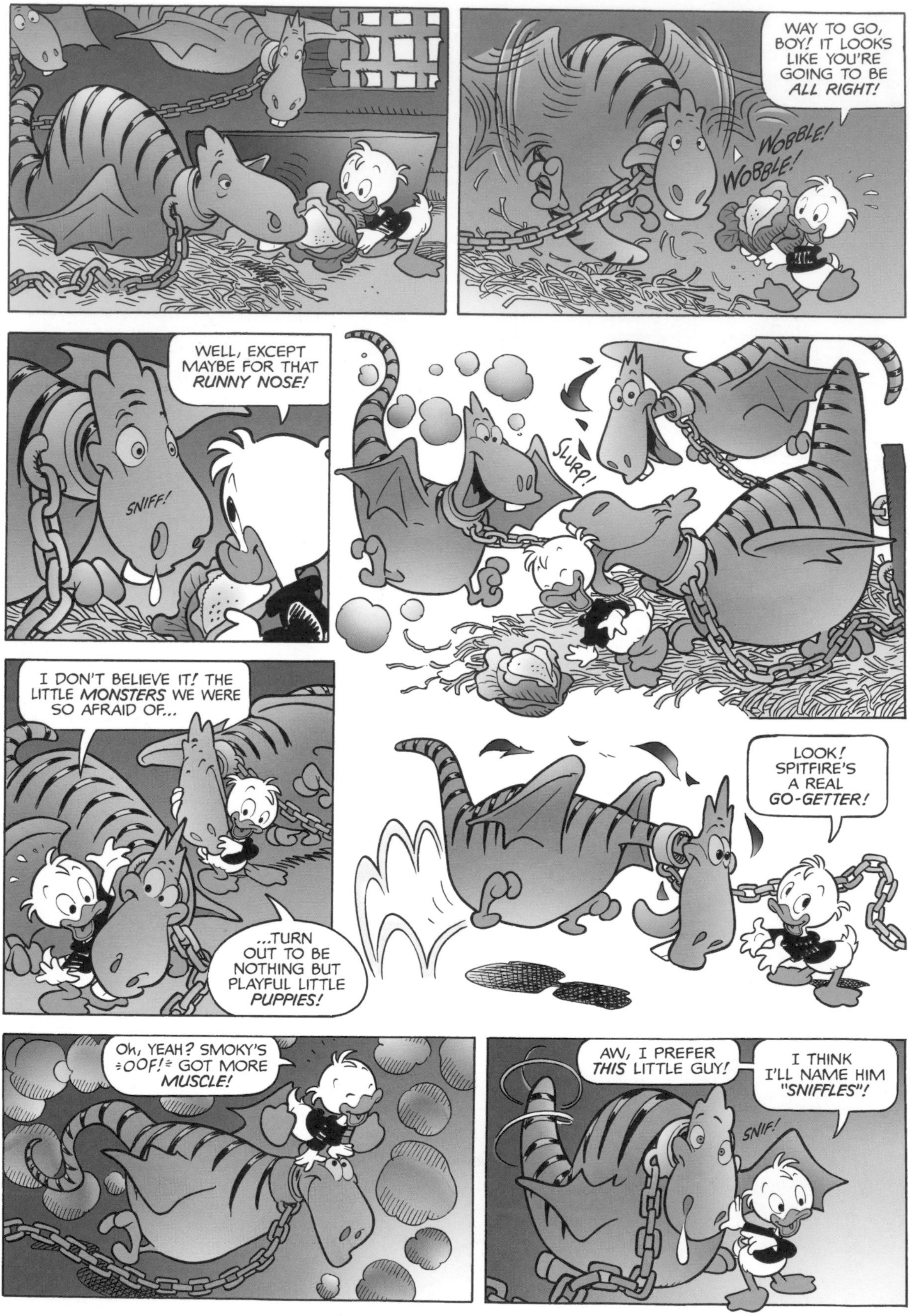
WAY TO GO, BOY! IT LOOKS LIKE YOU'RE GOING TO BE ALL RIGHT!
WOBBLE! WOBBLE!
WELL, EXCEPT MAYBE FOR THAT RUNNY NOSE!
SNIFF!
SLURP!
I DON'T BELIEVE IT! THE LITTLE MONSTERS WE WERE SO AFRAID OF...
...TURN OUT TO BE NOTHING BUT PLAYFUL LITTLE PUPPIES!
LOOK! SPITFIRE'S A REAL GO-GETTER!
Oh, YEAH? SMOKY'S =OOF!= GOT MORE MUSCLE!
AW, I PREFER THIS LITTLE GUY!
I THINK I'LL NAME HIM "SNIFFLES"!
SNIF!

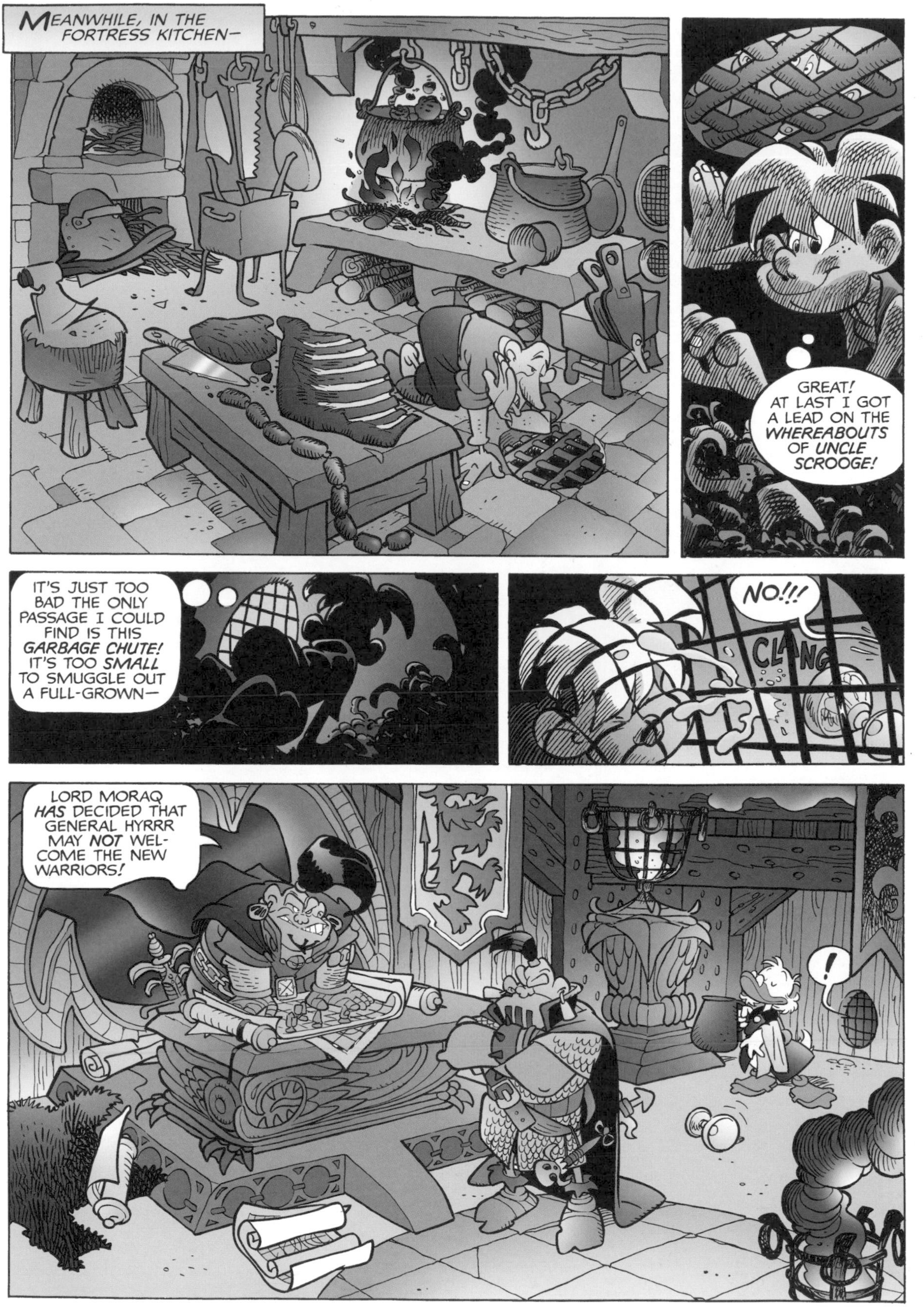
MEANWHILE, IN THE FORTRESS KITCHEN—
GREAT! AT LAST I GOT A LEAD ON THE WHEREABOUTS OF UNCLE SCROOGE!
IT'S JUST TOO BAD THE ONLY PASSAGE I COULD FIND IS THIS GARBAGE CHUTE! IT'S TOO SMALL TO SMUGGLE OUT A FULL-GROWN—
NO!!!
CLANG
LORD MORAQ HAS DECIDED THAT GENERAL HYRRR MAY NOT WELCOME THE NEW WARRIORS!
!

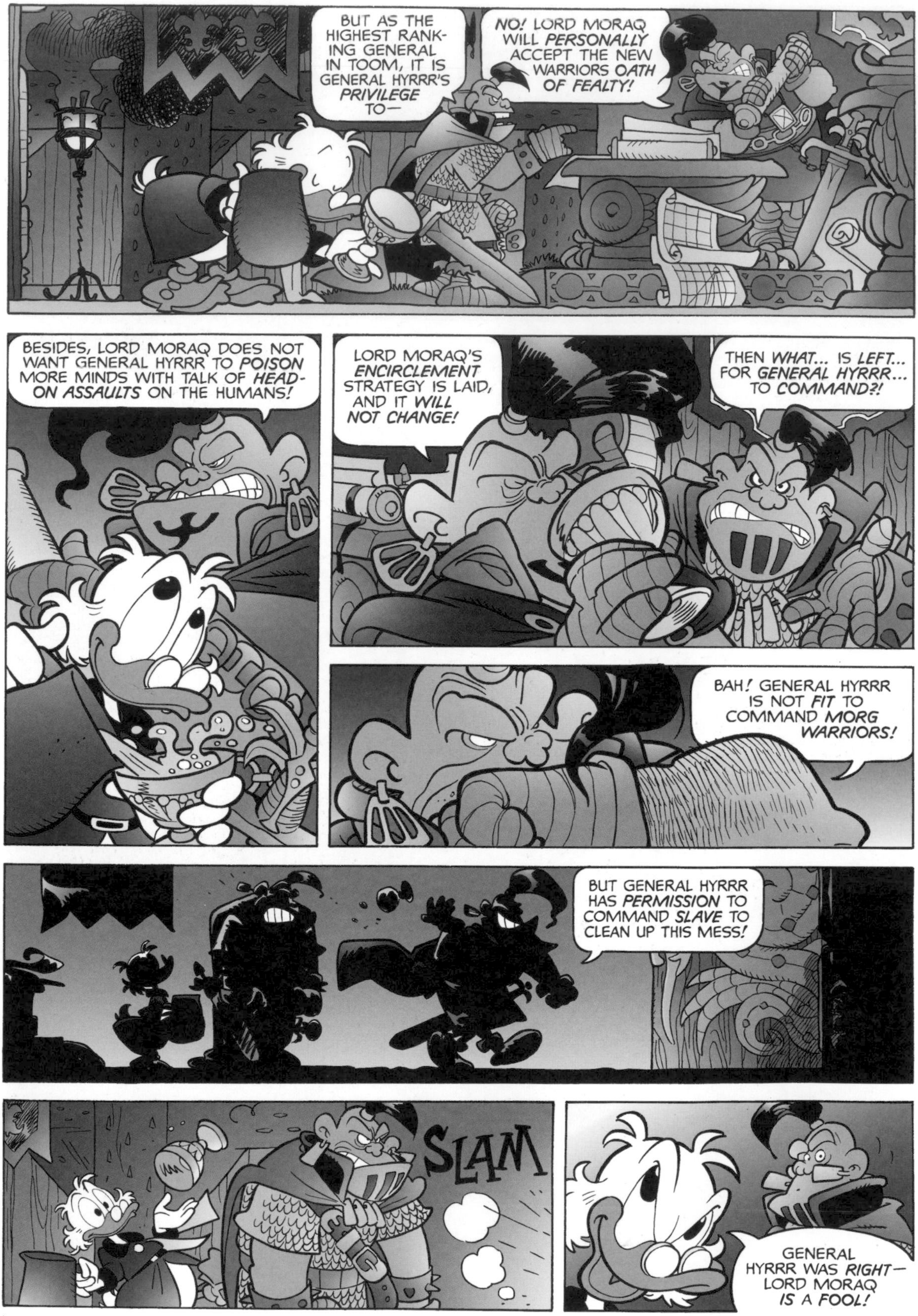
BUT AS THE HIGHEST RANKING GENERAL IN TOOM, IT IS GENERAL HYRRR'S PRIVILEGE TO—
NO! LORD MORAQ WILL PERSONALLY ACCEPT THE NEW WARRIORS OATH OF FEALTY!
BESIDES, LORD MORAQ DOES NOT WANT GENERAL HYRRR TO POISON MORE MINDS WITH TALK OF HEAD-ON ASSAULTS ON THE HUMANS!
LORD MORAQ'S ENCIRCLEMENT STRATEGY IS LAID, AND IT WILL NOT CHANGE!
THEN WHAT... IS LEFT... FOR GENERAL HYRRR... TO COMMAND?!
BAH! GENERAL HYRRR IS NOT FIT TO COMMAND MORG WARRIORS!
BUT GENERAL HYRRR HAS PERMISSION TO COMMAND SLAVE TO CLEAN UP THIS MESS!
SLAM
GENERAL HYRRR WAS RIGHT— LORD MORAQ IS A FOOL!

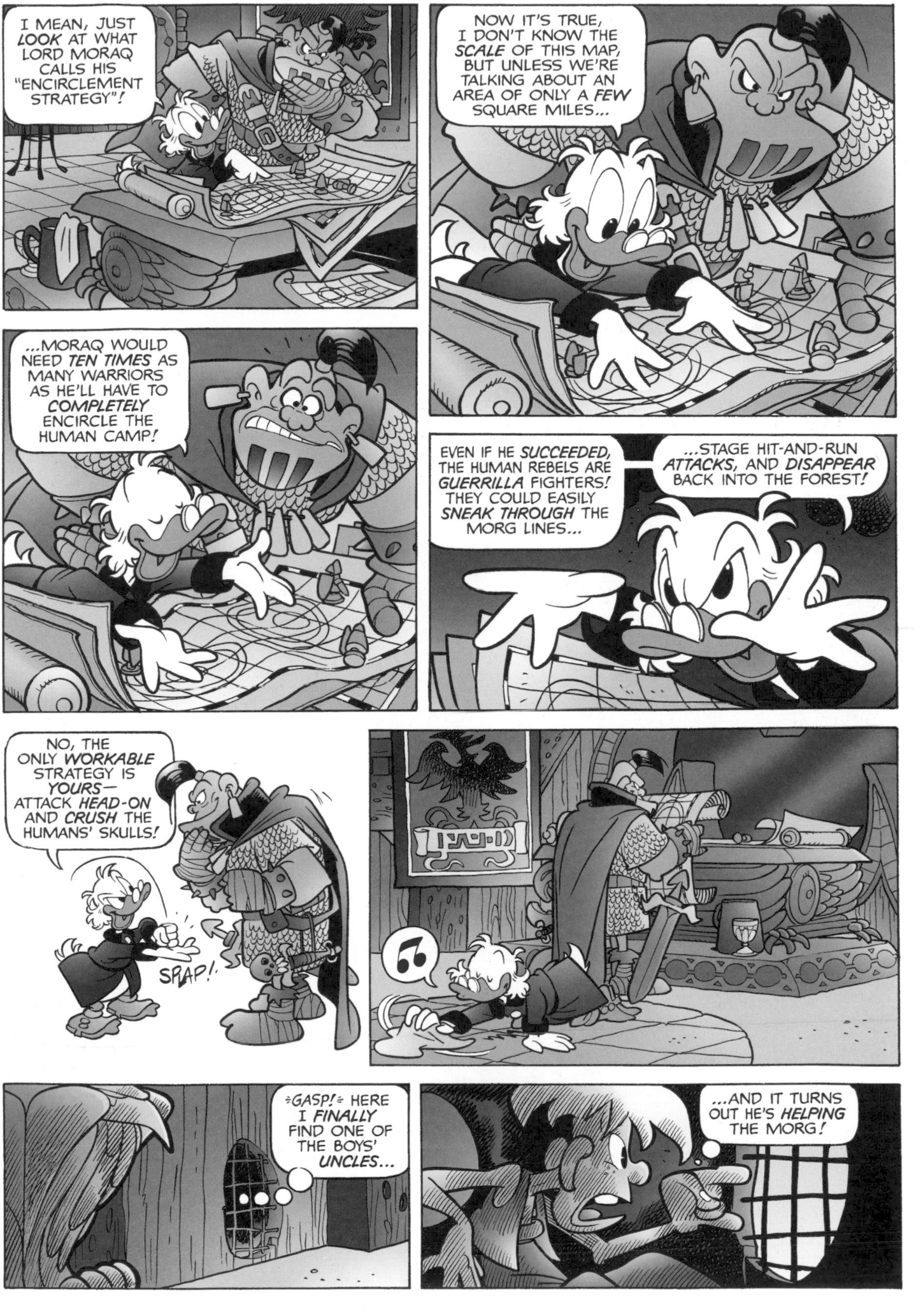
I MEAN, JUST LOOK AT WHAT LORD MORAQ CALLS HIS "ENCIRCLEMENT STRATEGY"!
NOW IT'S TRUE, I DON'T KNOW THE SCALE OF THIS MAP, BUT UNLESS WE'RE TALKING ABOUT AN AREA OF ONLY A FEW SQUARE MILES...
...MORAQ WOULD NEED TEN TIMES AS MANY WARRIORS AS HE'LL HAVE TO COMPLETELY ENCIRCLE THE HUMAN CAMP!
EVEN IF HE SUCCEEDED, THE HUMAN REBELS ARE GUERRILLA FIGHTERS! THEY COULD EASILY SNEAK THROUGH THE MORG LINES...
...STAGE HIT-AND-RUN ATTACKS, AND DISAPPEAR BACK INTO THE FOREST!
NO, THE ONLY WORKABLE STRATEGY IS YOURS— ATTACK HEAD-ON AND CRUSH THE HUMANS' SKULLS!
SPLAP!
GASP! HERE I FINALLY FIND ONE OF THE BOYS' UNCLES...
...AND IT TURNS OUT HE'S HELPING THE MORG!

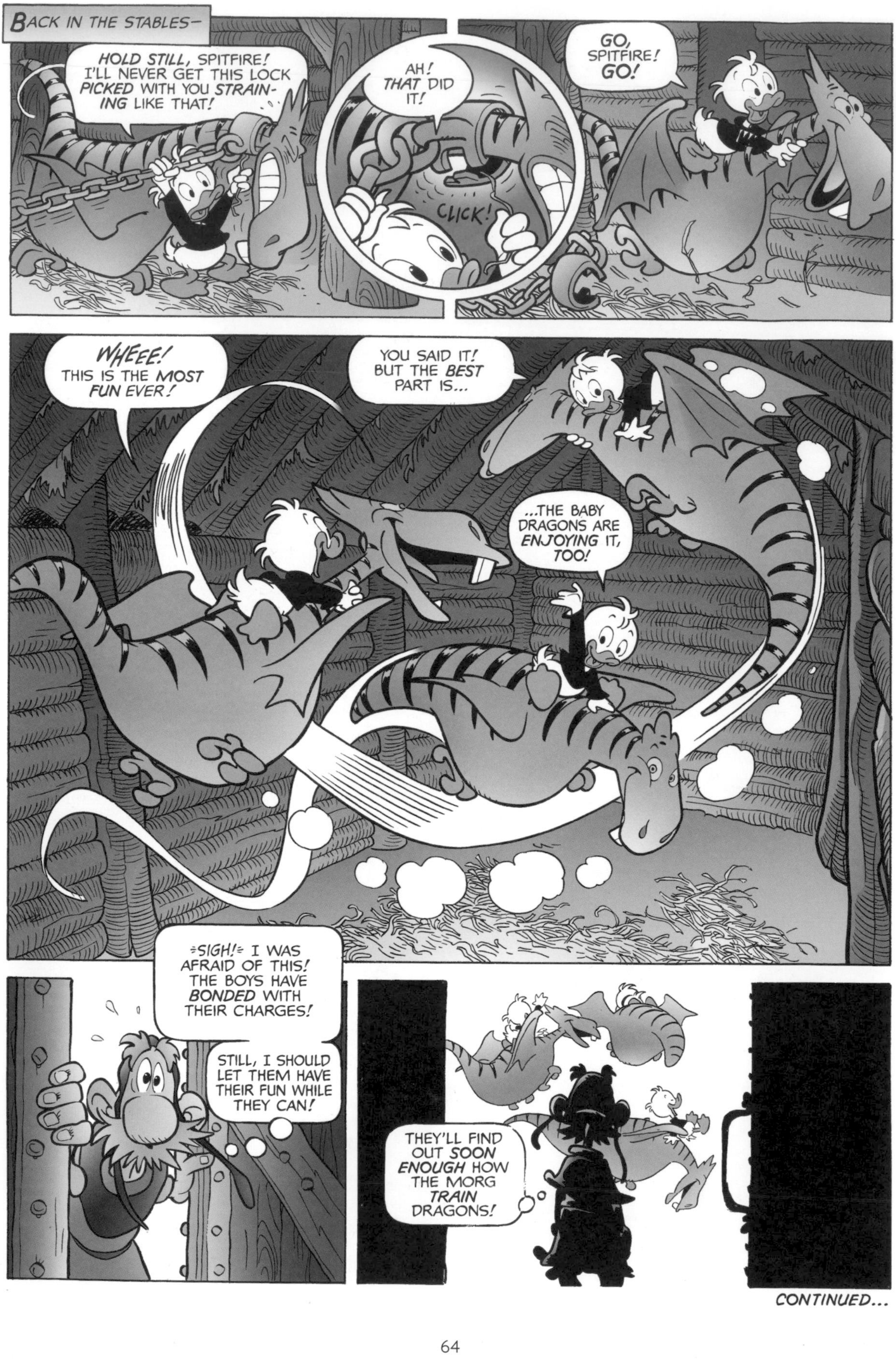
BACK IN THE STABLES—
HOLD STILL, SPITFIRE! I'LL NEVER GET THIS LOCK PICKED WITH YOU STRAINING LIKE THAT!
AH! THAT DID IT!
CLICK!
GO, SPITFIRE! GO!
WHEEE! THIS IS THE MOST FUN EVER!
YOU SAID IT! BUT THE BEST PART IS...
...THE BABY DRAGONS ARE ENJOYING IT, TOO!
≑SIGH!≑ I WAS AFRAID OF THIS! THE BOYS HAVE BONDED WITH THEIR CHARGES!
STILL, I SHOULD LET THEM HAVE THEIR FUN WHILE THEY CAN!
THEY'LL FIND OUT SOON ENOUGH HOW THE MORG TRAIN DRAGONS!
CONTINUED...

Cover drawing for Italian *Zio Paperone* 168 (2003), illustrating "Three for Three." Art by Marco Rota, color by Disney Italia.

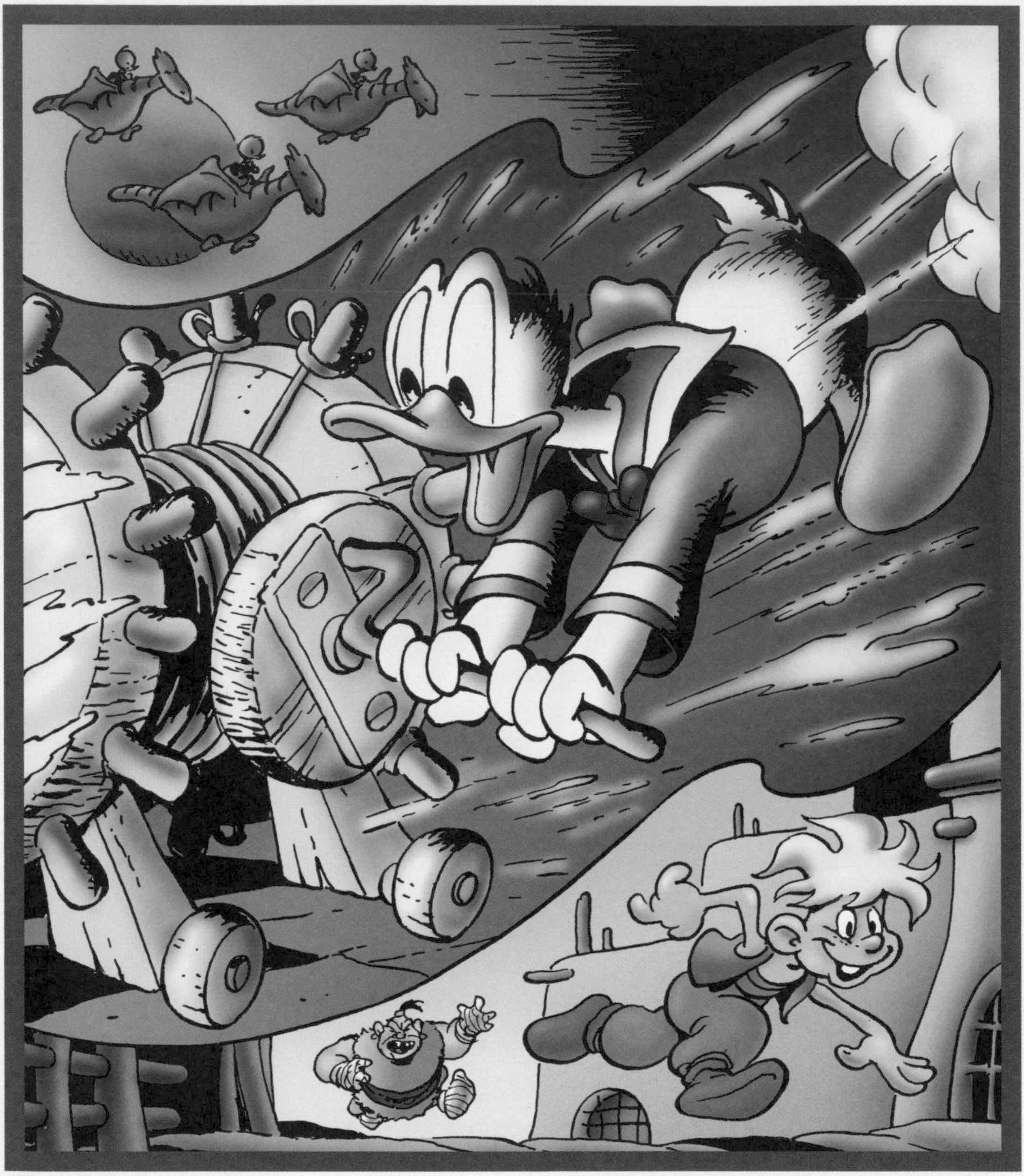

Cover drawing for Italian *Zio Paperone* 169 (2003), illustrating “Escape from the Morg.”
Art by Marco Rota, color by Disney Italia.

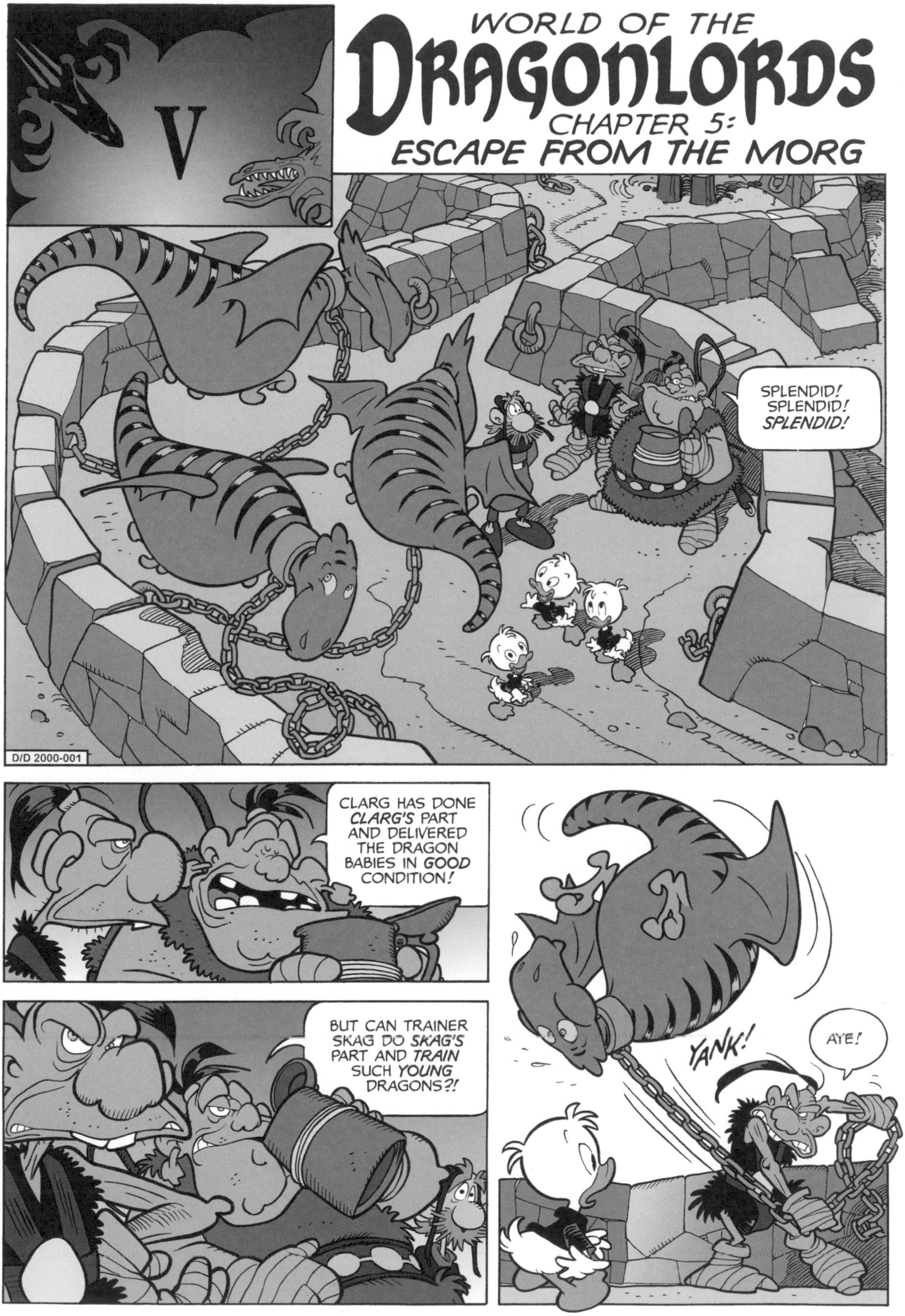
V
WORLD OF THE
DRAGONLORDS
CHAPTER 5:
ESCAPE FROM THE MORG
SPLENDID! SPLENDID! SPLENDID!
D/D 2000-001
CLARG HAS DONE CLARG'S PART AND DELIVERED THE DRAGON BABIES IN GOOD CONDITION!
BUT CAN TRAINER SKAG DO SKAG'S PART AND TRAIN SUCH YOUNG DRAGONS?!
YANK!
AYE!

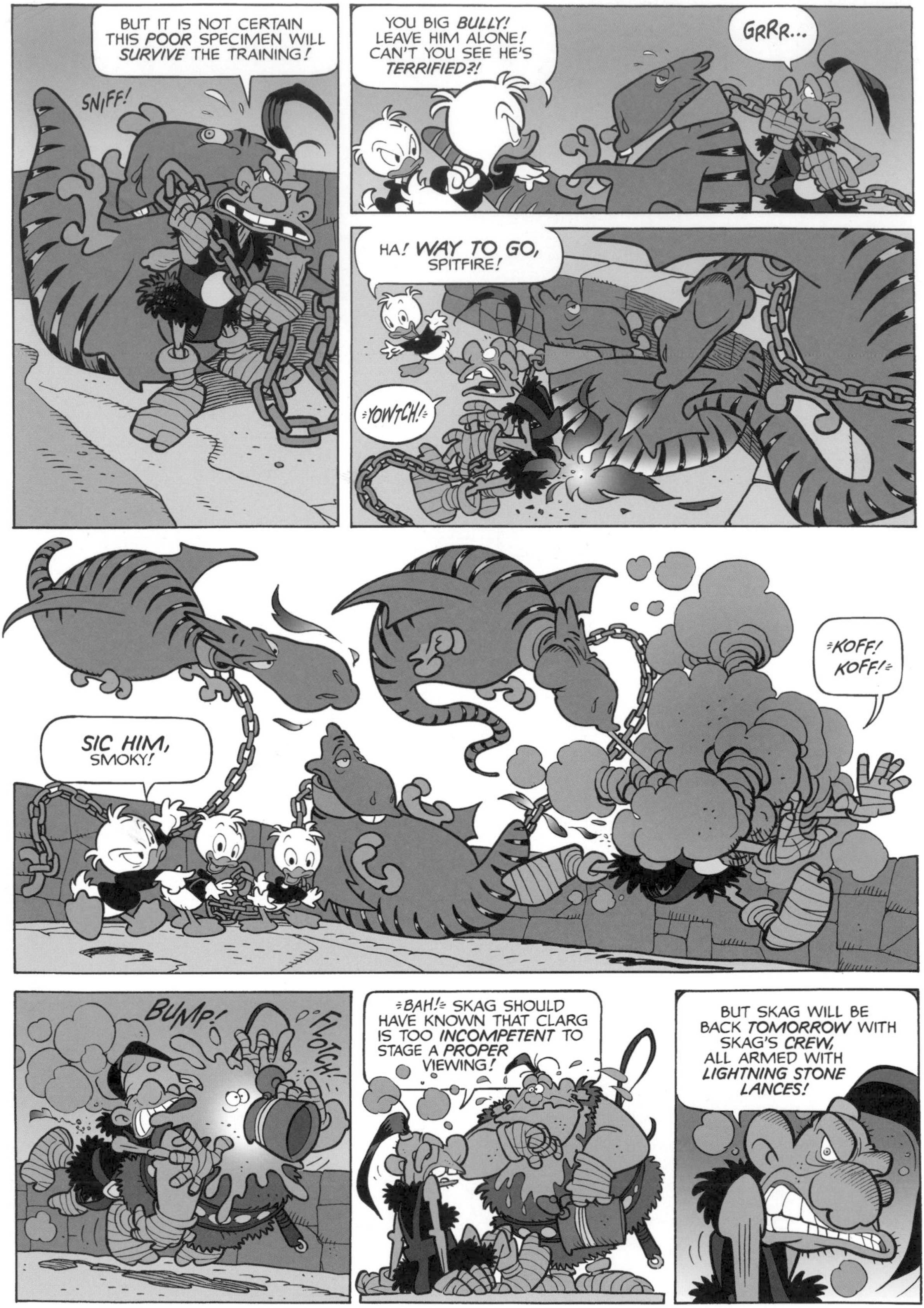

BUT IT IS NOT CERTAIN THIS POOR SPECIMEN WILL SURVIVE THE TRAINING!
SNIFF!
YOU BIG BULLY! LEAVE HIM ALONE! CAN'T YOU SEE HE'S TERRIFIED?!
GRRR...
HA! WAY TO GO, SPITFIRE!
YOWTCH!
SIC HIM, SMOKY!
KOFF! KOFF!
BUMP!
FLOTCH!
BAH! SKAG SHOULD HAVE KNOWN THAT CLARG IS TOO INCOMPETENT TO STAGE A PROPER VIEWING!
BUT SKAG WILL BE BACK TOMORROW WITH SKAG'S CREW, ALL ARMED WITH LIGHTNING STONE LANCES!

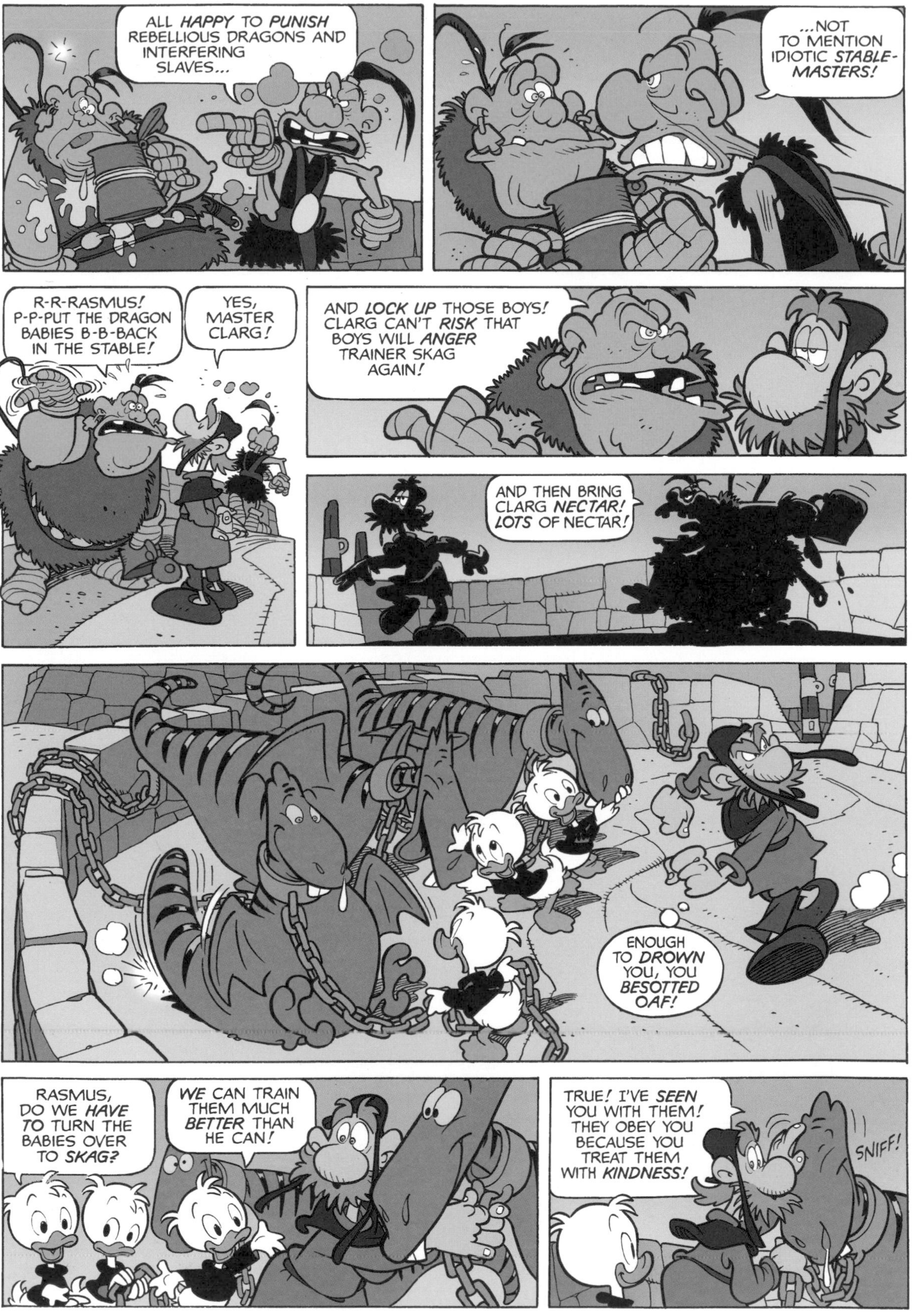
ALL HAPPY TO PUNISH REBELLIOUS DRAGONS AND INTERFERING SLAVES...
...NOT TO MENTION IDIOTIC STABLE-MASTERS!
R-R-RASMUS! P-P-PUT THE DRAGON BABIES B-B-BACK IN THE STABLE!
YES, MASTER CLARG!
AND LOCK UP THOSE BOYS! CLARG CAN'T RISK THAT BOYS WILL ANGER TRAINER SKAG AGAIN!
AND THEN BRING CLARG NECTAR! LOTS OF NECTAR!
ENOUGH TO DROWN YOU, YOU BESOTTED OAF!
RASMUS, DO WE HAVE TO TURN THE BABIES OVER TO SKAG?
WE CAN TRAIN THEM MUCH BETTER THAN HE CAN!
TRUE! I'VE SEEN YOU WITH THEM! THEY OBEY YOU BECAUSE YOU TREAT THEM WITH KINDNESS!
SNIFF!

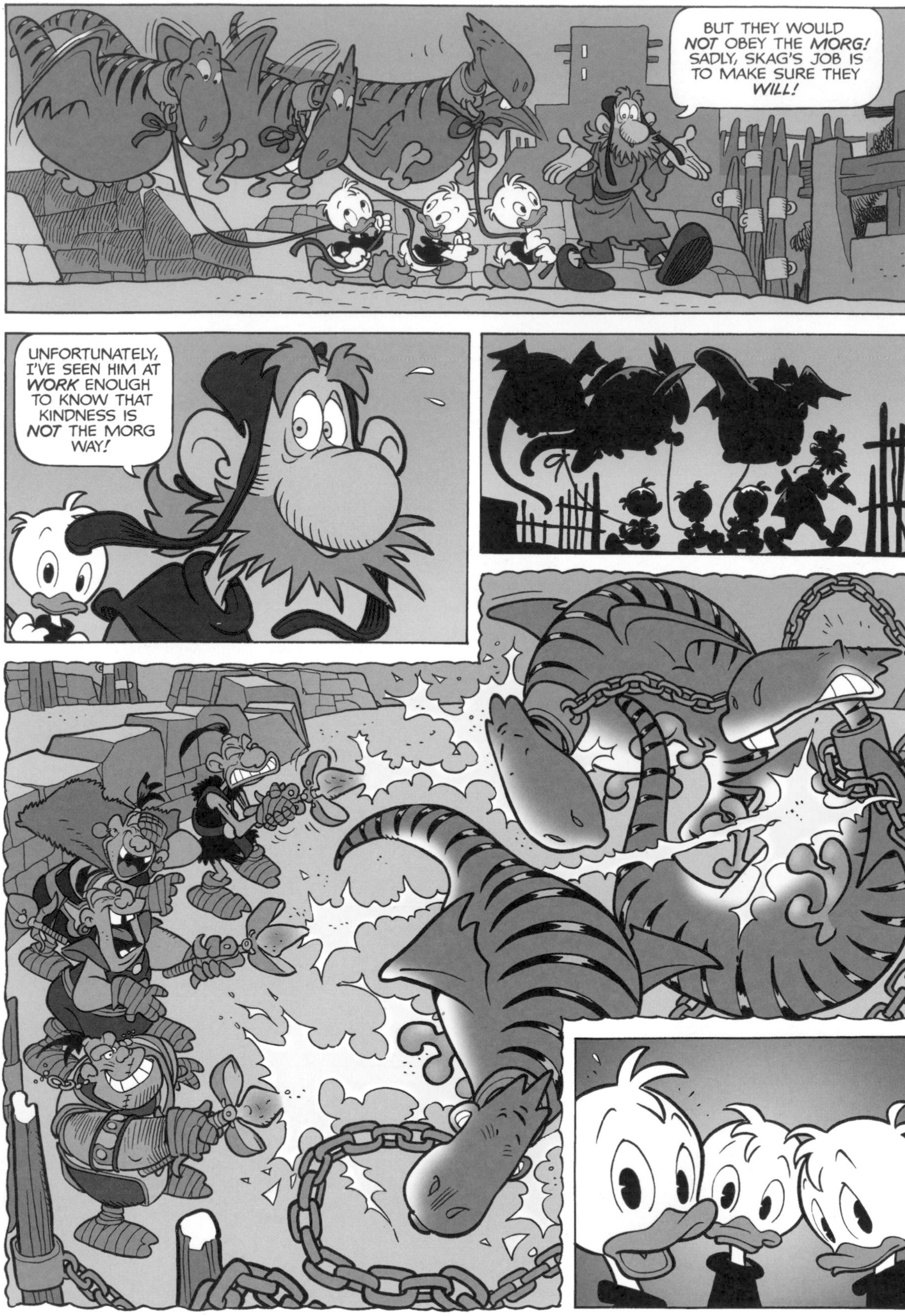
BUT THEY WOULD NOT OBEY THE MORG! SADLY, SKAG'S JOB IS TO MAKE SURE THEY WILL!
UNFORTUNATELY, I'VE SEEN HIM AT WORK ENOUGH TO KNOW THAT KINDNESS IS NOT THE MORG WAY!

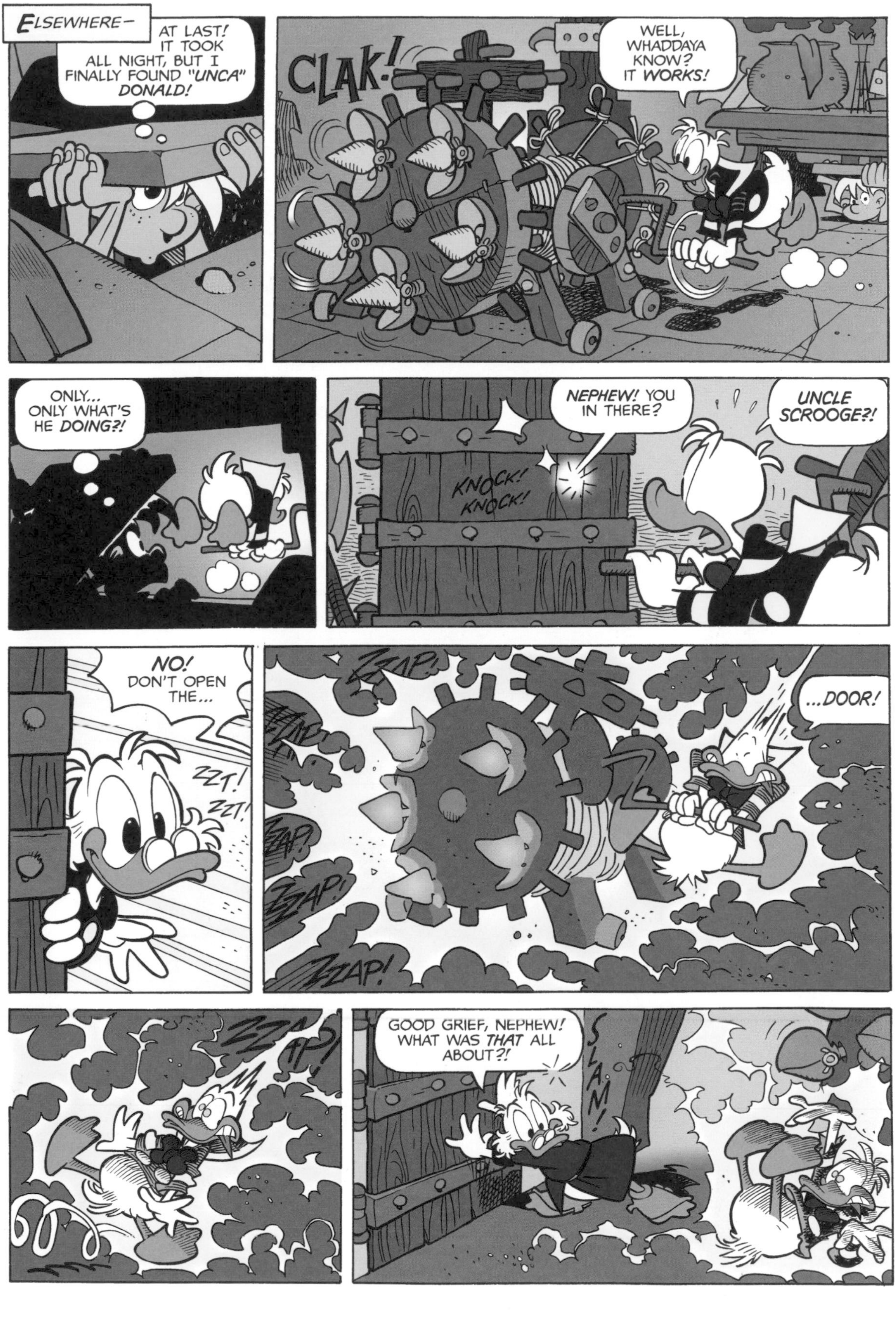
ELSEWHERE—
AT LAST! IT TOOK ALL NIGHT, BUT I FINALLY FOUND "UNCA" DONALD!
CLAK!
WELL, WHADDAYA KNOW? IT WORKS!
ONLY... ONLY WHAT'S HE DOING?!
NEPHEW! YOU IN THERE?
KNOCK! KNOCK!
UNCLE SCROOGE?!
NO! DON'T OPEN THE...
ZZT! ZZT!
ZZAP!
...DOOR!
ZZAP!
GOOD GRIEF, NEPHEW! WHAT WAS THAT ALL ABOUT?!
SLAM!

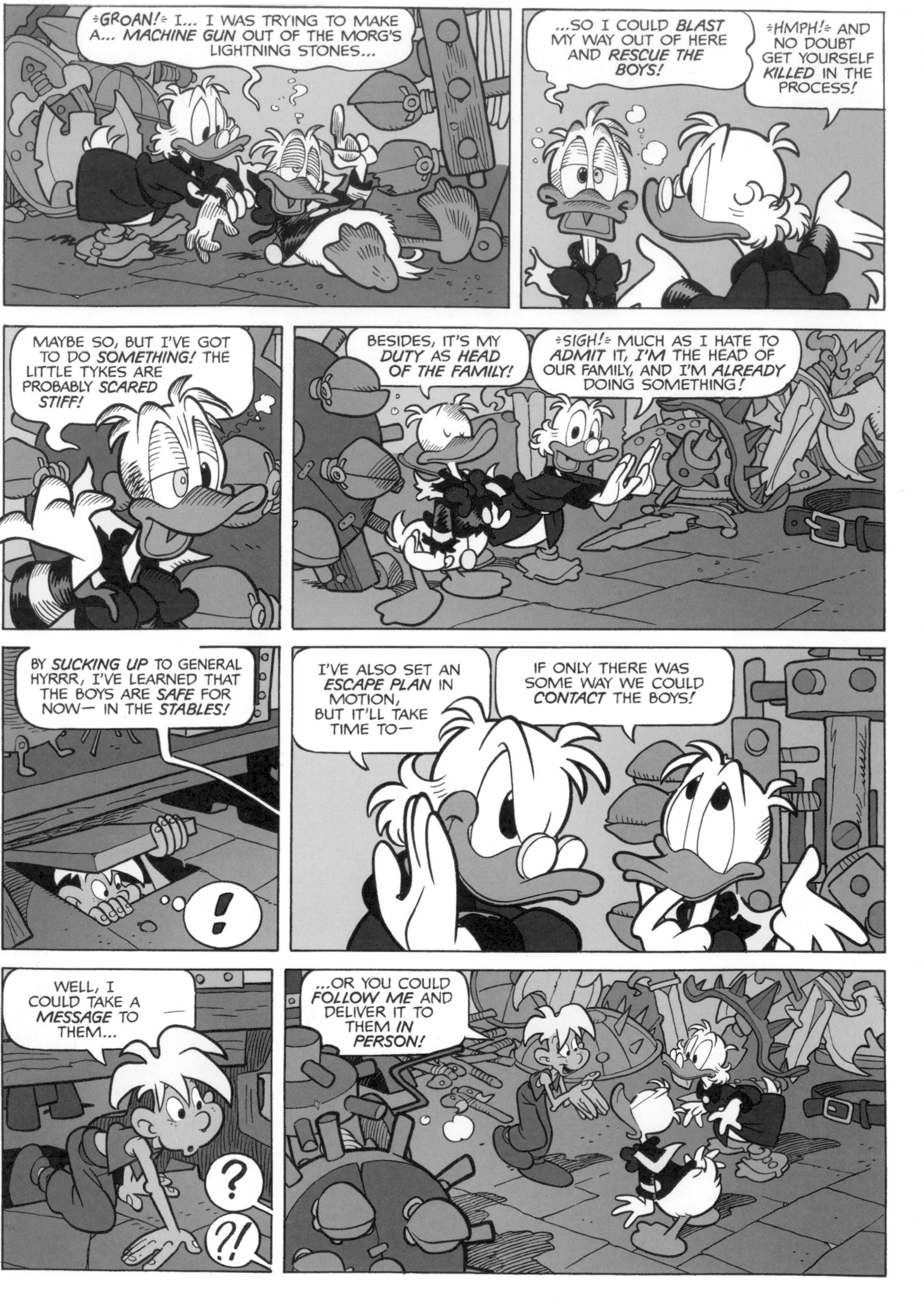

=GROAN!= I... I WAS TRYING TO MAKE A... MACHINE GUN OUT OF THE MORG'S LIGHTNING STONES...
...SO I COULD BLAST MY WAY OUT OF HERE AND RESCUE THE BOYS!
=HMPH!= AND NO DOUBT GET YOURSELF KILLED IN THE PROCESS!
MAYBE SO, BUT I'VE GOT TO DO SOMETHING! THE LITTLE TYKES ARE PROBABLY SCARED STIFF!
BESIDES, IT'S MY DUTY AS HEAD OF THE FAMILY!
=SIGH!= MUCH AS I HATE TO ADMIT IT, I'M THE HEAD OF OUR FAMILY, AND I'M ALREADY DOING SOMETHING!
BY SUCKING UP TO GENERAL HYRRR, I'VE LEARNED THAT THE BOYS ARE SAFE FOR NOW— IN THE STABLES!
!
I'VE ALSO SET AN ESCAPE PLAN IN MOTION, BUT IT'LL TAKE TIME TO—
IF ONLY THERE WAS SOME WAY WE COULD CONTACT THE BOYS!
WELL, I COULD TAKE A MESSAGE TO THEM...
?
?!
...OR YOU COULD FOLLOW ME AND DELIVER IT TO THEM IN PERSON!

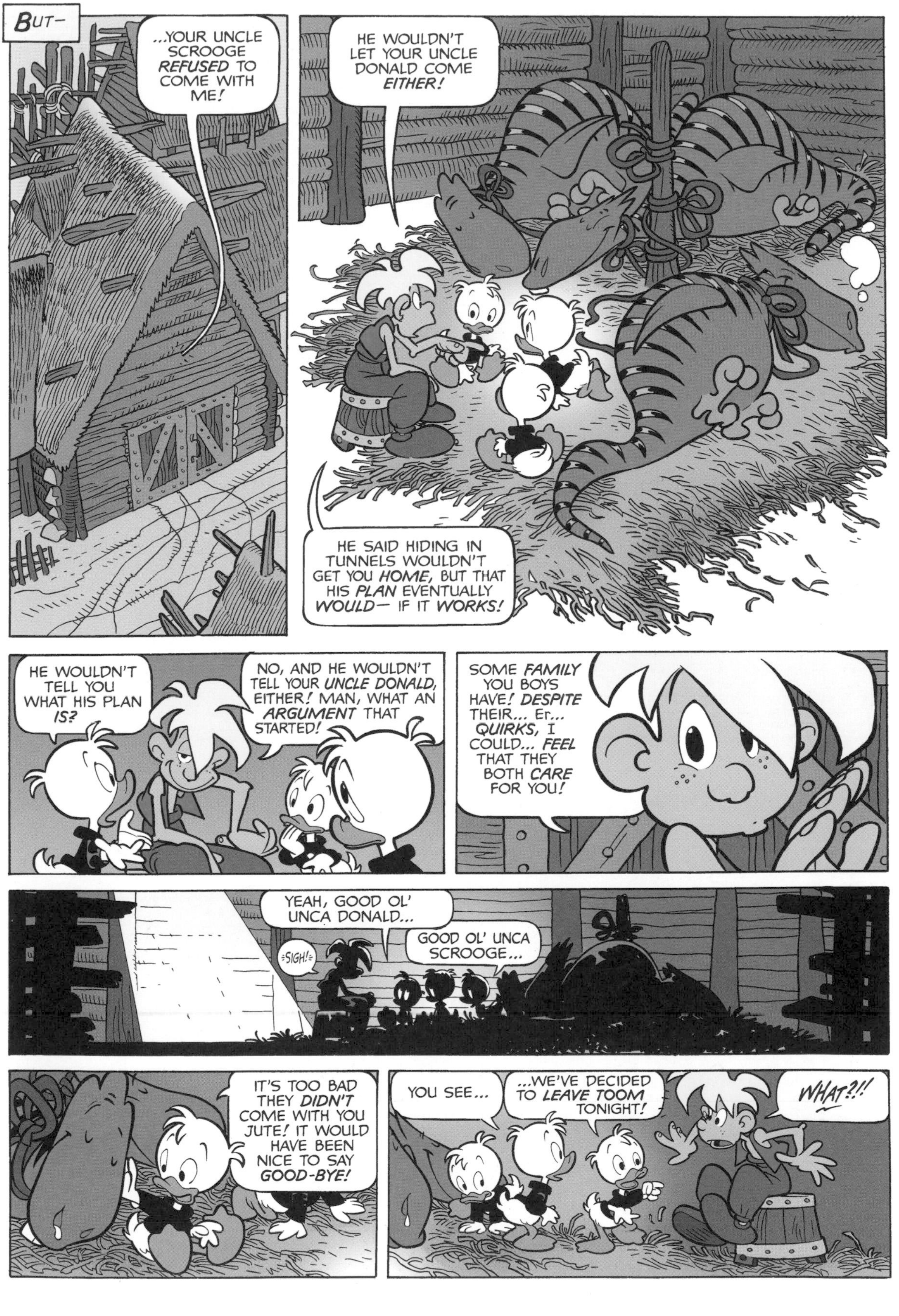

BUT—
...YOUR UNCLE SCROOGE REFUSED TO COME WITH ME!
HE WOULDN'T LET YOUR UNCLE DONALD COME EITHER!
HE SAID HIDING IN TUNNELS WOULDN'T GET YOU HOME, BUT THAT HIS PLAN EVENTUALLY WOULD— IF IT WORKS!
HE WOULDN'T TELL YOU WHAT HIS PLAN IS?
NO, AND HE WOULDN'T TELL YOUR UNCLE DONALD, EITHER! MAN, WHAT AN ARGUMENT THAT STARTED!
SOME FAMILY YOU BOYS HAVE! DESPITE THEIR... Er... QUIRKS, I COULD... FEEL THAT THEY BOTH CARE FOR YOU!
YEAH, GOOD OL' UNCA DONALD...
SIGH!
GOOD OL' UNCA SCROOGE...
IT'S TOO BAD THEY DIDN'T COME WITH YOU JUTE! IT WOULD HAVE BEEN NICE TO SAY GOOD-BYE!
YOU SEE...
...WE'VE DECIDED TO LEAVE TOOM TONIGHT!
WHAT?!!

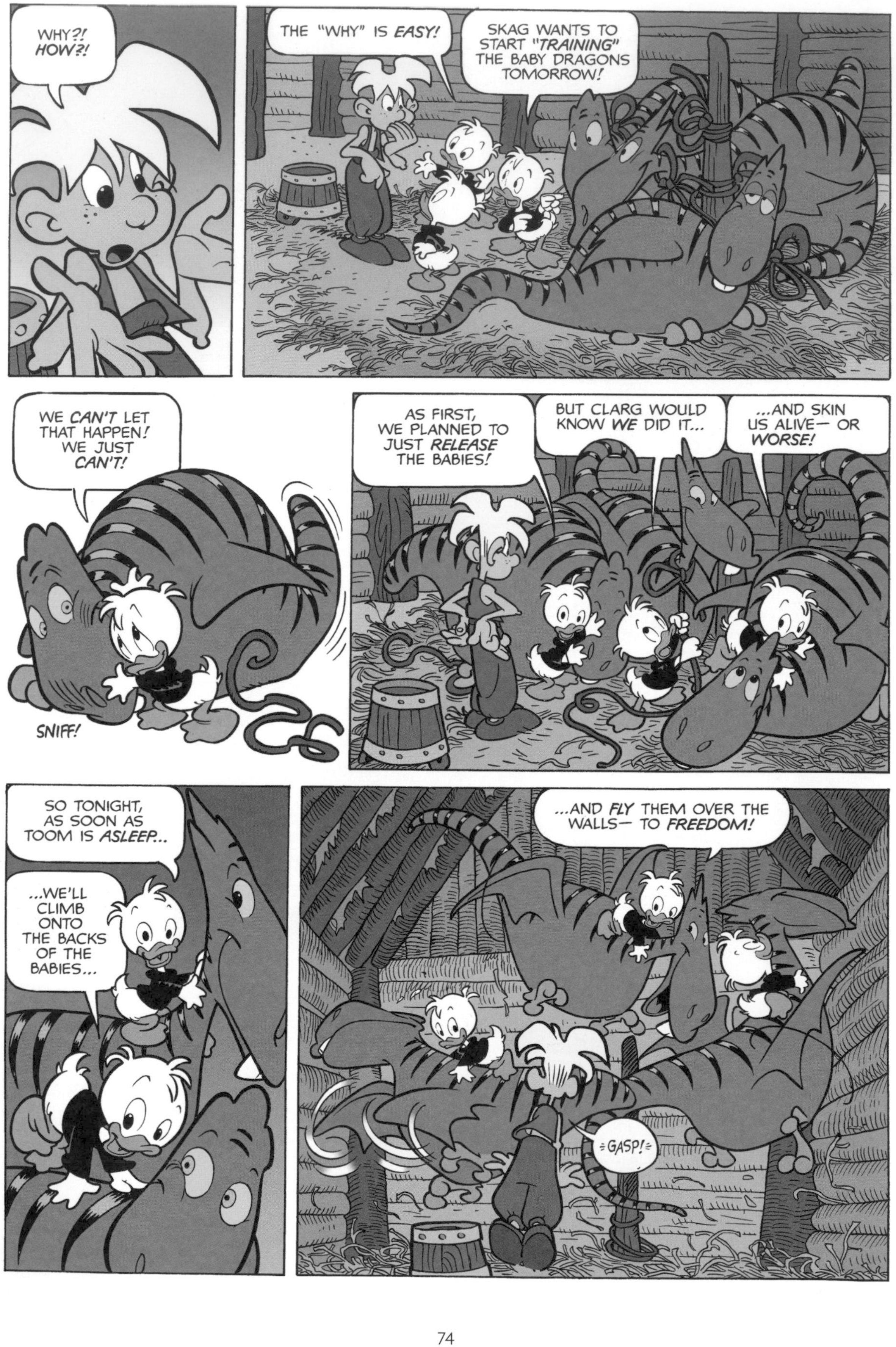
WHY?! HOW?!
THE "WHY" IS EASY!
SKAG WANTS TO START "TRAINING" THE BABY DRAGONS TOMORROW!
WE CAN'T LET THAT HAPPEN! WE JUST CAN'T!
SNIFF!
AS FIRST, WE PLANNED TO JUST RELEASE THE BABIES!
BUT CLARG WOULD KNOW WE DID IT...
...AND SKIN US ALIVE— OR WORSE!
SO TONIGHT, AS SOON AS TOOM IS ASLEEP...
...WE'LL CLIMB ONTO THE BACKS OF THE BABIES...
...AND FLY THEM OVER THE WALLS— TO FREEDOM!
GASP!

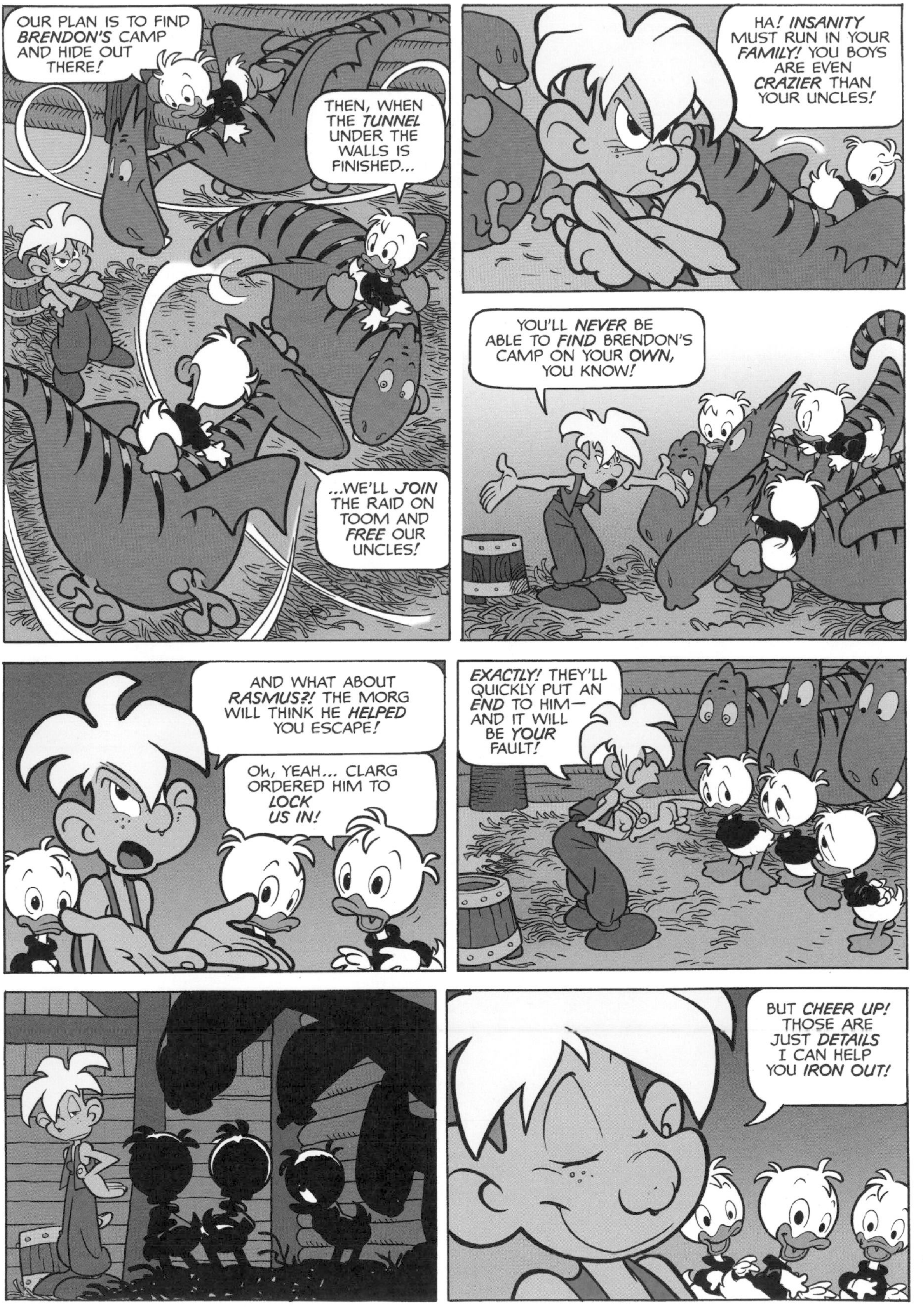
OUR PLAN IS TO FIND BRENDON'S CAMP AND HIDE OUT THERE!
THEN, WHEN THE TUNNEL UNDER THE WALLS IS FINISHED...
...WE'LL JOIN THE RAID ON TOOM AND FREE OUR UNCLES!
HA! INSANITY MUST RUN IN YOUR FAMILY! YOU BOYS ARE EVEN CRAZIER THAN YOUR UNCLES!
YOU'LL NEVER BE ABLE TO FIND BRENDON'S CAMP ON YOUR OWN, YOU KNOW!
AND WHAT ABOUT RASMUS?! THE MORG WILL THINK HE HELPED YOU ESCAPE!
Oh, YEAH... CLARG ORDERED HIM TO LOCK US IN!
EXACTLY! THEY'LL QUICKLY PUT AN END TO HIM— AND IT WILL BE YOUR FAULT!
BUT CHEER UP! THOSE ARE JUST DETAILS I CAN HELP YOU IRON OUT!

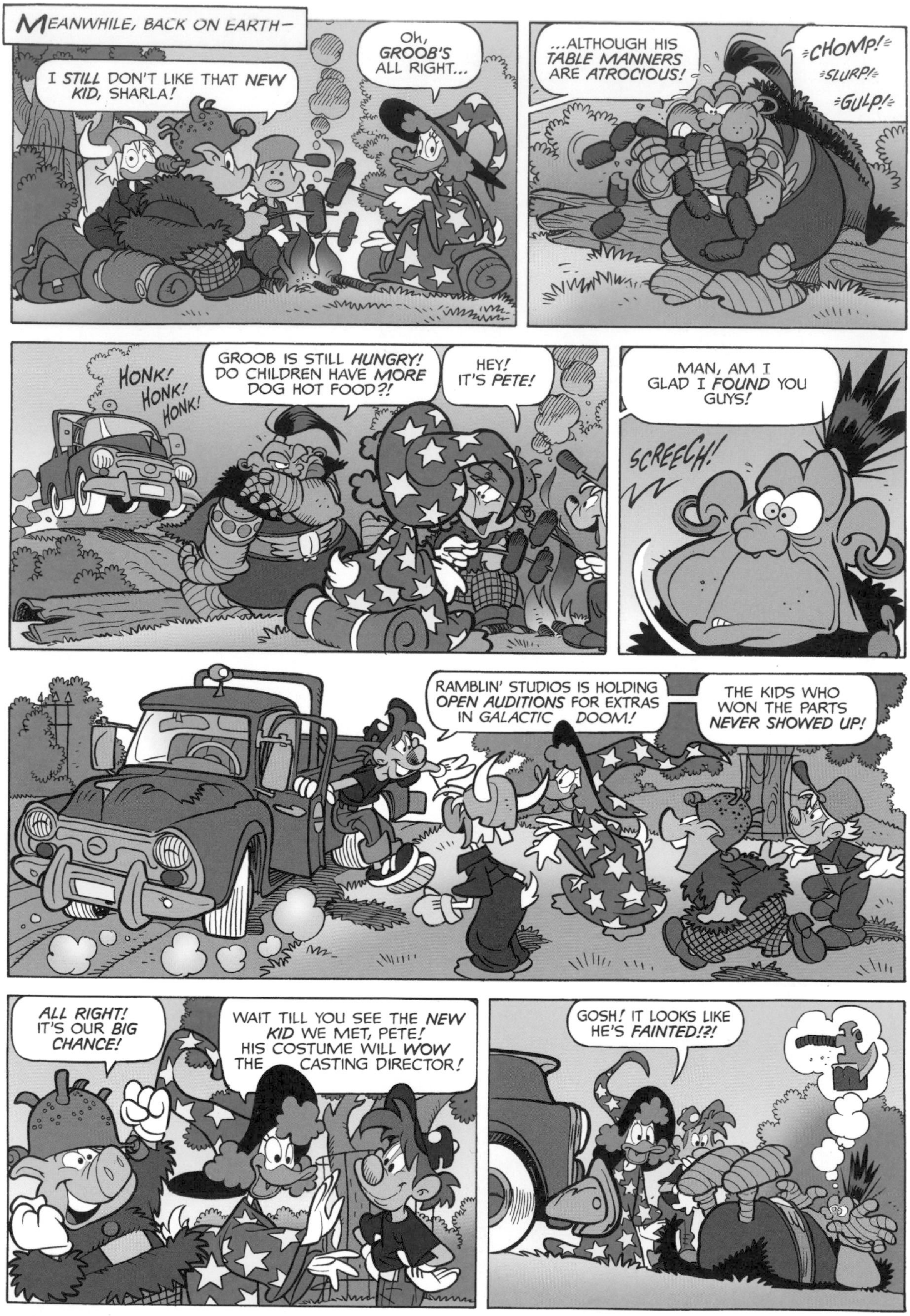

MEANWHILE, BACK ON EARTH–
I STILL DON'T LIKE THAT NEW KID, SHARLA!
Oh, GROOB'S ALL RIGHT...
...ALTHOUGH HIS TABLE MANNERS ARE ATROCIOUS!
CHOMP!
SLURP!
GULP!
HONK! HONK! HONK!
GROOB IS STILL HUNGRY! DO CHILDREN HAVE MORE DOG HOT FOOD?!
HEY! IT'S PETE!
MAN, AM I GLAD I FOUND YOU GUYS!
SCREECH!
RAMBLIN' STUDIOS IS HOLDING OPEN AUDITIONS FOR EXTRAS IN GALACTIC DOOM!
THE KIDS WHO WON THE PARTS NEVER SHOWED UP!
ALL RIGHT! IT'S OUR BIG CHANCE!
WAIT TILL YOU SEE THE NEW KID WE MET, PETE! HIS COSTUME WILL WOW THE CASTING DIRECTOR!
GOSH! IT LOOKS LIKE HE'S FAINTED!?!

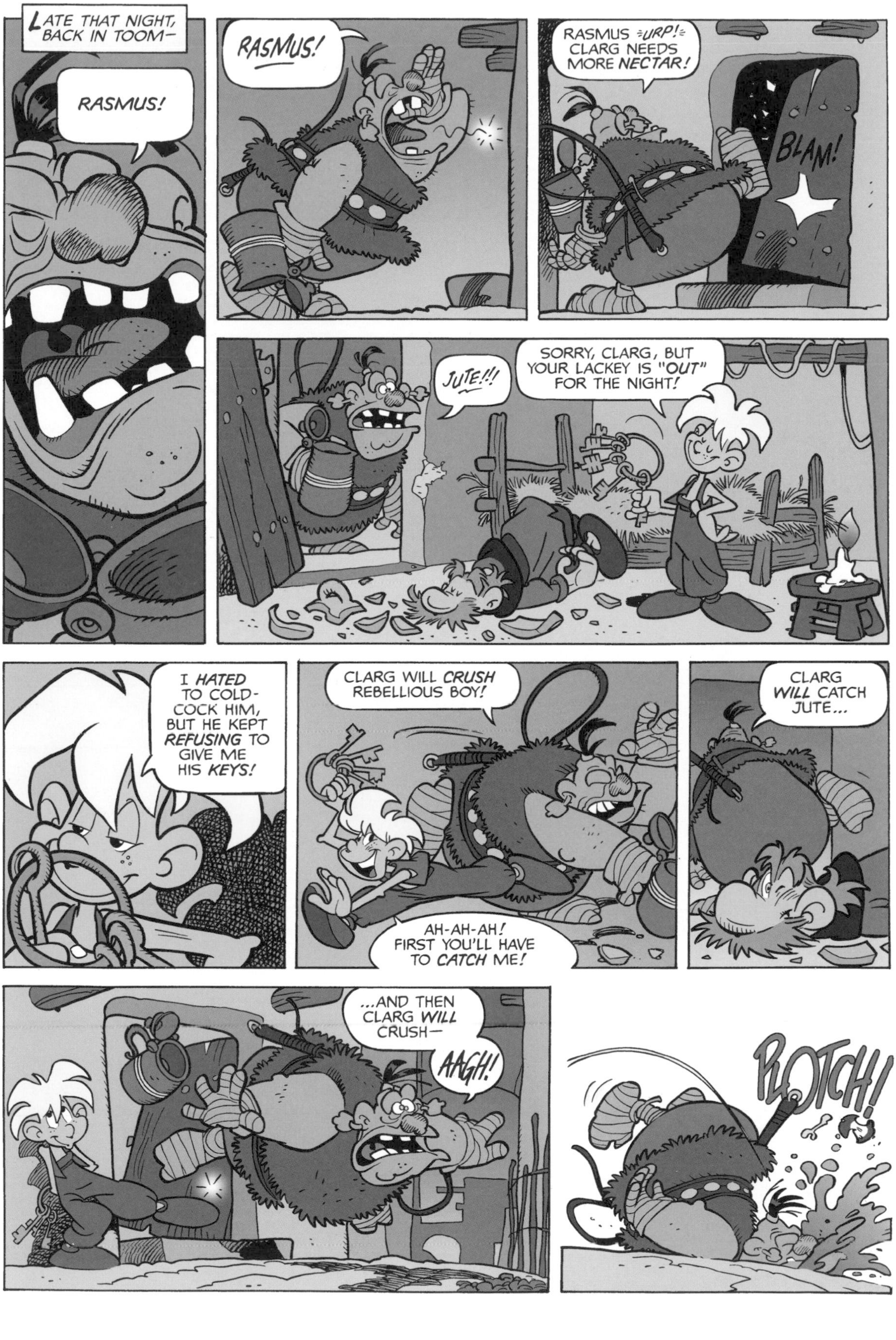
LATE THAT NIGHT, BACK IN TOOM—
RASMUS!
RASMUS!
RASMUS =URP!= CLARG NEEDS MORE NECTAR!
BLAM!
JUTE!!!
SORRY, CLARG, BUT YOUR LACKEY IS "OUT" FOR THE NIGHT!
I HATED TO COLD-COCK HIM, BUT HE KEPT REFUSING TO GIVE ME HIS KEYS!
CLARG WILL CRUSH REBELLIOUS BOY!
AH-AH-AH! FIRST YOU'LL HAVE TO CATCH ME!
CLARG WILL CATCH JUTE...
...AND THEN CLARG WILL CRUSH—
AAGH!
PLOTCH!

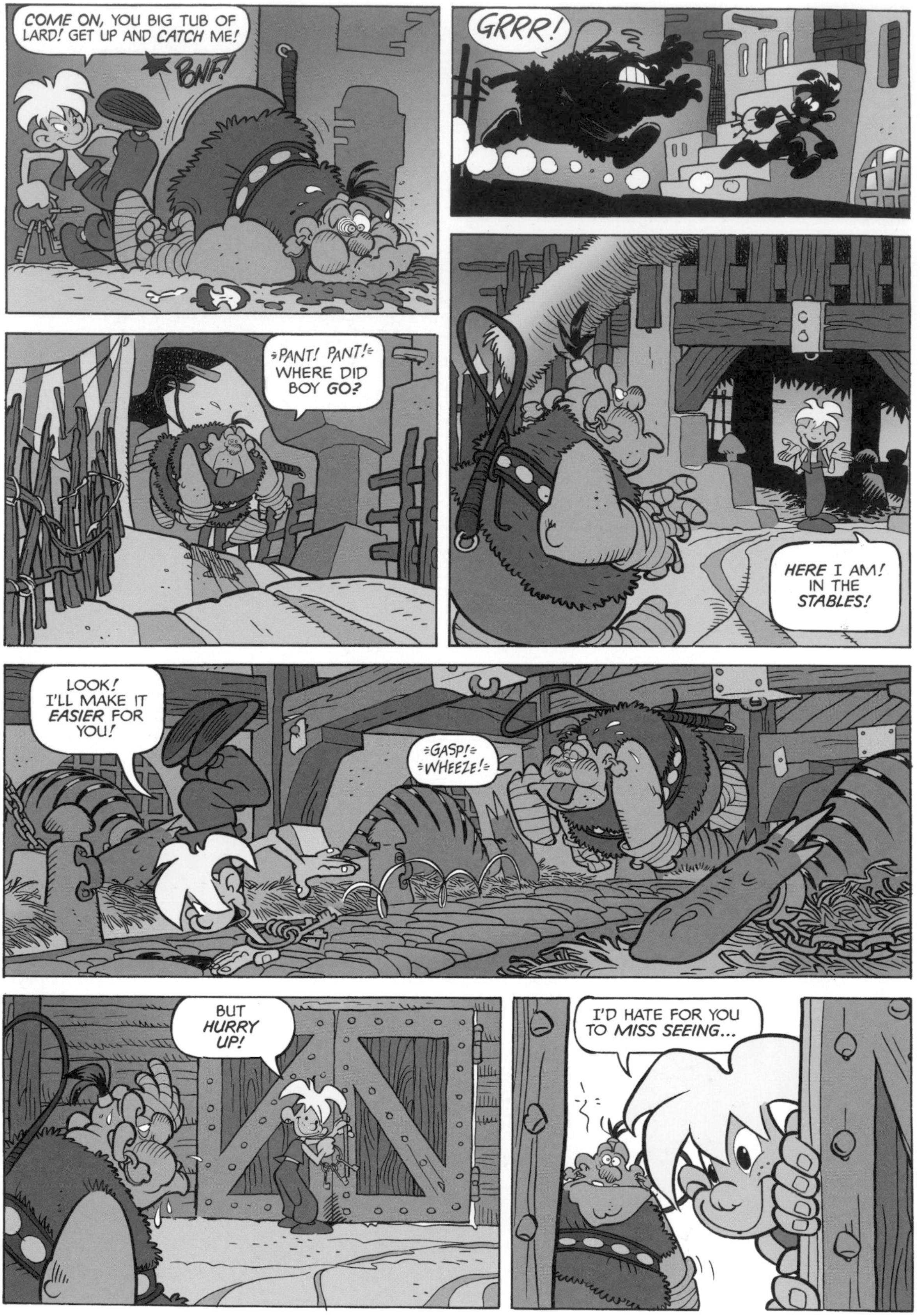

COME ON, YOU BIG TUB OF LARD! GET UP AND CATCH ME!
PONF!
GRRR!
PANT! PANT! WHERE DID BOY GO?
HERE I AM! IN THE STABLES!
LOOK! I'LL MAKE IT EASIER FOR YOU!
GASP! WHEEZE!
BUT HURRY UP!
I'D HATE FOR YOU TO MISS SEEING...

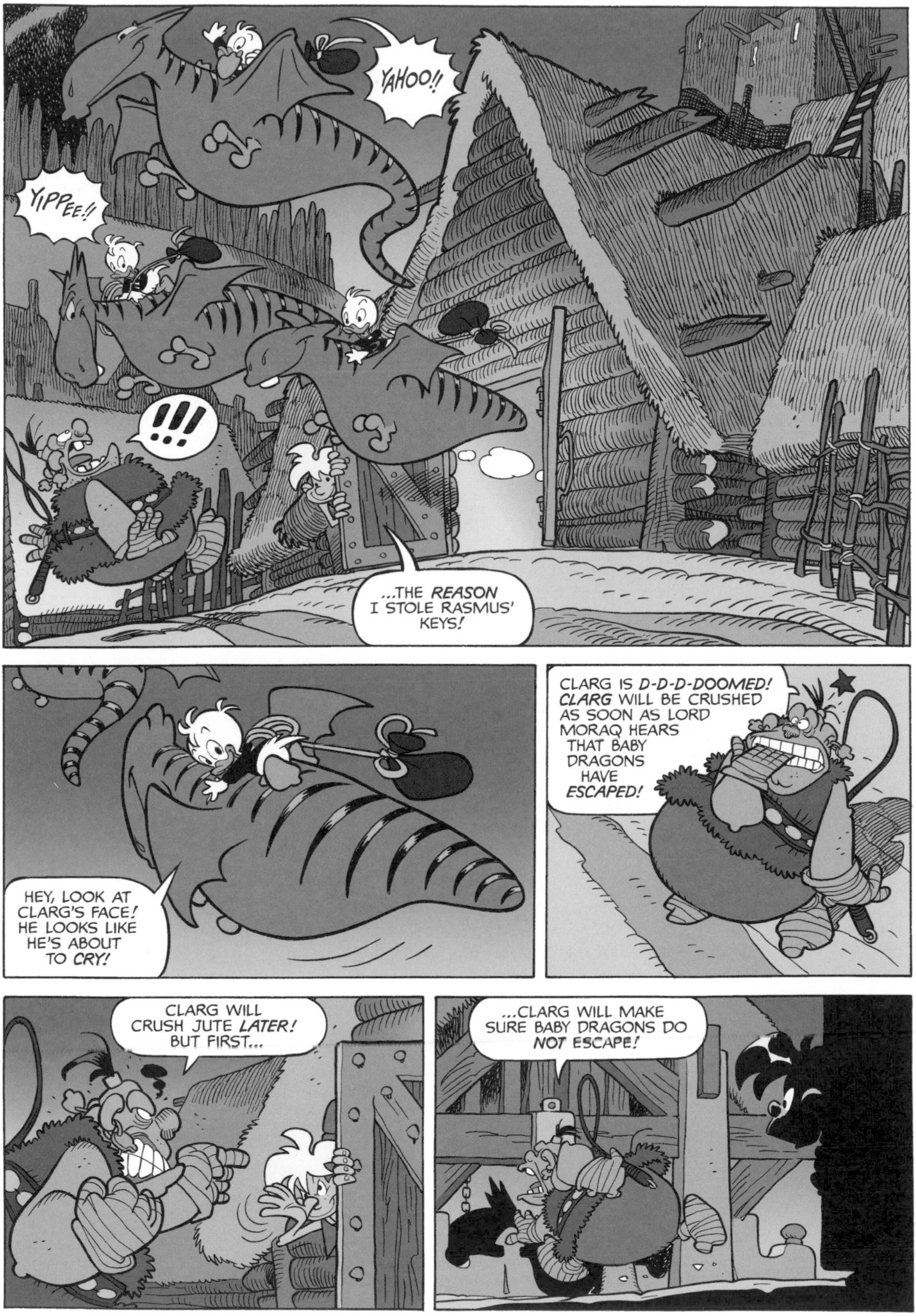
YAHOO!!
YIPPEE!!
!!!
...THE REASON I STOLE RASMUS' KEYS!
HEY, LOOK AT CLARG'S FACE! HE LOOKS LIKE HE'S ABOUT TO CRY!
CLARG IS D-D-D-DOOMED! CLARG WILL BE CRUSHED AS SOON AS LORD MORAQ HEARS THAT BABY DRAGONS HAVE ESCAPED!
CLARG WILL CRUSH JUTE LATER! BUT FIRST...
...CLARG WILL MAKE SURE BABY DRAGONS DO NOT ESCAPE!

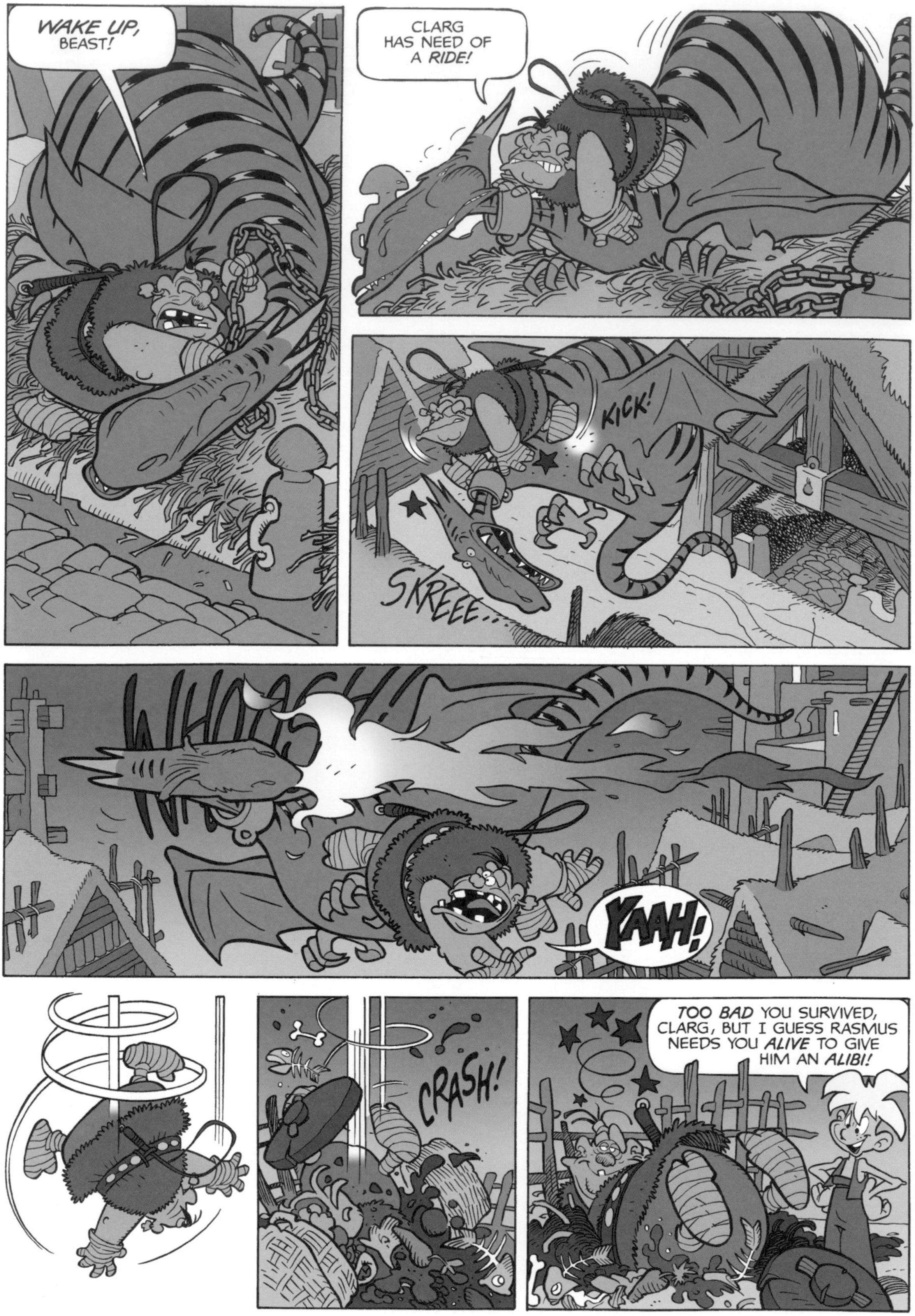
WAKE UP, BEAST!
CLARG HAS NEED OF A RIDE!
KICK!
SKREEE...
WHOOSH!
YAAH!
CRASH!
TOO BAD YOU SURVIVED, CLARG, BUT I GUESS RASMUS NEEDS YOU ALIVE TO GIVE HIM AN ALIBI!

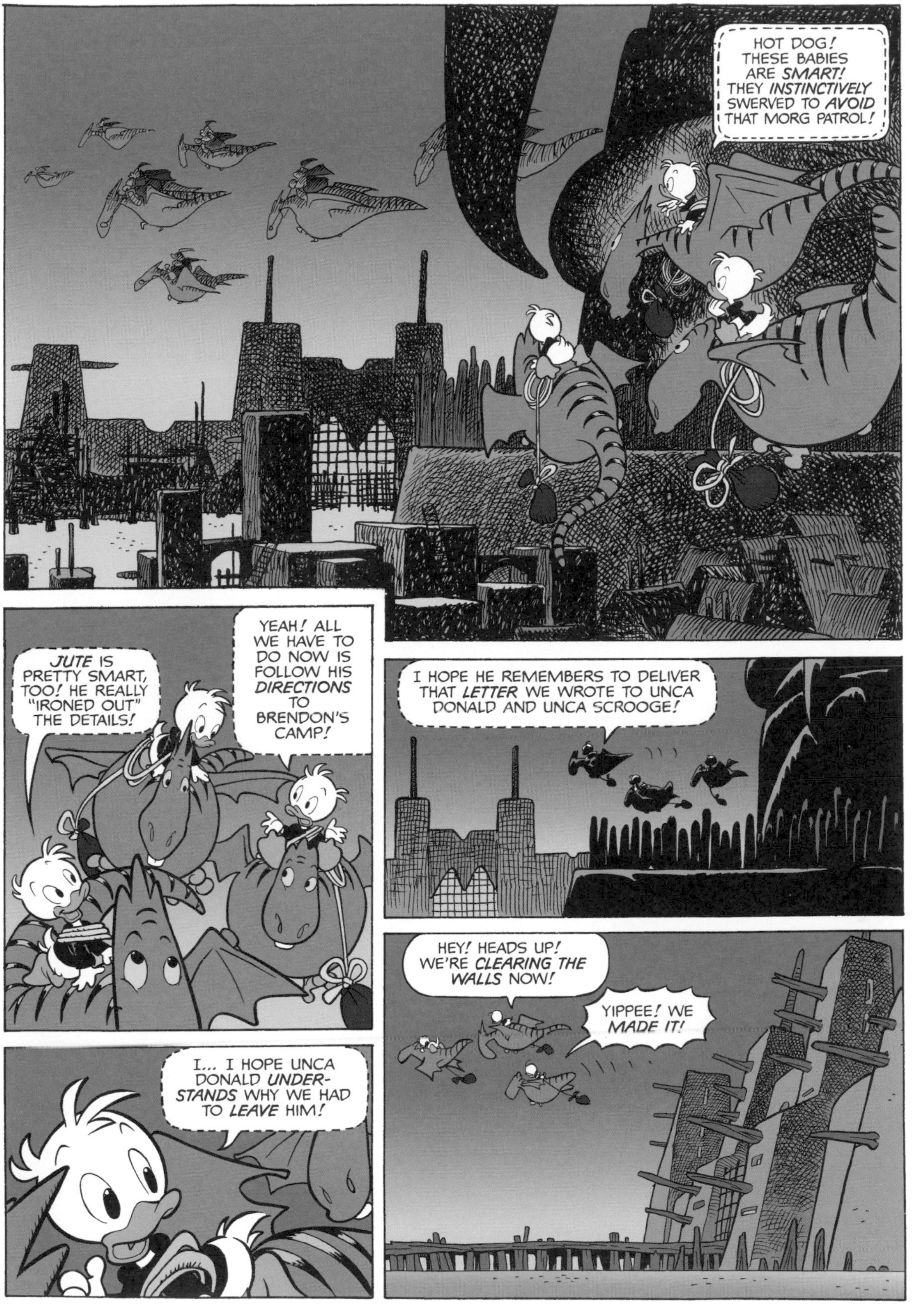
HOT DOG! THESE BABIES ARE SMART! THEY INSTINCTIVELY SWERVED TO AVOID THAT MORG PATROL!
JUTE IS PRETTY SMART, TOO! HE REALLY "IRONED OUT" THE DETAILS!
YEAH! ALL WE HAVE TO DO NOW IS FOLLOW HIS DIRECTIONS TO BRENDON'S CAMP!
I HOPE HE REMEMBERS TO DELIVER THAT LETTER WE WROTE TO UNCA DONALD AND UNCA SCROOGE!
I... I HOPE UNCA DONALD UNDER-STANDS WHY WE HAD TO LEAVE HIM!
HEY! HEADS UP! WE'RE CLEARING THE WALLS NOW!
YIPPEE! WE MADE IT!

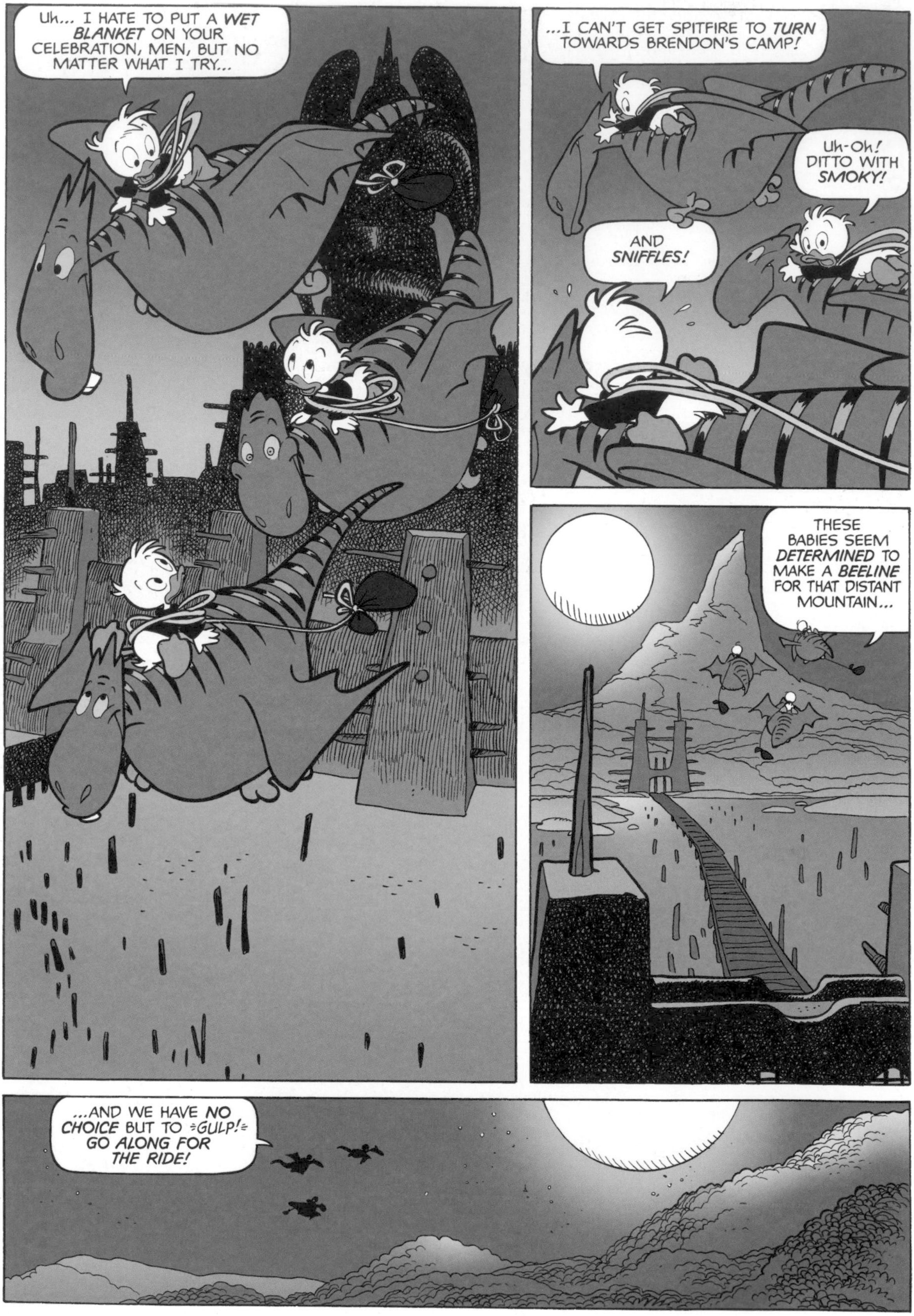
Uh... I HATE TO PUT A WET BLANKET ON YOUR CELEBRATION, MEN, BUT NO MATTER WHAT I TRY...
...I CAN'T GET SPITFIRE TO TURN TOWARDS BRENDON'S CAMP!
Uh-Oh! DITTO WITH SMOKY!
AND SNIFFLES!
THESE BABIES SEEM DETERMINED TO MAKE A BEELINE FOR THAT DISTANT MOUNTAIN...
...AND WE HAVE NO CHOICE BUT TO ≑GULP!≑ GO ALONG FOR THE RIDE!

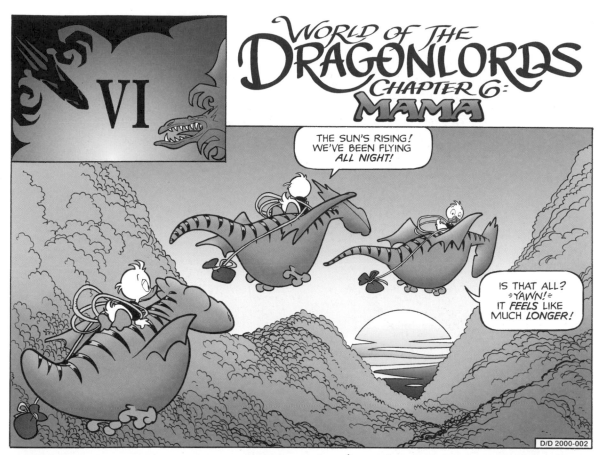

WORLD OF THE DRAGONLORDS
CHAPTER 6:
MAMA

VI

THE SUN'S RISING! WE'VE BEEN FLYING *ALL NIGHT!*

IS THAT ALL? *-YAWN!-* IT *FEELS* LIKE MUCH *LONGER!*

D/D 2000-002

I'M BETTING THAT *MOUNTAIN* IS WHERE THE BABIES ARE *TAKING* US!

YEAH... BUT WHAT *SAPS* WE WERE TO THINK WE COULD *CONTROL* THEM!

HEY, YOU GUYS! *HELP!!!*

SNIFFLES IS *EX-HAUSTED!*

SKREEÈ..

83

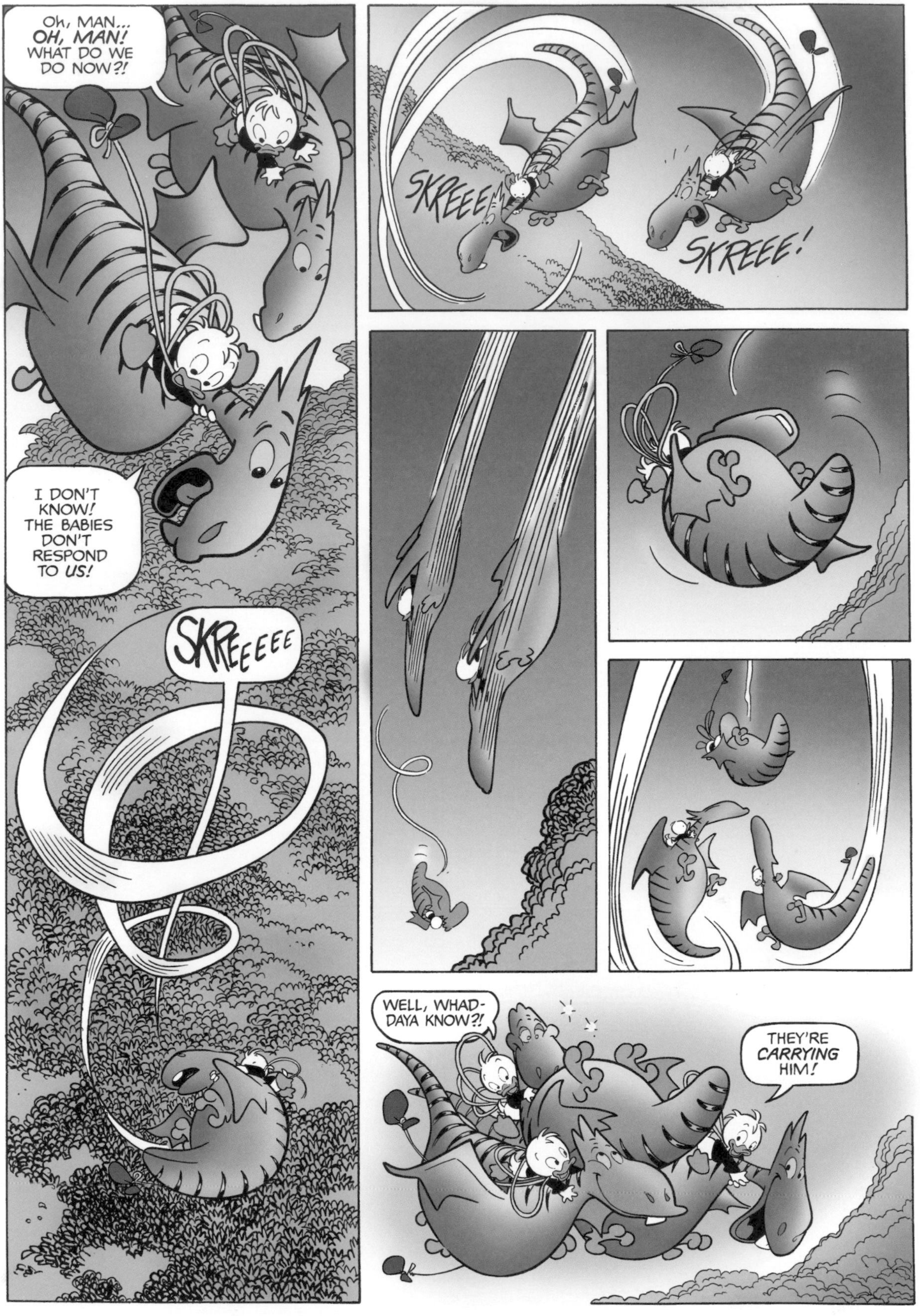

Oh, MAN... **OH, MAN!** WHAT DO WE DO NOW?!
I DON'T KNOW! THE BABIES DON'T RESPOND TO *US!*
SKREEEEEE
SKREEE
SKREEE!
WELL, WHAD-DAYA KNOW?!
THEY'RE *CARRYING* HIM!

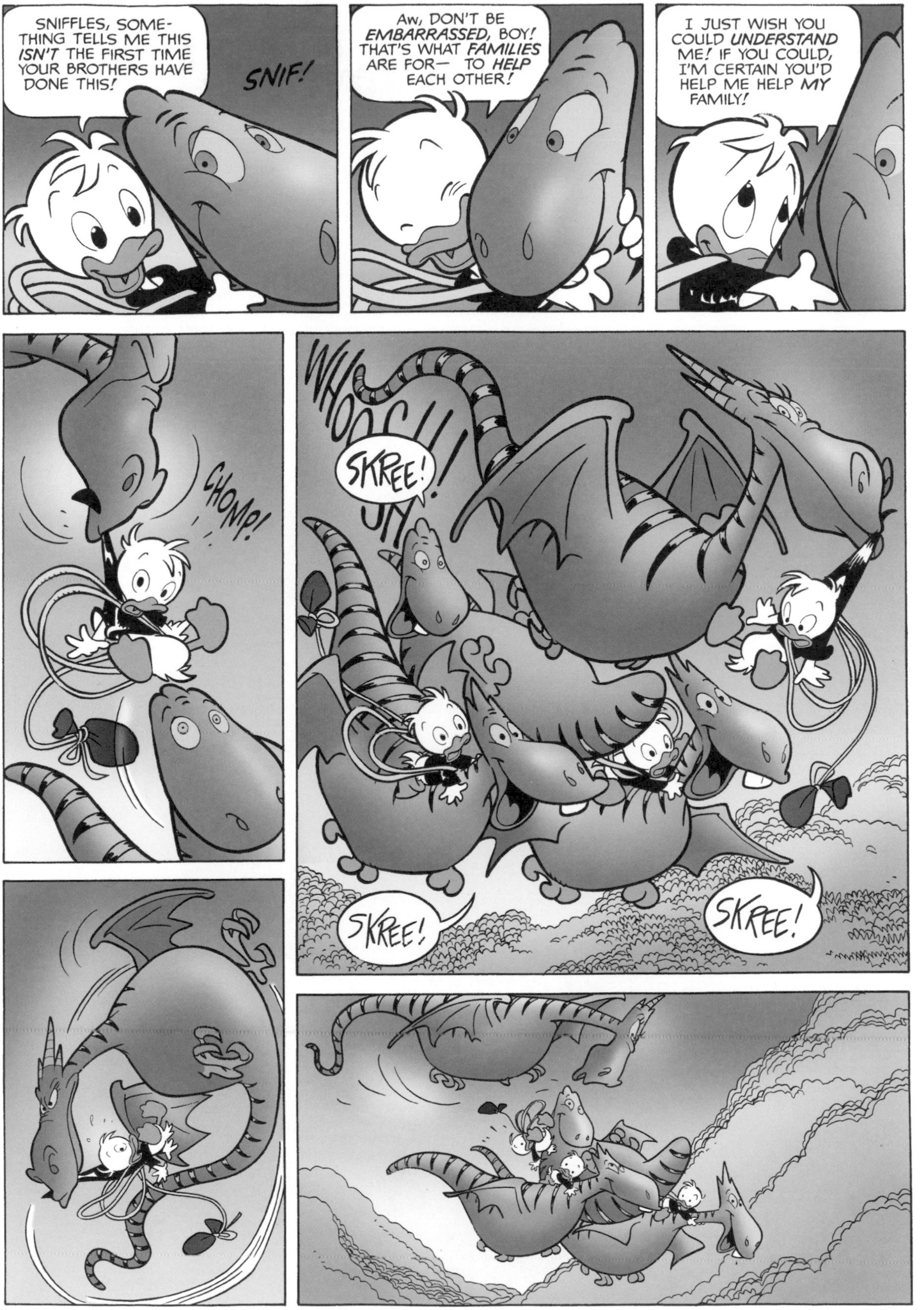
SNIFFLES, SOMETHING TELLS ME THIS ISN'T THE FIRST TIME YOUR BROTHERS HAVE DONE THIS!
SNIF!
AW, DON'T BE EMBARRASSED, BOY! THAT'S WHAT FAMILIES ARE FOR— TO HELP EACH OTHER!
I JUST WISH YOU COULD UNDERSTAND ME! IF YOU COULD, I'M CERTAIN YOU'D HELP ME HELP MY FAMILY!
CHOMP!
WHOOSH!!
SKREE!
SKREE!
SKREE!

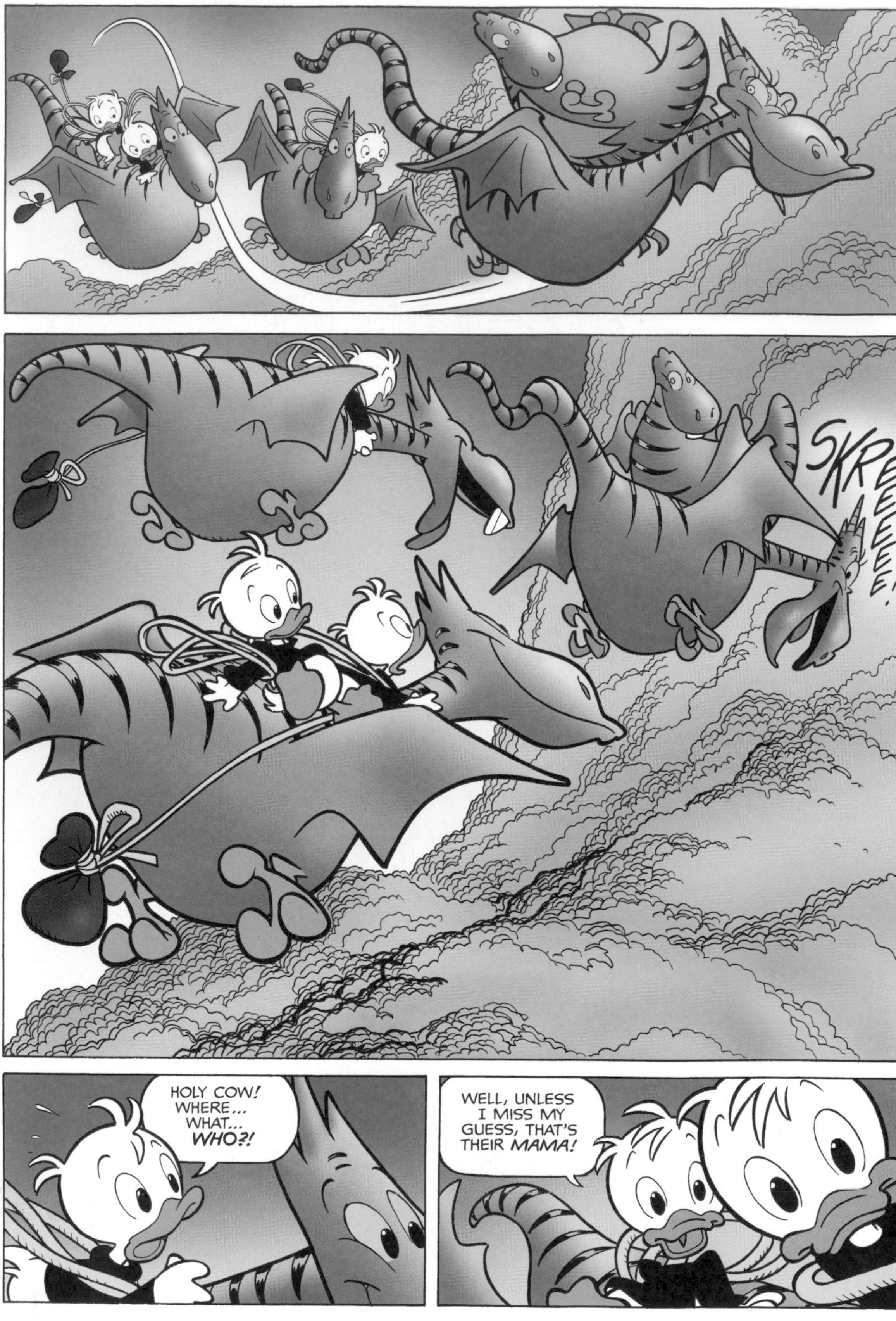
SKREEEEEE!
HOLY COW! WHERE... WHAT... *WHO?!*
WELL, UNLESS I MISS MY GUESS, THAT'S THEIR *MAMA!*

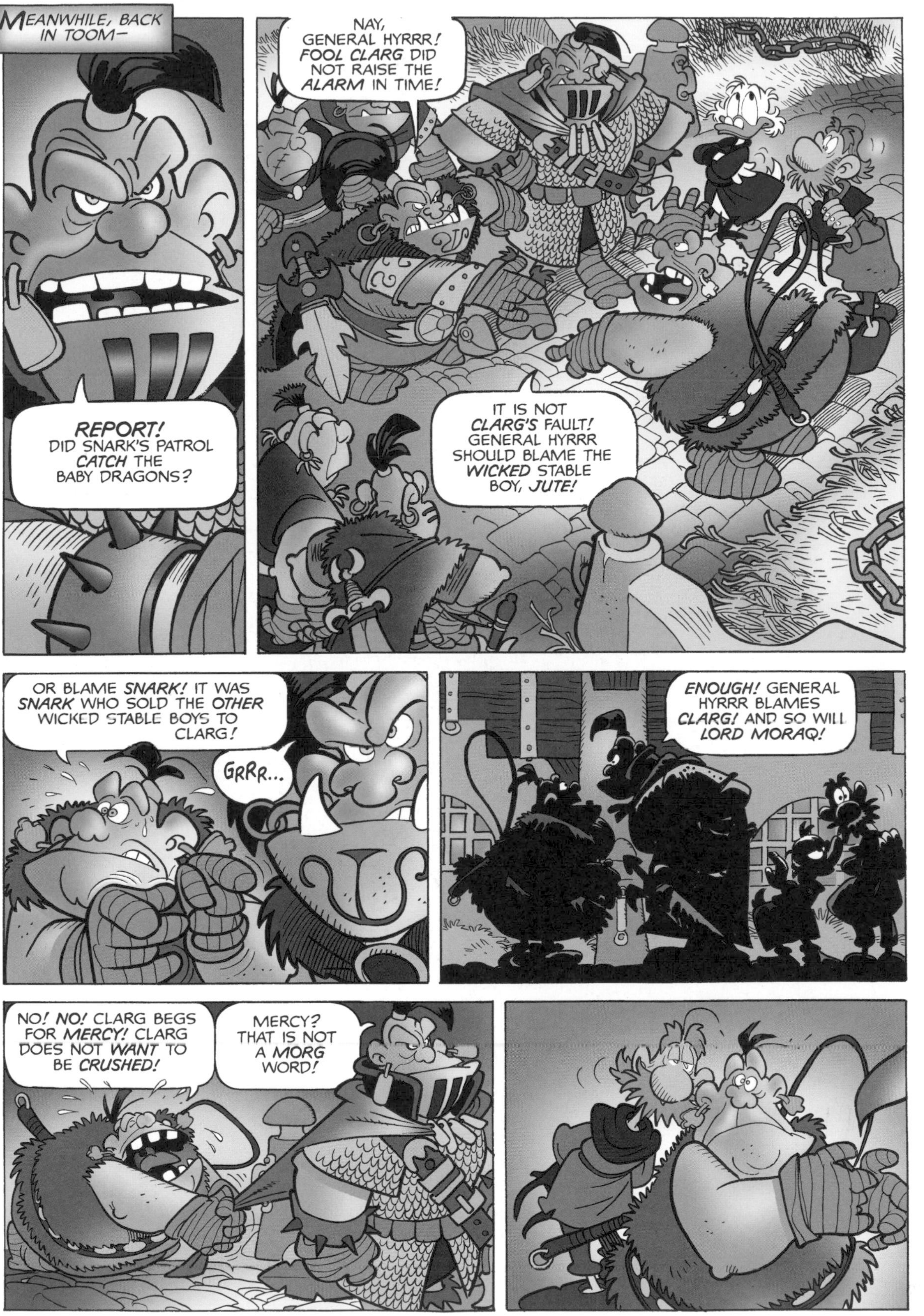
MEANWHILE, BACK IN TOOM—
REPORT! DID SNARK'S PATROL CATCH THE BABY DRAGONS?
NAY, GENERAL HYRRR! FOOL CLARG DID NOT RAISE THE ALARM IN TIME!
IT IS NOT CLARG'S FAULT! GENERAL HYRRR SHOULD BLAME THE WICKED STABLE BOY, JUTE!
OR BLAME SNARK! IT WAS SNARK WHO SOLD THE OTHER WICKED STABLE BOYS TO CLARG!
GRRR...
ENOUGH! GENERAL HYRRR BLAMES CLARG! AND SO WILL LORD MORAQ!
NO! NO! CLARG BEGS FOR MERCY! CLARG DOES NOT WANT TO BE CRUSHED!
MERCY? THAT IS NOT A MORG WORD!

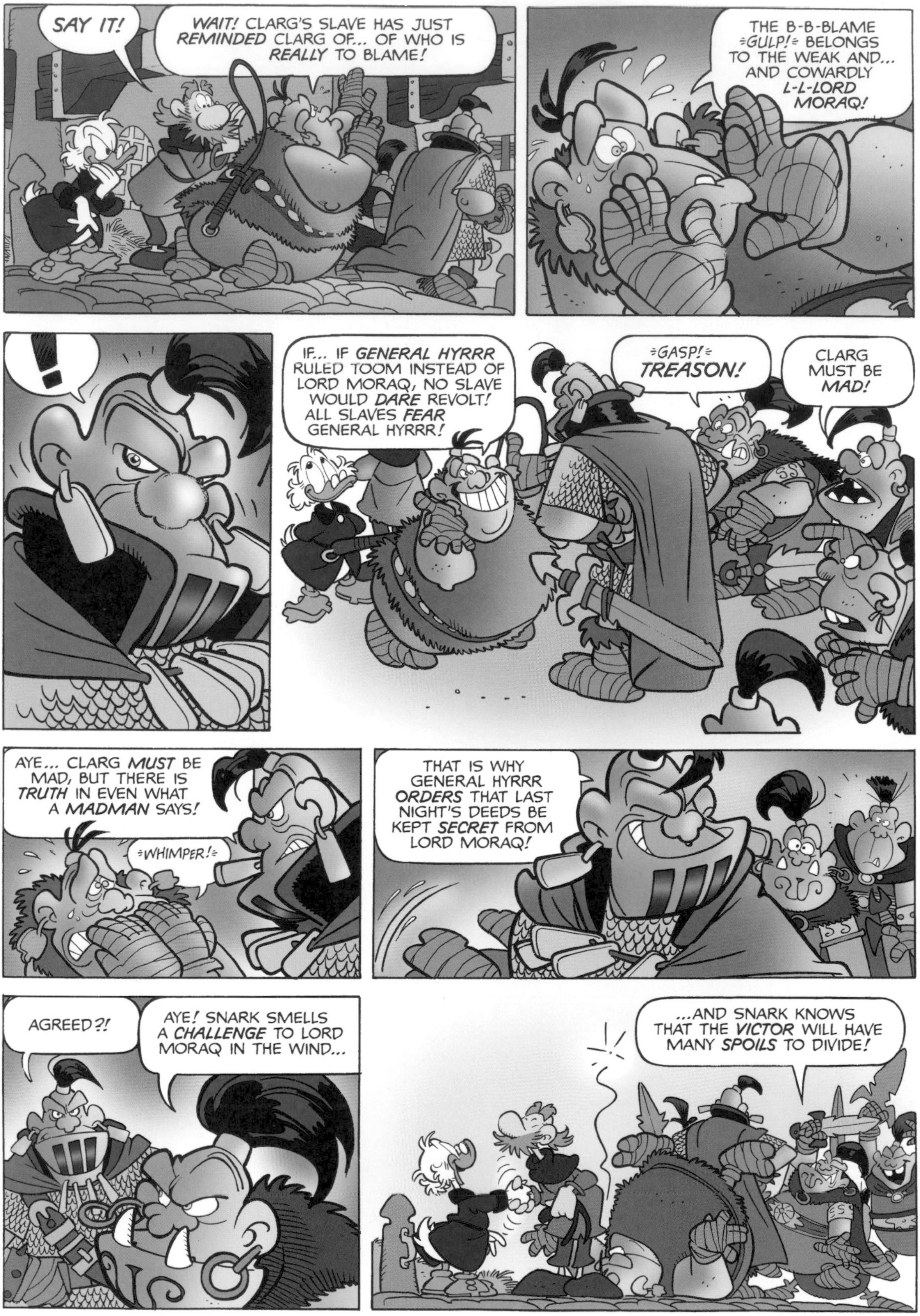
SAY IT!
WAIT! CLARG'S SLAVE HAS JUST REMINDED CLARG OF... OF WHO IS REALLY TO BLAME!
THE B-B-BLAME =GULP!= BELONGS TO THE WEAK AND... AND COWARDLY L-L-LORD MORAQ!
!
IF... IF GENERAL HYRRR RULED TOOM INSTEAD OF LORD MORAQ, NO SLAVE WOULD DARE REVOLT! ALL SLAVES FEAR GENERAL HYRRR!
=GASP!= TREASON!
CLARG MUST BE MAD!
AYE... CLARG MUST BE MAD, BUT THERE IS TRUTH IN EVEN WHAT A MADMAN SAYS!
=WHIMPER!=
THAT IS WHY GENERAL HYRRR ORDERS THAT LAST NIGHT'S DEEDS BE KEPT SECRET FROM LORD MORAQ!
AGREED?!
AYE! SNARK SMELLS A CHALLENGE TO LORD MORAQ IN THE WIND...
...AND SNARK KNOWS THAT THE VICTOR WILL HAVE MANY SPOILS TO DIVIDE!

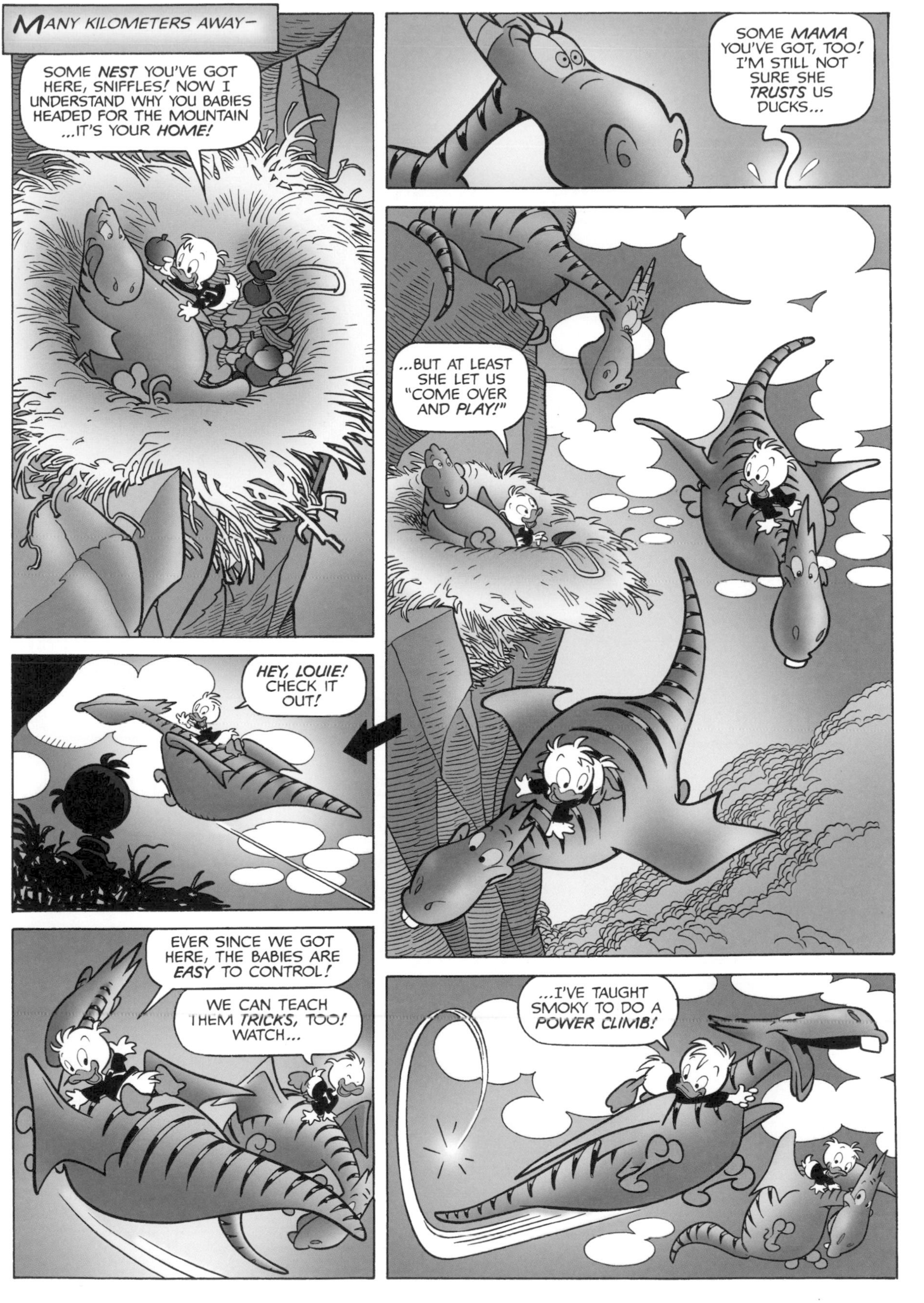
MANY KILOMETERS AWAY—
SOME NEST YOU'VE GOT HERE, SNIFFLES! NOW I UNDERSTAND WHY YOU BABIES HEADED FOR THE MOUNTAIN ...IT'S YOUR HOME!
SOME MAMA YOU'VE GOT, TOO! I'M STILL NOT SURE SHE TRUSTS US DUCKS...
...BUT AT LEAST SHE LET US "COME OVER AND PLAY!"
HEY, LOUIE! CHECK IT OUT!
EVER SINCE WE GOT HERE, THE BABIES ARE EASY TO CONTROL!
WE CAN TEACH THEM TRICKS, TOO! WATCH...
...I'VE TAUGHT SMOKY TO DO A POWER CLIMB!

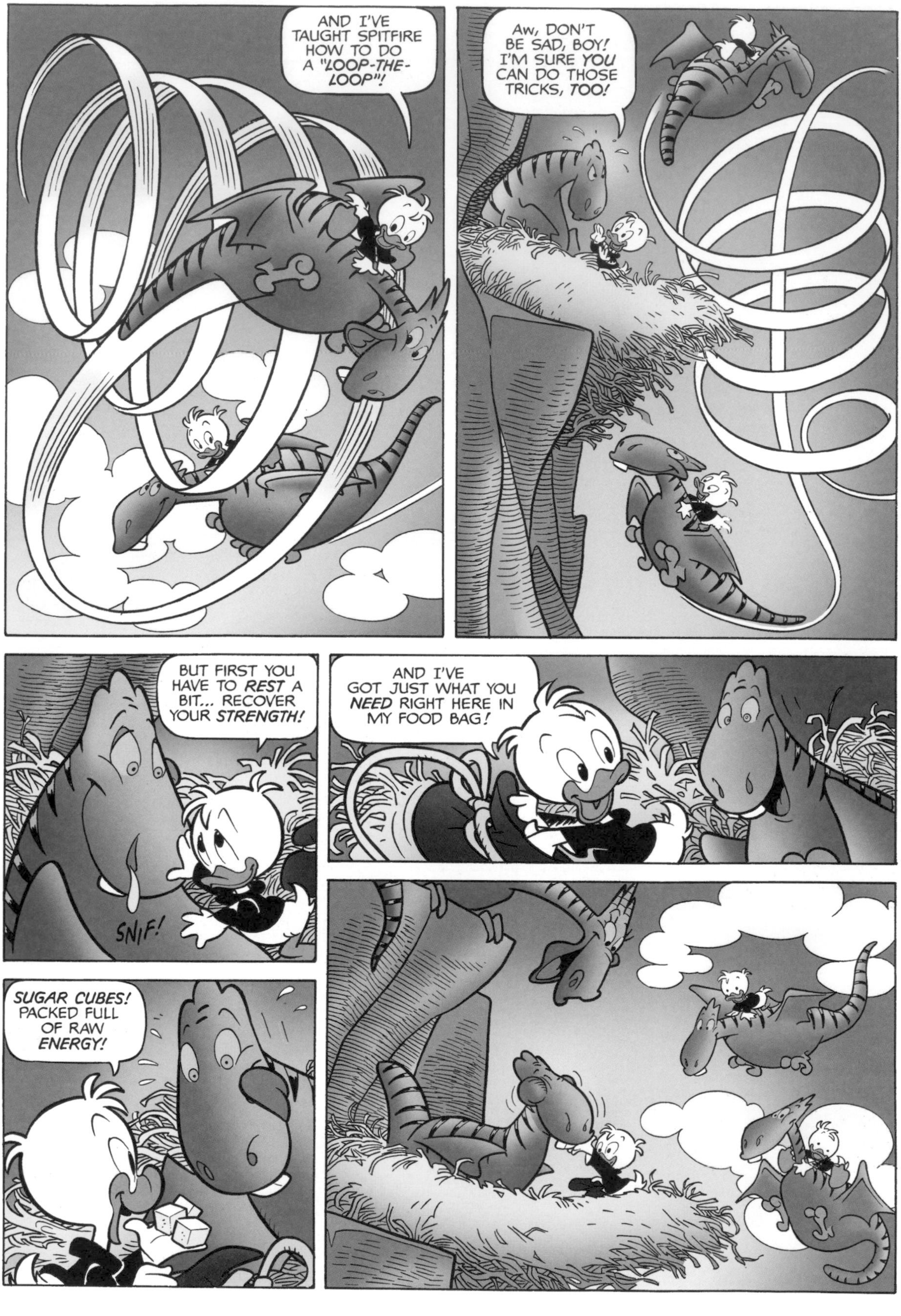
AND I'VE TAUGHT SPITFIRE HOW TO DO A "LOOP-THE-LOOP"!
AW, DON'T BE SAD, BOY! I'M SURE YOU CAN DO THOSE TRICKS, TOO!
BUT FIRST YOU HAVE TO REST A BIT... RECOVER YOUR STRENGTH!
SNIF!
AND I'VE GOT JUST WHAT YOU NEED RIGHT HERE IN MY FOOD BAG!
SUGAR CUBES! PACKED FULL OF RAW ENERGY!

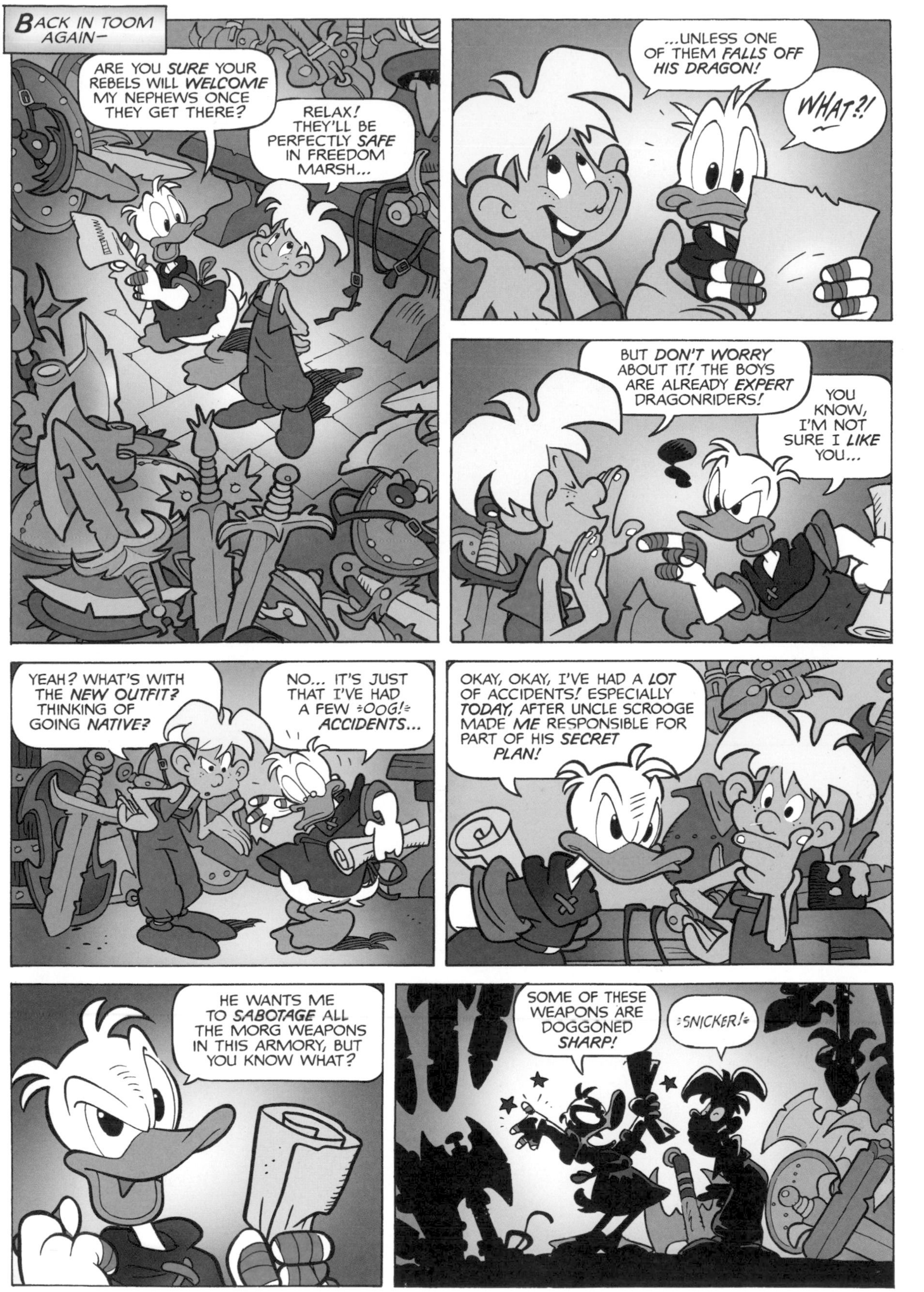

BACK IN TOOM AGAIN–
ARE YOU SURE YOUR REBELS WILL WELCOME MY NEPHEWS ONCE THEY GET THERE?
RELAX! THEY'LL BE PERFECTLY SAFE IN FREEDOM MARSH...
...UNLESS ONE OF THEM FALLS OFF HIS DRAGON!
WHAT?!
BUT DON'T WORRY ABOUT IT! THE BOYS ARE ALREADY EXPERT DRAGONRIDERS!
YOU KNOW, I'M NOT SURE I LIKE YOU...
YEAH? WHAT'S WITH THE NEW OUTFIT? THINKING OF GOING NATIVE?
NO... IT'S JUST THAT I'VE HAD A FEW =OOG!= ACCIDENTS...
OKAY, OKAY, I'VE HAD A LOT OF ACCIDENTS! ESPECIALLY TODAY, AFTER UNCLE SCROOGE MADE ME RESPONSIBLE FOR PART OF HIS SECRET PLAN!
HE WANTS ME TO SABOTAGE ALL THE MORG WEAPONS IN THIS ARMORY, BUT YOU KNOW WHAT?
SOME OF THESE WEAPONS ARE DOGGONED SHARP!
=SNICKER!=

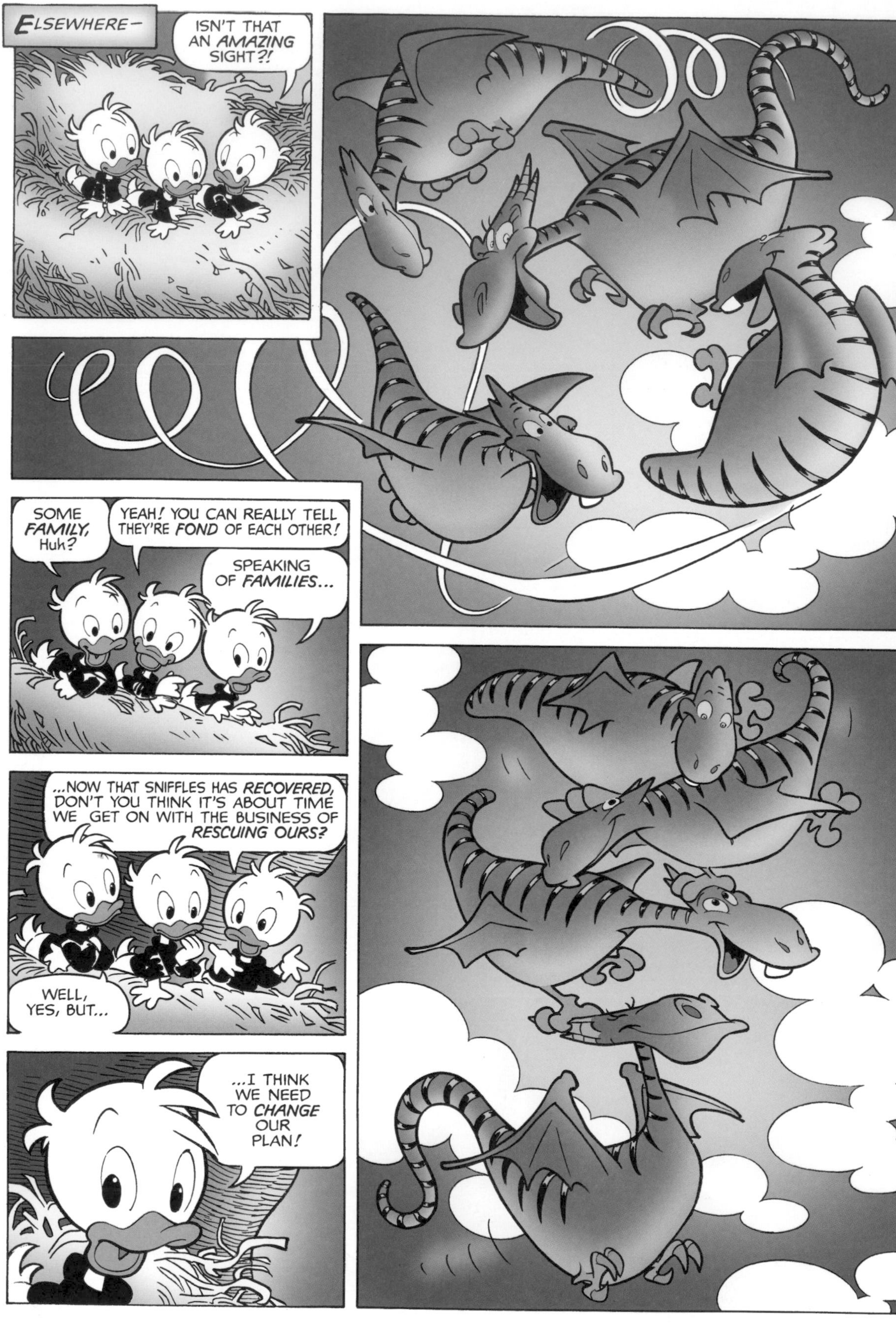

ELSEWHERE—
ISN'T THAT AN AMAZING SIGHT?!
SOME FAMILY, Huh?
YEAH! YOU CAN REALLY TELL THEY'RE FOND OF EACH OTHER!
SPEAKING OF FAMILIES...
...NOW THAT SNIFFLES HAS RECOVERED, DON'T YOU THINK IT'S ABOUT TIME WE GET ON WITH THE BUSINESS OF RESCUING OURS?
WELL, YES, BUT...
...I THINK WE NEED TO CHANGE OUR PLAN!

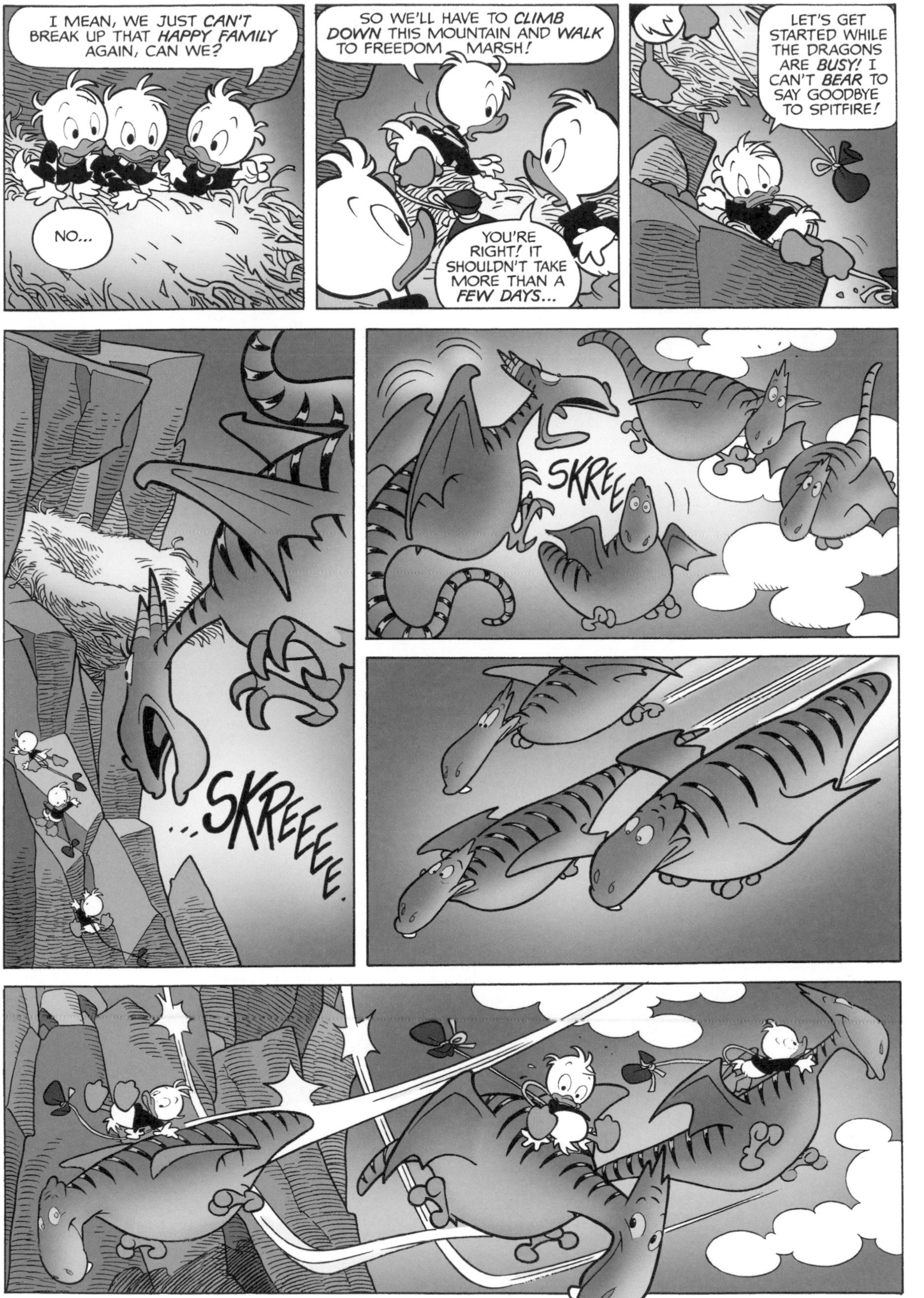

I MEAN, WE JUST CAN'T BREAK UP THAT HAPPY FAMILY AGAIN, CAN WE?
NO...
SO WE'LL HAVE TO CLIMB DOWN THIS MOUNTAIN AND WALK TO FREEDOM MARSH!
YOU'RE RIGHT! IT SHOULDN'T TAKE MORE THAN A FEW DAYS...
LET'S GET STARTED WHILE THE DRAGONS ARE BUSY! I CAN'T BEAR TO SAY GOODBYE TO SPITFIRE!
SKREEEEE.
SKREE

WELL, I'LL BE! IT... IT'S LIKE MAMA'S GIVING US *PERMISSION* TO BORROW HER SONS!

SKREEE

YES! SHE *IS!*

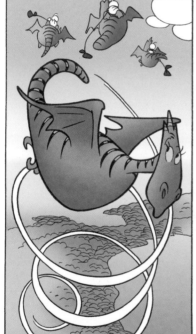

NEXT STOP, *FREEDOM MARSH!*

YAHOO!!!

CONTINUED...

Sketches

To prepare for illustrating *World of the Dragonlords*, Giorgio Cavazzano worked closely with Byron Erickson in fully fleshing out the characters. On these pages, and others throughout the balance of this book, we're pleased to reproduce a number of Cavazzano's preliminary sketches.

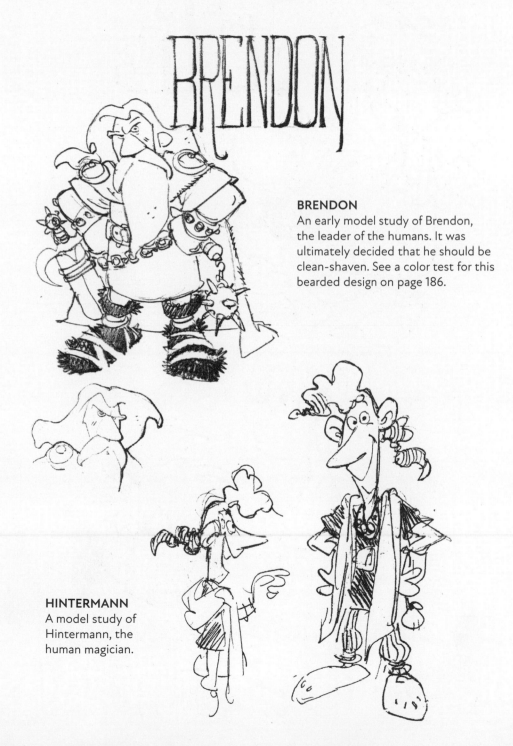

BRENDON
An early model study of Brendon, the leader of the humans. It was ultimately decided that he should be clean-shaven. See a color test for this bearded design on page 186.

HINTERMANN
A model study of Hintermann, the human magician.

Sketches

JUTE

JUTE
A model study
of the Ducks'
stable-boy ally.

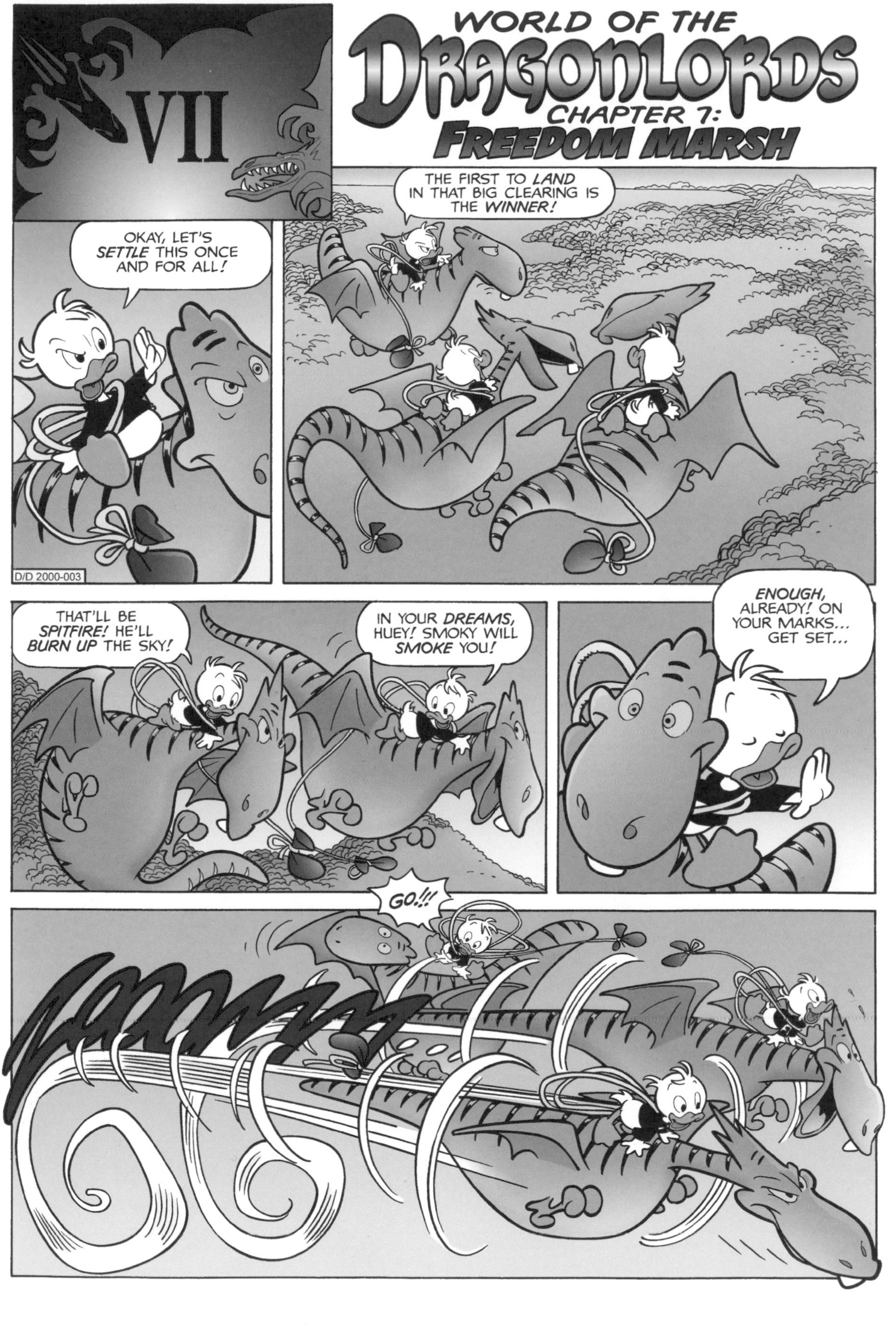
VII
WORLD OF THE
DRAGONLORDS
CHAPTER 7:
FREEDOM MARSH
OKAY, LET'S SETTLE THIS ONCE AND FOR ALL!
THE FIRST TO LAND IN THAT BIG CLEARING IS THE WINNER!
D/D 2000-003
THAT'LL BE SPITFIRE! HE'LL BURN UP THE SKY!
IN YOUR DREAMS, HUEY! SMOKY WILL SMOKE YOU!
ENOUGH, ALREADY! ON YOUR MARKS... GET SET...
GO!!!

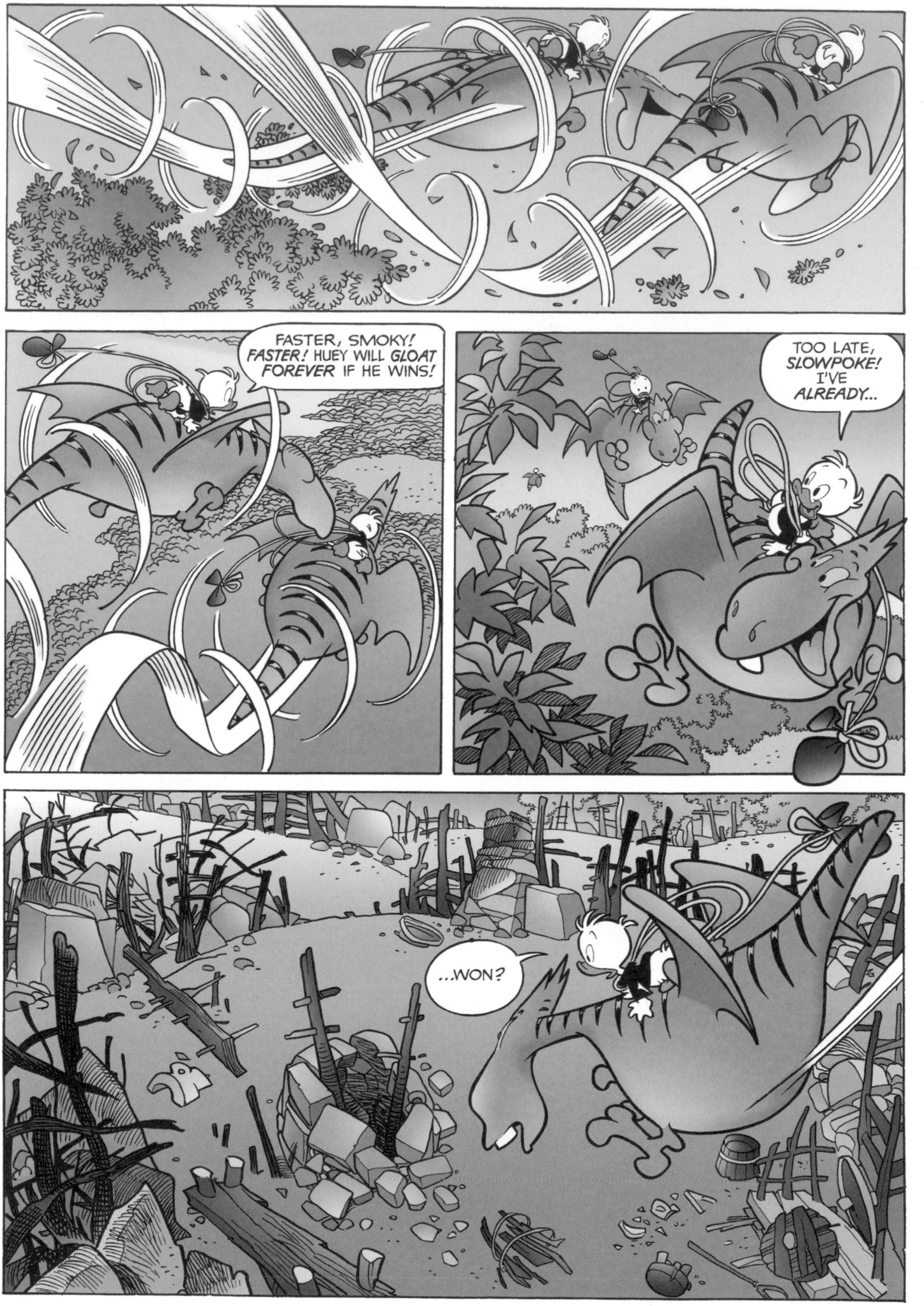
FASTER, SMOKY! FASTER! HUEY WILL GLOAT FOREVER IF HE WINS!
TOO LATE, SLOWPOKE! I'VE ALREADY...
...WON?

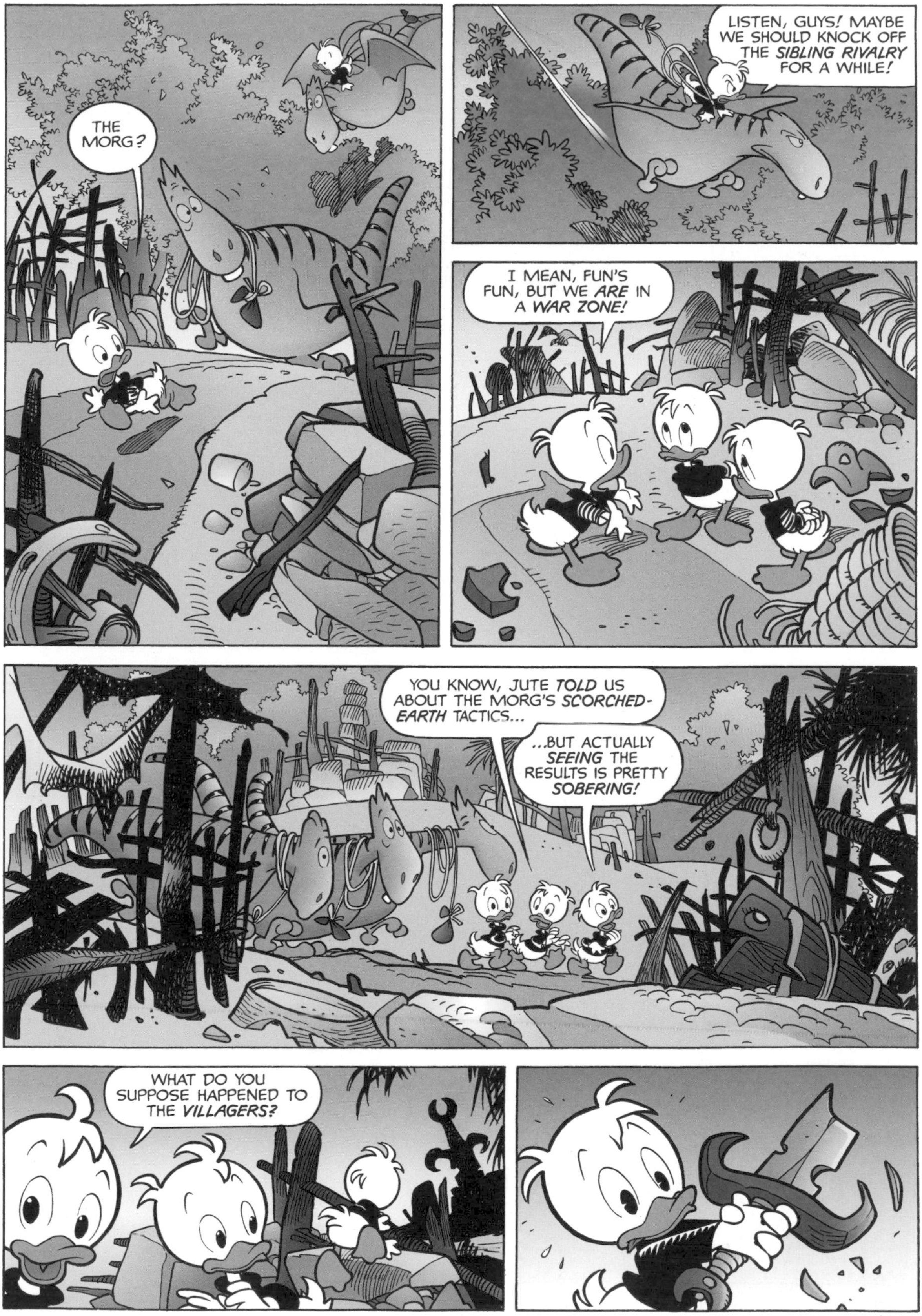
THE MORG?
LISTEN, GUYS! MAYBE WE SHOULD KNOCK OFF THE SIBLING RIVALRY FOR A WHILE!
I MEAN, FUN'S FUN, BUT WE ARE IN A WAR ZONE!
YOU KNOW, JUTE TOLD US ABOUT THE MORG'S SCORCHED-EARTH TACTICS...
...BUT ACTUALLY SEEING THE RESULTS IS PRETTY SOBERING!
WHAT DO YOU SUPPOSE HAPPENED TO THE VILLAGERS?

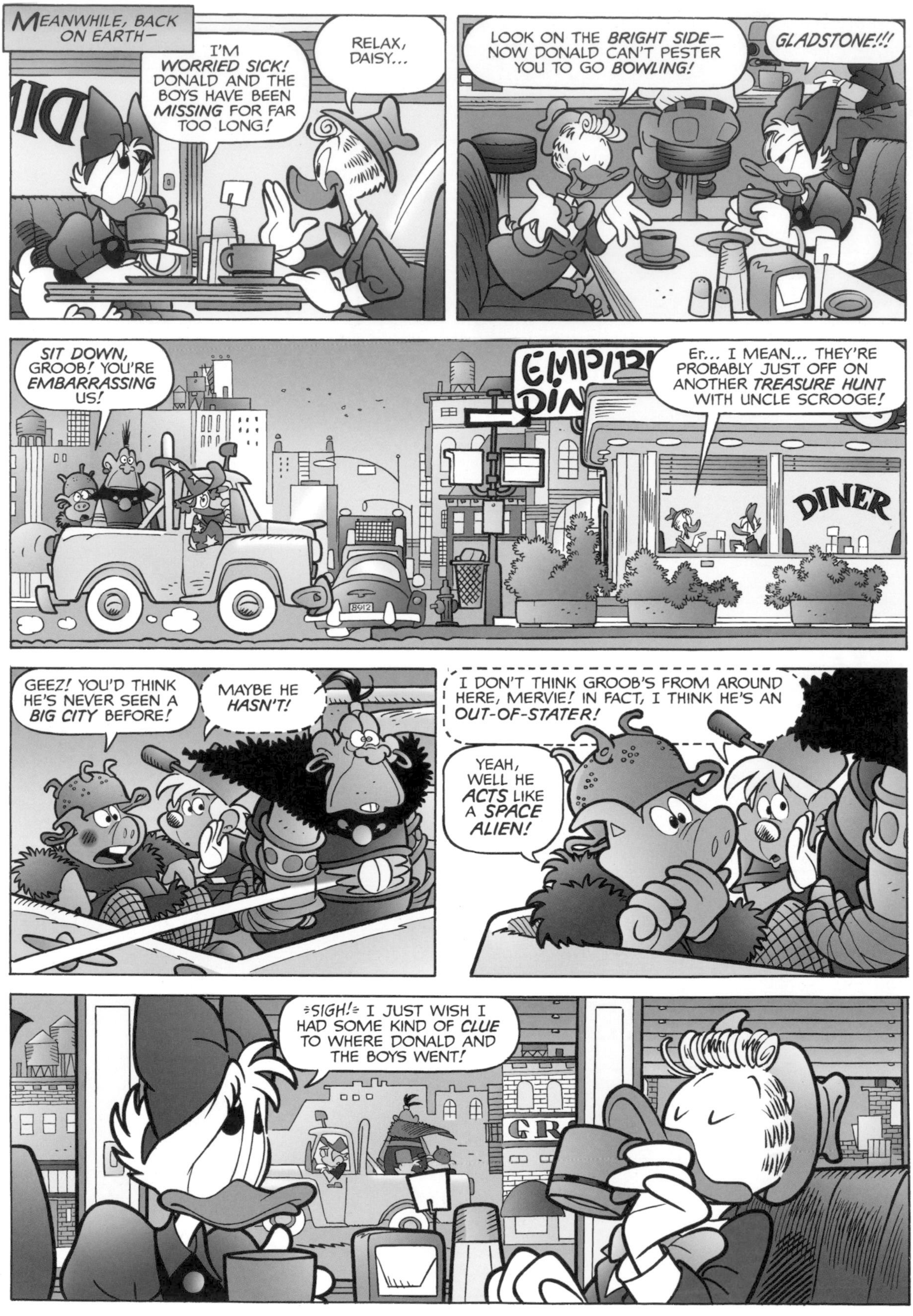
MEANWHILE, BACK ON EARTH—
I'M WORRIED SICK! DONALD AND THE BOYS HAVE BEEN MISSING FOR FAR TOO LONG!
RELAX, DAISY...
LOOK ON THE BRIGHT SIDE— NOW DONALD CAN'T PESTER YOU TO GO BOWLING!
GLADSTONE!!!
SIT DOWN, GROOB! YOU'RE EMBARRASSING US!
Er... I MEAN... THEY'RE PROBABLY JUST OFF ON ANOTHER TREASURE HUNT WITH UNCLE SCROOGE!
DINER
GEEZ! YOU'D THINK HE'S NEVER SEEN A BIG CITY BEFORE!
MAYBE HE HASN'T!
I DON'T THINK GROOB'S FROM AROUND HERE, MERVIE! IN FACT, I THINK HE'S AN OUT-OF-STATER!
YEAH, WELL HE ACTS LIKE A SPACE ALIEN!
≈SIGH!≈ I JUST WISH I HAD SOME KIND OF CLUE TO WHERE DONALD AND THE BOYS WENT!

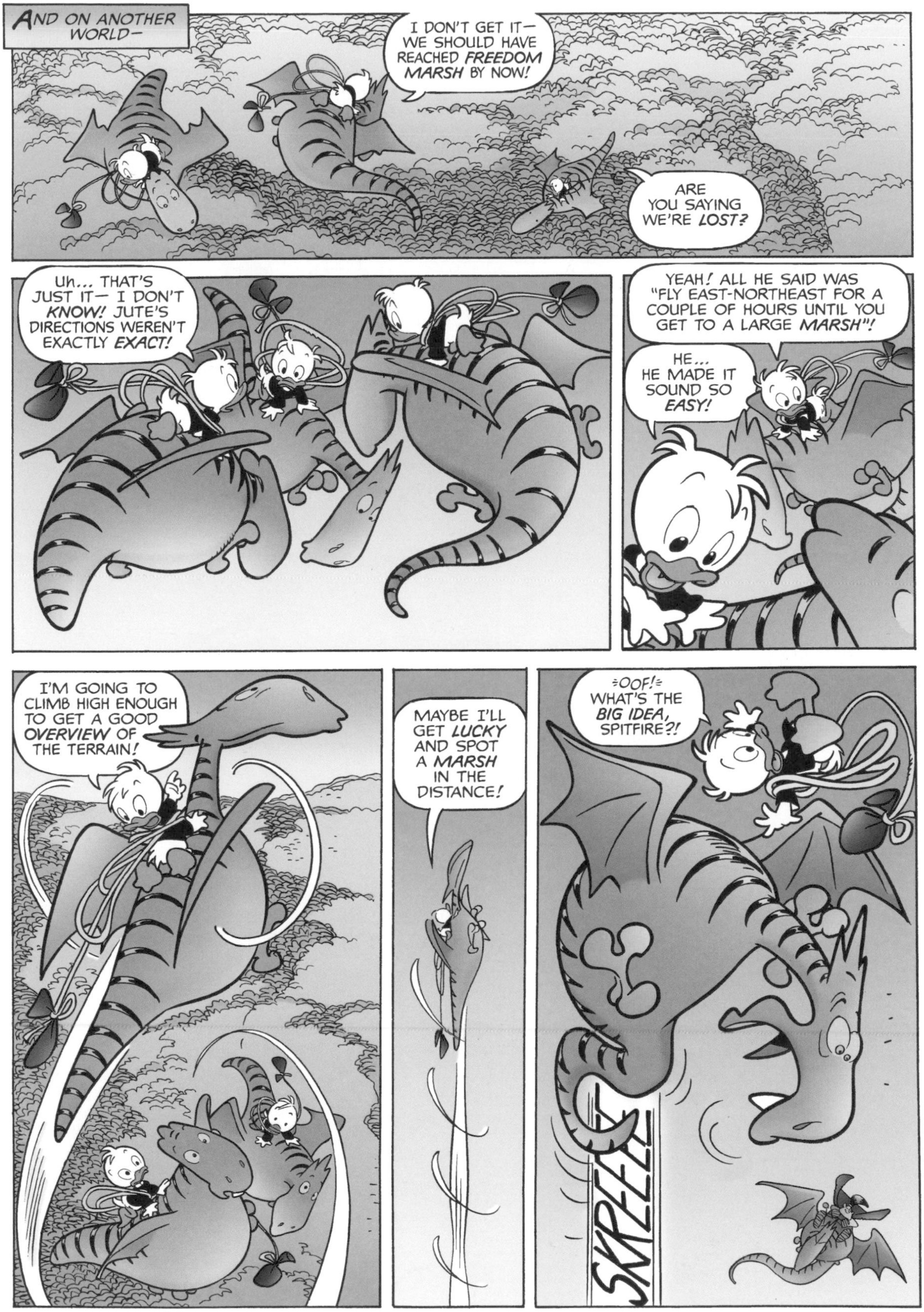
AND ON ANOTHER WORLD—
I DON'T GET IT— WE SHOULD HAVE REACHED FREEDOM MARSH BY NOW!
ARE YOU SAYING WE'RE LOST?
Uh... THAT'S JUST IT— I DON'T KNOW! JUTE'S DIRECTIONS WEREN'T EXACTLY EXACT!
YEAH! ALL HE SAID WAS "FLY EAST-NORTHEAST FOR A COUPLE OF HOURS UNTIL YOU GET TO A LARGE MARSH"!
HE... HE MADE IT SOUND SO EASY!
I'M GOING TO CLIMB HIGH ENOUGH TO GET A GOOD OVERVIEW OF THE TERRAIN!
MAYBE I'LL GET LUCKY AND SPOT A MARSH IN THE DISTANCE!
OOF! WHAT'S THE BIG IDEA, SPITFIRE?!
SKREEEE

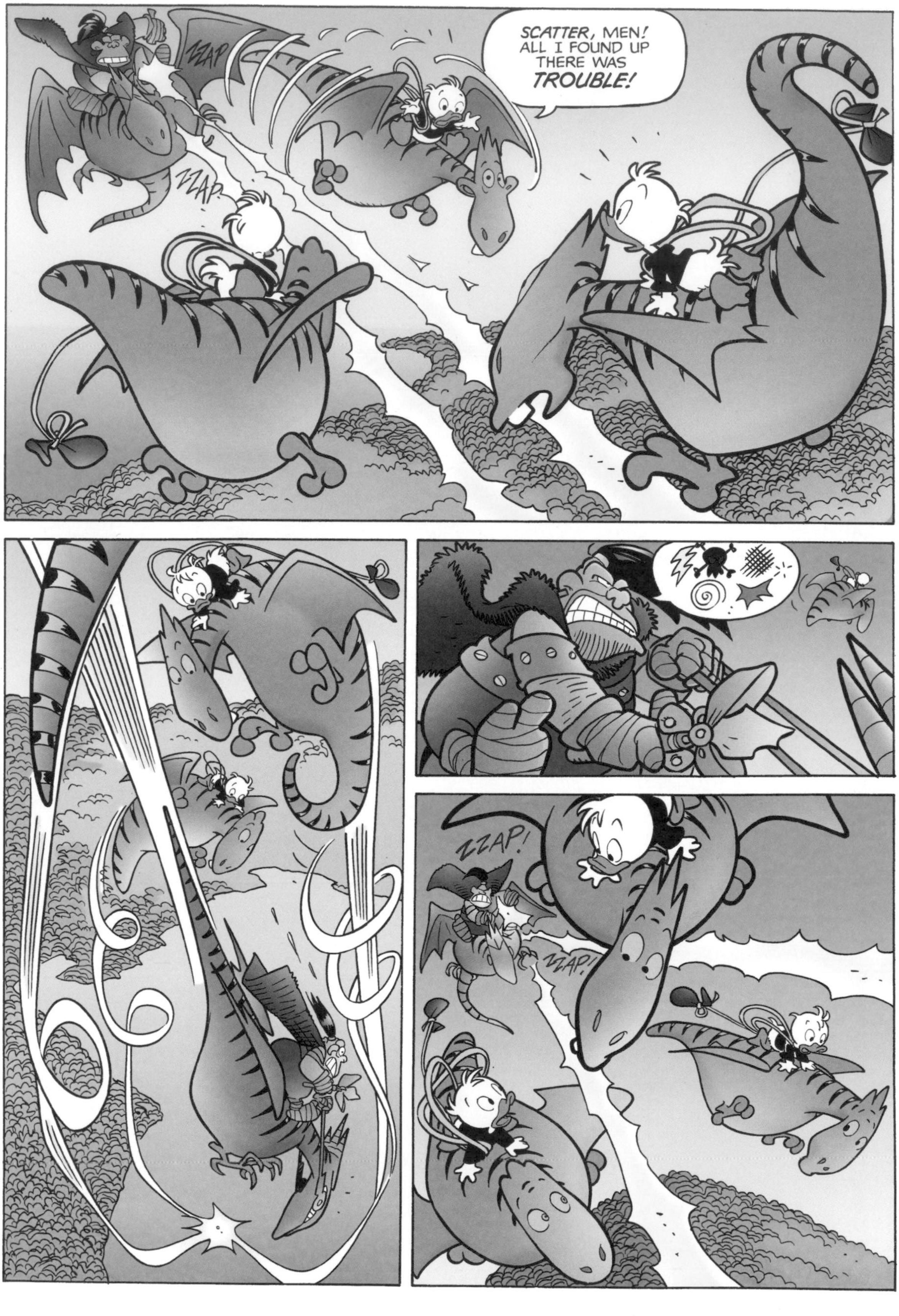

ZZAP
SCATTER, MEN! ALL I FOUND UP THERE WAS TROUBLE!
ZZAP
ZZAP!
ZZAP!

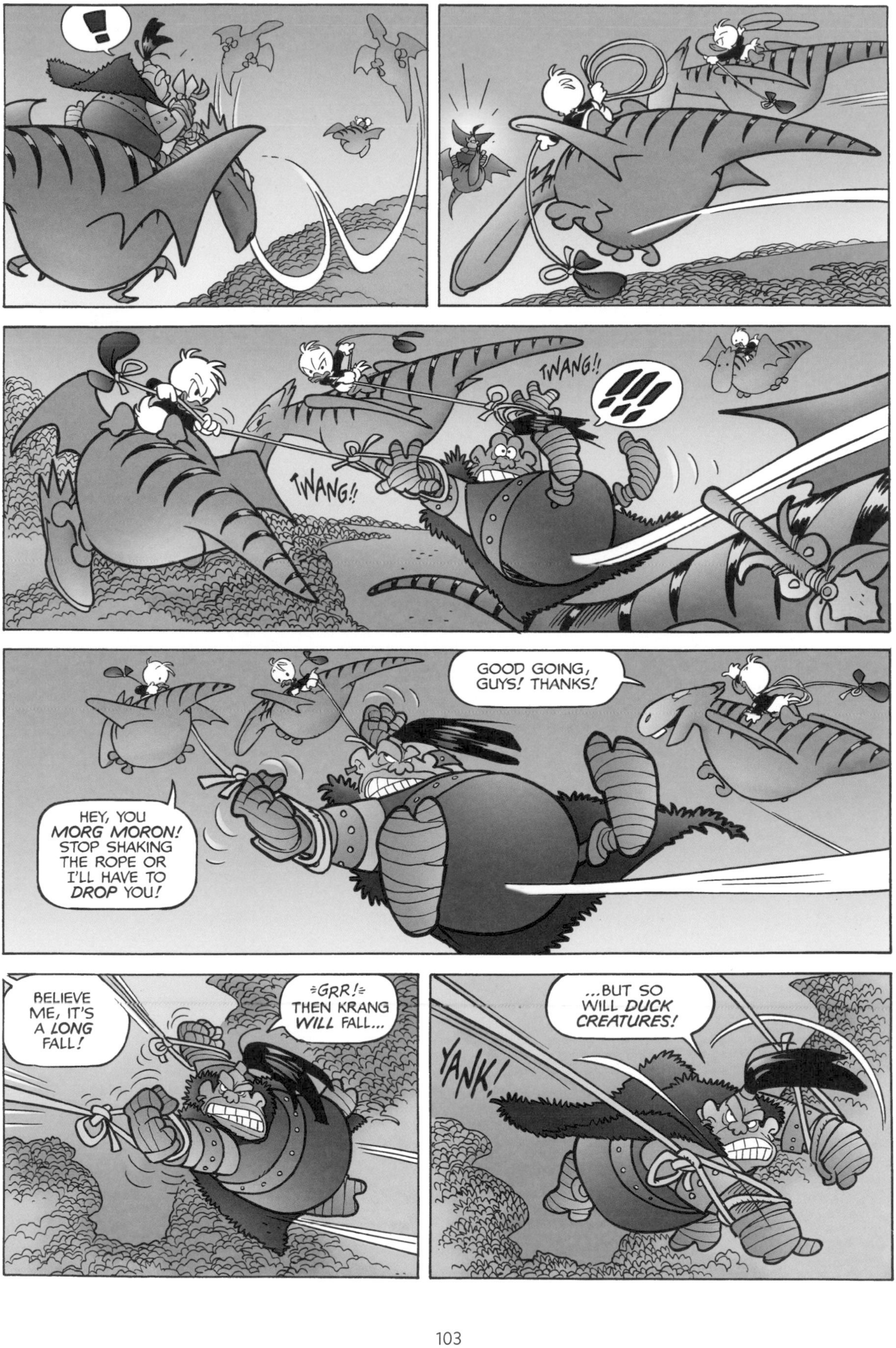
!
TWANG!!
!!!
TWANG!!
GOOD GOING, GUYS! THANKS!
HEY, YOU MORG MORON! STOP SHAKING THE ROPE OR I'LL HAVE TO DROP YOU!
BELIEVE ME, IT'S A LONG FALL!
GRR! THEN KRANG WILL FALL...
YANK!
...BUT SO WILL DUCK CREATURES!

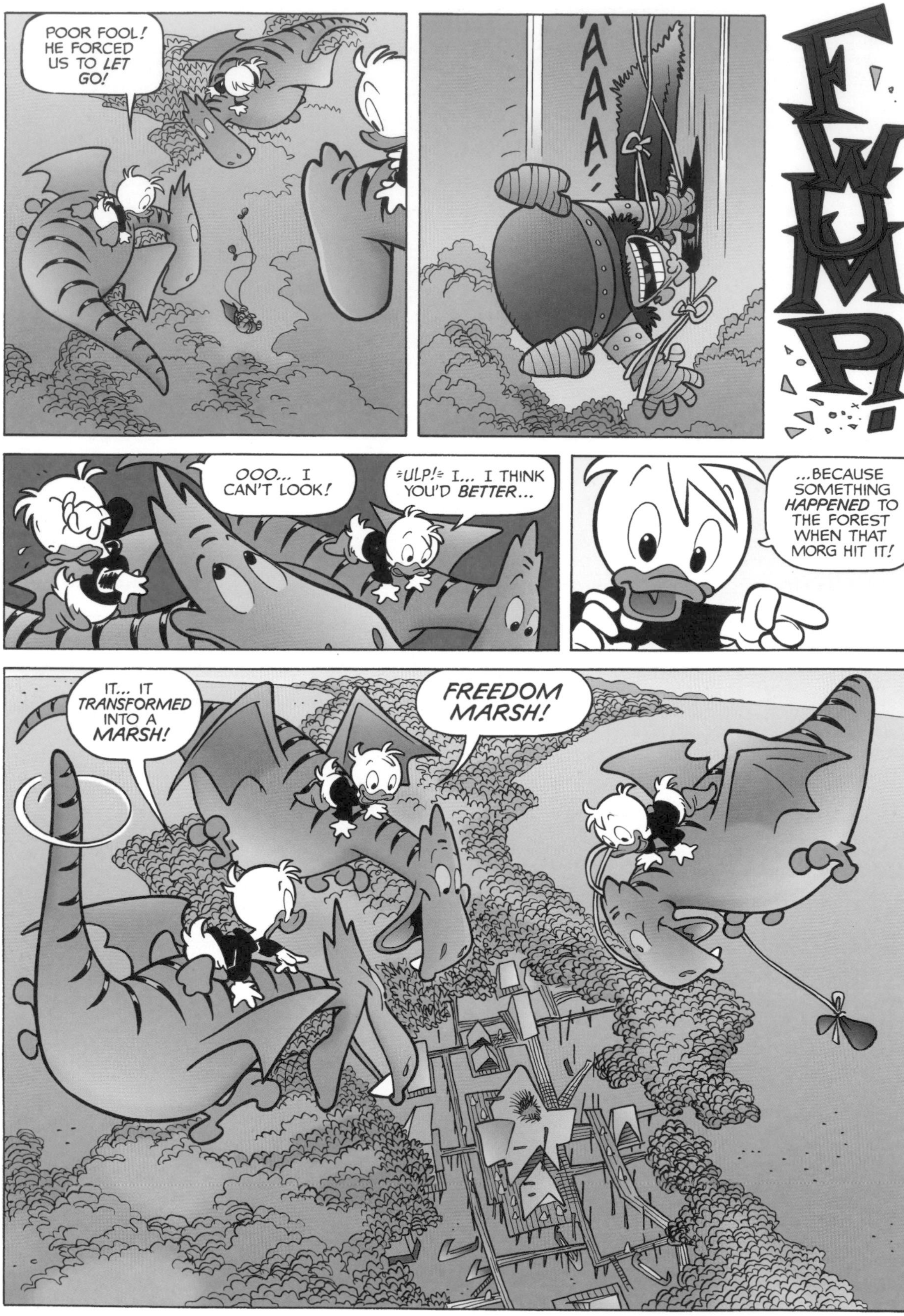

POOR FOOL! HE FORCED US TO *LET GO!*
AAAAA
FWUMP!
OOO... I CAN'T LOOK!
ULP! I... I THINK YOU'D *BETTER*...
...BECAUSE SOMETHING *HAPPENED* TO THE FOREST WHEN THAT MORG HIT IT!
IT... IT *TRANSFORMED* INTO A *MARSH!*
FREEDOM MARSH!

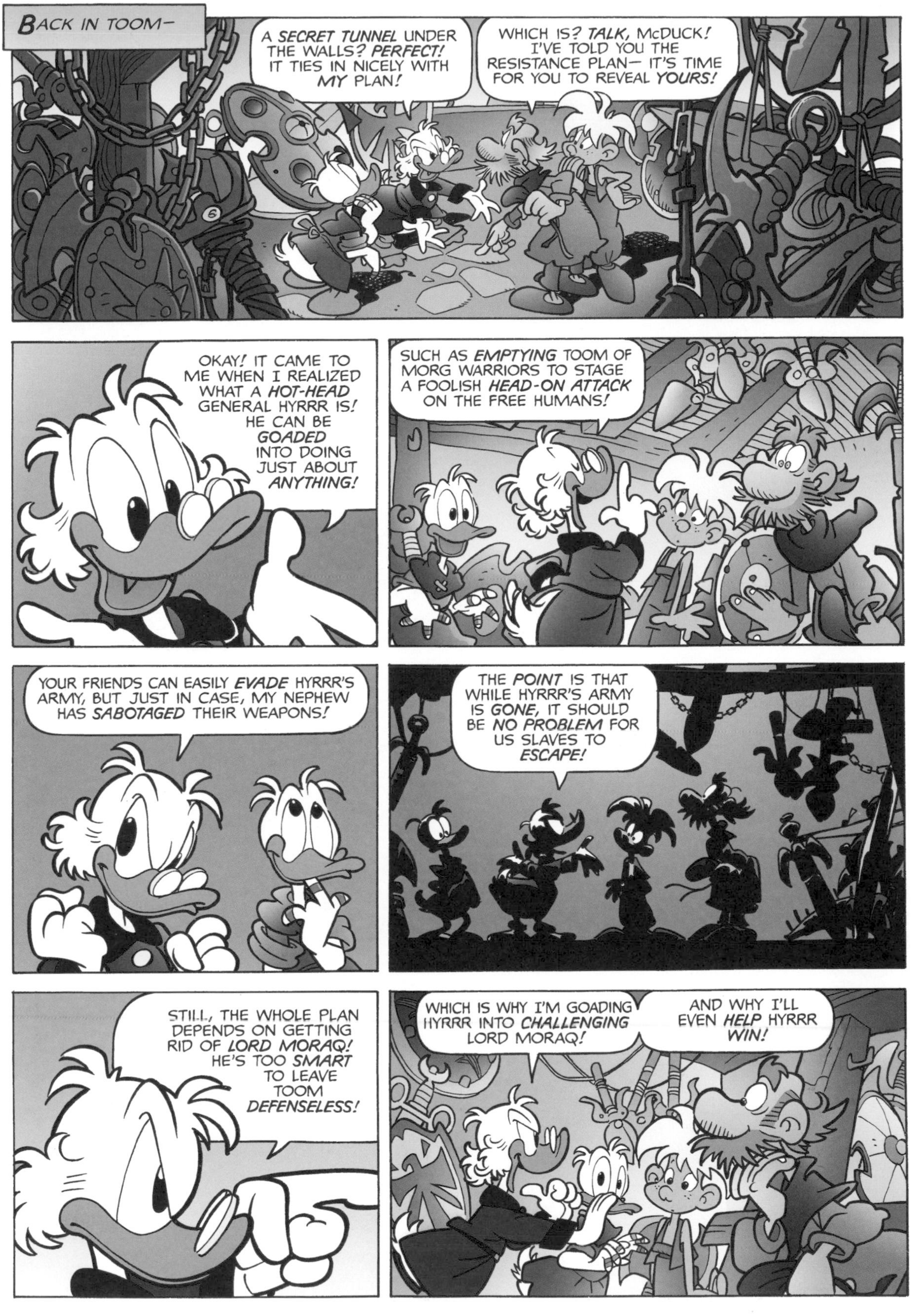
BACK IN TOOM—
A SECRET TUNNEL UNDER THE WALLS? PERFECT! IT TIES IN NICELY WITH MY PLAN!
WHICH IS? TALK, McDUCK! I'VE TOLD YOU THE RESISTANCE PLAN— IT'S TIME FOR YOU TO REVEAL YOURS!
OKAY! IT CAME TO ME WHEN I REALIZED WHAT A HOT-HEAD GENERAL HYRRR IS! HE CAN BE GOADED INTO DOING JUST ABOUT ANYTHING!
SUCH AS EMPTYING TOOM OF MORG WARRIORS TO STAGE A FOOLISH HEAD-ON ATTACK ON THE FREE HUMANS!
YOUR FRIENDS CAN EASILY EVADE HYRRR'S ARMY, BUT JUST IN CASE, MY NEPHEW HAS SABOTAGED THEIR WEAPONS!
THE POINT IS THAT WHILE HYRRR'S ARMY IS GONE, IT SHOULD BE NO PROBLEM FOR US SLAVES TO ESCAPE!
STILL, THE WHOLE PLAN DEPENDS ON GETTING RID OF LORD MORAQ! HE'S TOO SMART TO LEAVE TOOM DEFENSELESS!
WHICH IS WHY I'M GOADING HYRRR INTO CHALLENGING LORD MORAQ!
AND WHY I'LL EVEN HELP HYRRR WIN!

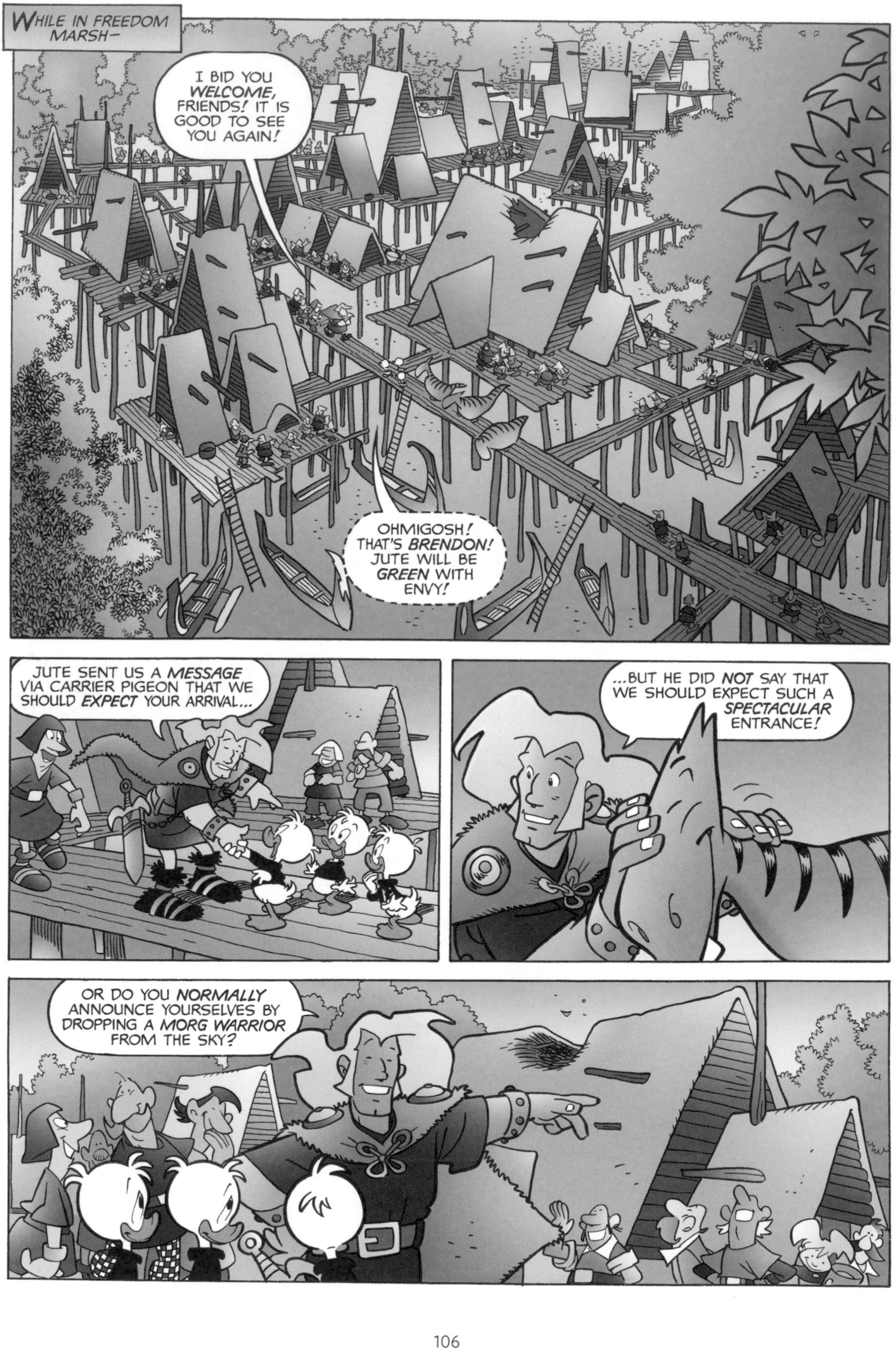
WHILE IN FREEDOM MARSH—
I BID YOU WELCOME, FRIENDS! IT IS GOOD TO SEE YOU AGAIN!
OHMIGOSH! THAT'S BRENDON! JUTE WILL BE GREEN WITH ENVY!
JUTE SENT US A MESSAGE VIA CARRIER PIGEON THAT WE SHOULD EXPECT YOUR ARRIVAL...
...BUT HE DID NOT SAY THAT WE SHOULD EXPECT SUCH A SPECTACULAR ENTRANCE!
OR DO YOU NORMALLY ANNOUNCE YOURSELVES BY DROPPING A MORG WARRIOR FROM THE SKY?

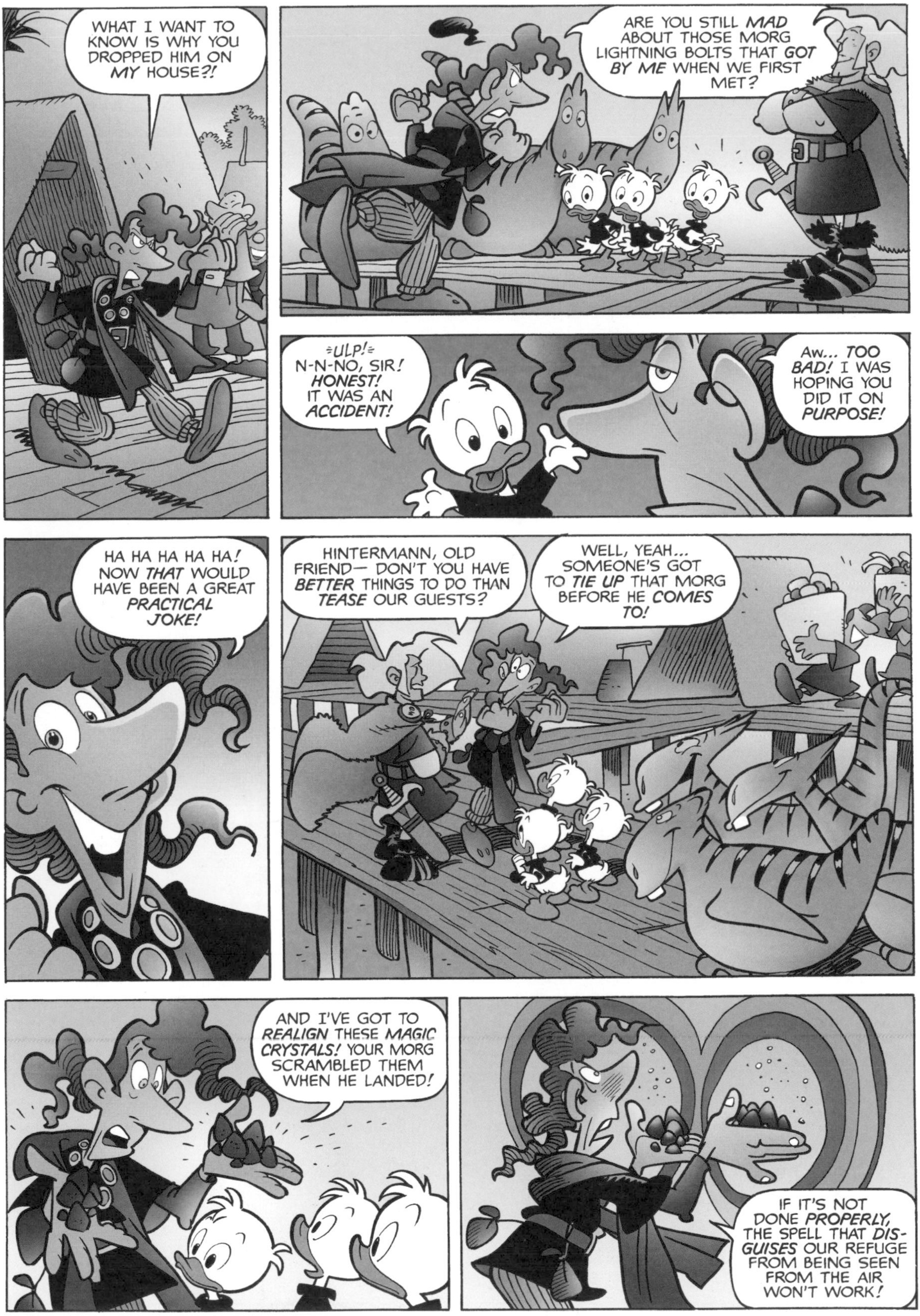
WHAT I WANT TO KNOW IS WHY YOU DROPPED HIM ON MY HOUSE?!
ARE YOU STILL MAD ABOUT THOSE MORG LIGHTNING BOLTS THAT GOT BY ME WHEN WE FIRST MET?
=ULP!= N-N-NO, SIR! HONEST! IT WAS AN ACCIDENT!
AW... TOO BAD! I WAS HOPING YOU DID IT ON PURPOSE!
HA HA HA HA HA! NOW THAT WOULD HAVE BEEN A GREAT PRACTICAL JOKE!
HINTERMANN, OLD FRIEND— DON'T YOU HAVE BETTER THINGS TO DO THAN TEASE OUR GUESTS?
WELL, YEAH... SOMEONE'S GOT TO TIE UP THAT MORG BEFORE HE COMES TO!
AND I'VE GOT TO REALIGN THESE MAGIC CRYSTALS! YOUR MORG SCRAMBLED THEM WHEN HE LANDED!
IF IT'S NOT DONE PROPERLY, THE SPELL THAT DISGUISES OUR REFUGE FROM BEING SEEN FROM THE AIR WON'T WORK!

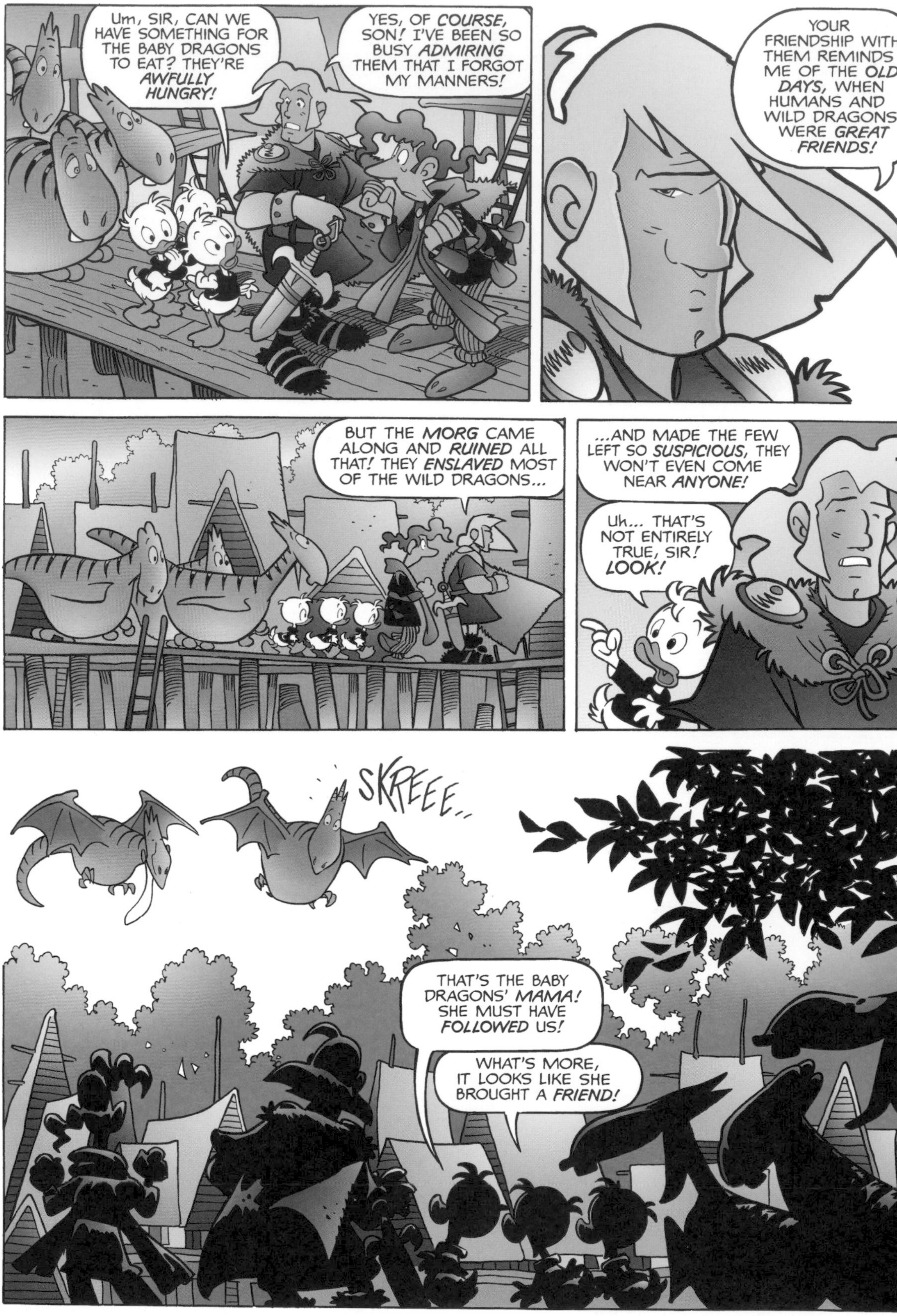
Um, SIR, CAN WE HAVE SOMETHING FOR THE BABY DRAGONS TO EAT? THEY'RE AWFULLY HUNGRY!
YES, OF COURSE, SON! I'VE BEEN SO BUSY ADMIRING THEM THAT I FORGOT MY MANNERS!
YOUR FRIENDSHIP WITH THEM REMINDS ME OF THE OLD DAYS, WHEN HUMANS AND WILD DRAGONS WERE GREAT FRIENDS!
BUT THE MORG CAME ALONG AND RUINED ALL THAT! THEY ENSLAVED MOST OF THE WILD DRAGONS...
...AND MADE THE FEW LEFT SO SUSPICIOUS, THEY WON'T EVEN COME NEAR ANYONE!
Uh... THAT'S NOT ENTIRELY TRUE, SIR! LOOK!
SKREEEE...
THAT'S THE BABY DRAGONS' MAMA! SHE MUST HAVE FOLLOWED US!
WHAT'S MORE, IT LOOKS LIKE SHE BROUGHT A FRIEND!

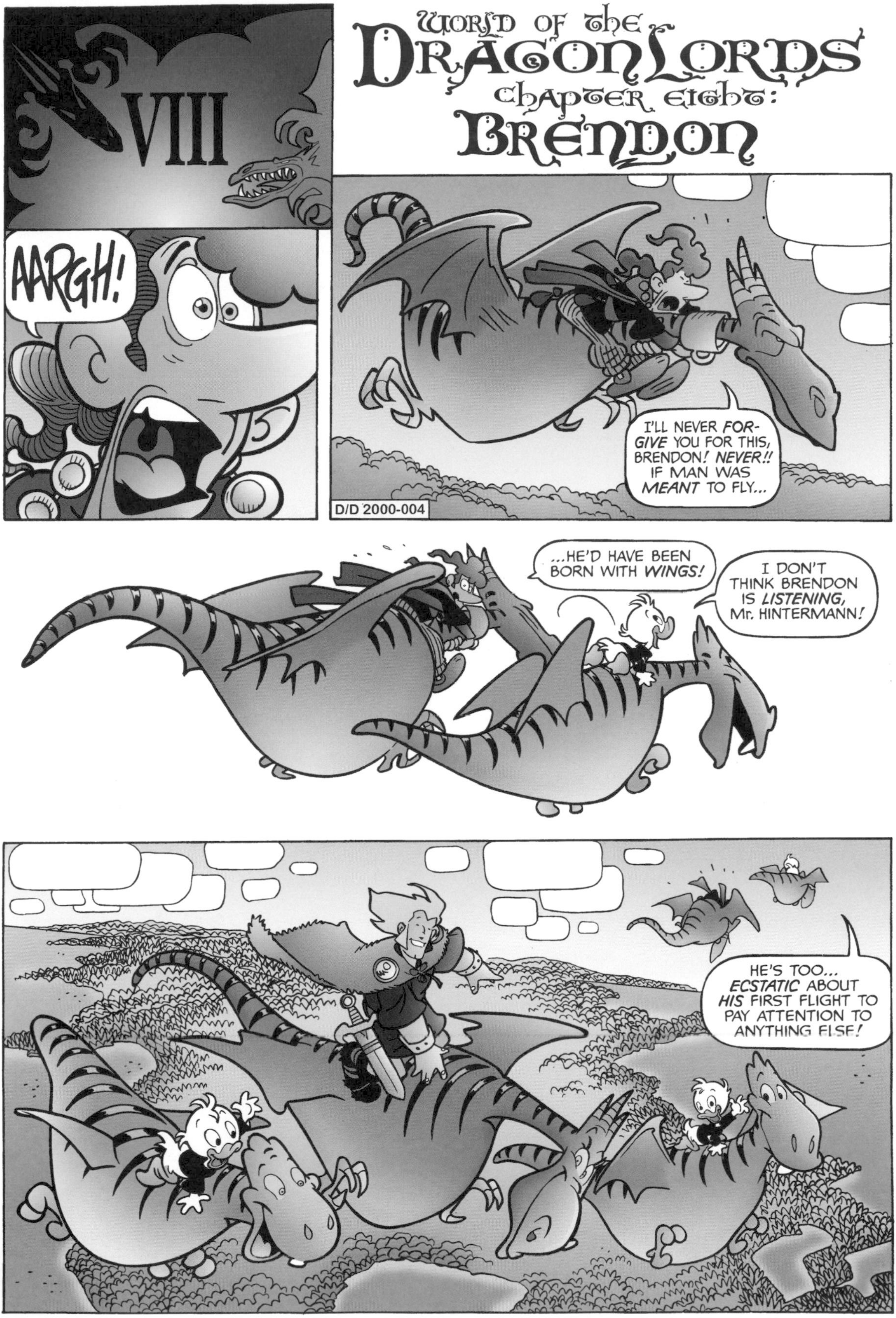

WORLD OF THE DRAGONLORDS
CHAPTER EIGHT: BRENDON
VIII
AARGH!
I'LL NEVER FORGIVE YOU FOR THIS, BRENDON! NEVER!! IF MAN WAS MEANT TO FLY...
D/D 2000-004
...HE'D HAVE BEEN BORN WITH WINGS!
I DON'T THINK BRENDON IS LISTENING, Mr. HINTERMANN!
HE'S TOO... ECSTATIC ABOUT HIS FIRST FLIGHT TO PAY ATTENTION TO ANYTHING ELSE!

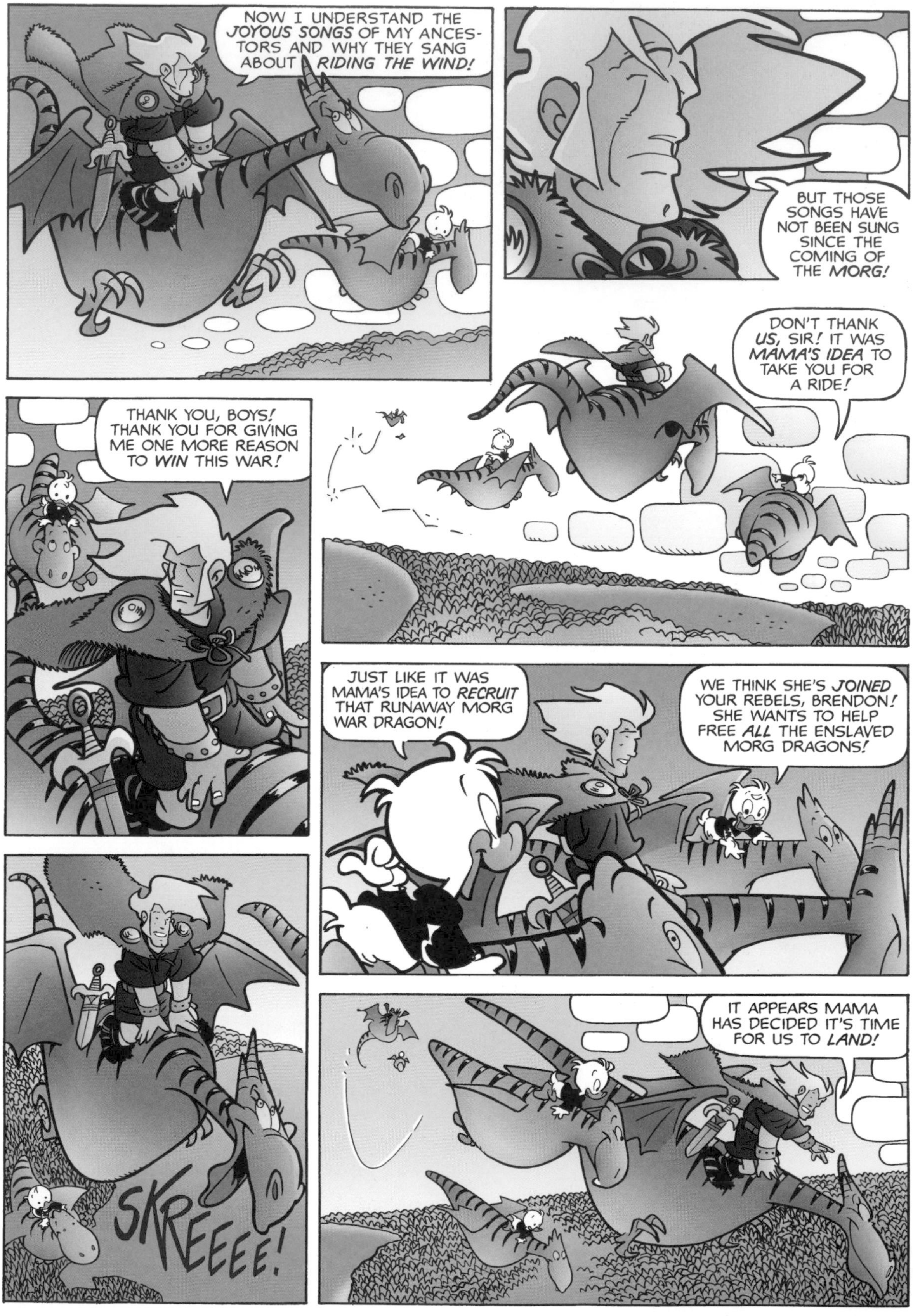

NOW I UNDERSTAND THE *JOYOUS SONGS* OF MY ANCESTORS AND WHY THEY SANG ABOUT *RIDING THE WIND!*
BUT THOSE SONGS HAVE NOT BEEN SUNG SINCE THE COMING OF THE *MORG!*
THANK YOU, BOYS! THANK YOU FOR GIVING ME ONE MORE REASON TO *WIN* THIS WAR!
DON'T THANK *US*, SIR! IT WAS *MAMA'S IDEA* TO TAKE YOU FOR A RIDE!
JUST LIKE IT WAS MAMA'S IDEA TO *RECRUIT* THAT RUNAWAY MORG WAR DRAGON!
WE THINK SHE'S *JOINED* YOUR REBELS, BRENDON! SHE WANTS TO HELP FREE *ALL* THE ENSLAVED MORG DRAGONS!
SKREEEEE!
IT APPEARS MAMA HAS DECIDED IT'S TIME FOR US TO *LAND!*

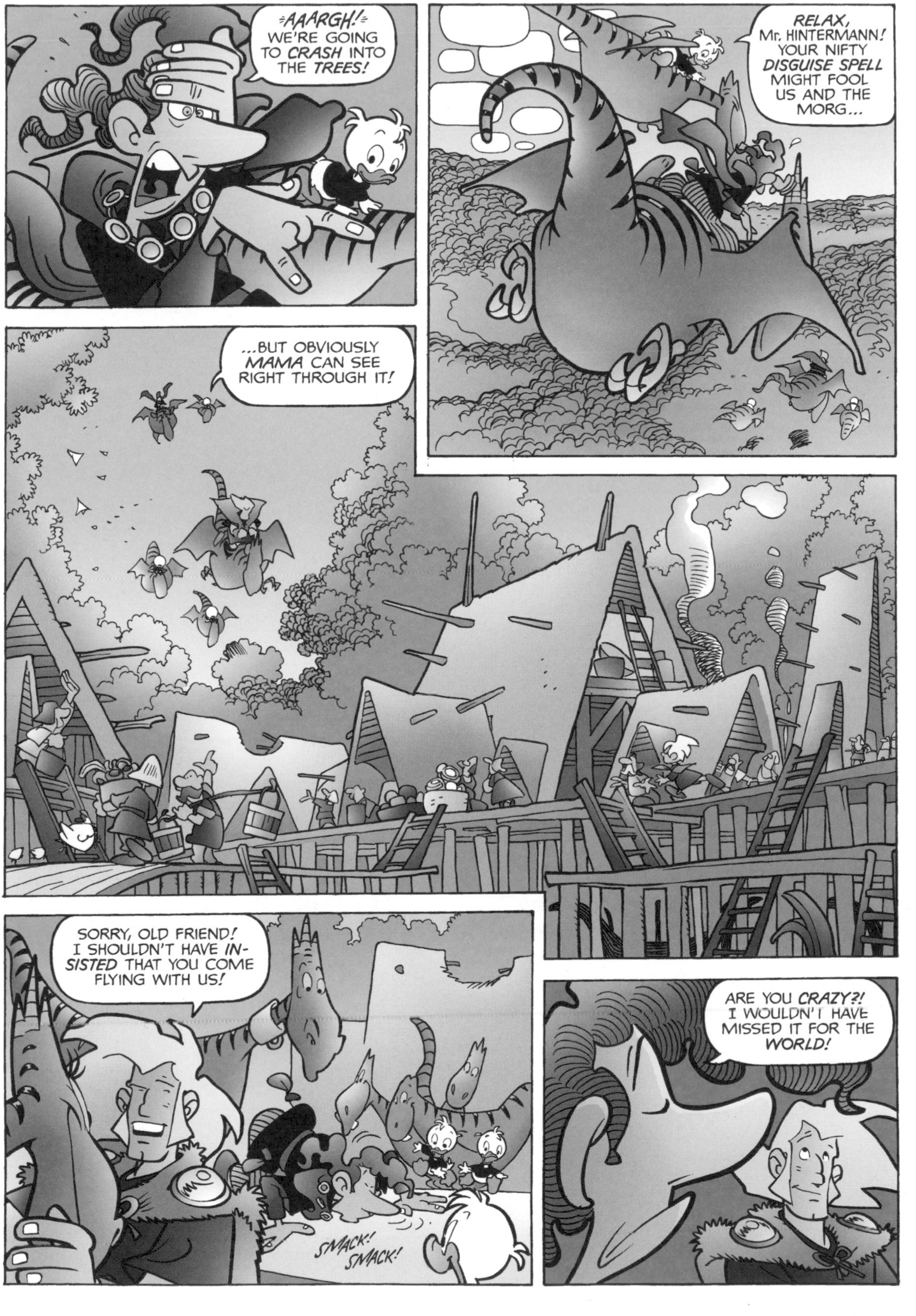

AAARGH! WE'RE GOING TO CRASH INTO THE TREES!
RELAX, Mr. HINTERMANN! YOUR NIFTY DISGUISE SPELL MIGHT FOOL US AND THE MORG...
...BUT OBVIOUSLY MAMA CAN SEE RIGHT THROUGH IT!
SORRY, OLD FRIEND! I SHOULDN'T HAVE INSISTED THAT YOU COME FLYING WITH US!
SMACK! SMACK!
ARE YOU CRAZY?! I WOULDN'T HAVE MISSED IT FOR THE WORLD!

Oh, SURE, I *PRETENDED* TO BE SCARED, BUT THAT MADE THE RIDE EVEN *MORE* FUN!
DADDY!
YOU WERE *WONDER-FUL!*
THE *DRAGONS* ARE WONDER-FUL, SILIA!
Huh? BRENDON HAS A *DAUGHTER?!*
ARE... ARE HEROES *ALLOWED* TO HAVE FAMILIES?!
DOESN'T SHE LOOK KIND OF *FAMILIAR?*
ADOPTED DAUGHTER, ACTUALLY! BRENDON *RESCUED* HER FROM THE MORG...
...BUT ONLY AFTER THEY HAD *DESTROYED* HER VILLAGE!
Uh... SPEAKING OF THE MORG, WHAT DID YOU *DO* WITH THE ONE WE DROP-PED ON YOUR HOUSE?!
ULP!
IN ALL THE EXCITEMENT, I *FORGOT* ABOUT HIM! IF HE SHOULD COME TO—!!!

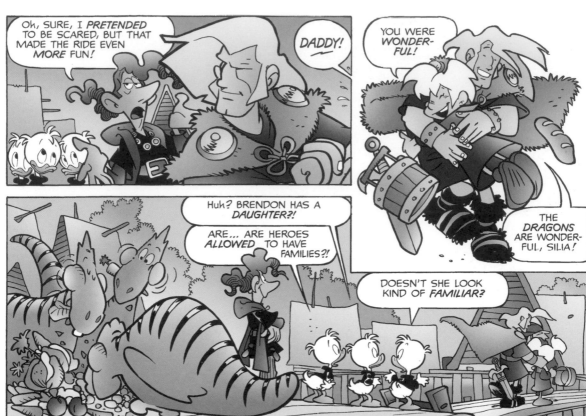

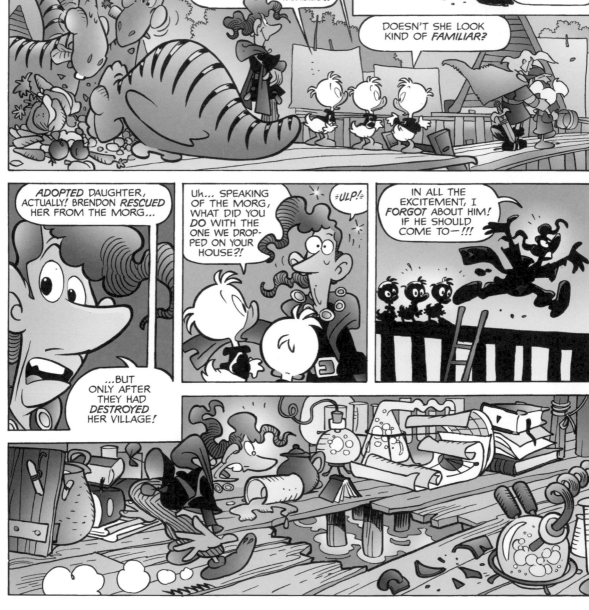

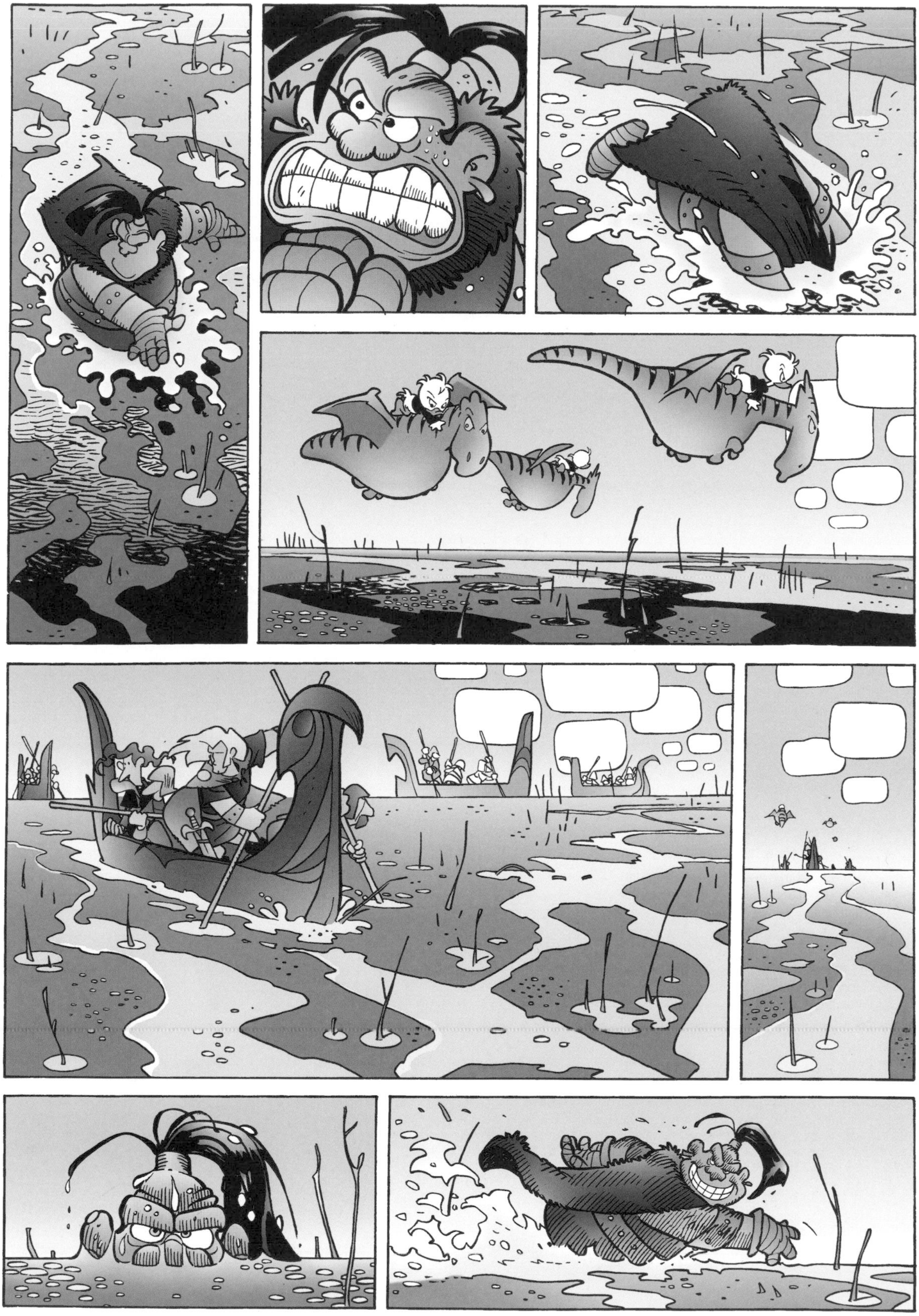

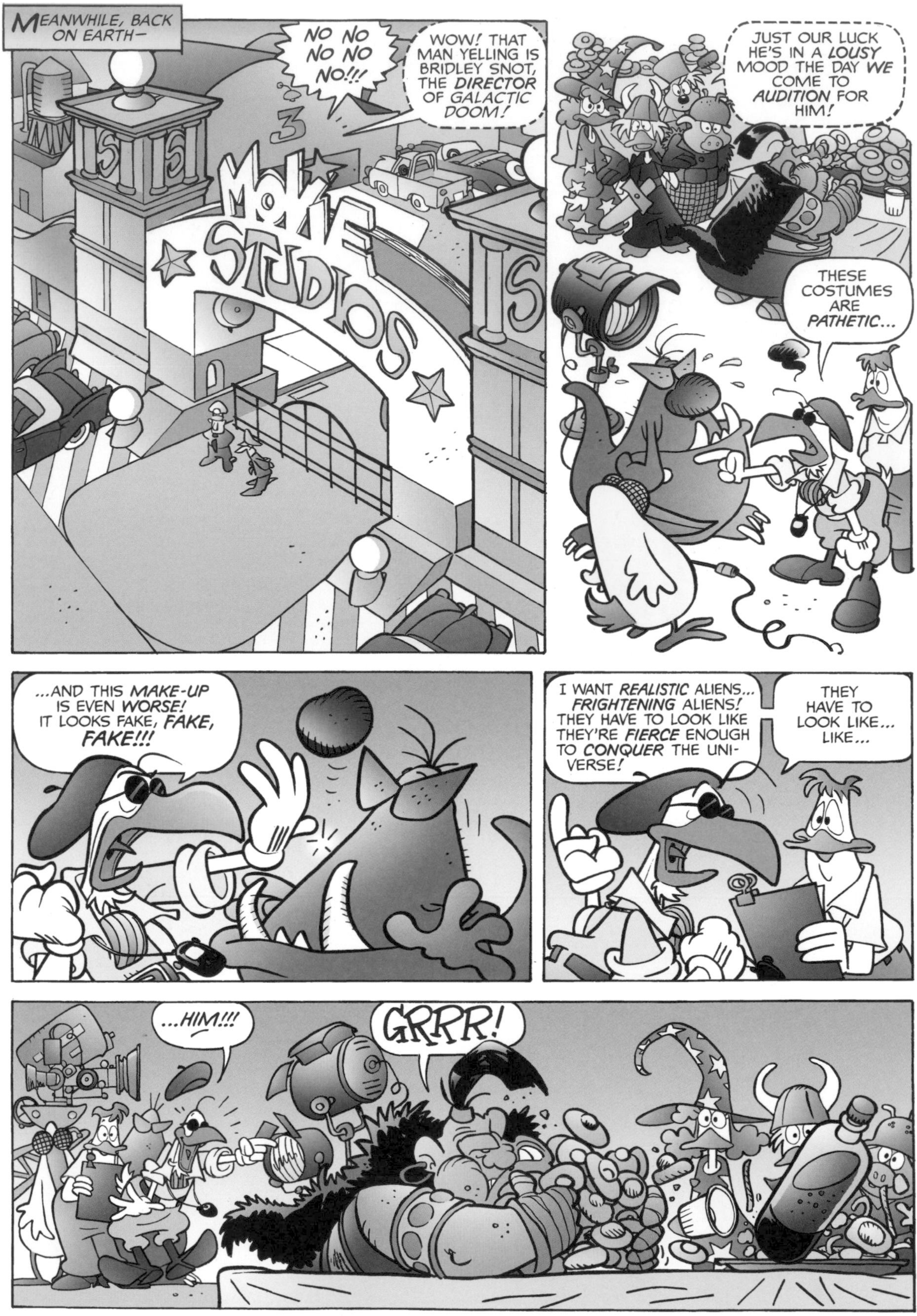
MEANWHILE, BACK ON EARTH–
NO NO NO NO NO!!!
WOW! THAT MAN YELLING IS BRIDLEY SNOT, THE DIRECTOR OF GALACTIC DOOM!
MOVIE STUDIOS
JUST OUR LUCK HE'S IN A LOUSY MOOD THE DAY WE COME TO AUDITION FOR HIM!
THESE COSTUMES ARE PATHETIC...
...AND THIS MAKE-UP IS EVEN WORSE! IT LOOKS FAKE, FAKE, FAKE!!!
I WANT REALISTIC ALIENS... FRIGHTENING ALIENS! THEY HAVE TO LOOK LIKE THEY'RE FIERCE ENOUGH TO CONQUER THE UNIVERSE!
THEY HAVE TO LOOK LIKE... LIKE...
...HIM!!!
GRRR!

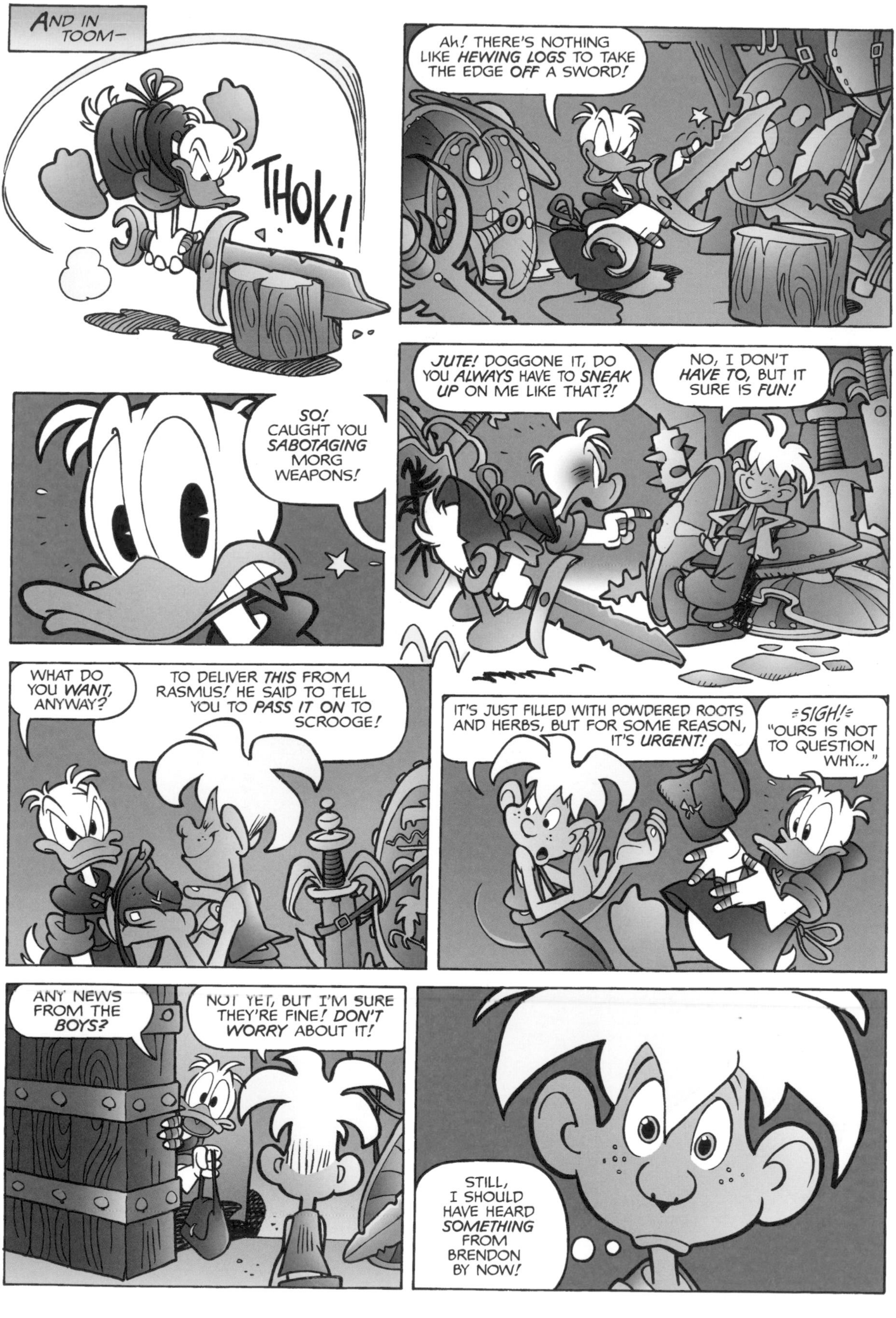
AND IN TOOM—
THOK!
AH! THERE'S NOTHING LIKE HEWING LOGS TO TAKE THE EDGE OFF A SWORD!
SO! CAUGHT YOU SABOTAGING MORG WEAPONS!
JUTE! DOGGONE IT, DO YOU ALWAYS HAVE TO SNEAK UP ON ME LIKE THAT?!
NO, I DON'T HAVE TO, BUT IT SURE IS FUN!
WHAT DO YOU WANT, ANYWAY?
TO DELIVER THIS FROM RASMUS! HE SAID TO TELL YOU TO PASS IT ON TO SCROOGE!
IT'S JUST FILLED WITH POWDERED ROOTS AND HERBS, BUT FOR SOME REASON, IT'S URGENT!
SIGH!
"OURS IS NOT TO QUESTION WHY..."
ANY NEWS FROM THE BOYS?
NOT YET, BUT I'M SURE THEY'RE FINE! DON'T WORRY ABOUT IT!
STILL, I SHOULD HAVE HEARD SOMETHING FROM BRENDON BY NOW!

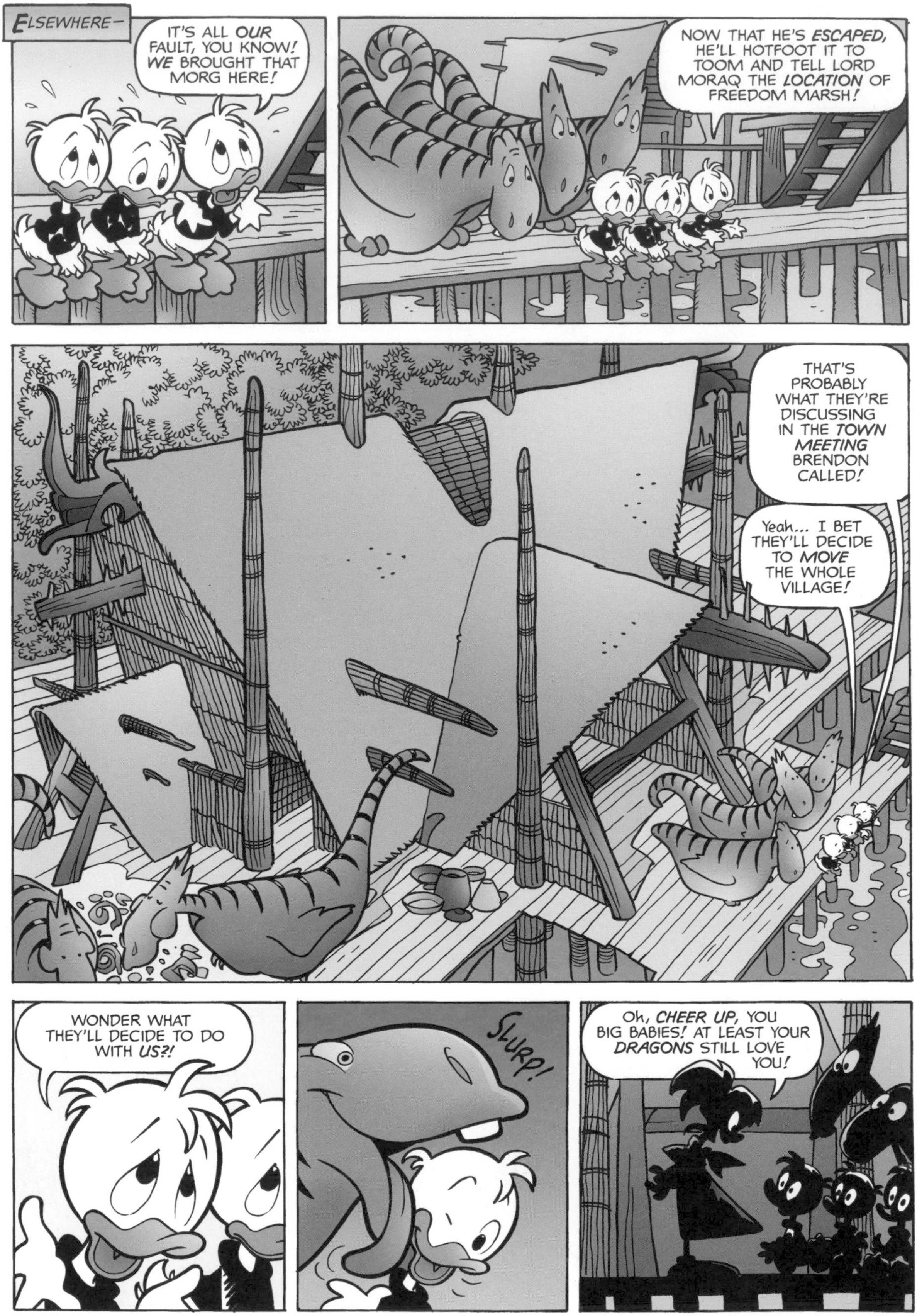
ELSEWHERE–
IT'S ALL OUR FAULT, YOU KNOW! WE BROUGHT THAT MORG HERE!
NOW THAT HE'S ESCAPED, HE'LL HOTFOOT IT TO TOOM AND TELL LORD MORAQ THE LOCATION OF FREEDOM MARSH!
THAT'S PROBABLY WHAT THEY'RE DISCUSSING IN THE TOWN MEETING BRENDON CALLED!
Yeah... I BET THEY'LL DECIDE TO MOVE THE WHOLE VILLAGE!
WONDER WHAT THEY'LL DECIDE TO DO WITH US?!
SLURP!
Oh, CHEER UP, YOU BIG BABIES! AT LEAST YOUR DRAGONS STILL LOVE YOU!

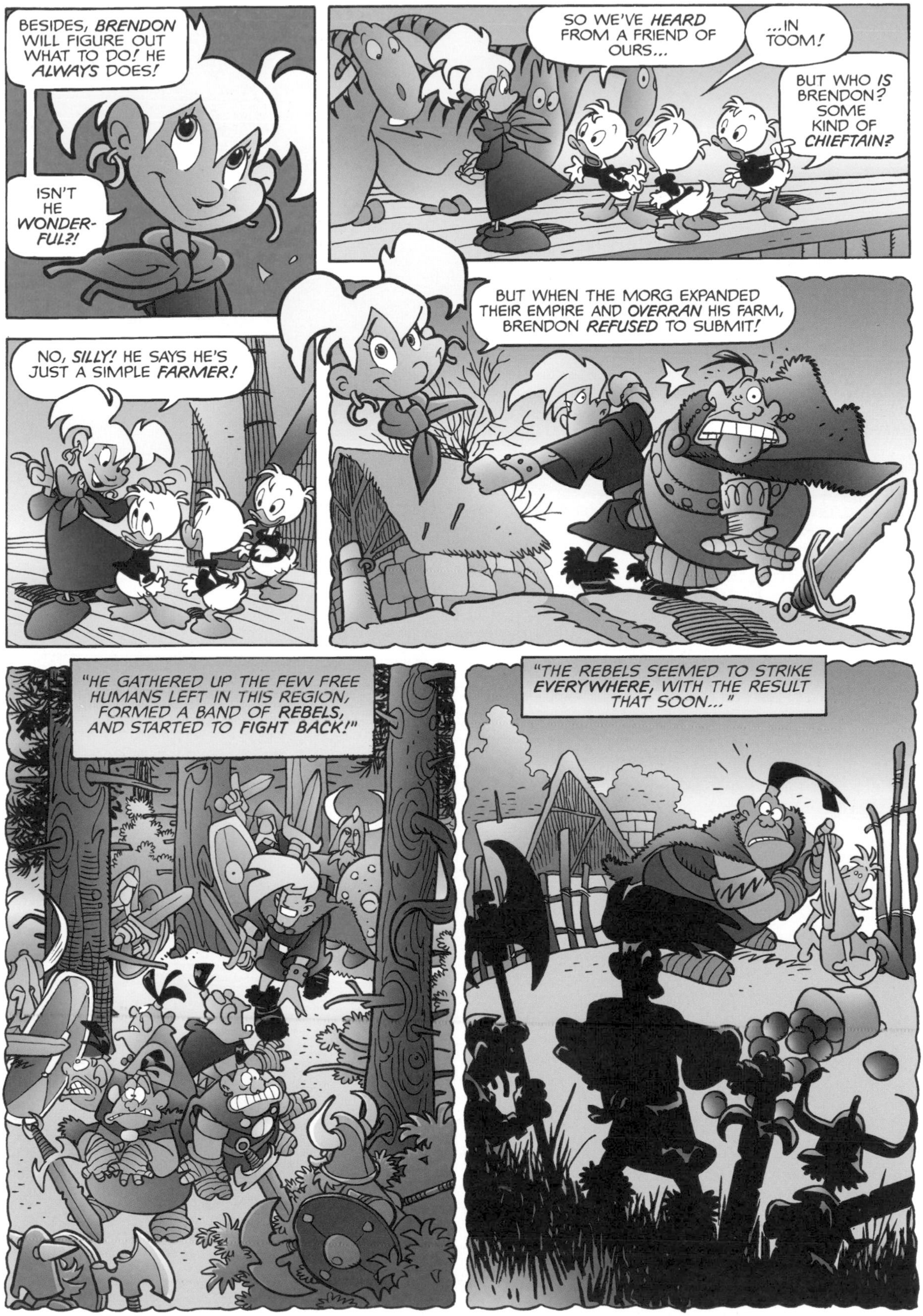
BESIDES, BRENDON WILL FIGURE OUT WHAT TO DO! HE ALWAYS DOES!
ISN'T HE WONDER-FUL?!
SO WE'VE HEARD FROM A FRIEND OF OURS...
...IN TOOM!
BUT WHO IS BRENDON? SOME KIND OF CHIEFTAIN?
NO, SILLY! HE SAYS HE'S JUST A SIMPLE FARMER!
BUT WHEN THE MORG EXPANDED THEIR EMPIRE AND OVERRAN HIS FARM, BRENDON REFUSED TO SUBMIT!
"HE GATHERED UP THE FEW FREE HUMANS LEFT IN THIS REGION, FORMED A BAND OF REBELS, AND STARTED TO FIGHT BACK!"
"THE REBELS SEEMED TO STRIKE EVERYWHERE, WITH THE RESULT THAT SOON..."

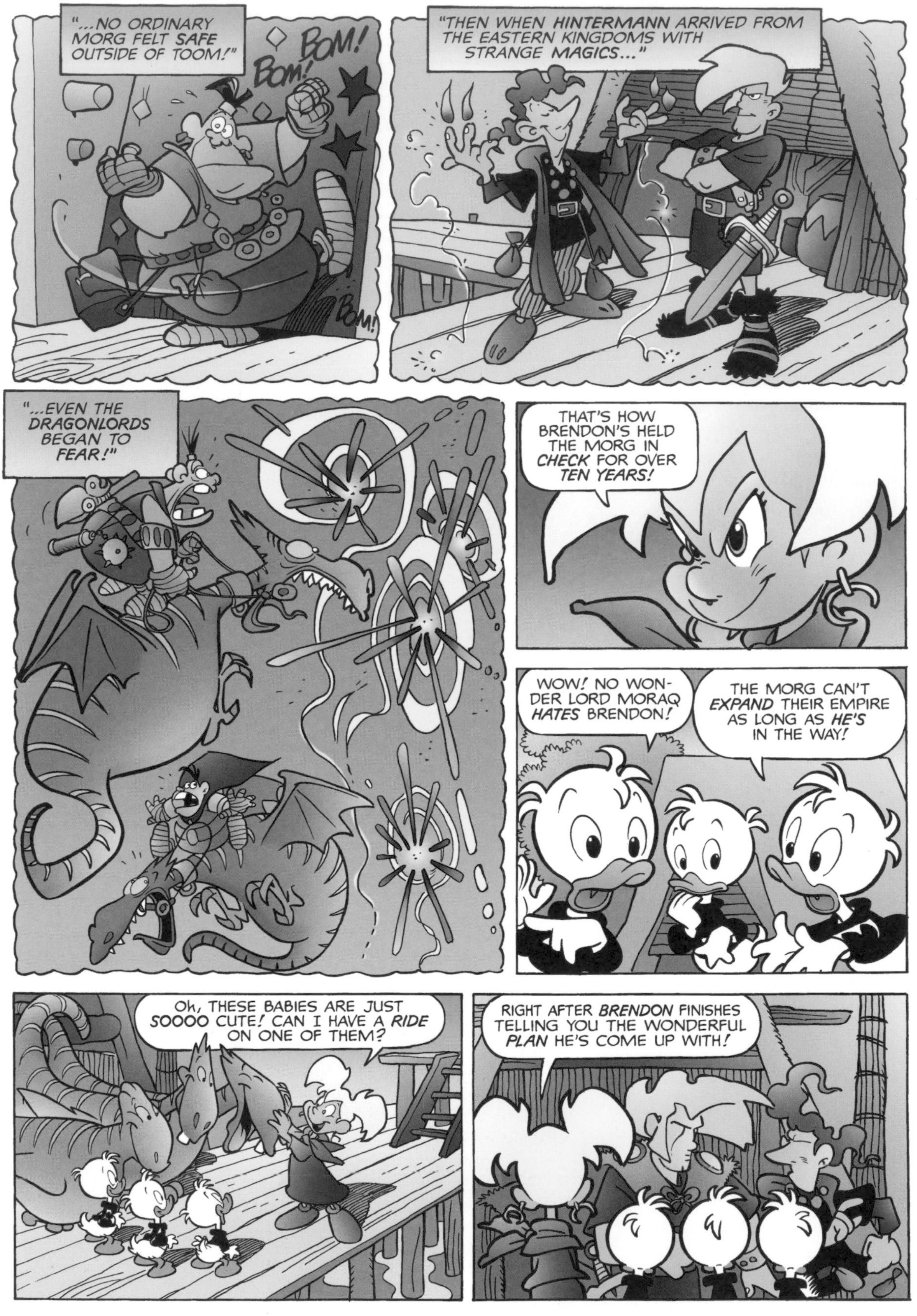
"...NO ORDINARY MORG FELT SAFE OUTSIDE OF TOOM!"
BOM! BOM!
BOM!
"THEN WHEN HINTERMANN ARRIVED FROM THE EASTERN KINGDOMS WITH STRANGE MAGICS..."
"...EVEN THE DRAGONLORDS BEGAN TO FEAR!"
THAT'S HOW BRENDON'S HELD THE MORG IN CHECK FOR OVER TEN YEARS!
WOW! NO WONDER LORD MORAQ HATES BRENDON!
THE MORG CAN'T EXPAND THEIR EMPIRE AS LONG AS HE'S IN THE WAY!
Oh, THESE BABIES ARE JUST SOOOO CUTE! CAN I HAVE A RIDE ON ONE OF THEM?
RIGHT AFTER BRENDON FINISHES TELLING YOU THE WONDERFUL PLAN HE'S COME UP WITH!

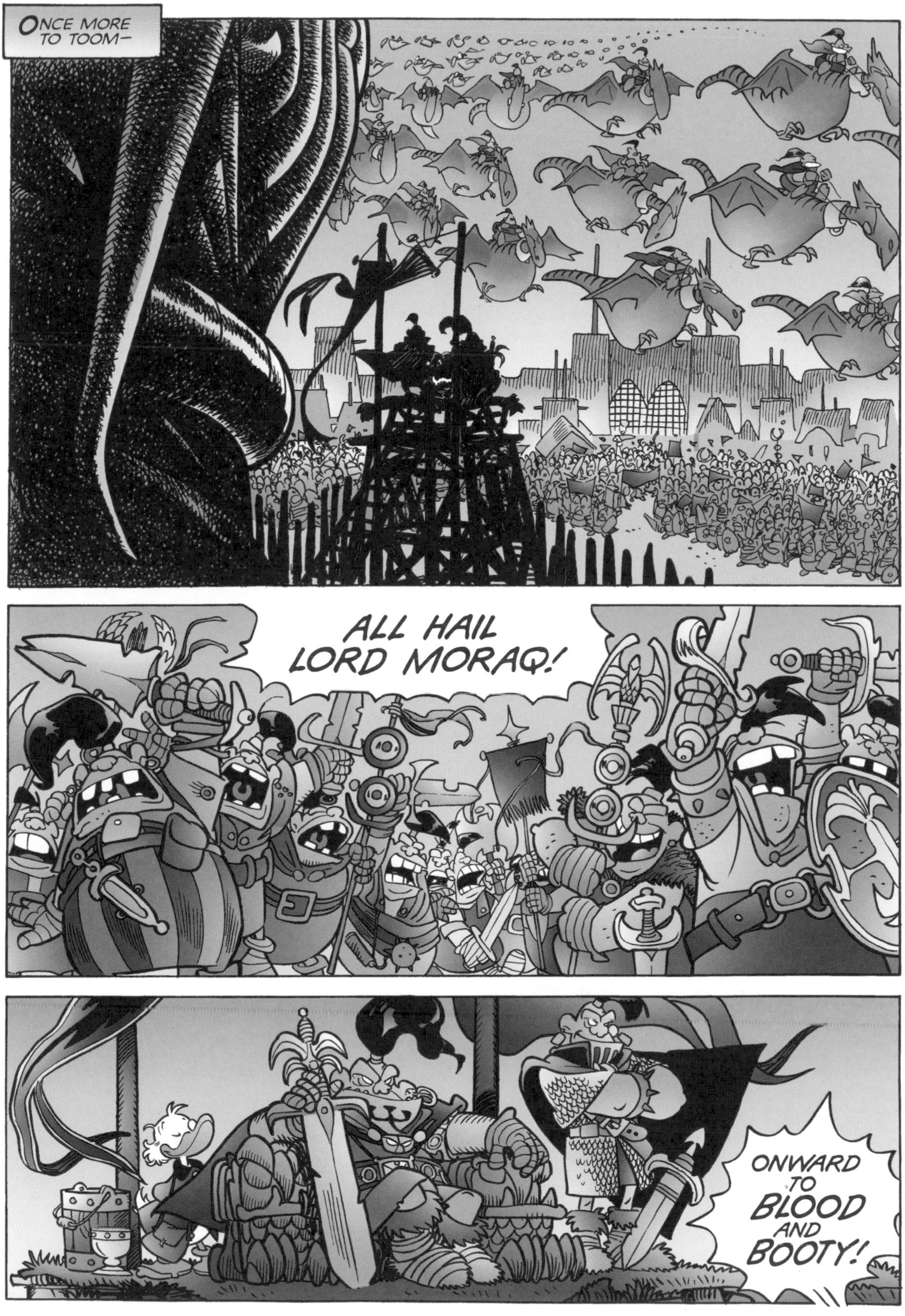
ONCE MORE TO TOOM—
ALL HAIL LORD MORAQ!
ONWARD TO BLOOD AND BOOTY!

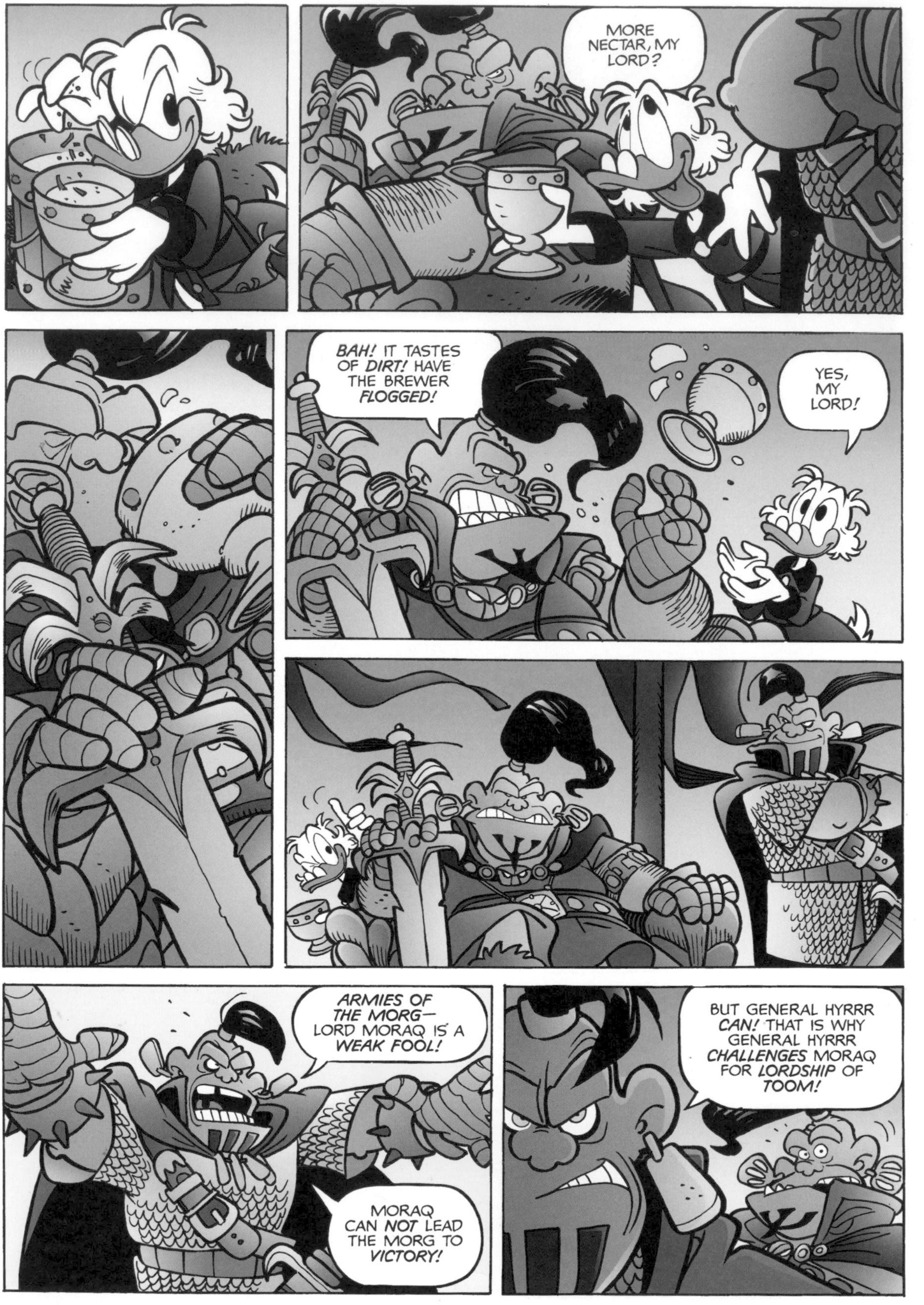
MORE NECTAR, MY LORD?
BAH! IT TASTES OF DIRT! HAVE THE BREWER FLOGGED!
YES, MY LORD!
ARMIES OF THE MORG— LORD MORAQ IS A WEAK FOOL!
MORAQ CAN NOT LEAD THE MORG TO VICTORY!
BUT GENERAL HYRRR CAN! THAT IS WHY GENERAL HYRRR CHALLENGES MORAQ FOR LORDSHIP OF TOOM!

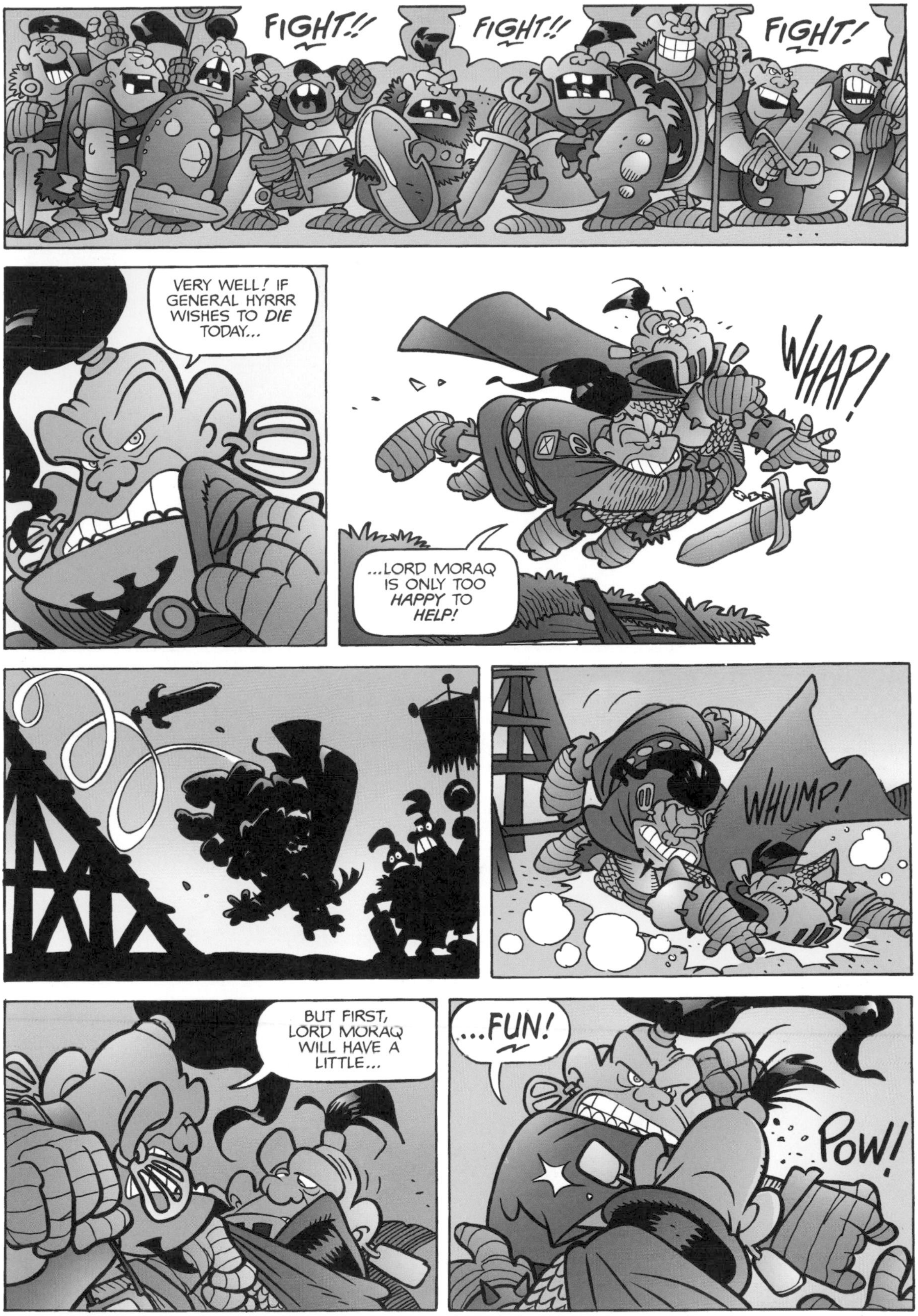
FIGHT!!
FIGHT!!
FIGHT!
VERY WELL! IF GENERAL HYRRR WISHES TO DIE TODAY...
WHAP!
...LORD MORAQ IS ONLY TOO HAPPY TO HELP!
WHUMP!
BUT FIRST, LORD MORAQ WILL HAVE A LITTLE...
...FUN!
POW!

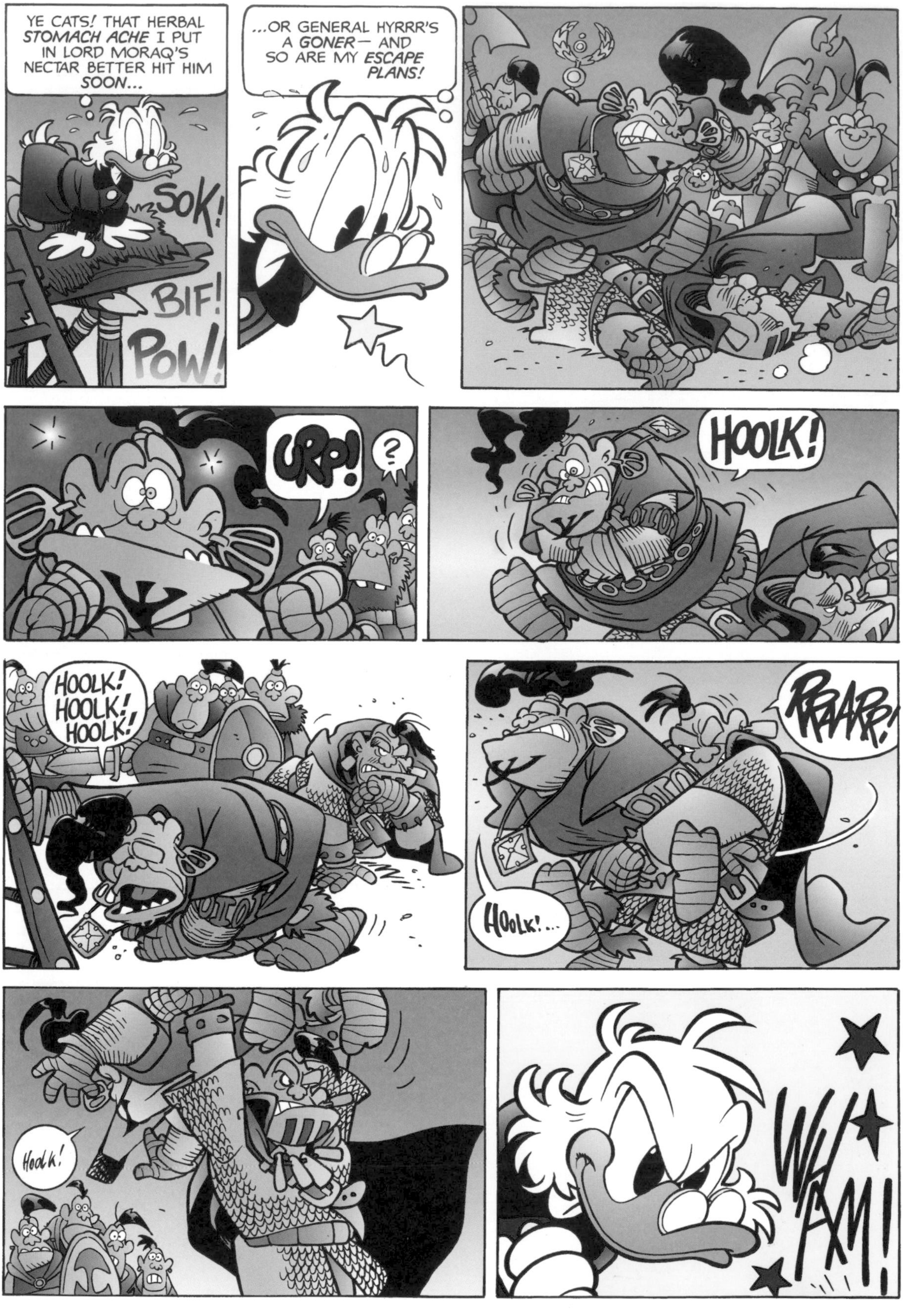

YE CATS! THAT HERBAL STOMACH ACHE I PUT IN LORD MORAQ'S NECTAR BETTER HIT HIM SOON...
SOK!
BIF!
POW!
...OR GENERAL HYRRR'S A GONER— AND SO ARE MY ESCAPE PLANS!
URP!
?
HOOLK!
HOOLK! HOOLK! HOOLK!
RRAARR!
HOOLK!...
Hoolk!
WHAM!

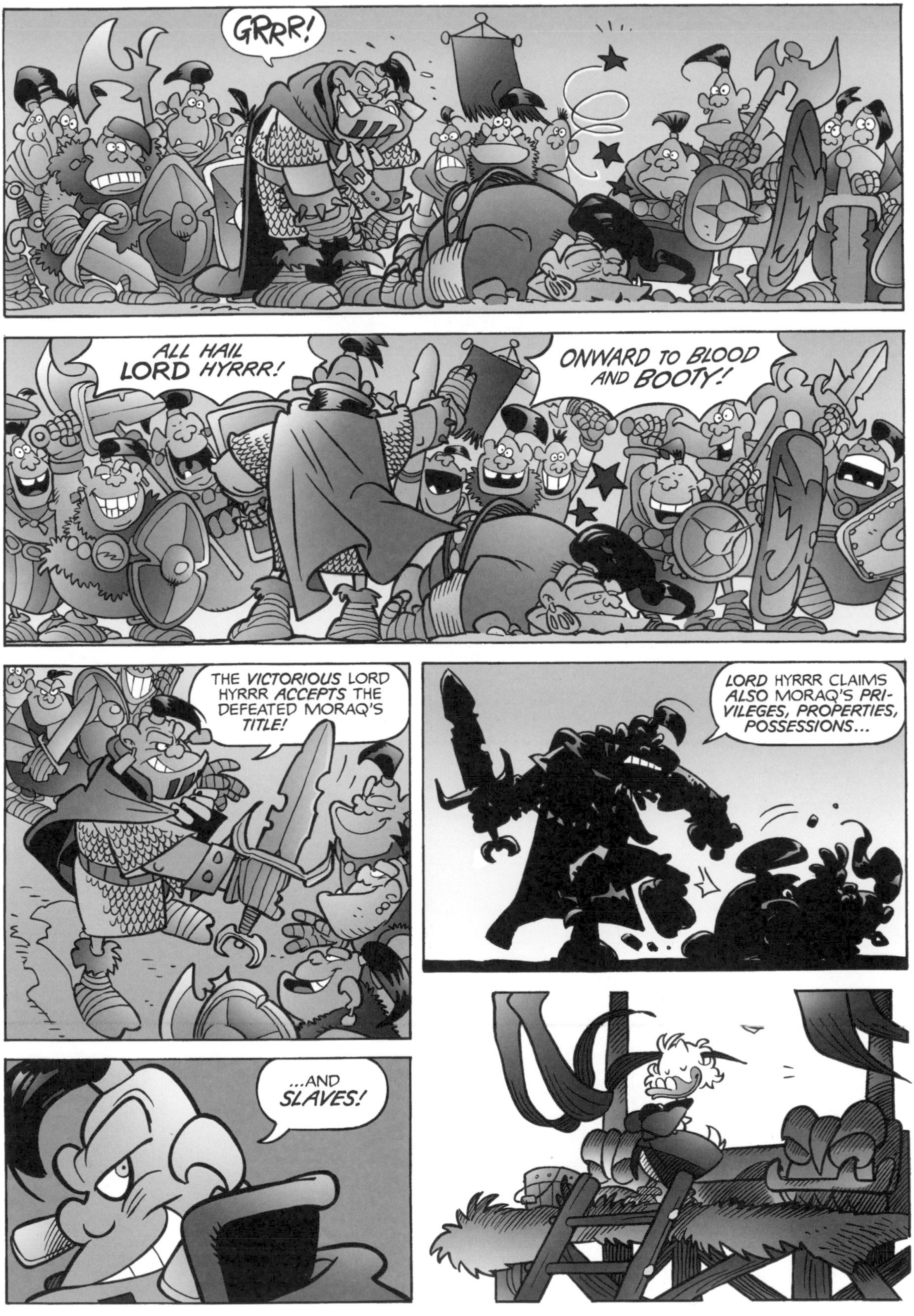
GRRR!
ALL HAIL LORD HYRRR!
ONWARD TO BLOOD AND BOOTY!
THE VICTORIOUS LORD HYRRR ACCEPTS THE DEFEATED MORAQ'S TITLE!
LORD HYRRR CLAIMS ALSO MORAQ'S PRIVILEGES, PROPERTIES, POSSESSIONS...
...AND SLAVES!

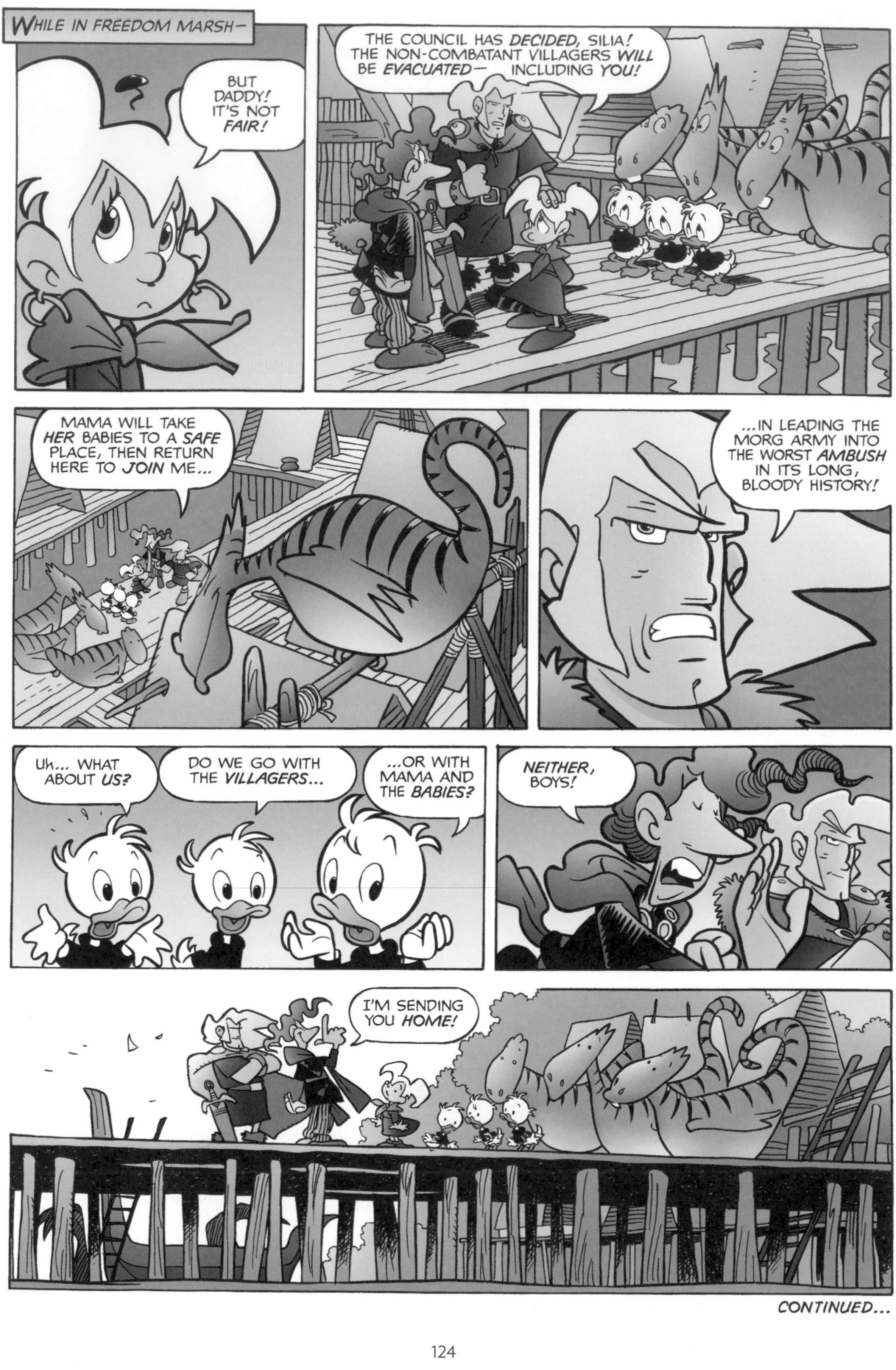
WHILE IN FREEDOM MARSH—
BUT DADDY! IT'S NOT FAIR!
THE COUNCIL HAS DECIDED, SILIA! THE NON-COMBATANT VILLAGERS WILL BE EVACUATED— INCLUDING YOU!
MAMA WILL TAKE HER BABIES TO A SAFE PLACE, THEN RETURN HERE TO JOIN ME...
...IN LEADING THE MORG ARMY INTO THE WORST AMBUSH IN ITS LONG, BLOODY HISTORY!
Uh... WHAT ABOUT US?
DO WE GO WITH THE VILLAGERS...
...OR WITH MAMA AND THE BABIES?
NEITHER, BOYS!
I'M SENDING YOU HOME!
CONTINUED...

Sketches

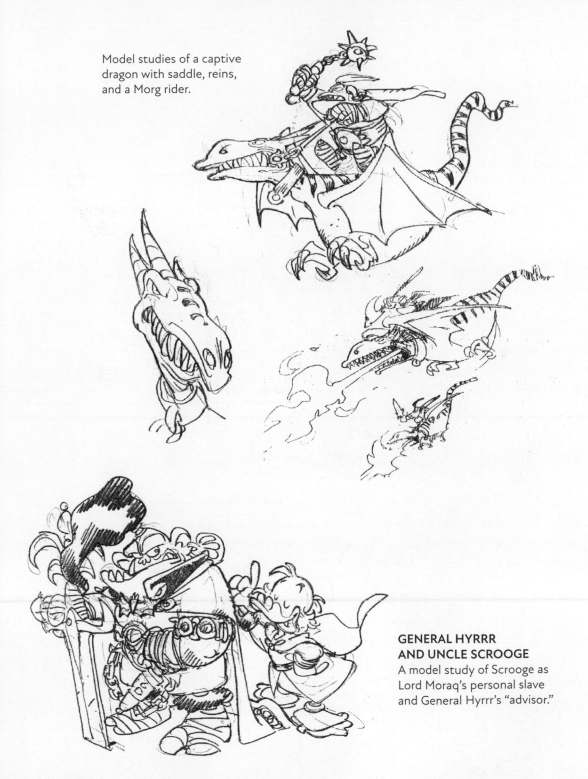

Model studies of a captive dragon with saddle, reins, and a Morg rider.

GENERAL HYRRR AND UNCLE SCROOGE
A model study of Scrooge as Lord Moraq's personal slave and General Hyrrr's "advisor."

SILIA
A model study of Brendon's adopted daughter.

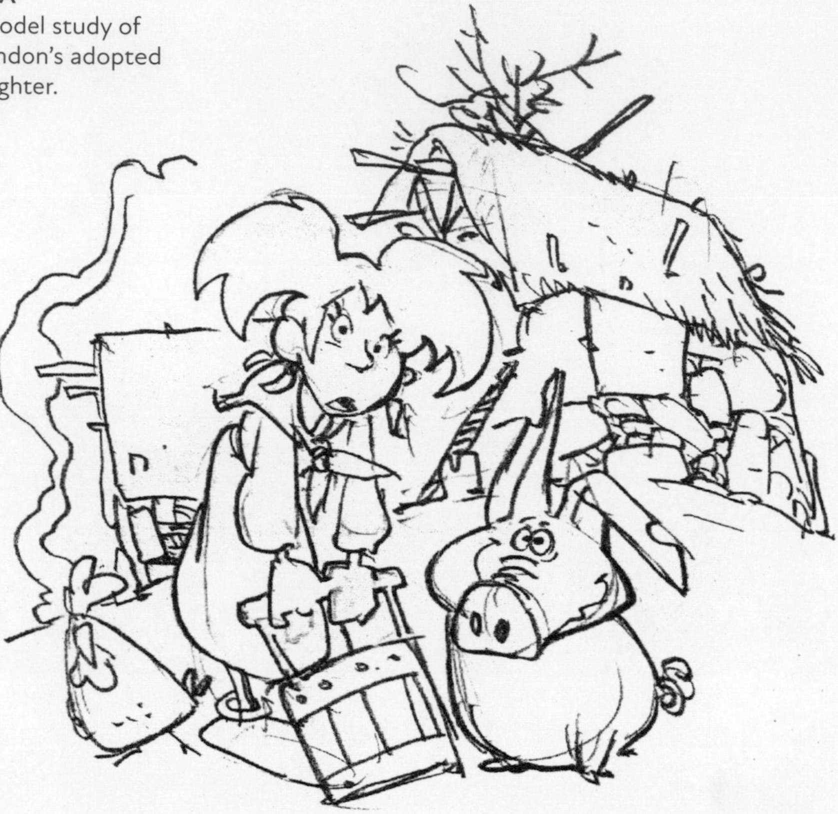

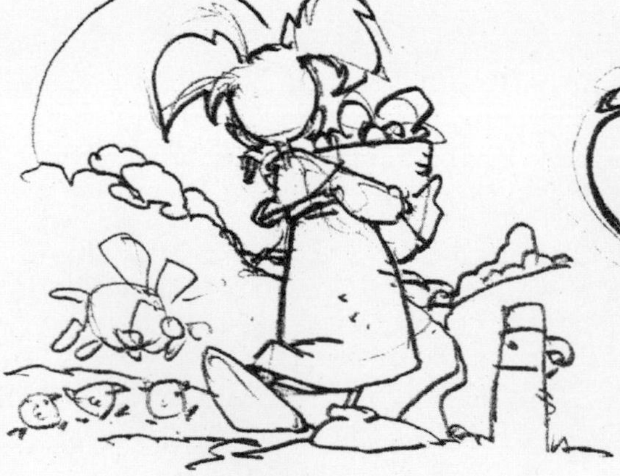

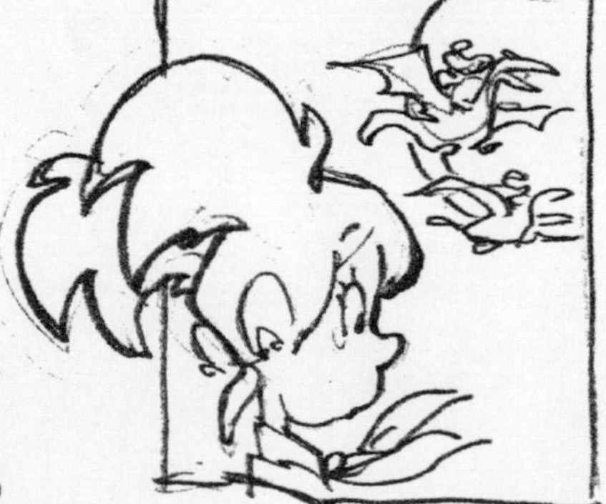

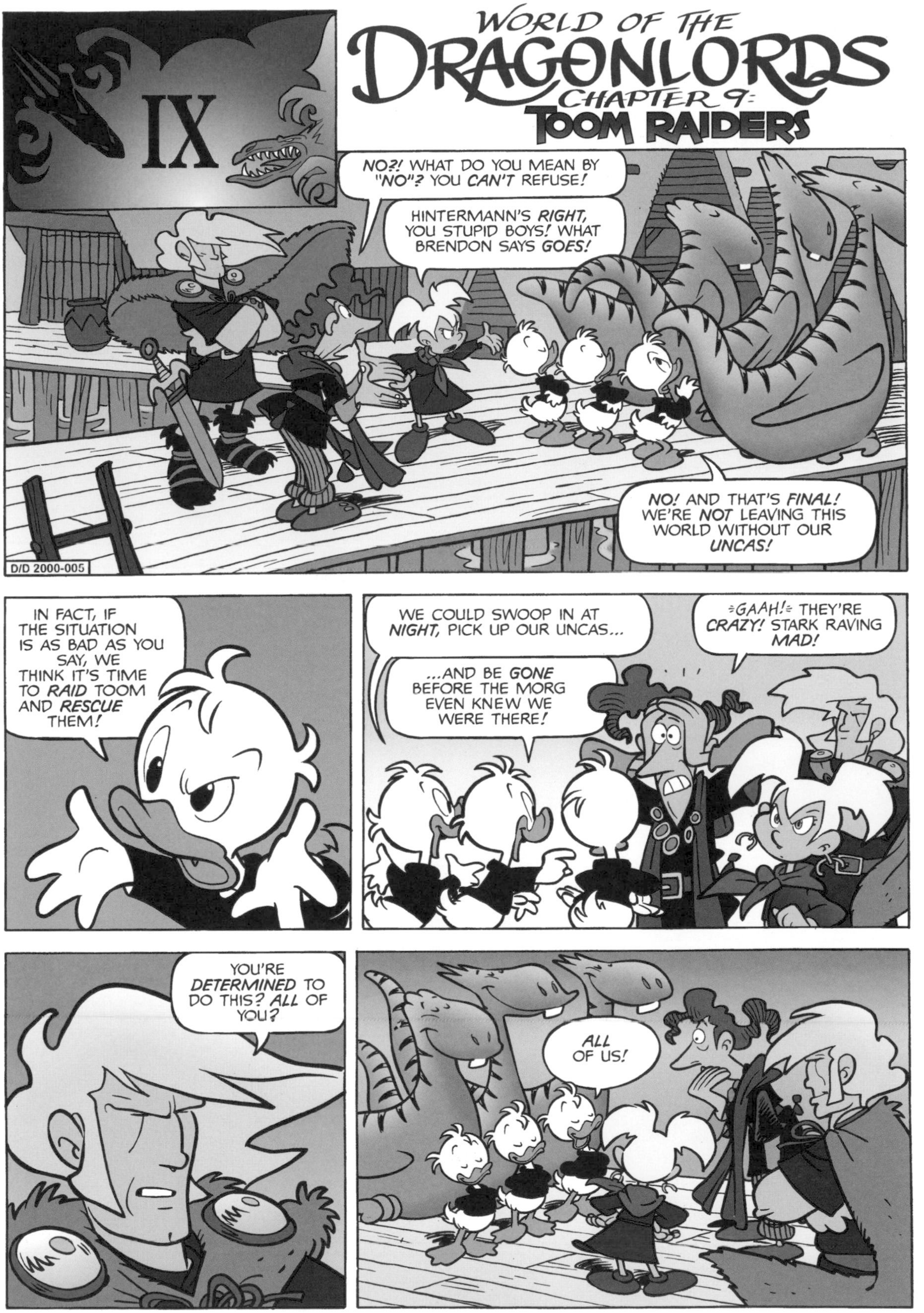

IX
WORLD OF THE DRAGONLORDS
CHAPTER 9:
TOOM RAIDERS
NO?! WHAT DO YOU MEAN BY "NO"? YOU CAN'T REFUSE!
HINTERMANN'S RIGHT, YOU STUPID BOYS! WHAT BRENDON SAYS GOES!
NO! AND THAT'S FINAL! WE'RE NOT LEAVING THIS WORLD WITHOUT OUR UNCAS!
D/D 2000-005
IN FACT, IF THE SITUATION IS AS BAD AS YOU SAY, WE THINK IT'S TIME TO RAID TOOM AND RESCUE THEM!
WE COULD SWOOP IN AT NIGHT, PICK UP OUR UNCAS...
...AND BE GONE BEFORE THE MORG EVEN KNEW WE WERE THERE!
GAAH! THEY'RE CRAZY! STARK RAVING MAD!
YOU'RE DETERMINED TO DO THIS? ALL OF YOU?
ALL OF US!

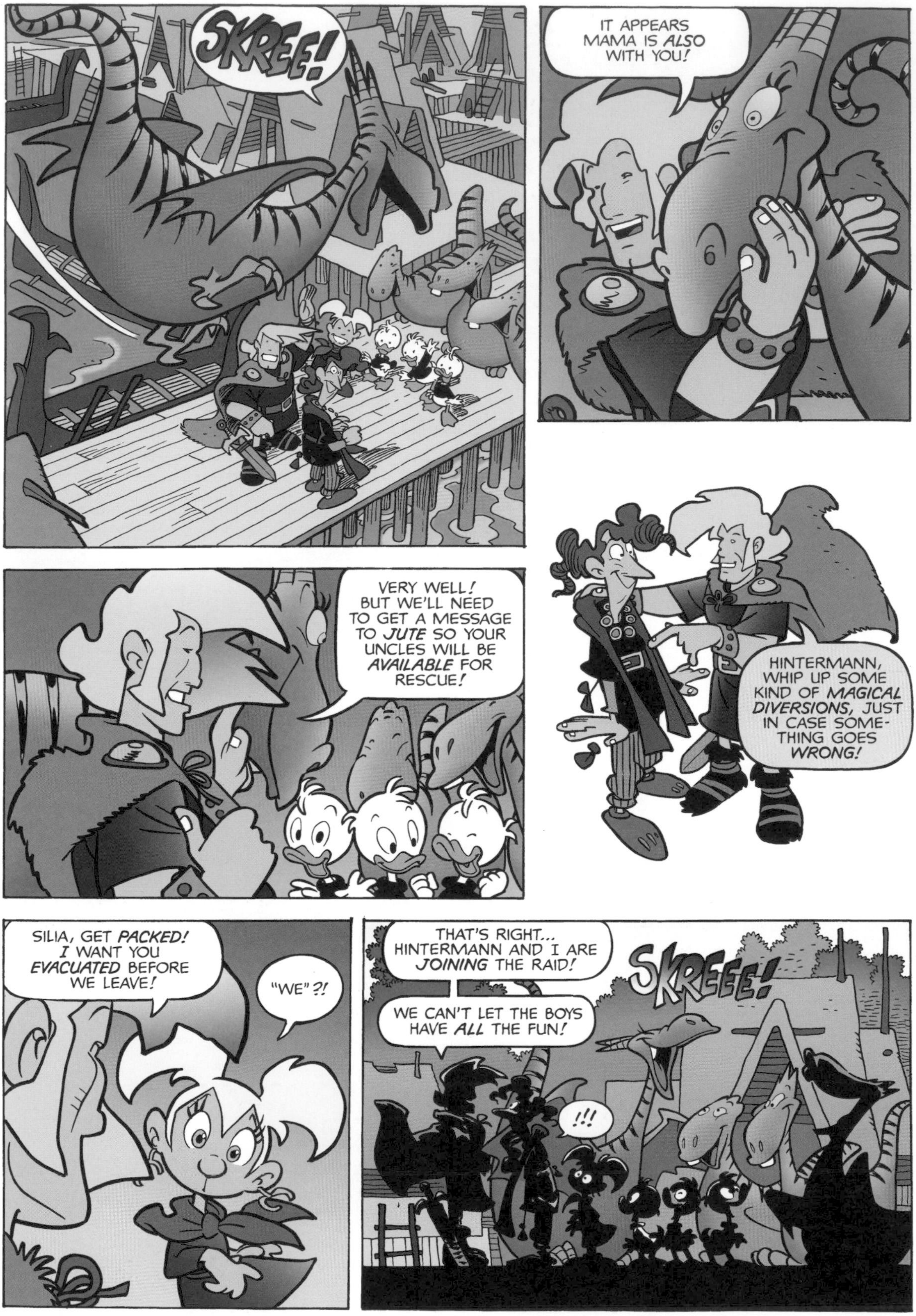
SKREE!
IT APPEARS MAMA IS ALSO WITH YOU!
VERY WELL! BUT WE'LL NEED TO GET A MESSAGE TO JUTE SO YOUR UNCLES WILL BE AVAILABLE FOR RESCUE!
HINTERMANN, WHIP UP SOME KIND OF MAGICAL DIVERSIONS, JUST IN CASE SOME-THING GOES WRONG!
SILIA, GET PACKED! I WANT YOU EVACUATED BEFORE WE LEAVE!
"WE"?!
THAT'S RIGHT... HINTERMANN AND I ARE JOINING THE RAID!
WE CAN'T LET THE BOYS HAVE ALL THE FUN!
SKREEE!
!!!

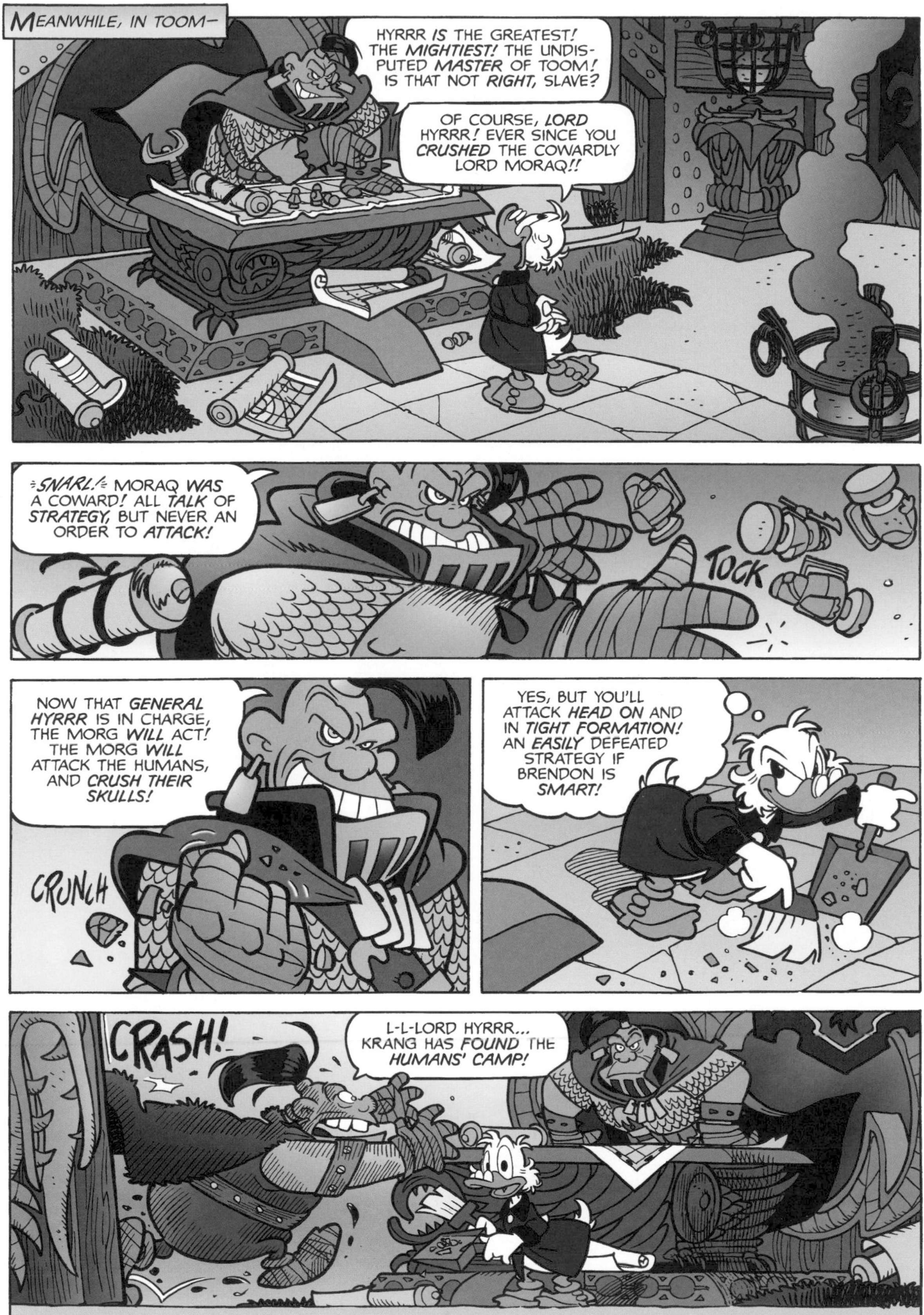

MEANWHILE, IN TOOM—
HYRRR IS THE GREATEST! THE MIGHTIEST! THE UNDISPUTED MASTER OF TOOM! IS THAT NOT RIGHT, SLAVE?
OF COURSE, LORD HYRRR! EVER SINCE YOU CRUSHED THE COWARDLY LORD MORAQ!!
SNARL! MORAQ WAS A COWARD! ALL TALK OF STRATEGY, BUT NEVER AN ORDER TO ATTACK!
TOCK
NOW THAT GENERAL HYRRR IS IN CHARGE, THE MORG WILL ACT! THE MORG WILL ATTACK THE HUMANS, AND CRUSH THEIR SKULLS!
CRUNCH
YES, BUT YOU'LL ATTACK HEAD ON AND IN TIGHT FORMATION! AN EASILY DEFEATED STRATEGY IF BRENDON IS SMART!
CRASH!
L-L-LORD HYRRR... KRANG HAS FOUND THE HUMANS' CAMP!

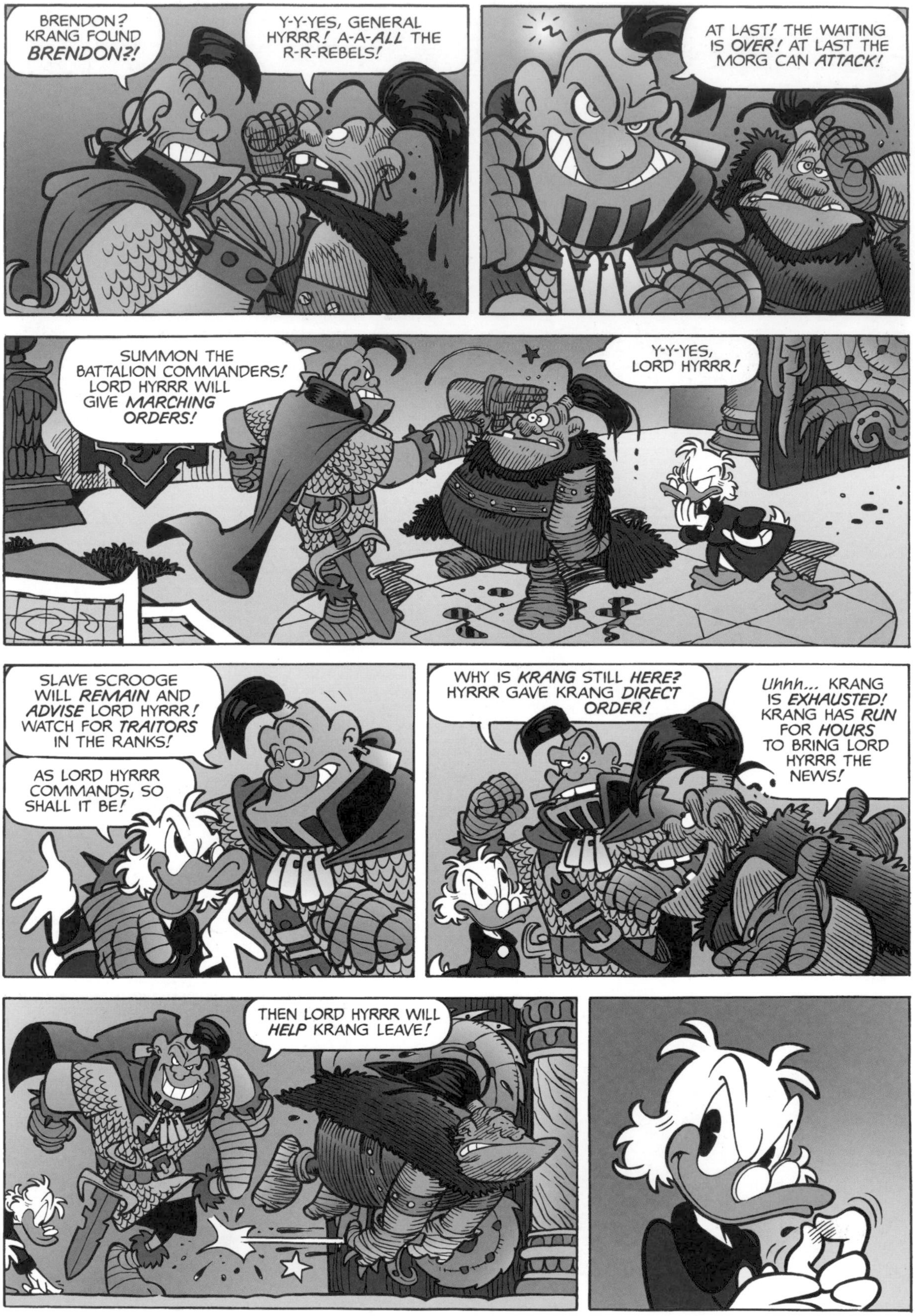
BRENDON? KRANG FOUND BRENDON?!
Y-Y-YES, GENERAL HYRRR! A-A-ALL THE R-R-REBELS!
AT LAST! THE WAITING IS OVER! AT LAST THE MORG CAN ATTACK!
SUMMON THE BATTALION COMMANDERS! LORD HYRRR WILL GIVE MARCHING ORDERS!
Y-Y-YES, LORD HYRRR!
SLAVE SCROOGE WILL REMAIN AND ADVISE LORD HYRRR! WATCH FOR TRAITORS IN THE RANKS!
AS LORD HYRRR COMMANDS, SO SHALL IT BE!
WHY IS KRANG STILL HERE? HYRRR GAVE KRANG DIRECT ORDER!
Uhhh... KRANG IS EXHAUSTED! KRANG HAS RUN FOR HOURS TO BRING LORD HYRRR THE NEWS!
THEN LORD HYRRR WILL HELP KRANG LEAVE!

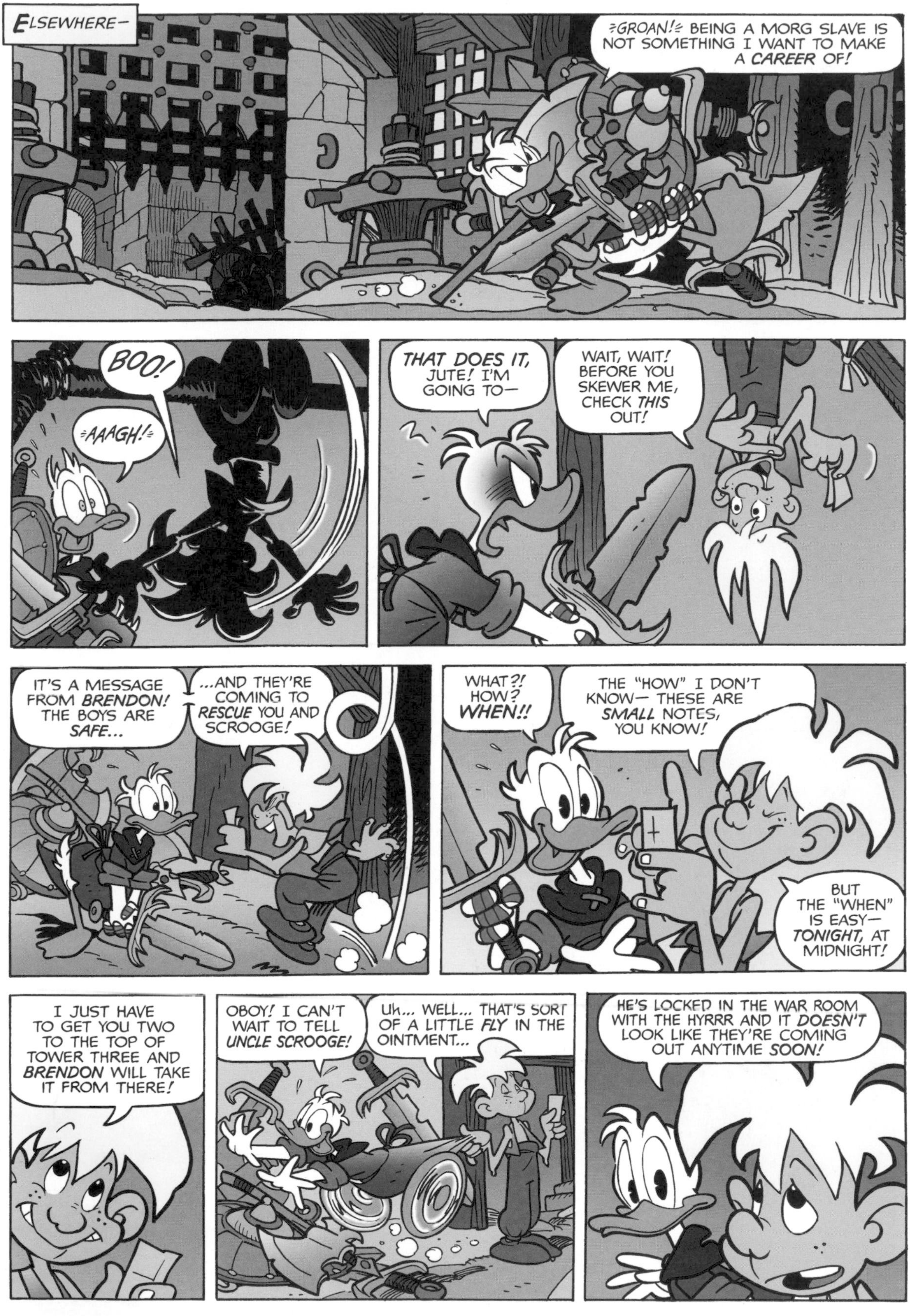
ELSEWHERE—
GROAN! BEING A MORG SLAVE IS NOT SOMETHING I WANT TO MAKE A CAREER OF!
BOO!
AAAGH!
THAT DOES IT, JUTE! I'M GOING TO—
WAIT, WAIT! BEFORE YOU SKEWER ME, CHECK THIS OUT!
IT'S A MESSAGE FROM BRENDON! THE BOYS ARE SAFE...
...AND THEY'RE COMING TO RESCUE YOU AND SCROOGE!
WHAT?! HOW? WHEN!!
THE "HOW" I DON'T KNOW— THESE ARE SMALL NOTES, YOU KNOW!
BUT THE "WHEN" IS EASY— TONIGHT, AT MIDNIGHT!
I JUST HAVE TO GET YOU TWO TO THE TOP OF TOWER THREE AND BRENDON WILL TAKE IT FROM THERE!
OBOY! I CAN'T WAIT TO TELL UNCLE SCROOGE!
Uh... WELL... THAT'S SORT OF A LITTLE FLY IN THE OINTMENT...
HE'S LOCKED IN THE WAR ROOM WITH THE HYRRR AND IT DOESN'T LOOK LIKE THEY'RE COMING OUT ANYTIME SOON!

BACK IN DUCKBURG—

YOU'RE RIGHT, GYRO... WE CAN'T START LOOKING UNTIL WE KNOW *WHERE* TO START, BUT STILL...

ALL RIGHT... YES, YOU TOO... TALK TO YOU LATER!

MAYBE THE *ENTERTAINMENT NEWS* WILL GET MY MIND OFF THEM...

CLICK!

...NEW *CHARACTER ACTOR* HAS CAUSED SUCH A *SENSATION* THAT "GALACTIC DOOM" IS BEING *REWRITTEN* TO GIVE HIM A *BIGGER* ROLE!

GROOB, TELL THE FANS ABOUT YOURSELF!

GROOB DOES NOT KNOW WHAT "FANS" IS! GROOB IS *MORG WARRIOR*, ARRIVED ON STUPID PLANET THROUGH *GLOWING HOLE IN SKY!*

GROOB FOUGHT *TWO* HUMANS AND *FIVE* DUCK CREATURES! GROOB WAS *CHEATED!* GROOB *LOST!*

WHEN GROOB CAME TO, HUMANS AND DUCK CREATURES WERE *GONE*, AND SO WAS HOLE IN SKY! GROOB IS *STRANDED* HERE!

WHERE IS FOOD? GROOB IS HUNGRY!

ISN'T HE *AMAZING?!* HE NEVER *BREAKS CHARACTER!*

FIVE DUCKS?

GYRO! THE TRAIL JUST GOT *VERY HOT!*

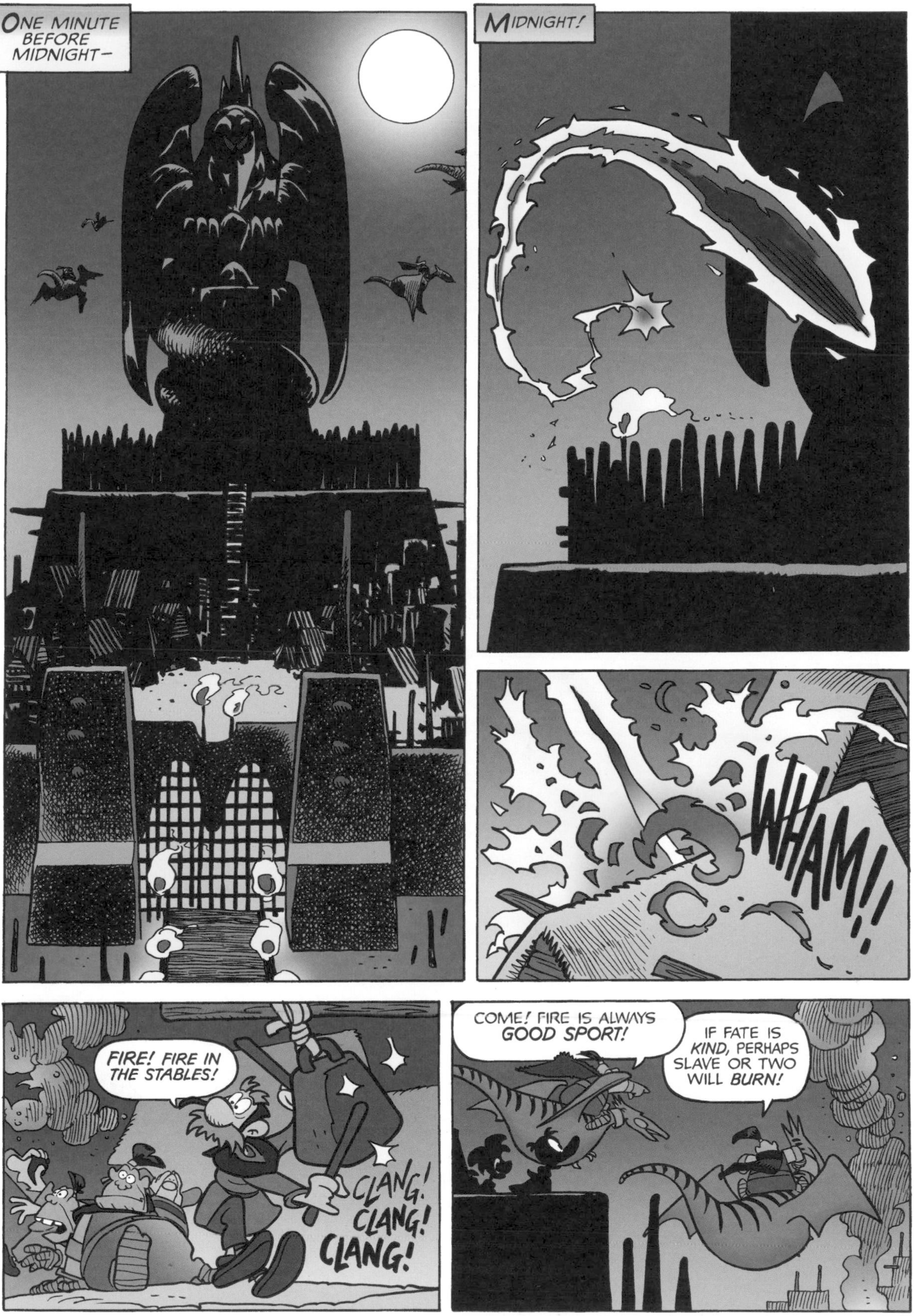

ONE MINUTE BEFORE MIDNIGHT—
MIDNIGHT!
WHAM!!
FIRE! FIRE IN THE STABLES!
CLANG! CLANG! CLANG!
COME! FIRE IS ALWAYS GOOD SPORT!
IF FATE IS KIND, PERHAPS SLAVE OR TWO WILL BURN!

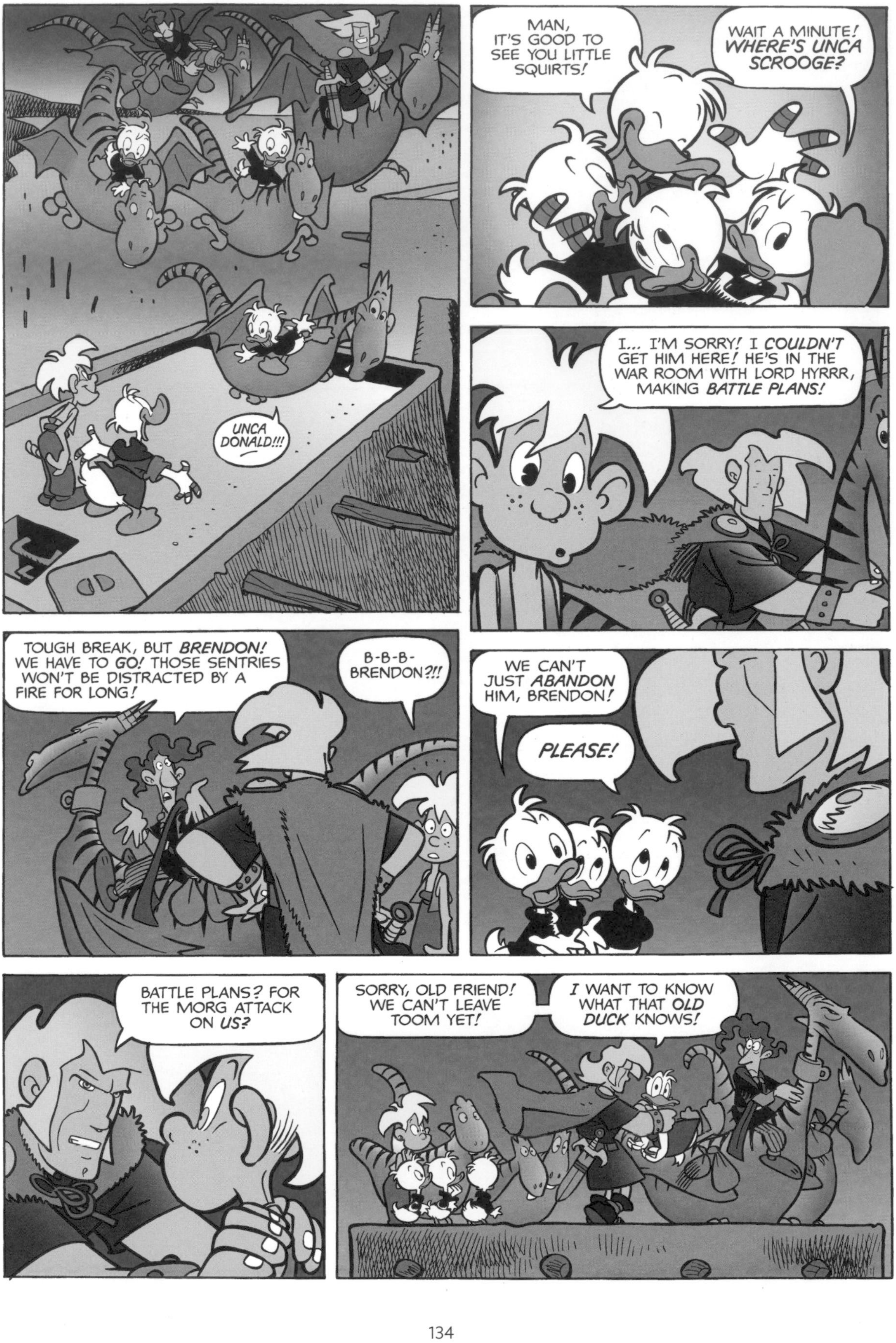
UNCA DONALD!!!
MAN, IT'S GOOD TO SEE YOU LITTLE SQUIRTS!
WAIT A MINUTE! WHERE'S UNCA SCROOGE?
I... I'M SORRY! I COULDN'T GET HIM HERE! HE'S IN THE WAR ROOM WITH LORD HYRRR, MAKING BATTLE PLANS!
TOUGH BREAK, BUT BRENDON! WE HAVE TO GO! THOSE SENTRIES WON'T BE DISTRACTED BY A FIRE FOR LONG!
B-B-B-BRENDON?!!
WE CAN'T JUST ABANDON HIM, BRENDON!
PLEASE!
BATTLE PLANS? FOR THE MORG ATTACK ON US?
SORRY, OLD FRIEND! WE CAN'T LEAVE TOOM YET!
I WANT TO KNOW WHAT THAT OLD DUCK KNOWS!

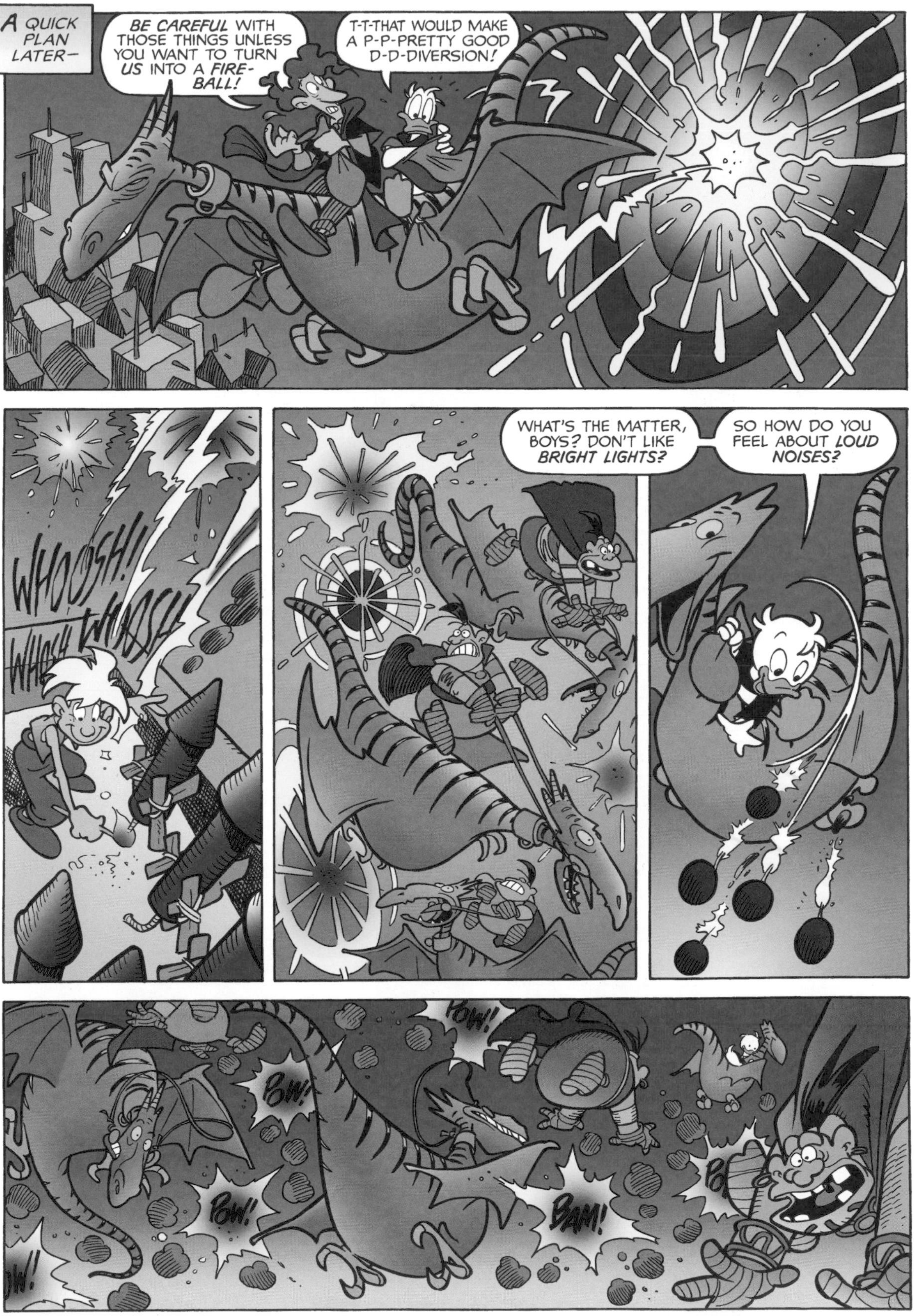
A QUICK PLAN LATER—
BE CAREFUL WITH THOSE THINGS UNLESS YOU WANT TO TURN US INTO A FIRE-BALL!
T-T-THAT WOULD MAKE A P-P-PRETTY GOOD D-D-DIVERSION!
WHOOSH!
WHOOSH
WHOOSH
WHAT'S THE MATTER, BOYS? DON'T LIKE BRIGHT LIGHTS?
SO HOW DO YOU FEEL ABOUT LOUD NOISES?
POW!
POW!
POW!
BAM!
POW!

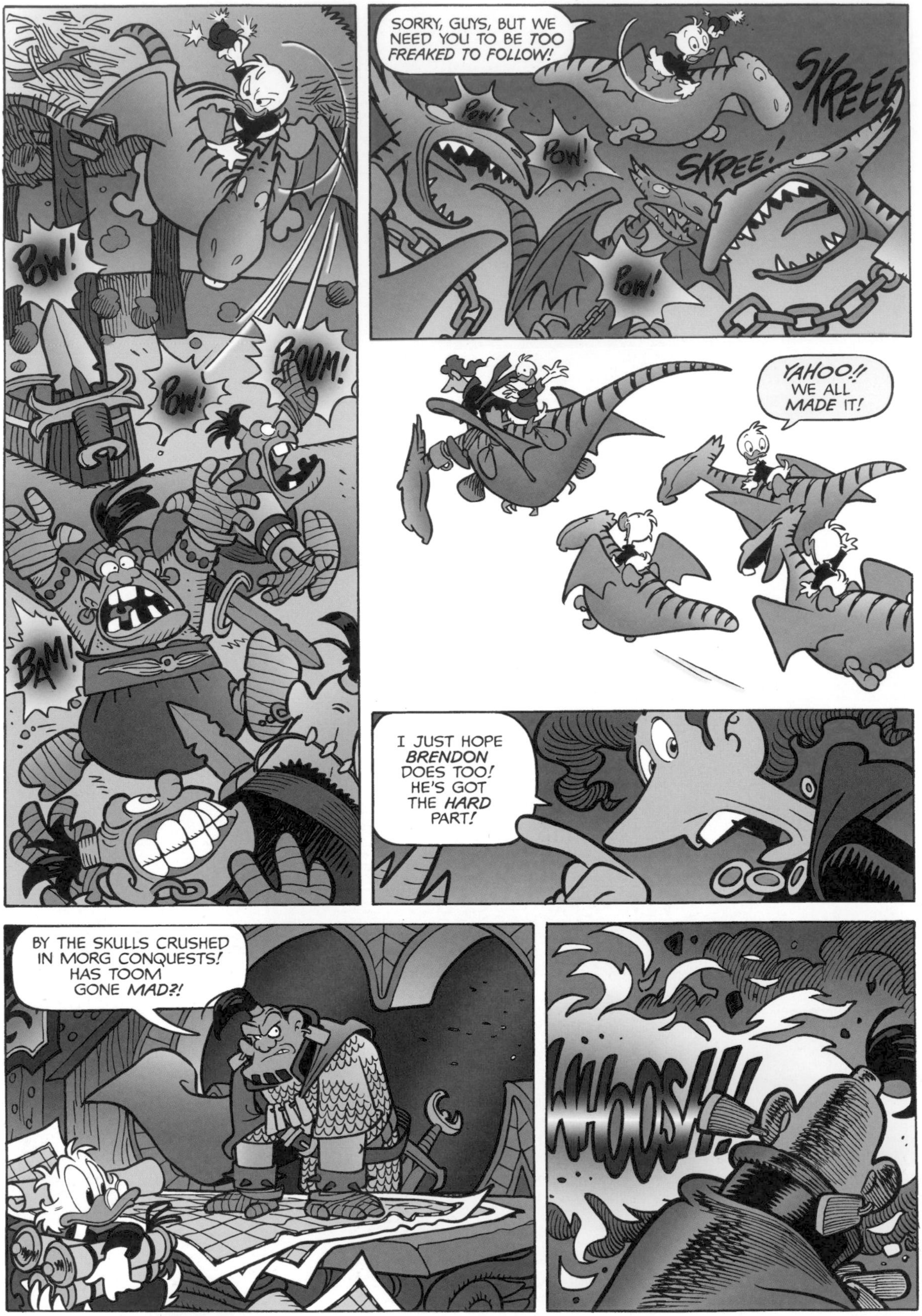
POW!
BOOM!
POW!
BAM!
SORRY, GUYS, BUT WE NEED YOU TO BE TOO FREAKED TO FOLLOW!
SKREEE
POW!
POW!
SKREE!
POW!
YAHOO!! WE ALL MADE IT!
I JUST HOPE BRENDON DOES TOO! HE'S GOT THE HARD PART!
BY THE SKULLS CRUSHED IN MORG CONQUESTS! HAS TOOM GONE MAD?!
WHOOSH!!

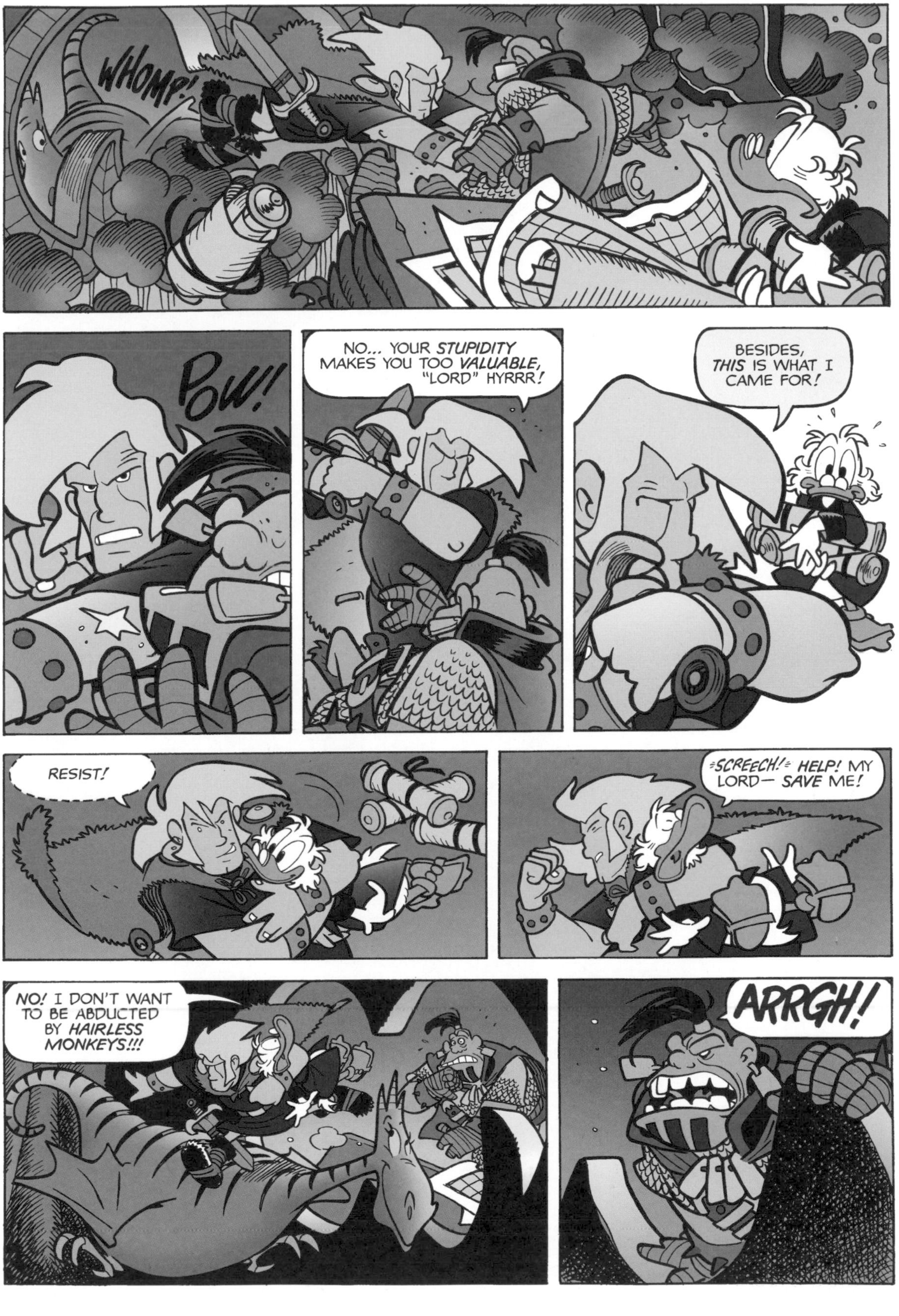
WHOMP!
POW!
NO... YOUR STUPIDITY MAKES YOU TOO VALUABLE, "LORD" HYRRR!
BESIDES, THIS IS WHAT I CAME FOR!
RESIST!
SCREECH! HELP! MY LORD— SAVE ME!
NO! I DON'T WANT TO BE ABDUCTED BY HAIRLESS MONKEYS!!!
ARRGH!

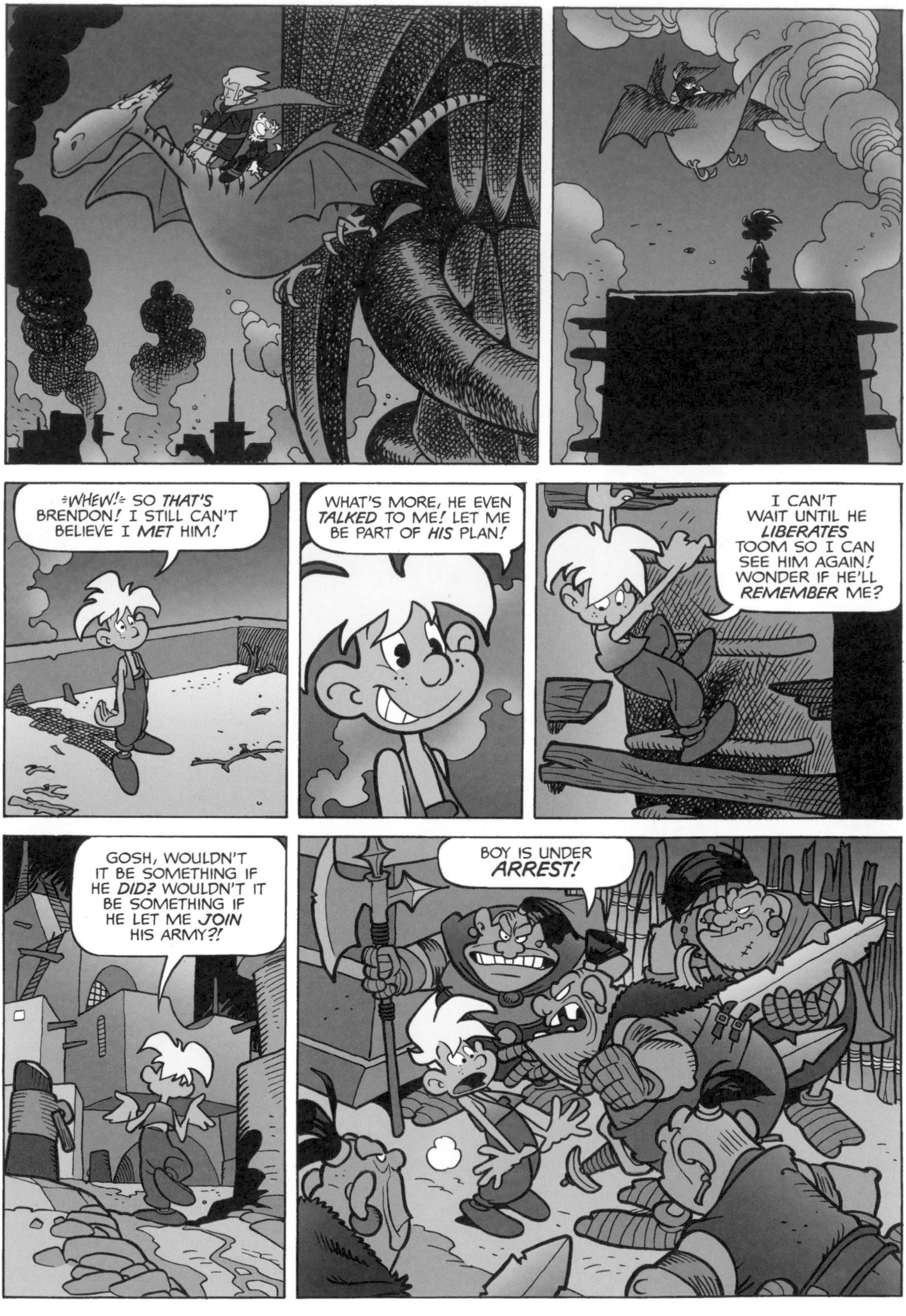
=WHEW!= SO THAT'S BRENDON! I STILL CAN'T BELIEVE I MET HIM!
WHAT'S MORE, HE EVEN TALKED TO ME! LET ME BE PART OF HIS PLAN!
I CAN'T WAIT UNTIL HE LIBERATES TOOM SO I CAN SEE HIM AGAIN! WONDER IF HE'LL REMEMBER ME?
GOSH, WOULDN'T IT BE SOMETHING IF HE DID? WOULDN'T IT BE SOMETHING IF HE LET ME JOIN HIS ARMY?!
BOY IS UNDER ARREST!

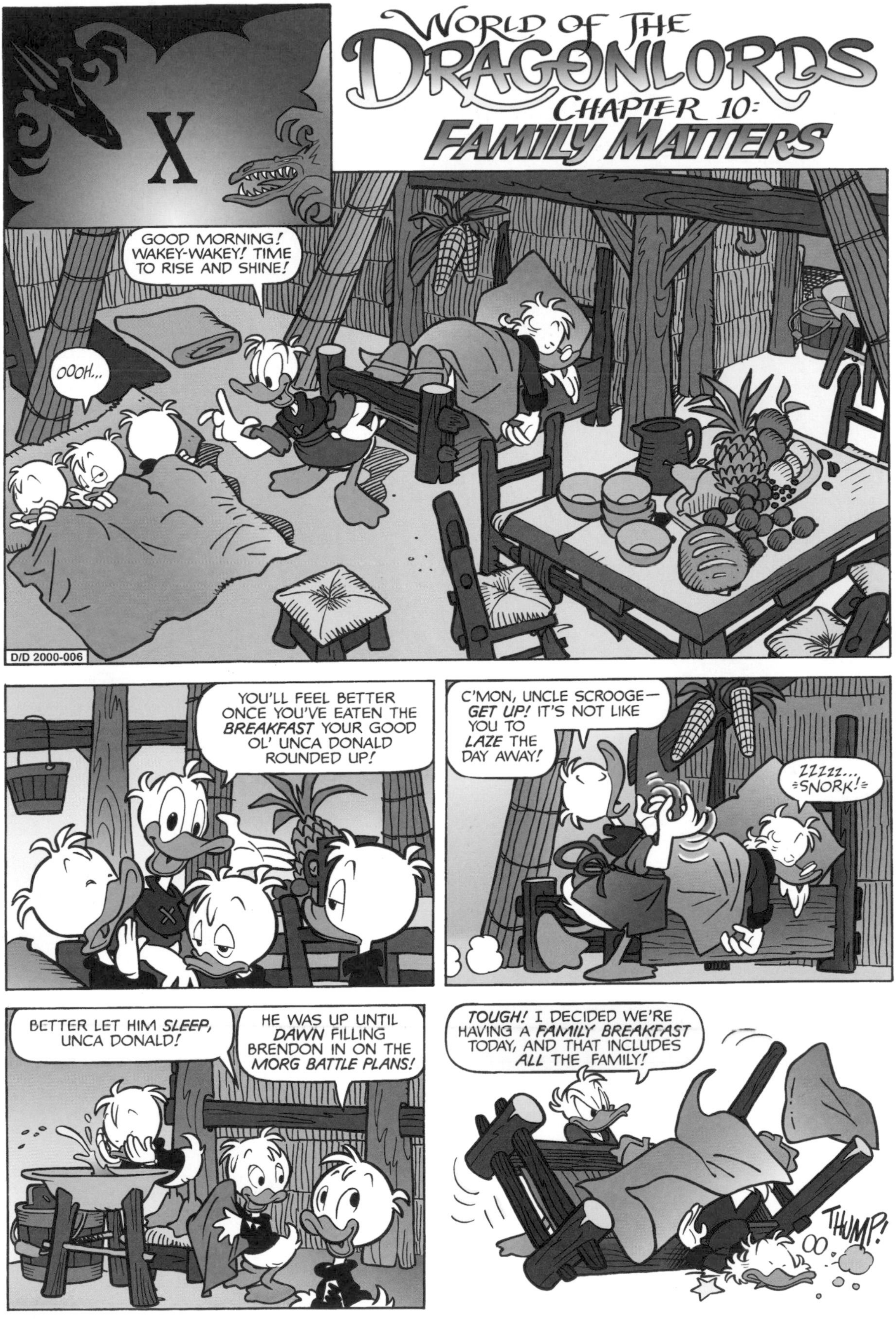

WORLD OF THE DRAGONLORDS
CHAPTER 10:
FAMILY MATTERS
X
GOOD MORNING! WAKEY-WAKEY! TIME TO RISE AND SHINE!
OOOH...
D/D 2000-006
YOU'LL FEEL BETTER ONCE YOU'VE EATEN THE BREAKFAST YOUR GOOD OL' UNCA DONALD ROUNDED UP!
C'MON, UNCLE SCROOGE— GET UP! IT'S NOT LIKE YOU TO LAZE THE DAY AWAY!
ZZZZZ... SNORK!
BETTER LET HIM SLEEP, UNCA DONALD!
HE WAS UP UNTIL DAWN FILLING BRENDON IN ON THE MORG BATTLE PLANS!
TOUGH! I DECIDED WE'RE HAVING A FAMILY BREAKFAST TODAY, AND THAT INCLUDES ALL THE FAMILY!
THUMP!
OO

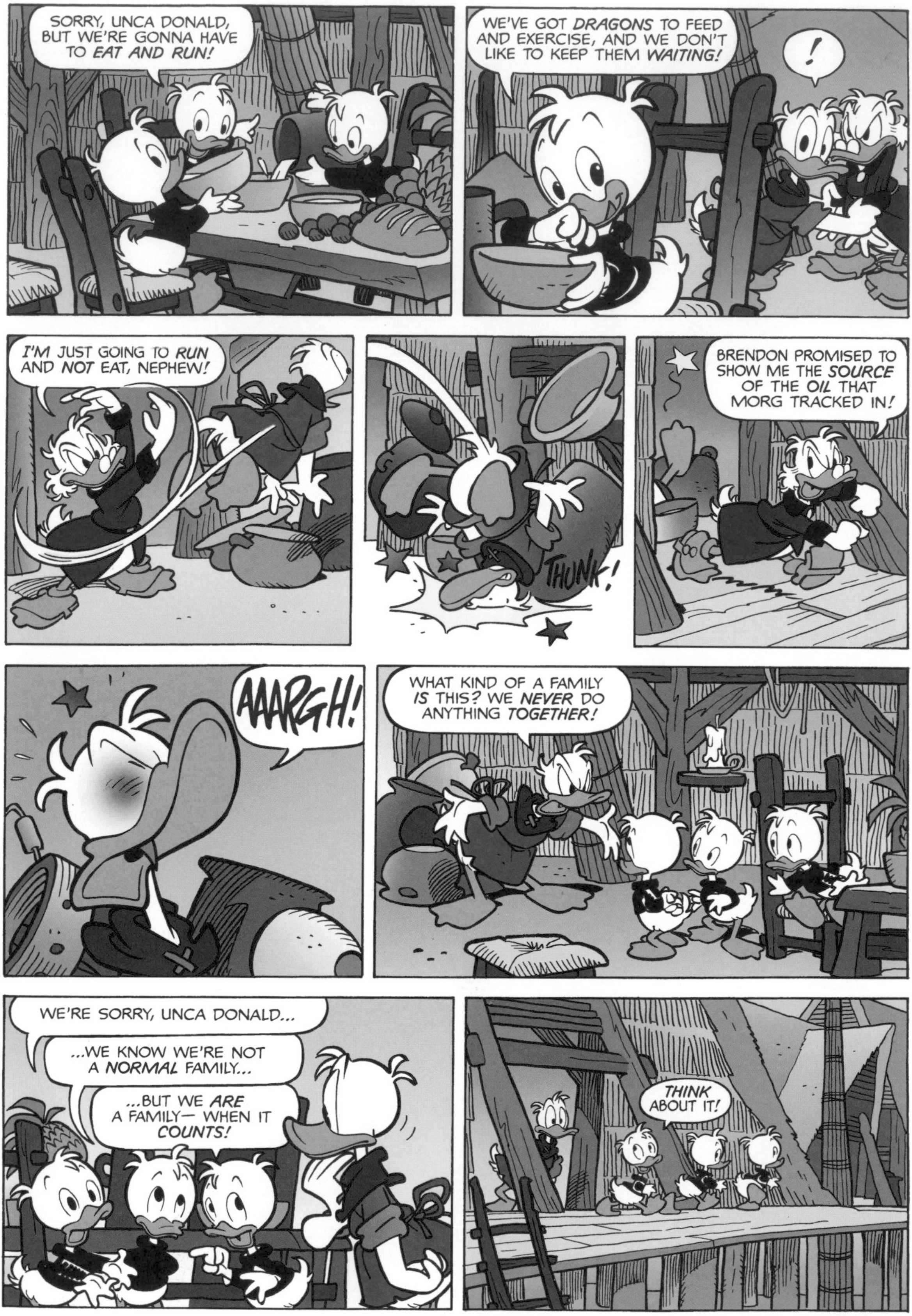
SORRY, UNCA DONALD, BUT WE'RE GONNA HAVE TO EAT AND RUN!
WE'VE GOT DRAGONS TO FEED AND EXERCISE, AND WE DON'T LIKE TO KEEP THEM WAITING!
!
I'M JUST GOING TO RUN AND NOT EAT, NEPHEW!
THUNK!
BRENDON PROMISED TO SHOW ME THE SOURCE OF THE OIL THAT MORG TRACKED IN!
AAARGH!
WHAT KIND OF A FAMILY IS THIS? WE NEVER DO ANYTHING TOGETHER!
WE'RE SORRY, UNCA DONALD...
...WE KNOW WE'RE NOT A NORMAL FAMILY...
...BUT WE ARE A FAMILY— WHEN IT COUNTS!
THINK ABOUT IT!

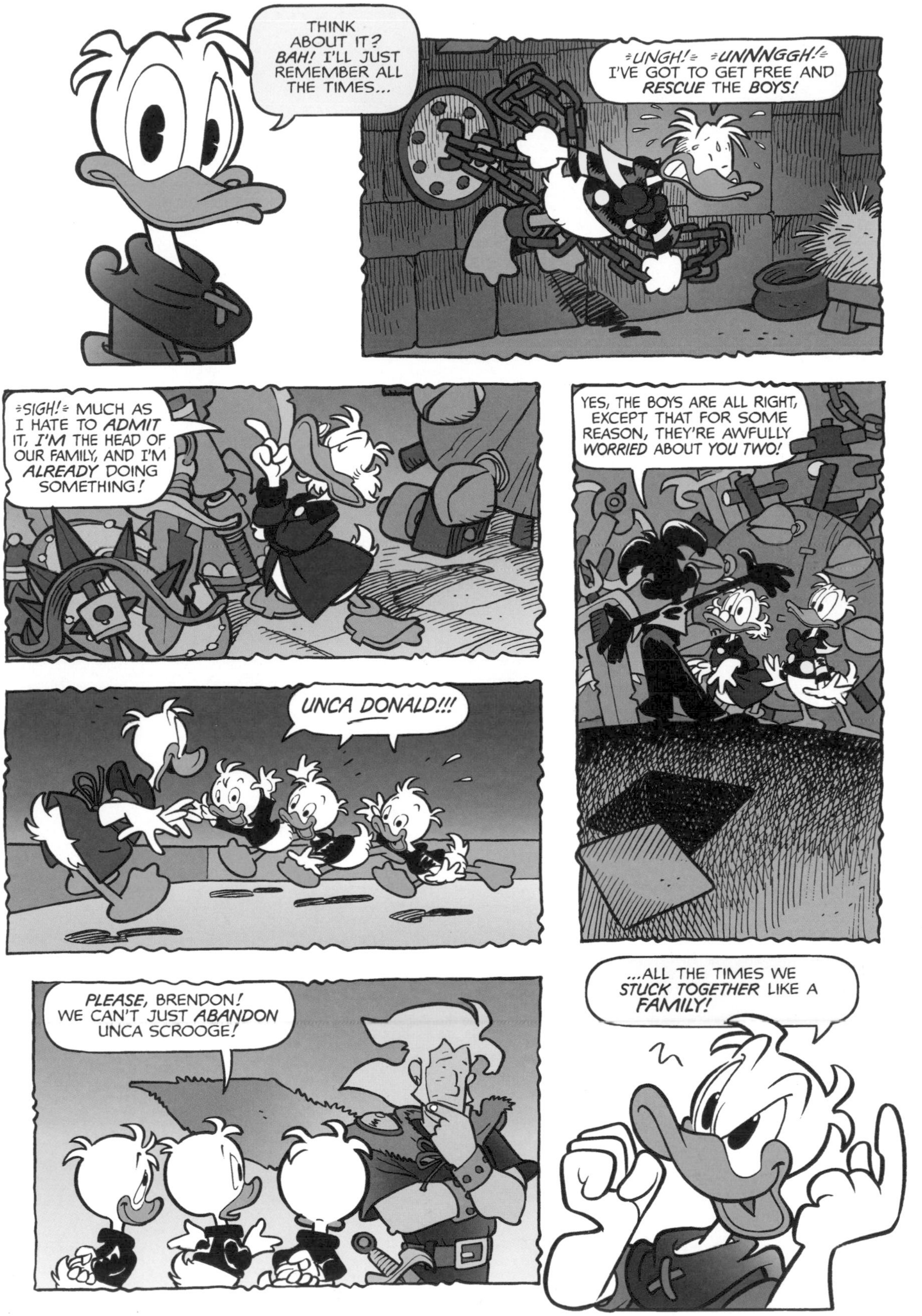
THINK ABOUT IT? BAH! I'LL JUST REMEMBER ALL THE TIMES...
=UNGH!= =UNNNGGH!= I'VE GOT TO GET FREE AND RESCUE THE BOYS!
=SIGH!= MUCH AS I HATE TO ADMIT IT, I'M THE HEAD OF OUR FAMILY, AND I'M ALREADY DOING SOMETHING!
YES, THE BOYS ARE ALL RIGHT, EXCEPT THAT FOR SOME REASON, THEY'RE AWFULLY WORRIED ABOUT YOU TWO!
UNCA DONALD!!!
PLEASE, BRENDON! WE CAN'T JUST ABANDON UNCA SCROOGE!
...ALL THE TIMES WE STUCK TOGETHER LIKE A FAMILY!

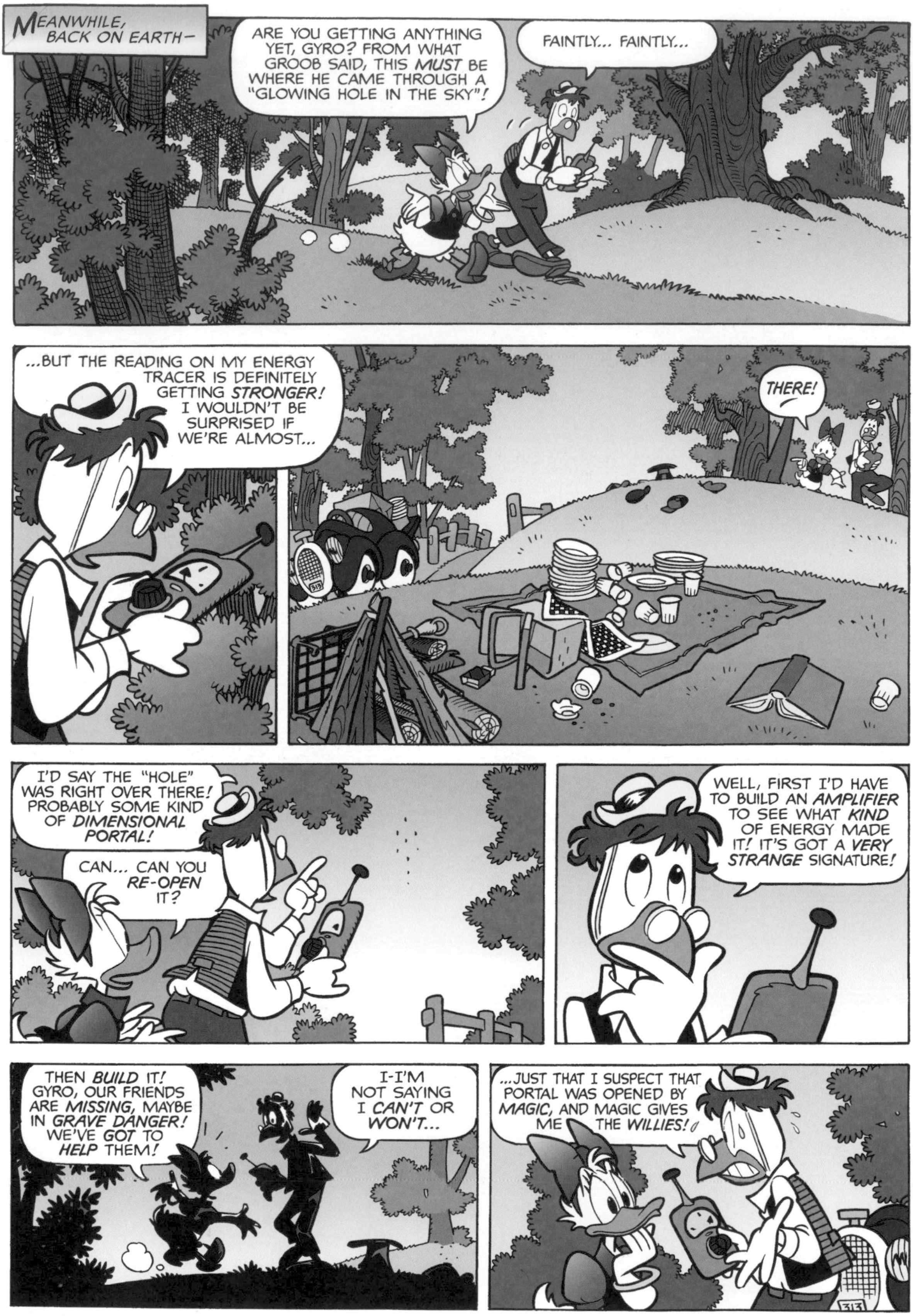
MEANWHILE, BACK ON EARTH—
ARE YOU GETTING ANYTHING YET, GYRO? FROM WHAT GROOB SAID, THIS *MUST* BE WHERE HE CAME THROUGH A "GLOWING HOLE IN THE SKY"!
FAINTLY... FAINTLY...
...BUT THE READING ON MY ENERGY TRACER IS DEFINITELY GETTING *STRONGER!* I WOULDN'T BE SURPRISED IF WE'RE ALMOST...
THERE!
I'D SAY THE "HOLE" WAS RIGHT OVER THERE! PROBABLY SOME KIND OF *DIMENSIONAL PORTAL!*
CAN... CAN YOU *RE-OPEN* IT?
WELL, FIRST I'D HAVE TO BUILD AN *AMPLIFIER* TO SEE WHAT *KIND* OF ENERGY MADE IT! IT'S GOT A *VERY STRANGE* SIGNATURE!
THEN *BUILD* IT! GYRO, OUR FRIENDS ARE *MISSING*, MAYBE IN *GRAVE DANGER!* WE'VE *GOT* TO *HELP* THEM!
I-I'M NOT SAYING I *CAN'T* OR *WON'T*...
...JUST THAT I SUSPECT THAT PORTAL WAS OPENED BY *MAGIC*, AND MAGIC GIVES ME THE *WILLIES!*

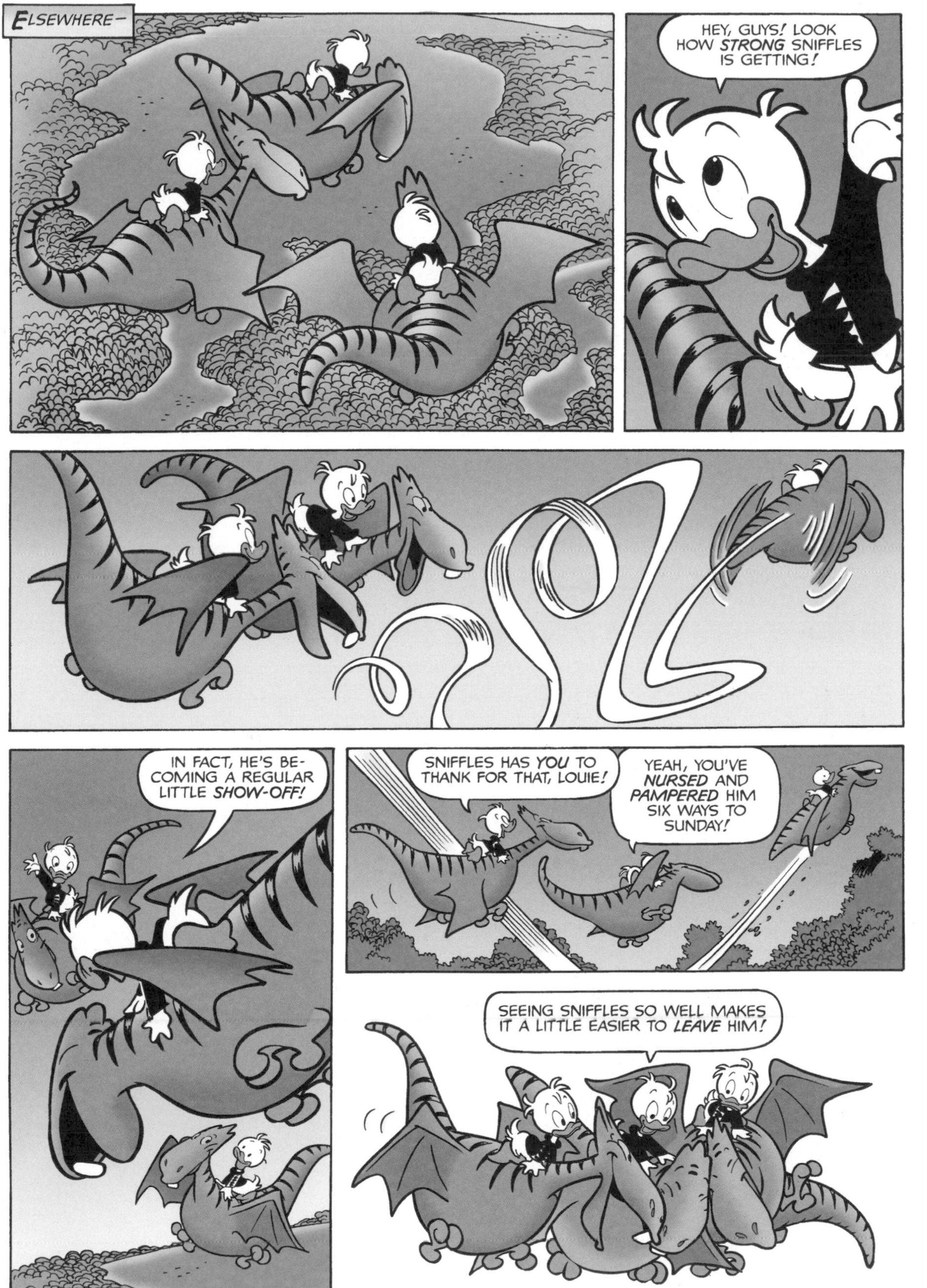
ELSEWHERE—
HEY, GUYS! LOOK HOW STRONG SNIFFLES IS GETTING!
IN FACT, HE'S BE-COMING A REGULAR LITTLE SHOW-OFF!
SNIFFLES HAS YOU TO THANK FOR THAT, LOUIE!
YEAH, YOU'VE NURSED AND PAMPERED HIM SIX WAYS TO SUNDAY!
SEEING SNIFFLES SO WELL MAKES IT A LITTLE EASIER TO LEAVE HIM!

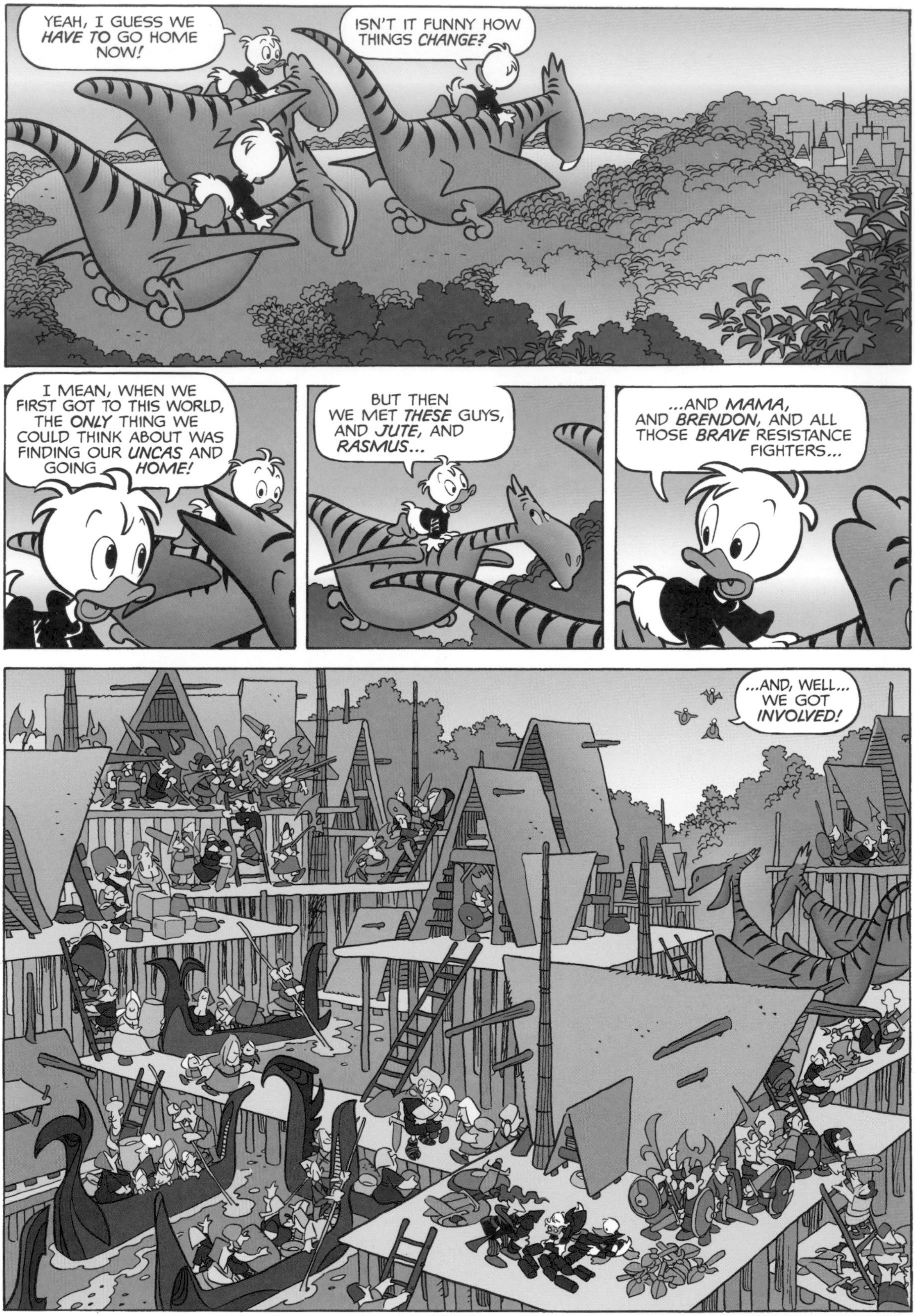
YEAH, I GUESS WE *HAVE TO* GO HOME NOW!
ISN'T IT FUNNY HOW THINGS *CHANGE?*
I MEAN, WHEN WE FIRST GOT TO THIS WORLD, THE *ONLY* THING WE COULD THINK ABOUT WAS FINDING OUR *UNCAS* AND GOING *HOME!*
BUT THEN WE MET *THESE* GUYS, AND *JUTE*, AND *RASMUS*...
...AND *MAMA*, AND *BRENDON*, AND ALL THOSE *BRAVE* RESISTANCE FIGHTERS...
...AND, WELL... WE GOT *INVOLVED!*

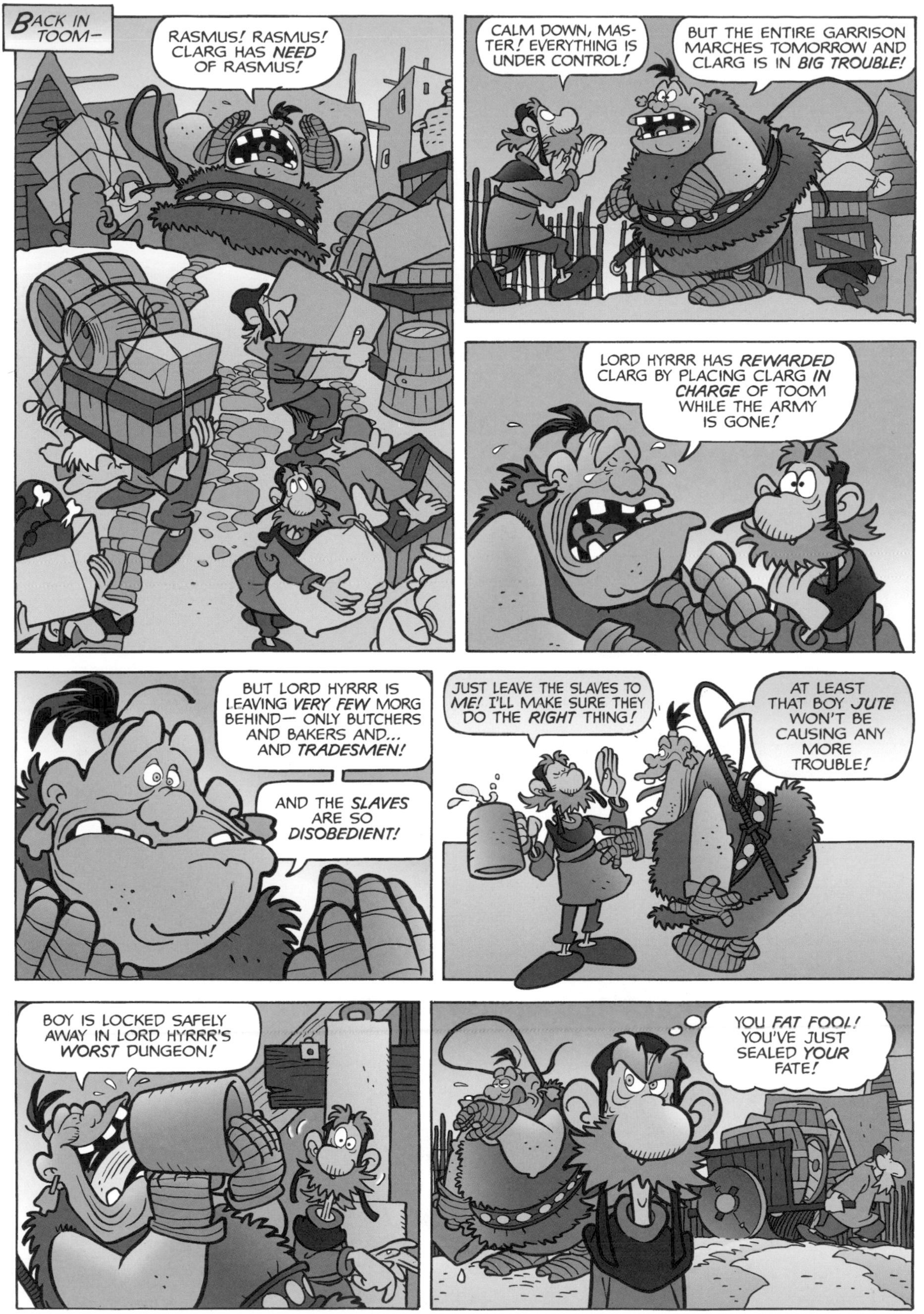
BACK IN TOOM–
RASMUS! RASMUS! CLARG HAS NEED OF RASMUS!
CALM DOWN, MASTER! EVERYTHING IS UNDER CONTROL!
BUT THE ENTIRE GARRISON MARCHES TOMORROW AND CLARG IS IN BIG TROUBLE!
LORD HYRRR HAS REWARDED CLARG BY PLACING CLARG IN CHARGE OF TOOM WHILE THE ARMY IS GONE!
BUT LORD HYRRR IS LEAVING VERY FEW MORG BEHIND– ONLY BUTCHERS AND BAKERS AND... AND TRADESMEN!
AND THE SLAVES ARE SO DISOBEDIENT!
JUST LEAVE THE SLAVES TO ME! I'LL MAKE SURE THEY DO THE RIGHT THING!
AT LEAST THAT BOY JUTE WON'T BE CAUSING ANY MORE TROUBLE!
BOY IS LOCKED SAFELY AWAY IN LORD HYRRR'S WORST DUNGEON!
YOU FAT FOOL! YOU'VE JUST SEALED YOUR FATE!

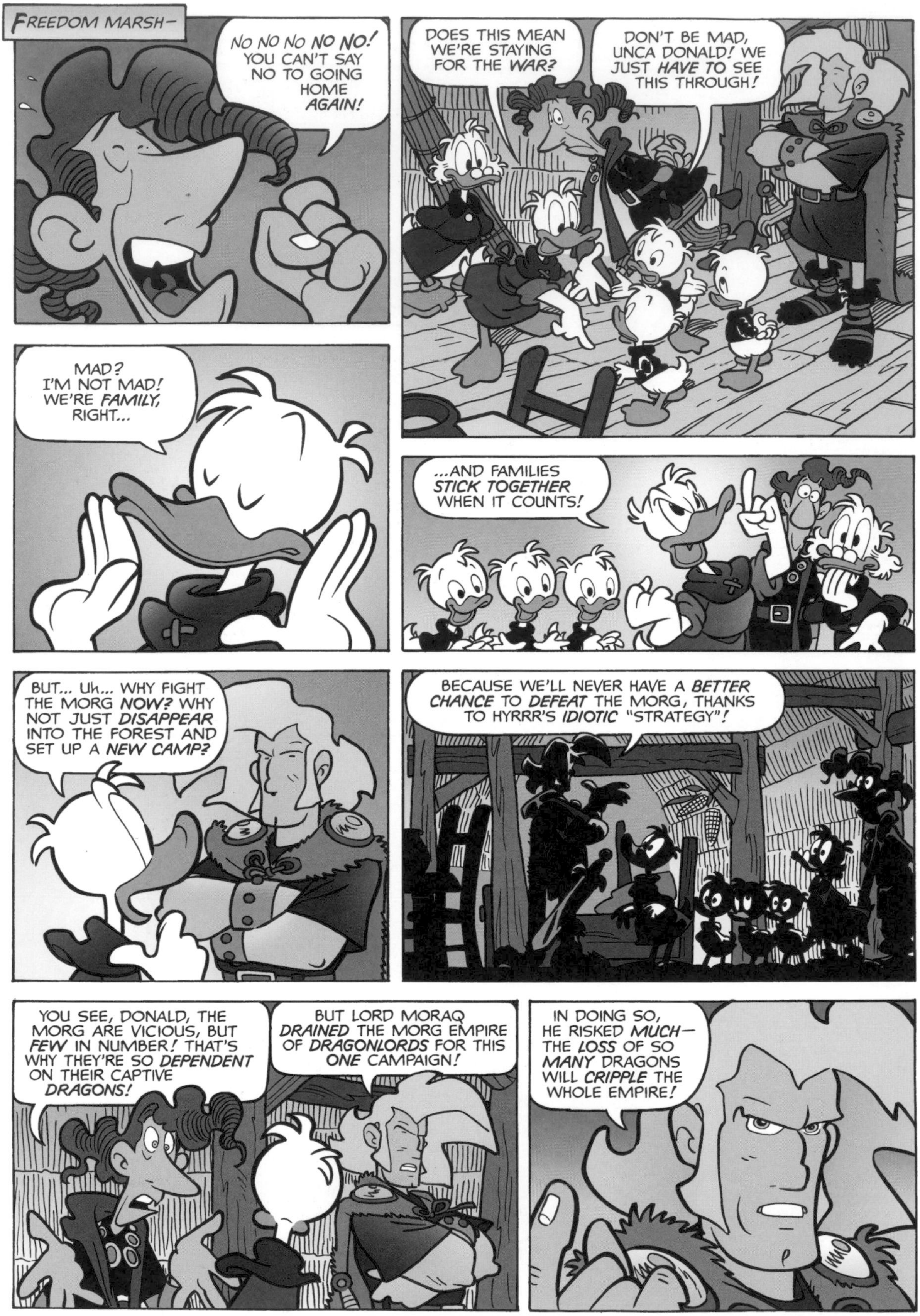
FREEDOM MARSH—
NO NO NO NO NO! YOU CAN'T SAY NO TO GOING HOME AGAIN!
DOES THIS MEAN WE'RE STAYING FOR THE WAR?
DON'T BE MAD, UNCA DONALD! WE JUST HAVE TO SEE THIS THROUGH!
MAD? I'M NOT MAD! WE'RE FAMILY, RIGHT...
...AND FAMILIES STICK TOGETHER WHEN IT COUNTS!
BUT... Uh... WHY FIGHT THE MORG NOW? WHY NOT JUST DISAPPEAR INTO THE FOREST AND SET UP A NEW CAMP?
BECAUSE WE'LL NEVER HAVE A BETTER CHANCE TO DEFEAT THE MORG, THANKS TO HYRRR'S IDIOTIC "STRATEGY"!
YOU SEE, DONALD, THE MORG ARE VICIOUS, BUT FEW IN NUMBER! THAT'S WHY THEY'RE SO DEPENDENT ON THEIR CAPTIVE DRAGONS!
BUT LORD MORAQ DRAINED THE MORG EMPIRE OF DRAGONLORDS FOR THIS ONE CAMPAIGN!
IN DOING SO, HE RISKED MUCH— THE LOSS OF SO MANY DRAGONS WILL CRIPPLE THE WHOLE EMPIRE!

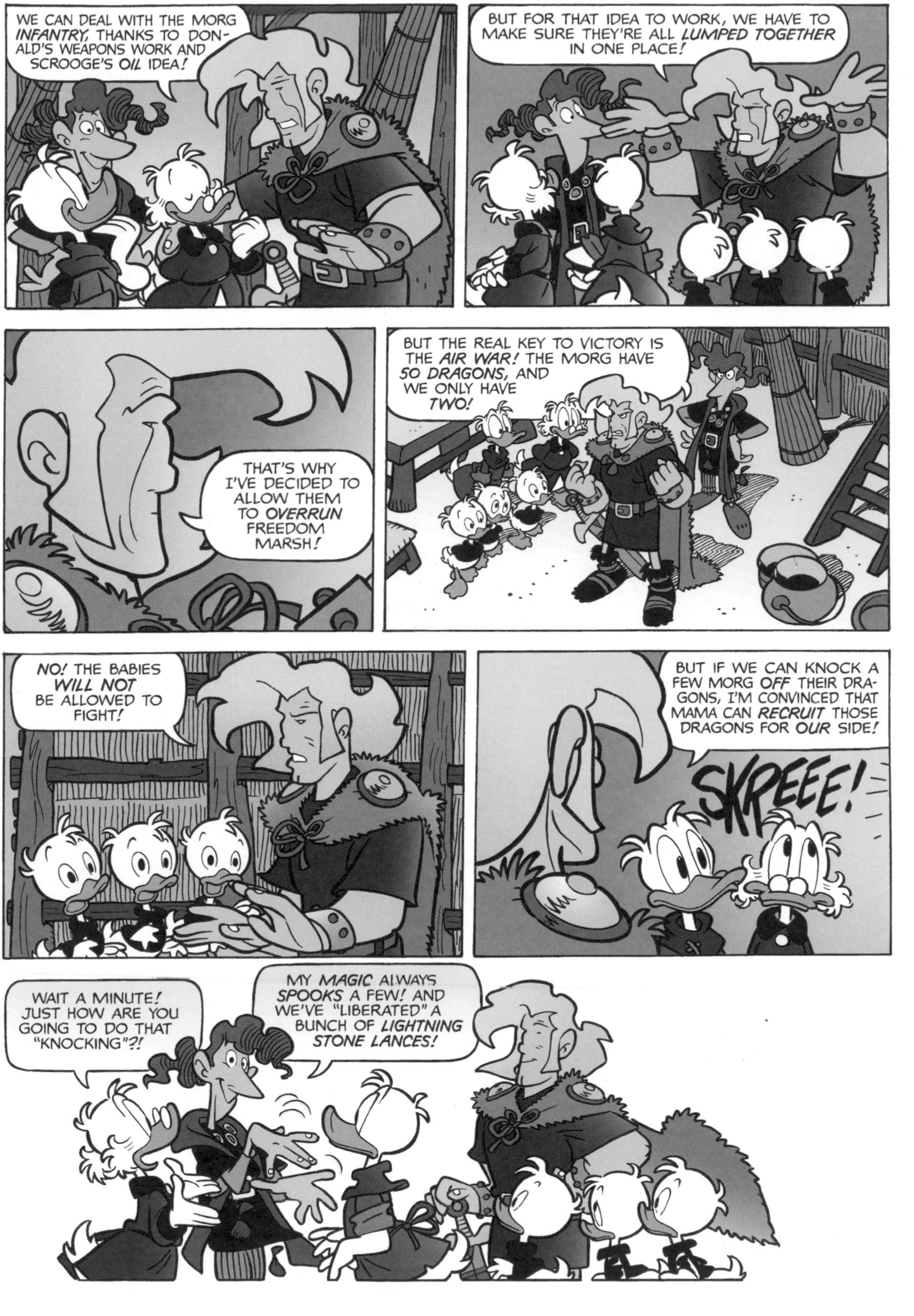
WE CAN DEAL WITH THE MORG INFANTRY, THANKS TO DONALD'S WEAPONS WORK AND SCROOGE'S OIL IDEA!
BUT FOR THAT IDEA TO WORK, WE HAVE TO MAKE SURE THEY'RE ALL LUMPED TOGETHER IN ONE PLACE!
THAT'S WHY I'VE DECIDED TO ALLOW THEM TO OVERRUN FREEDOM MARSH!
BUT THE REAL KEY TO VICTORY IS THE AIR WAR! THE MORG HAVE 50 DRAGONS, AND WE ONLY HAVE TWO!
NO! THE BABIES WILL NOT BE ALLOWED TO FIGHT!
BUT IF WE CAN KNOCK A FEW MORG OFF THEIR DRAGONS, I'M CONVINCED THAT MAMA CAN RECRUIT THOSE DRAGONS FOR OUR SIDE!
SKREEE!
WAIT A MINUTE! JUST HOW ARE YOU GOING TO DO THAT "KNOCKING"?!
MY MAGIC ALWAYS SPOOKS A FEW! AND WE'VE "LIBERATED" A BUNCH OF LIGHTNING STONE LANCES!

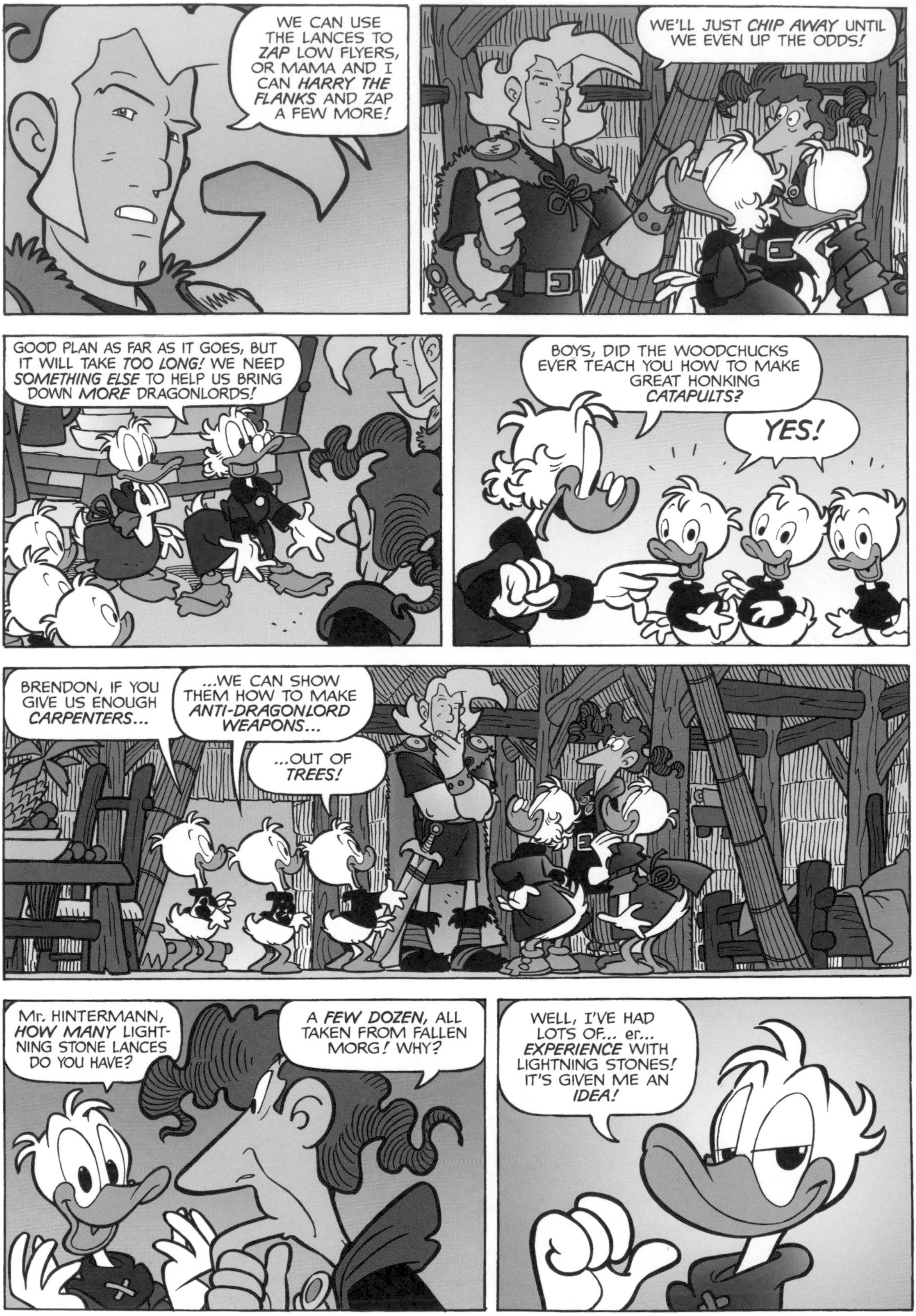

WE CAN USE THE LANCES TO ZAP LOW FLYERS, OR MAMA AND I CAN HARRY THE FLANKS AND ZAP A FEW MORE!
WE'LL JUST CHIP AWAY UNTIL WE EVEN UP THE ODDS!
GOOD PLAN AS FAR AS IT GOES, BUT IT WILL TAKE TOO LONG! WE NEED SOMETHING ELSE TO HELP US BRING DOWN MORE DRAGONLORDS!
BOYS, DID THE WOODCHUCKS EVER TEACH YOU HOW TO MAKE GREAT HONKING CATAPULTS?
YES!
BRENDON, IF YOU GIVE US ENOUGH CARPENTERS...
...WE CAN SHOW THEM HOW TO MAKE ANTI-DRAGONLORD WEAPONS...
...OUT OF TREES!
Mr. HINTERMANN, HOW MANY LIGHT-NING STONE LANCES DO YOU HAVE?
A FEW DOZEN, ALL TAKEN FROM FALLEN MORG! WHY?
WELL, I'VE HAD LOTS OF... er... EXPERIENCE WITH LIGHTNING STONES! IT'S GIVEN ME AN IDEA!

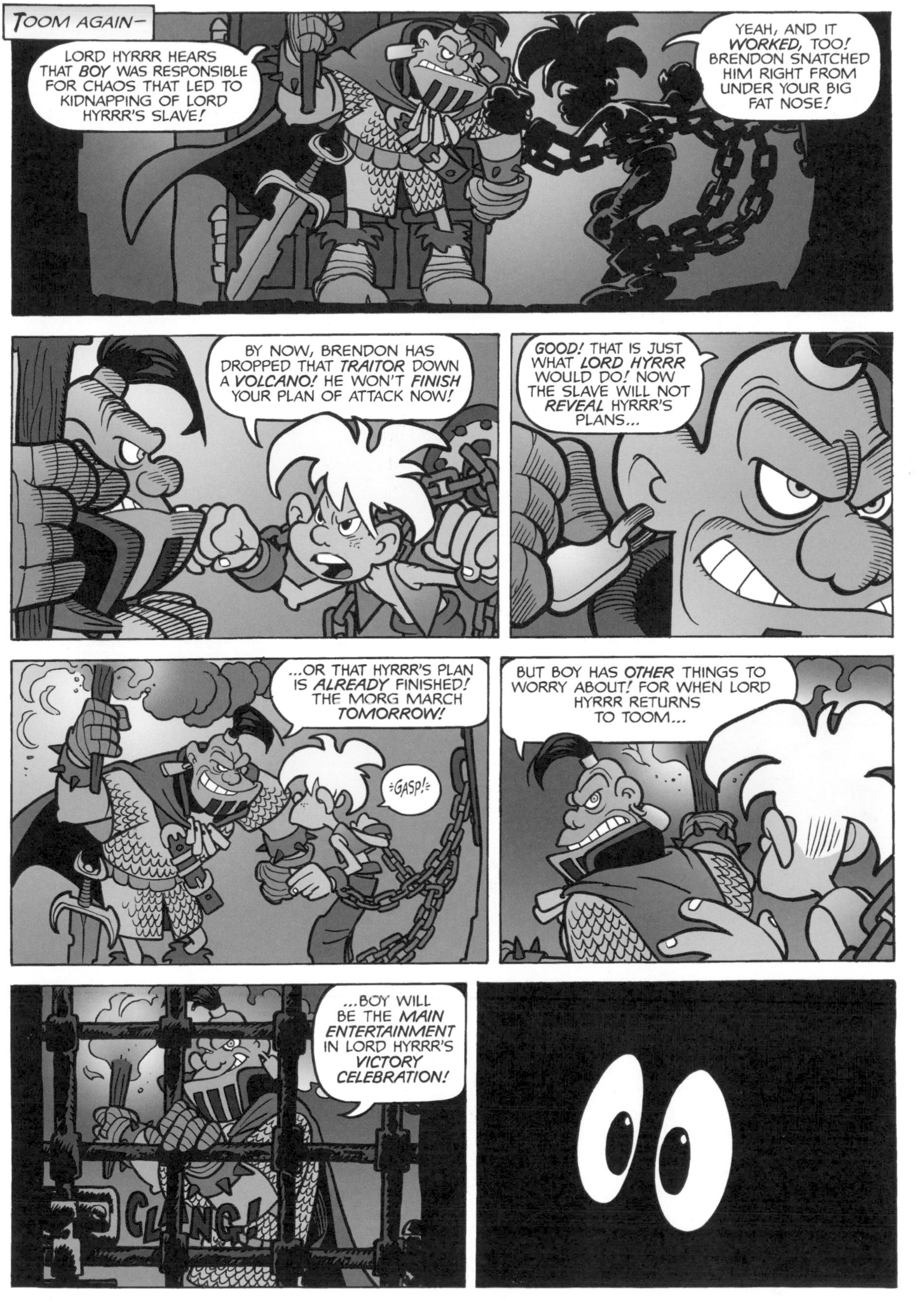
TOOM AGAIN—
LORD HYRRR HEARS THAT BOY WAS RESPONSIBLE FOR CHAOS THAT LED TO KIDNAPPING OF LORD HYRRR'S SLAVE!
YEAH, AND IT WORKED, TOO! BRENDON SNATCHED HIM RIGHT FROM UNDER YOUR BIG FAT NOSE!
BY NOW, BRENDON HAS DROPPED THAT TRAITOR DOWN A VOLCANO! HE WON'T FINISH YOUR PLAN OF ATTACK NOW!
GOOD! THAT IS JUST WHAT LORD HYRRR WOULD DO! NOW THE SLAVE WILL NOT REVEAL HYRRR'S PLANS...
...OR THAT HYRRR'S PLAN IS ALREADY FINISHED! THE MORG MARCH TOMORROW!
GASP!
BUT BOY HAS OTHER THINGS TO WORRY ABOUT! FOR WHEN LORD HYRRR RETURNS TO TOOM...
...BOY WILL BE THE MAIN ENTERTAINMENT IN LORD HYRRR'S VICTORY CELEBRATION!
CLANG!

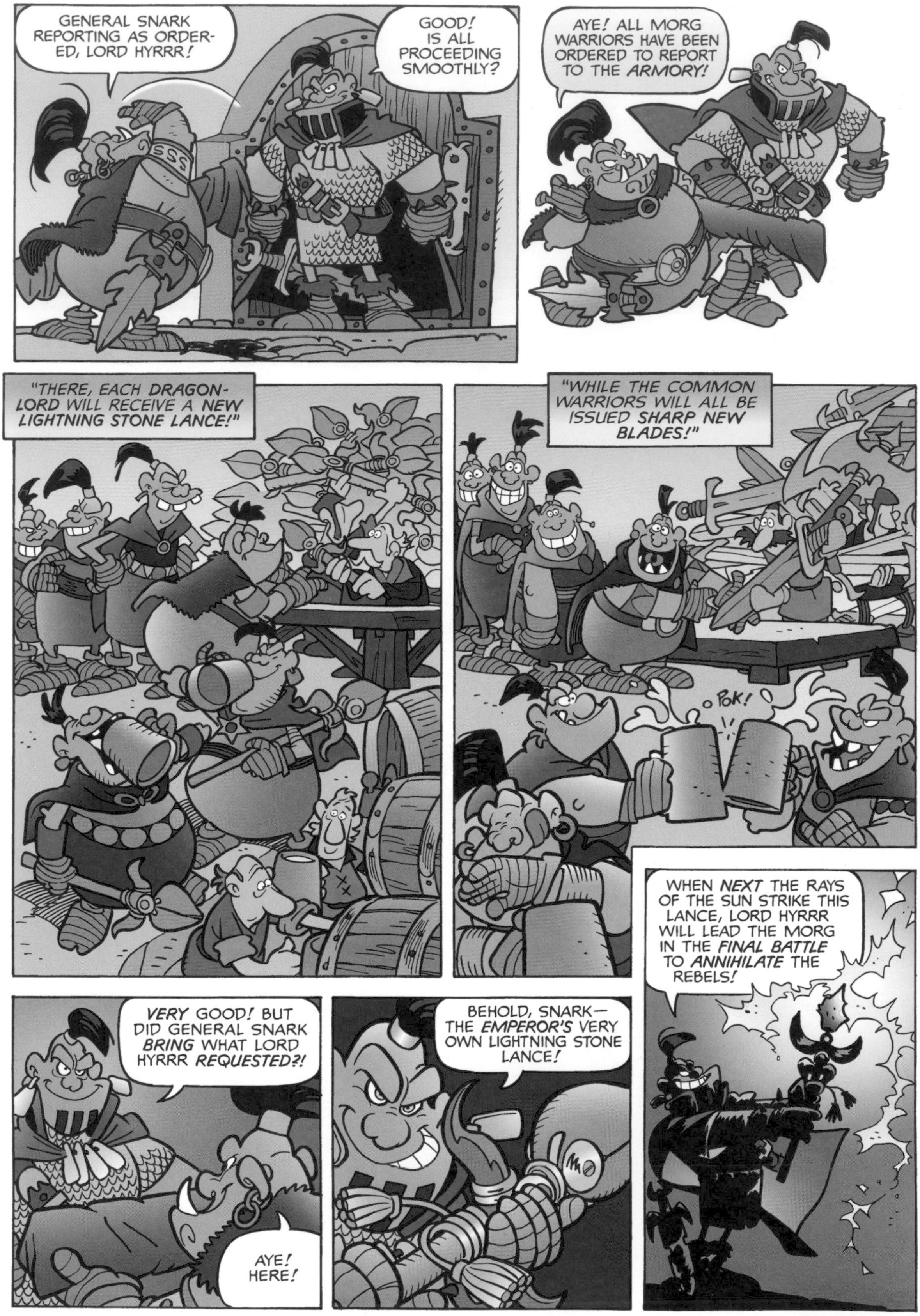
GENERAL SNARK REPORTING AS ORDERED, LORD HYRRR!
GOOD! IS ALL PROCEEDING SMOOTHLY?
AYE! ALL MORG WARRIORS HAVE BEEN ORDERED TO REPORT TO THE ARMORY!
"THERE, EACH DRAGON-LORD WILL RECEIVE A NEW LIGHTNING STONE LANCE!"
"WHILE THE COMMON WARRIORS WILL ALL BE ISSUED SHARP NEW BLADES!"
POK!
VERY GOOD! BUT DID GENERAL SNARK BRING WHAT LORD HYRRR REQUESTED?!
AYE! HERE!
BEHOLD, SNARK— THE EMPEROR'S VERY OWN LIGHTNING STONE LANCE!
WHEN NEXT THE RAYS OF THE SUN STRIKE THIS LANCE, LORD HYRRR WILL LEAD THE MORG IN THE FINAL BATTLE TO ANNIHILATE THE REBELS!

CONTINUED...

Sketches

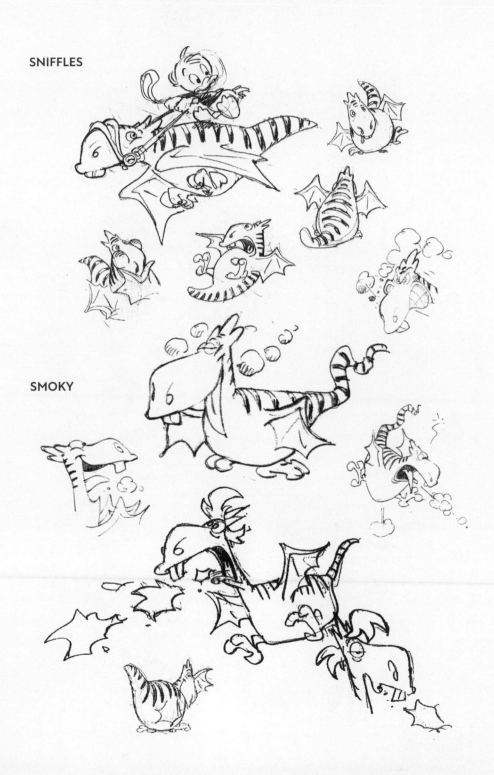

SNIFFLES

SMOKY

Sketches

SPITFIRE

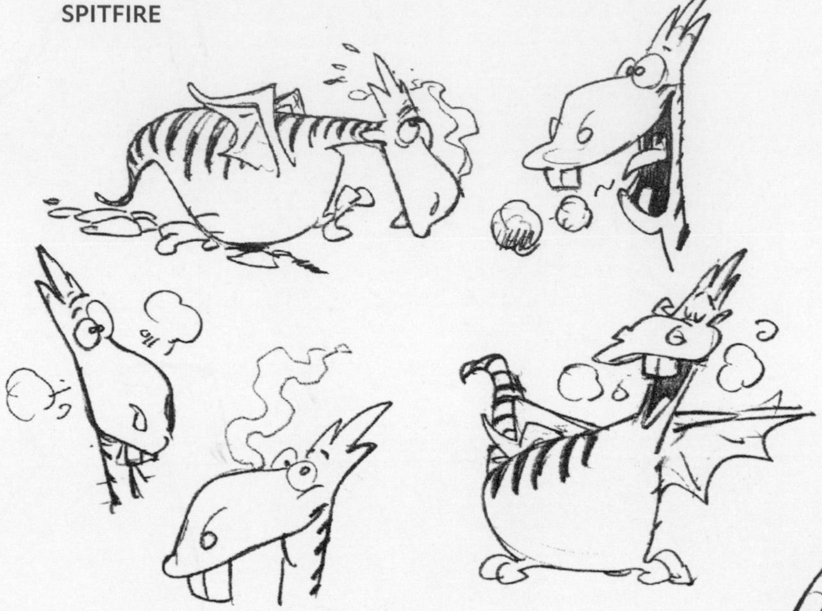

MAMA

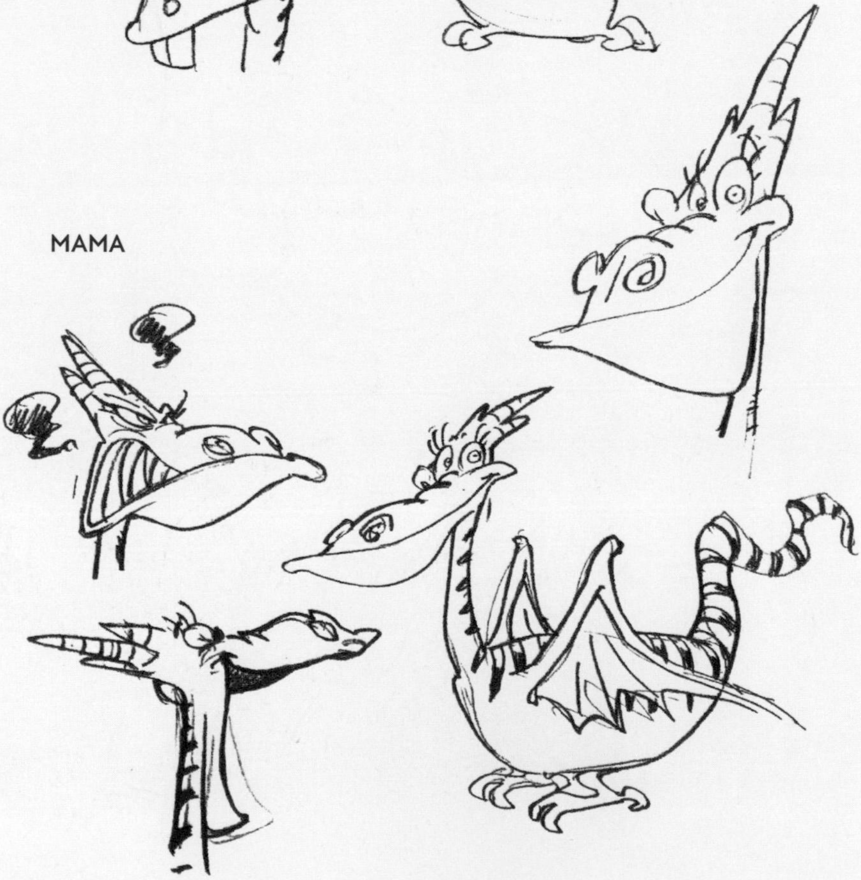

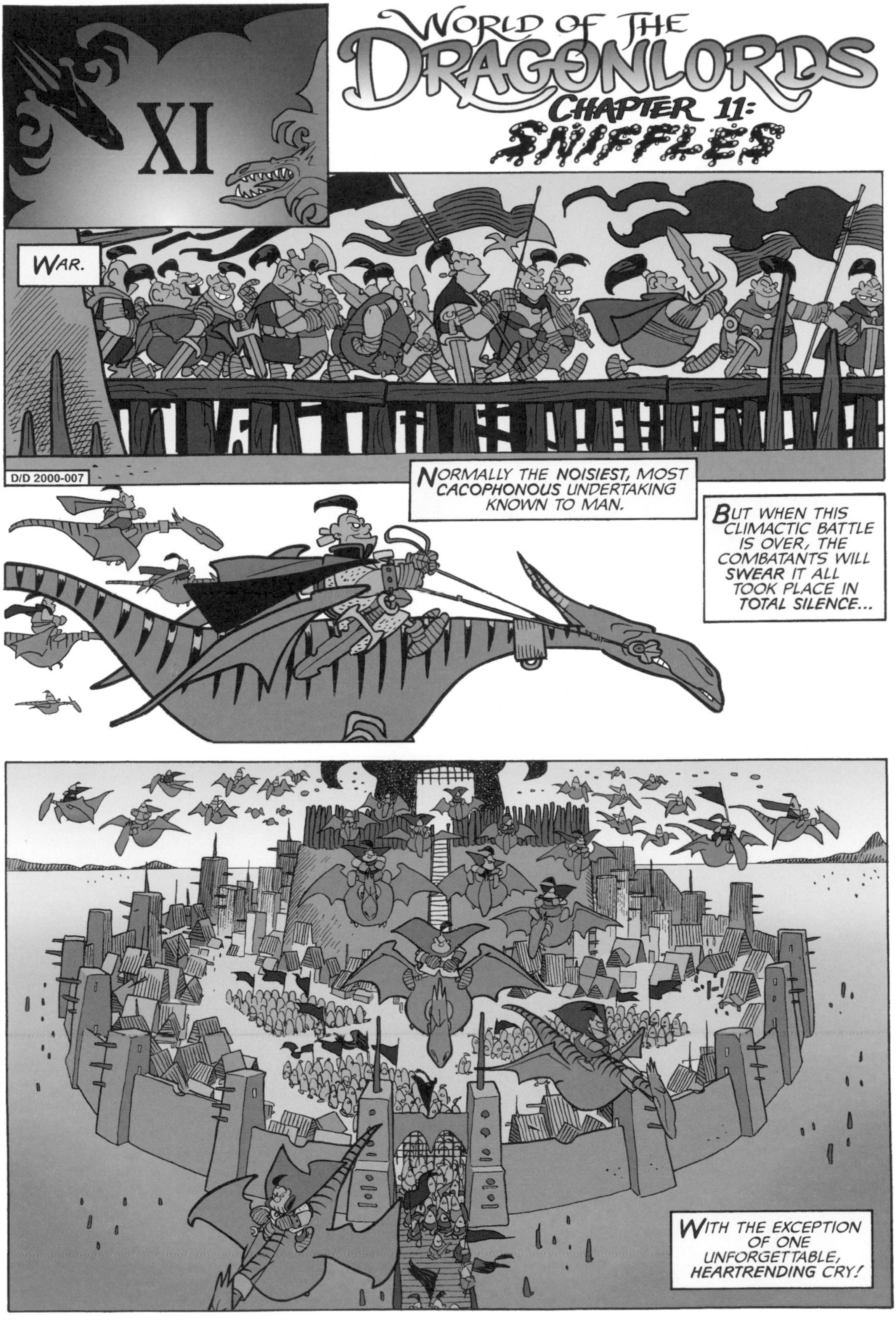
XI
WORLD OF THE DRAGONLORDS
CHAPTER 11: SNIFFLES
WAR.
D/D 2000-007
NORMALLY THE NOISIEST, MOST CACOPHONOUS UNDERTAKING KNOWN TO MAN.
BUT WHEN THIS CLIMACTIC BATTLE IS OVER, THE COMBATANTS WILL SWEAR IT ALL TOOK PLACE IN TOTAL SILENCE...
WITH THE EXCEPTION OF ONE UNFORGETTABLE, HEARTRENDING CRY!

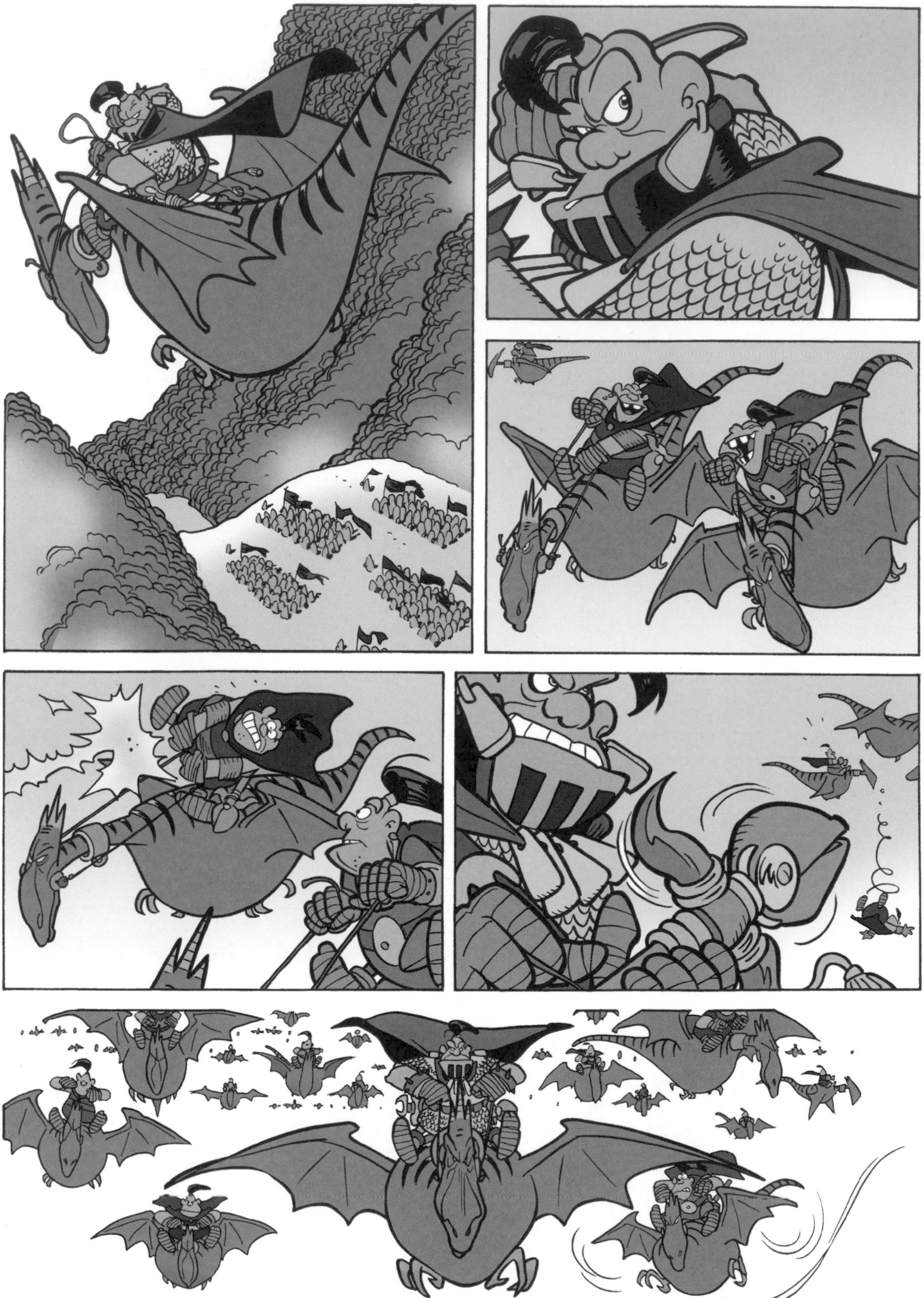

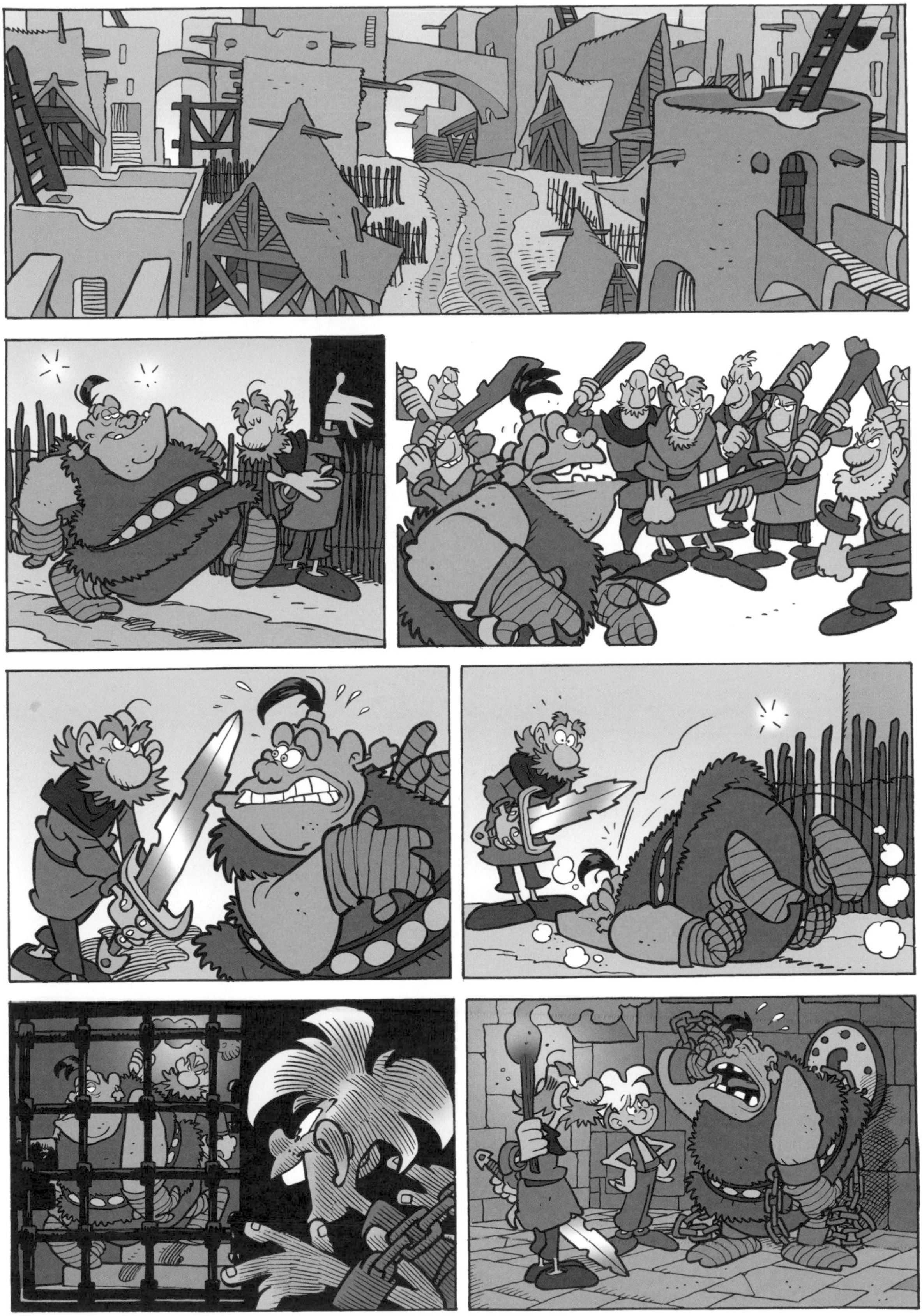

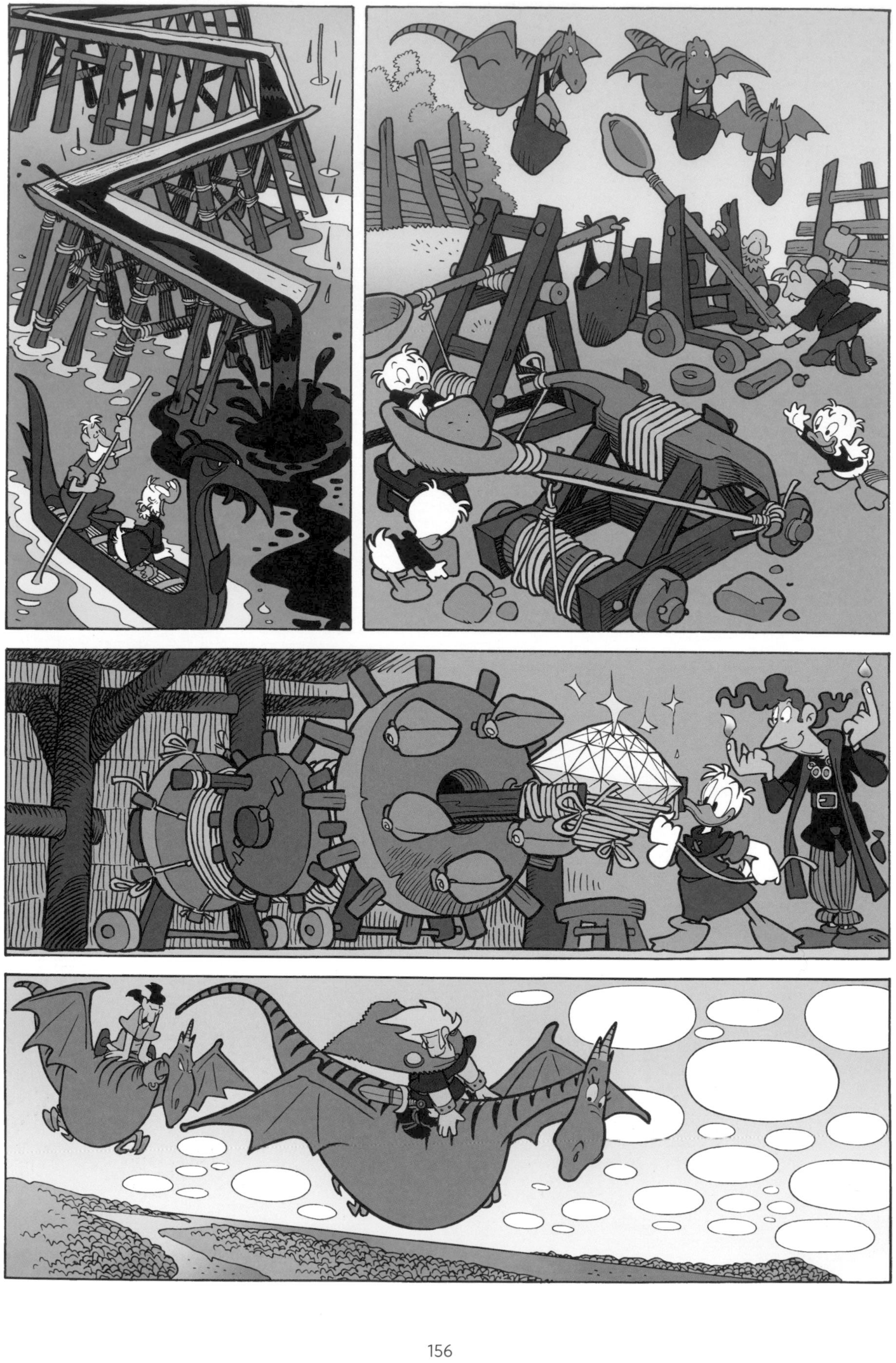

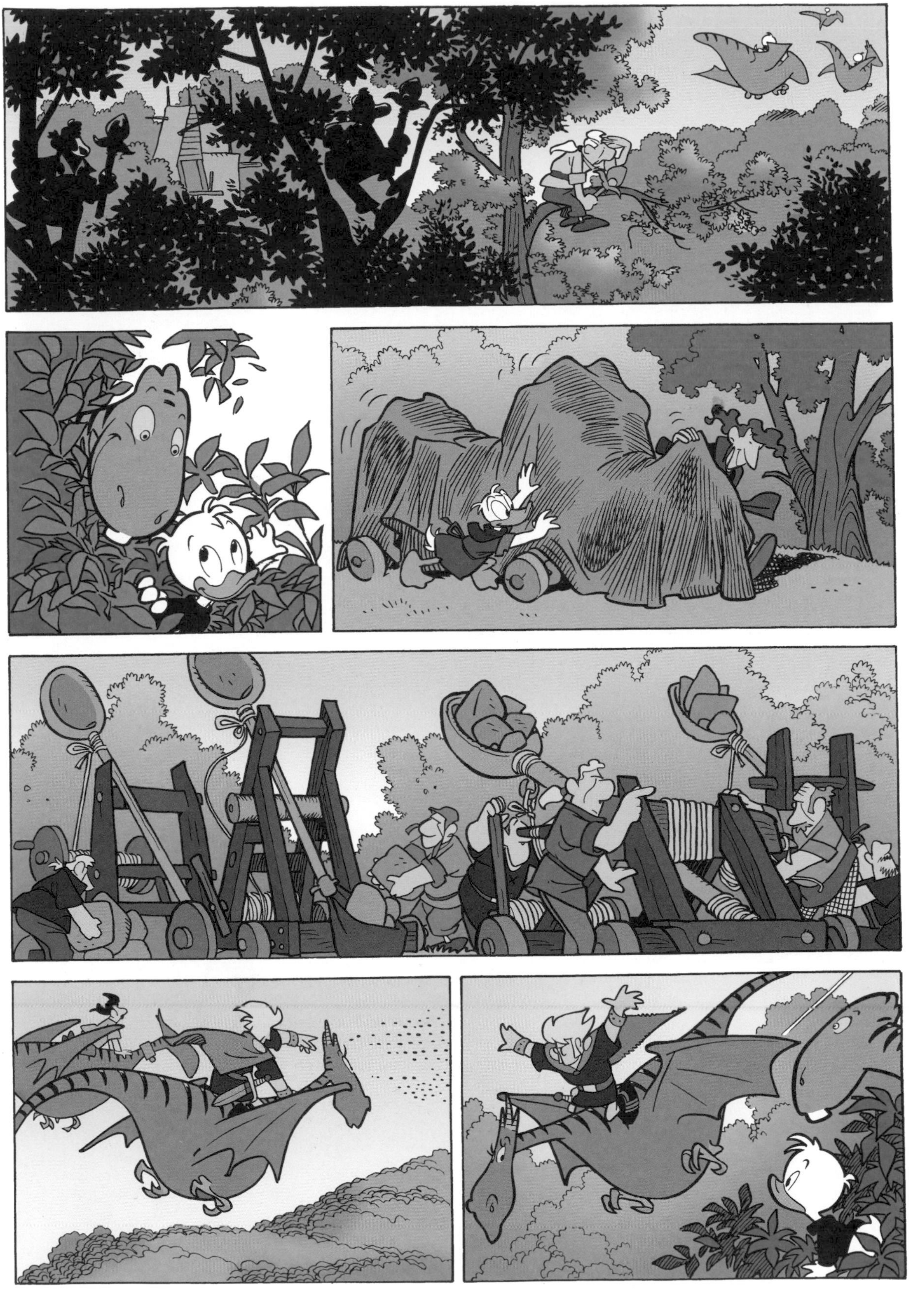

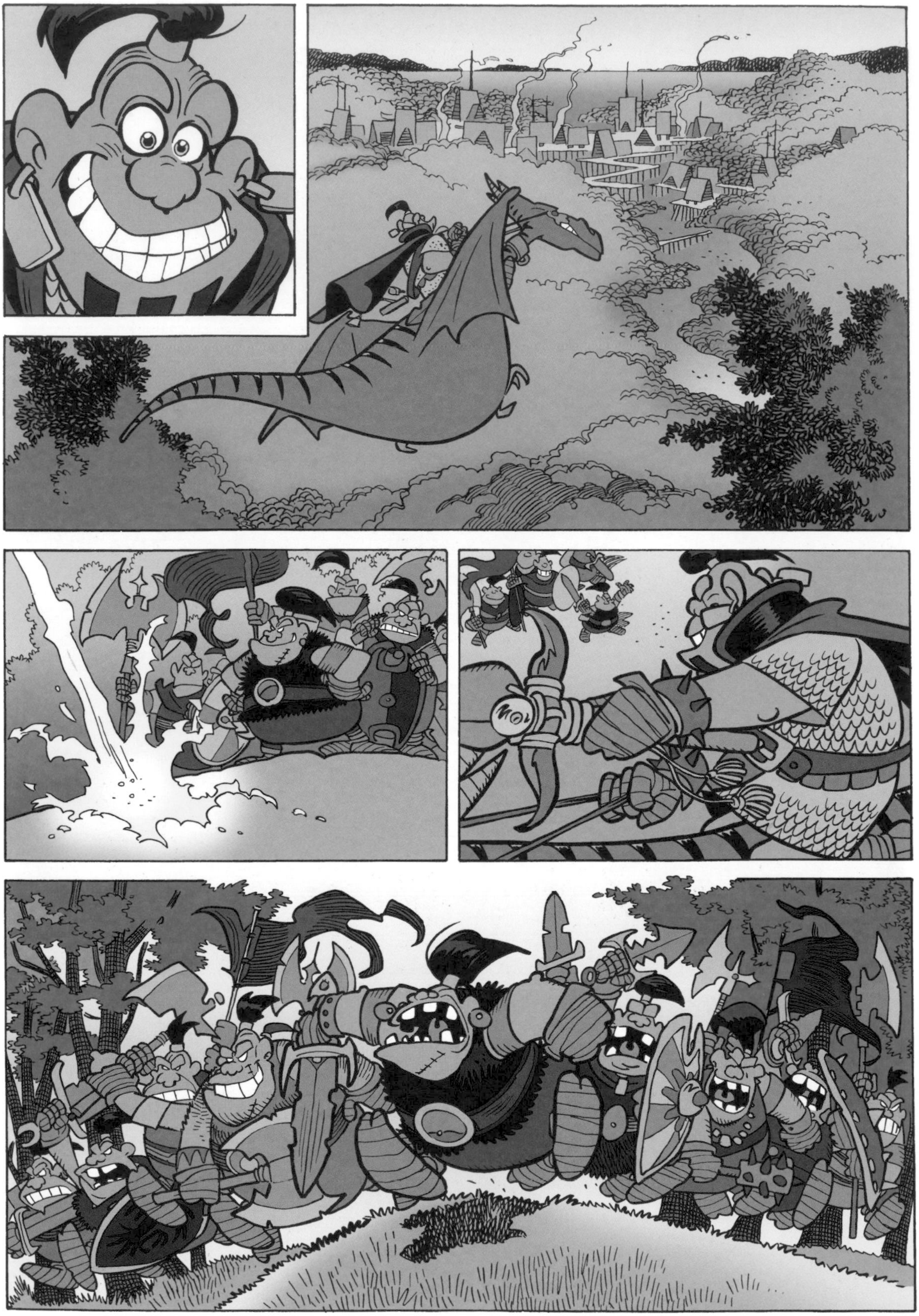

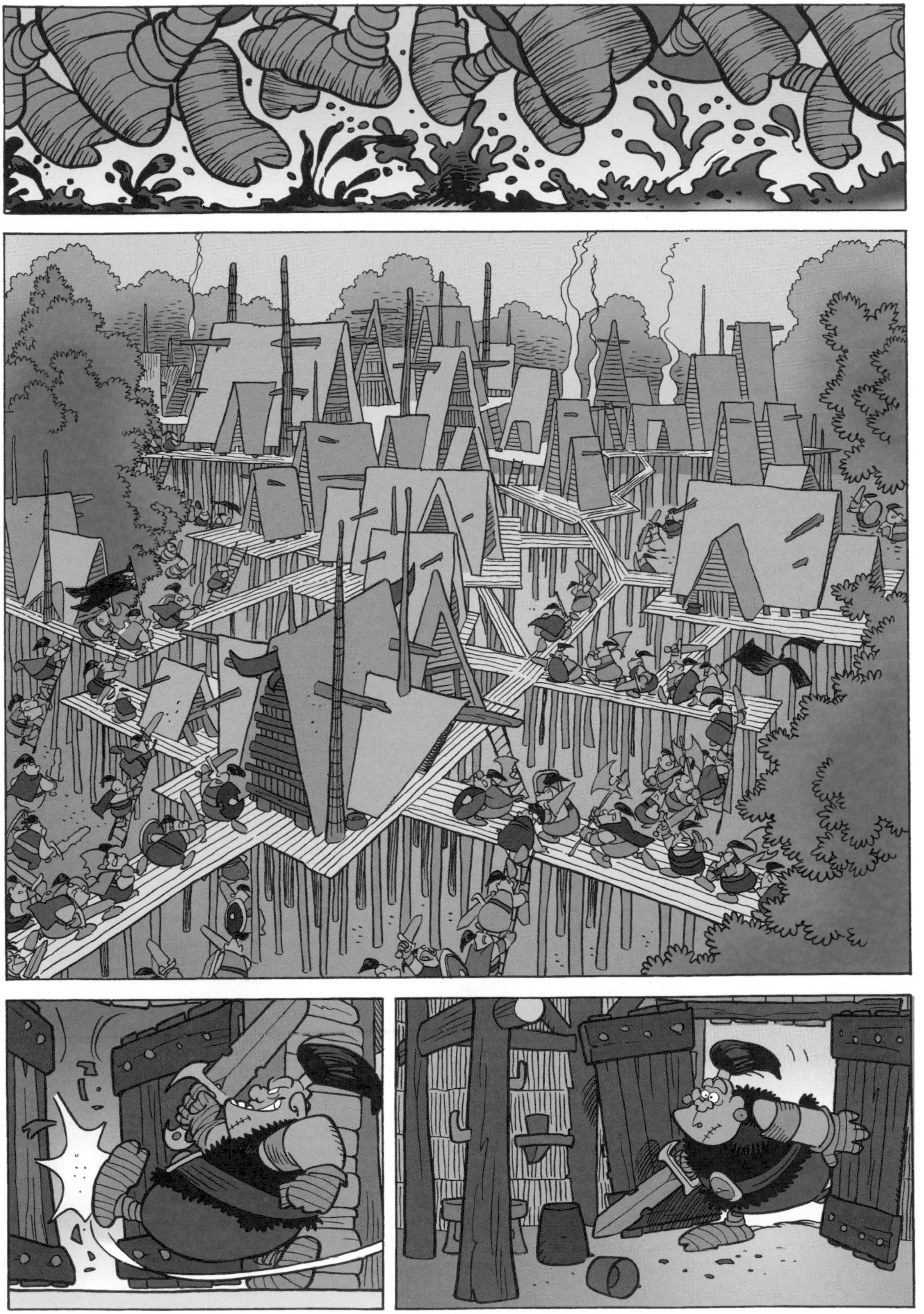

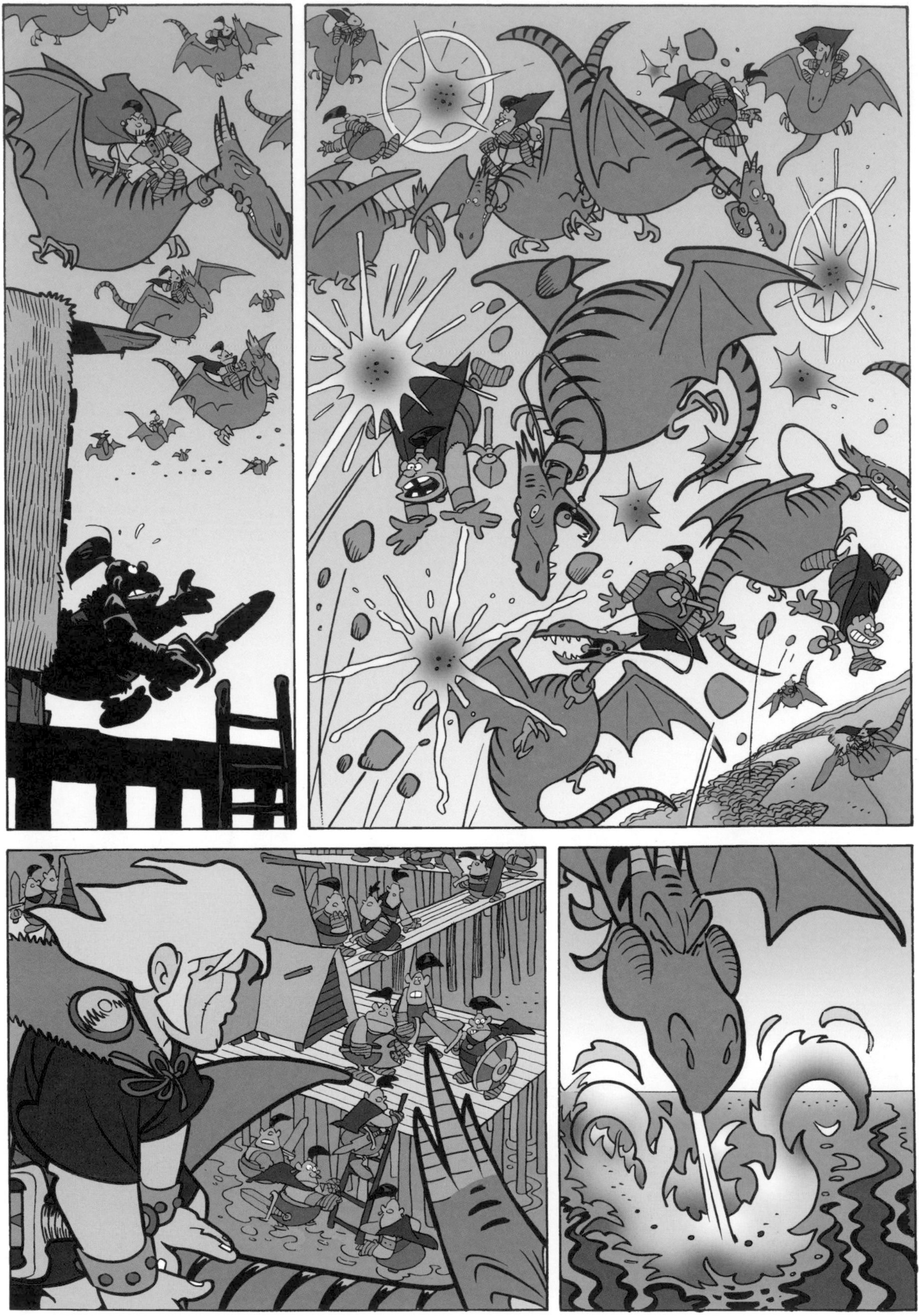

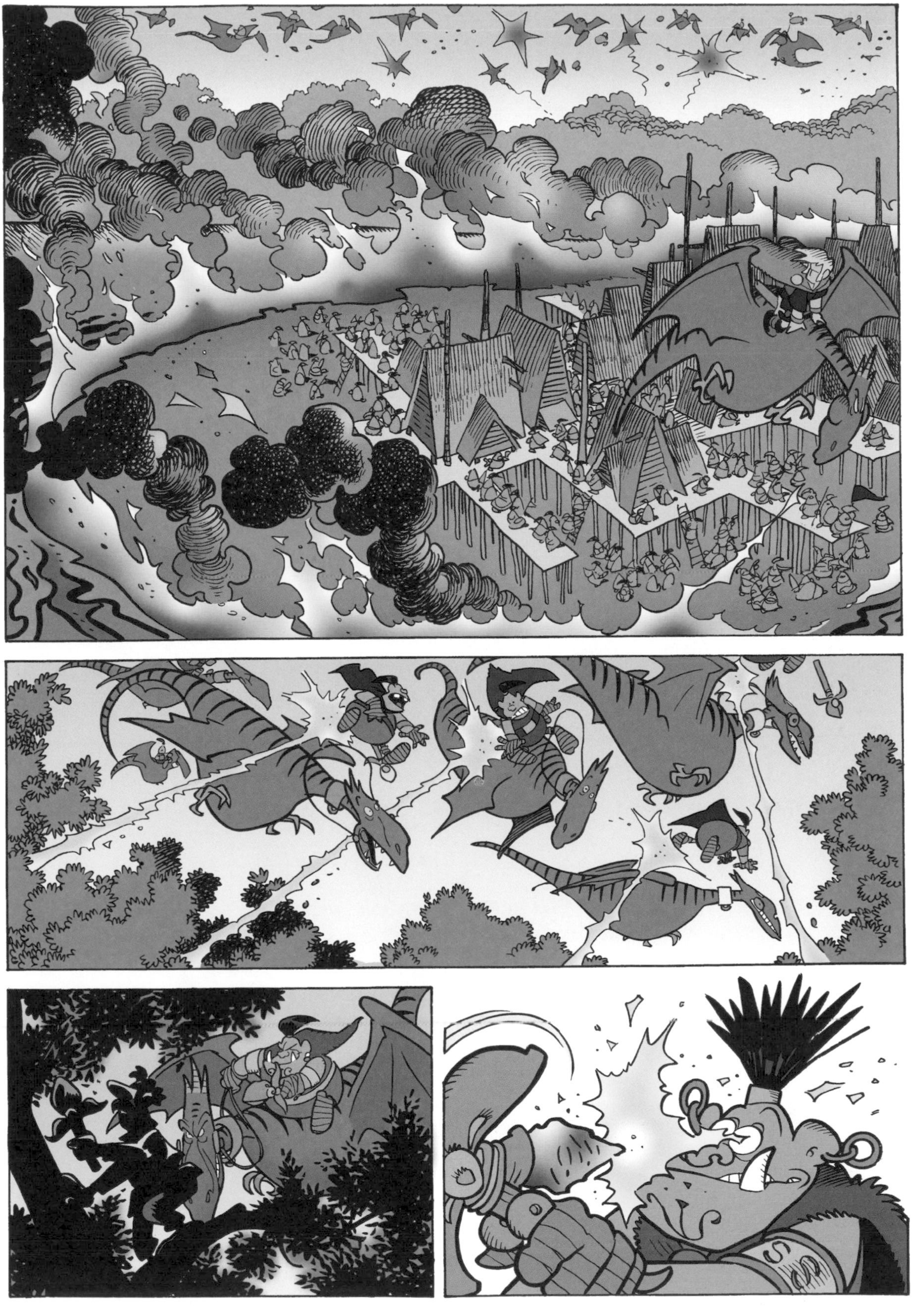

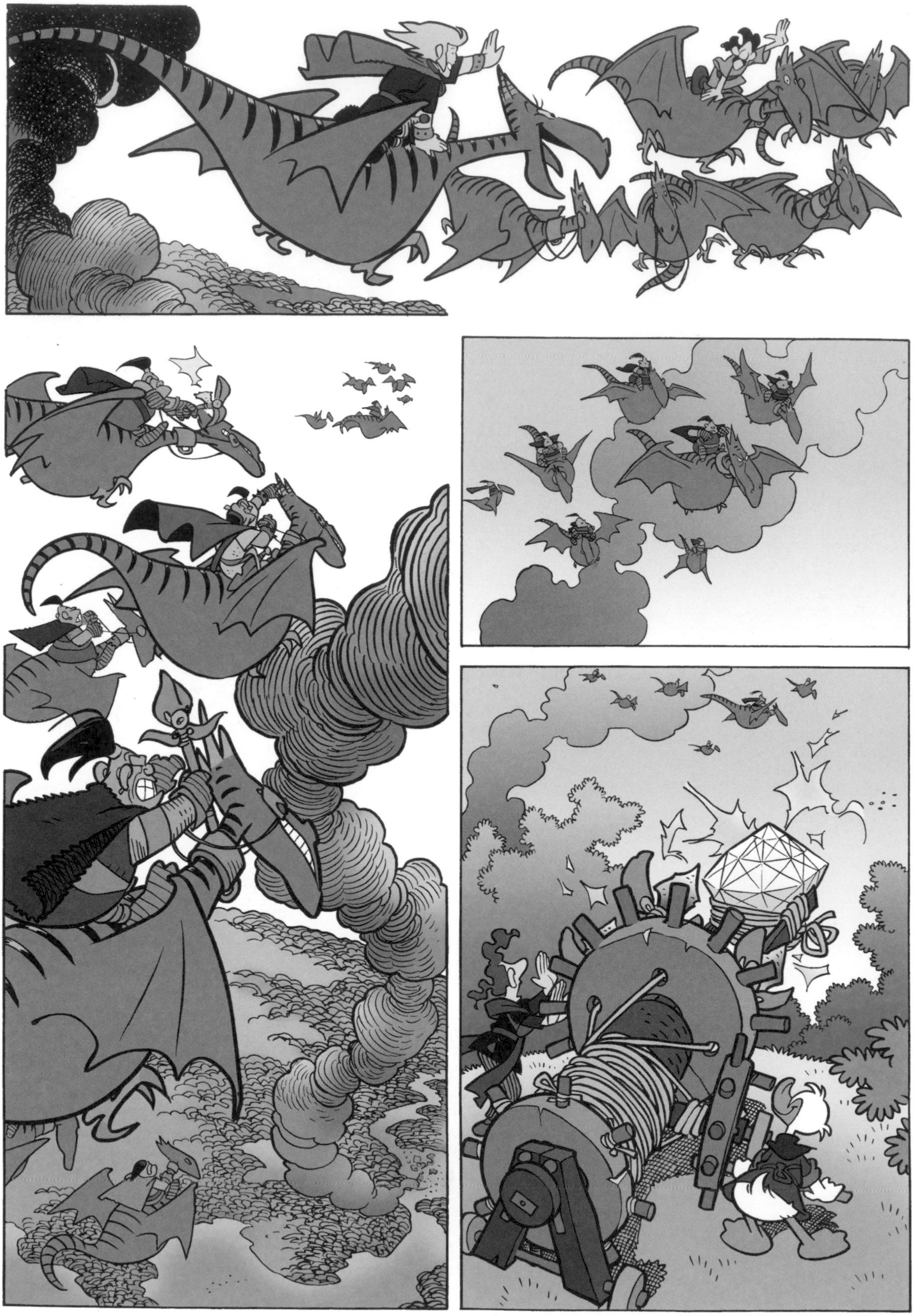

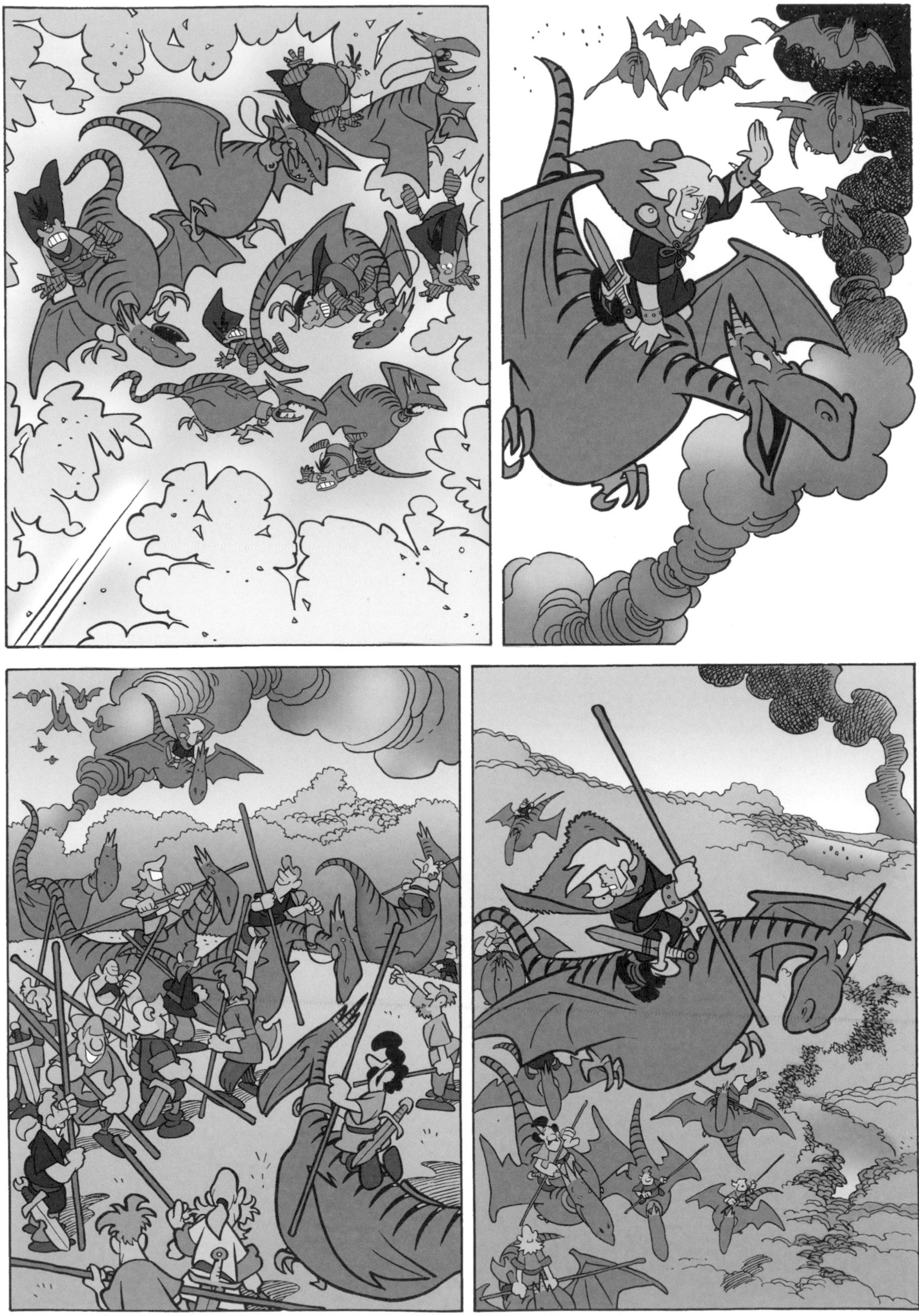

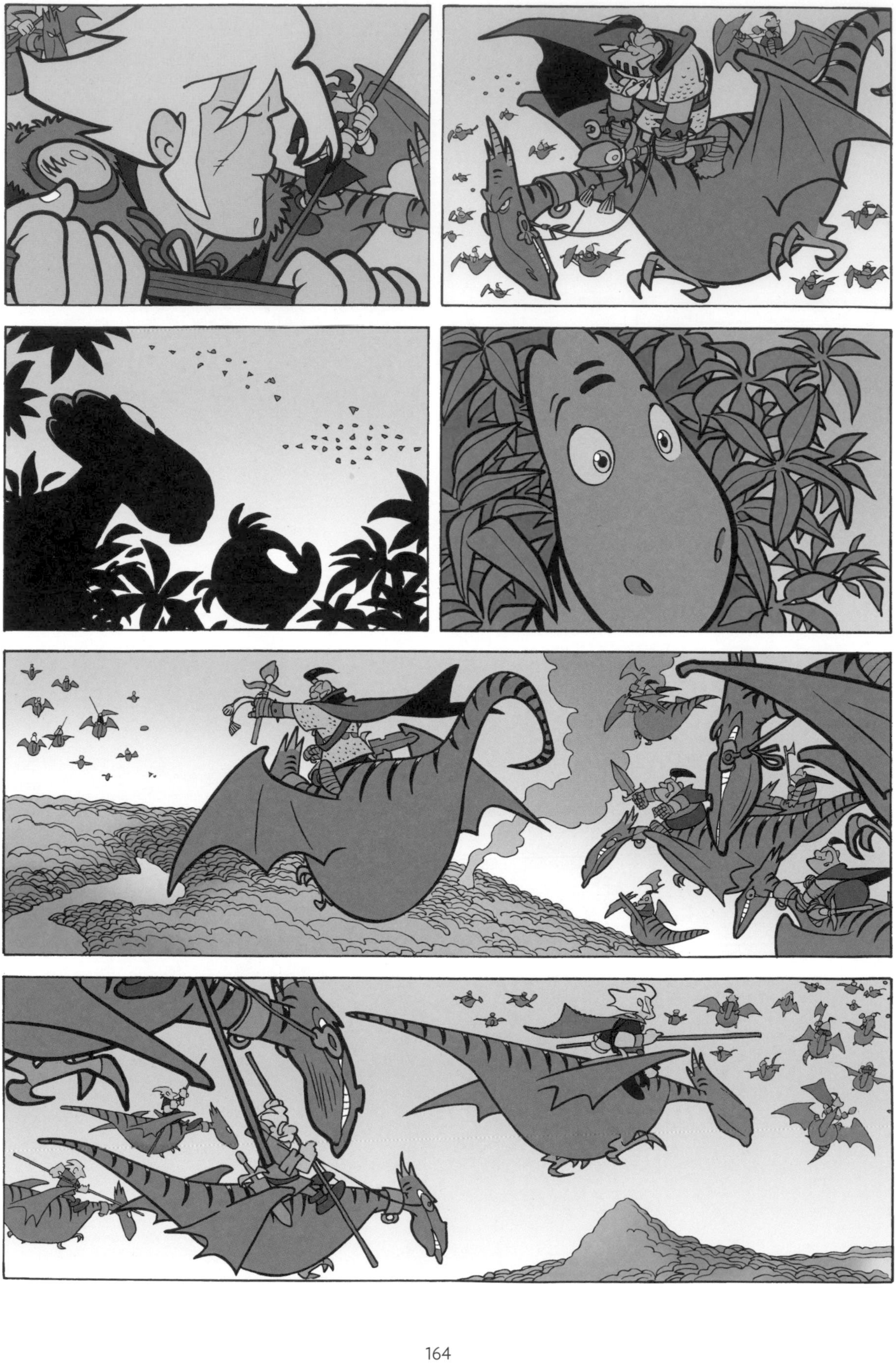

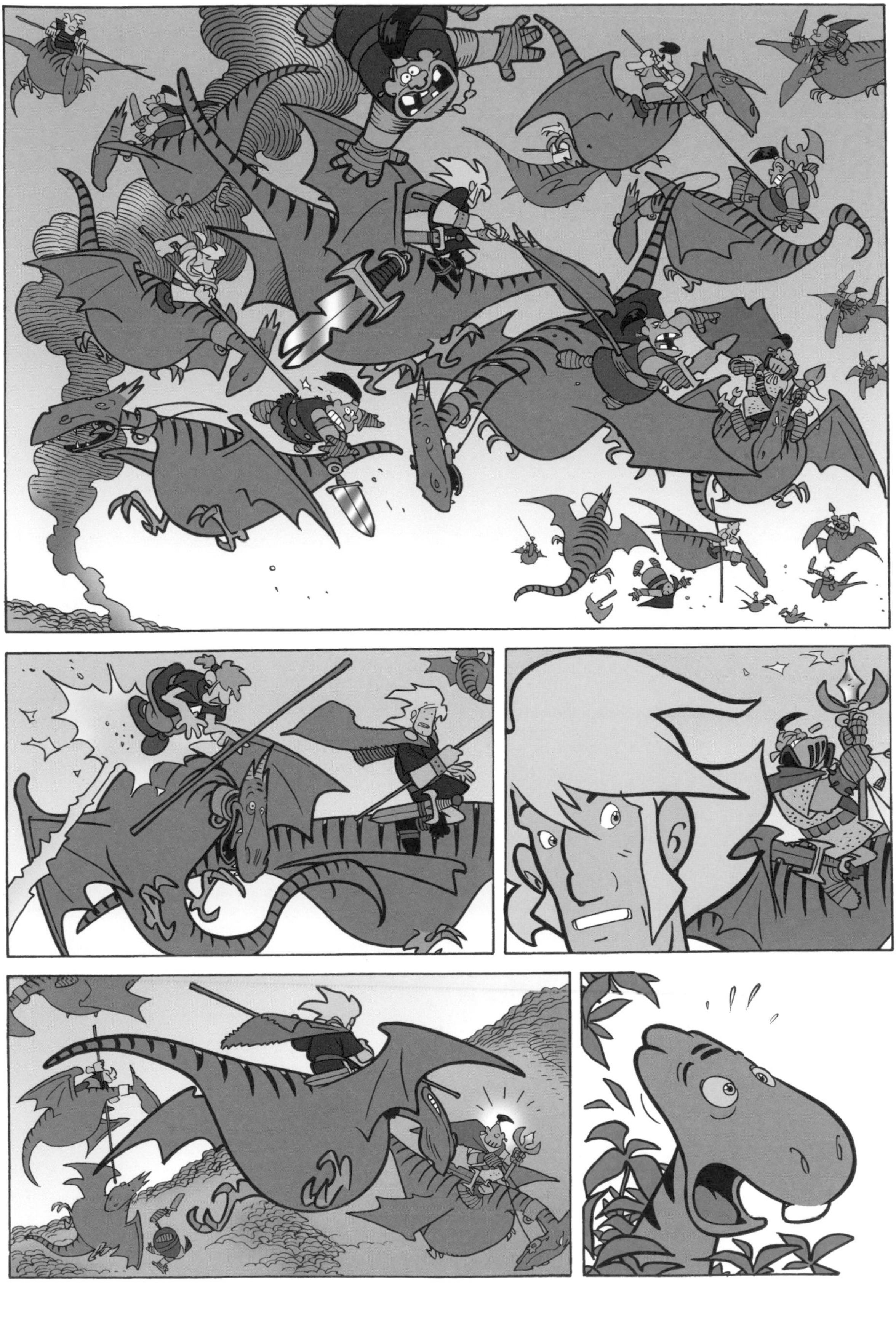

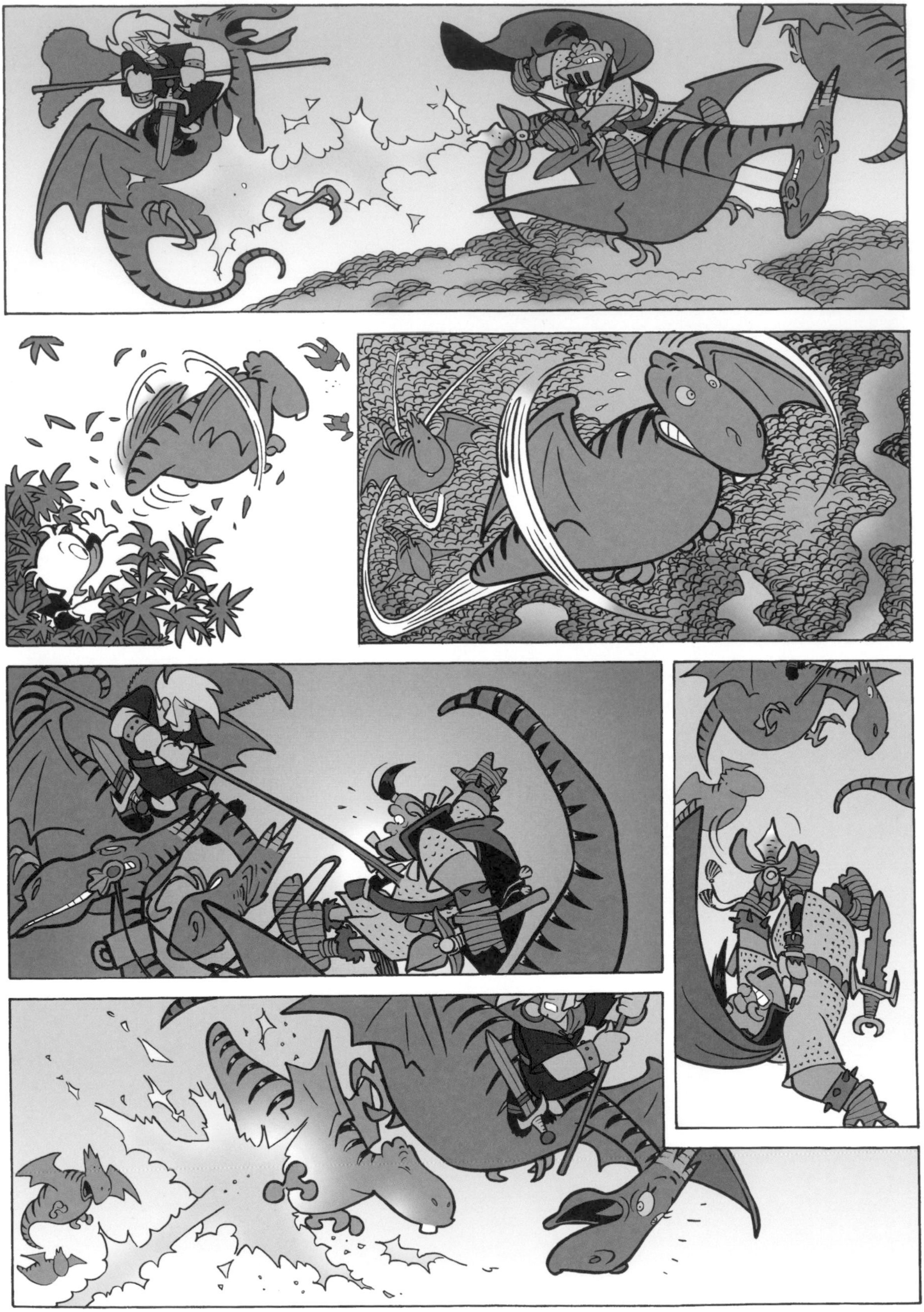

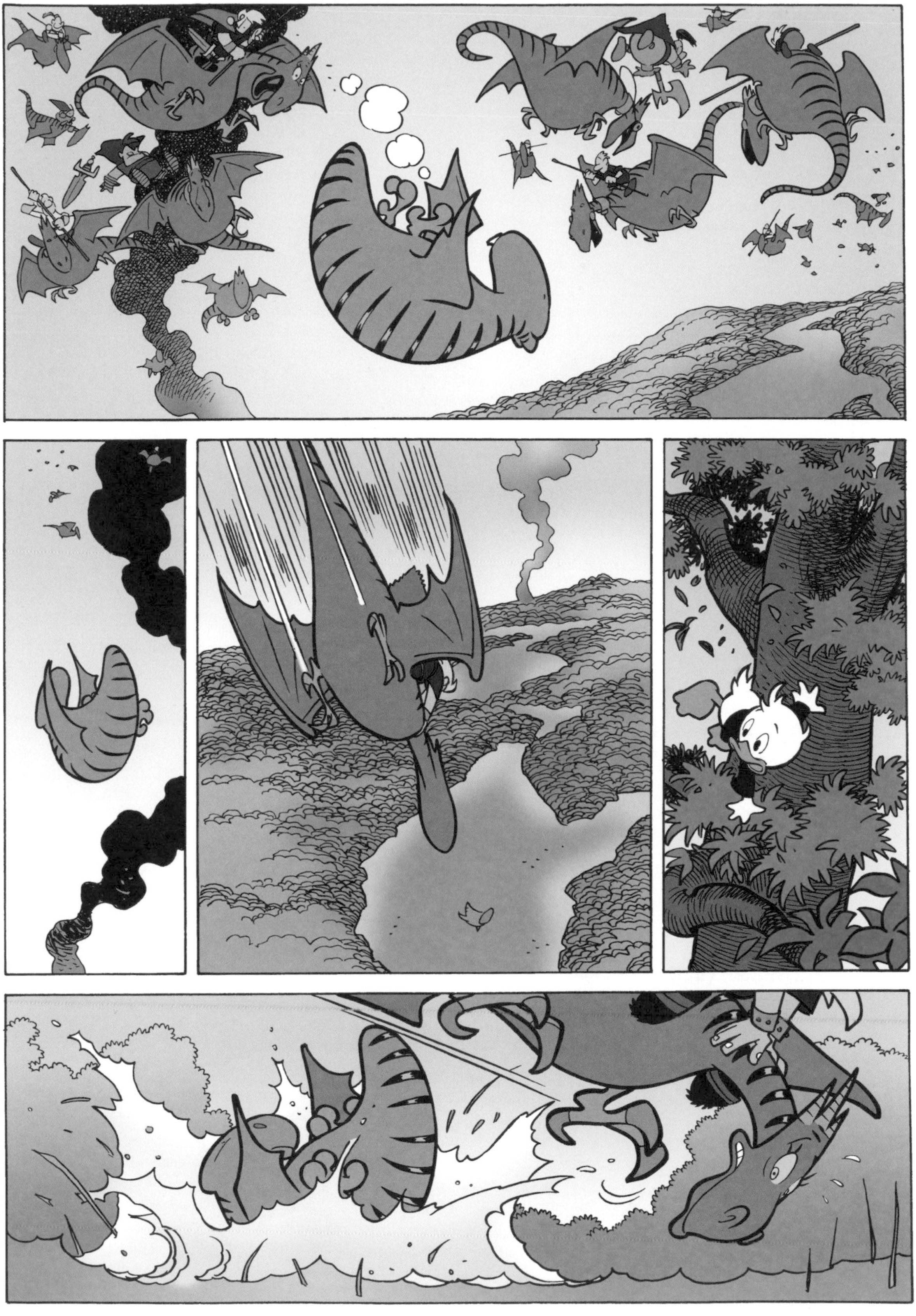

SKREEEE!

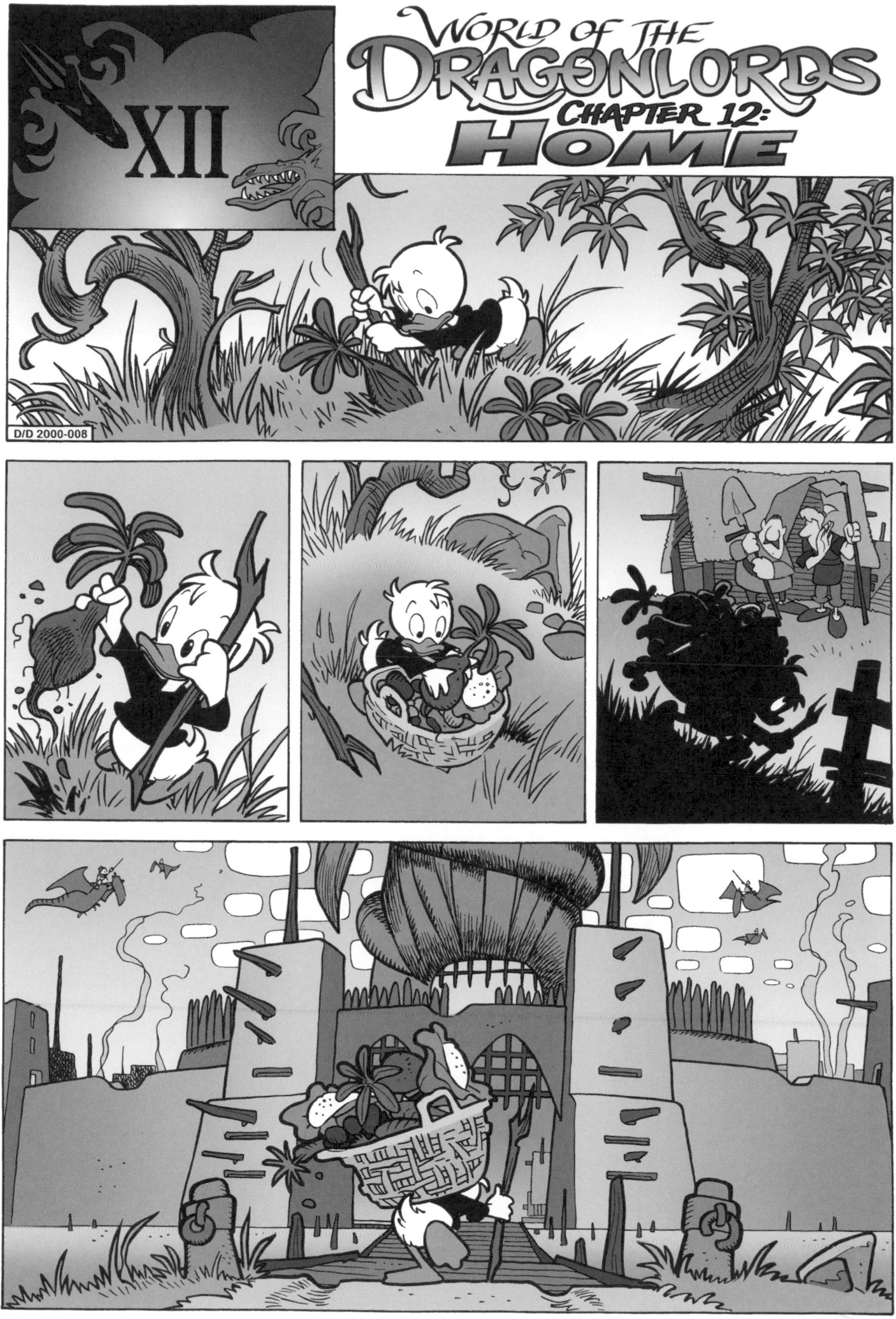
XII
World of the Dragonlords
Chapter 12:
Home
D/D 2000-008

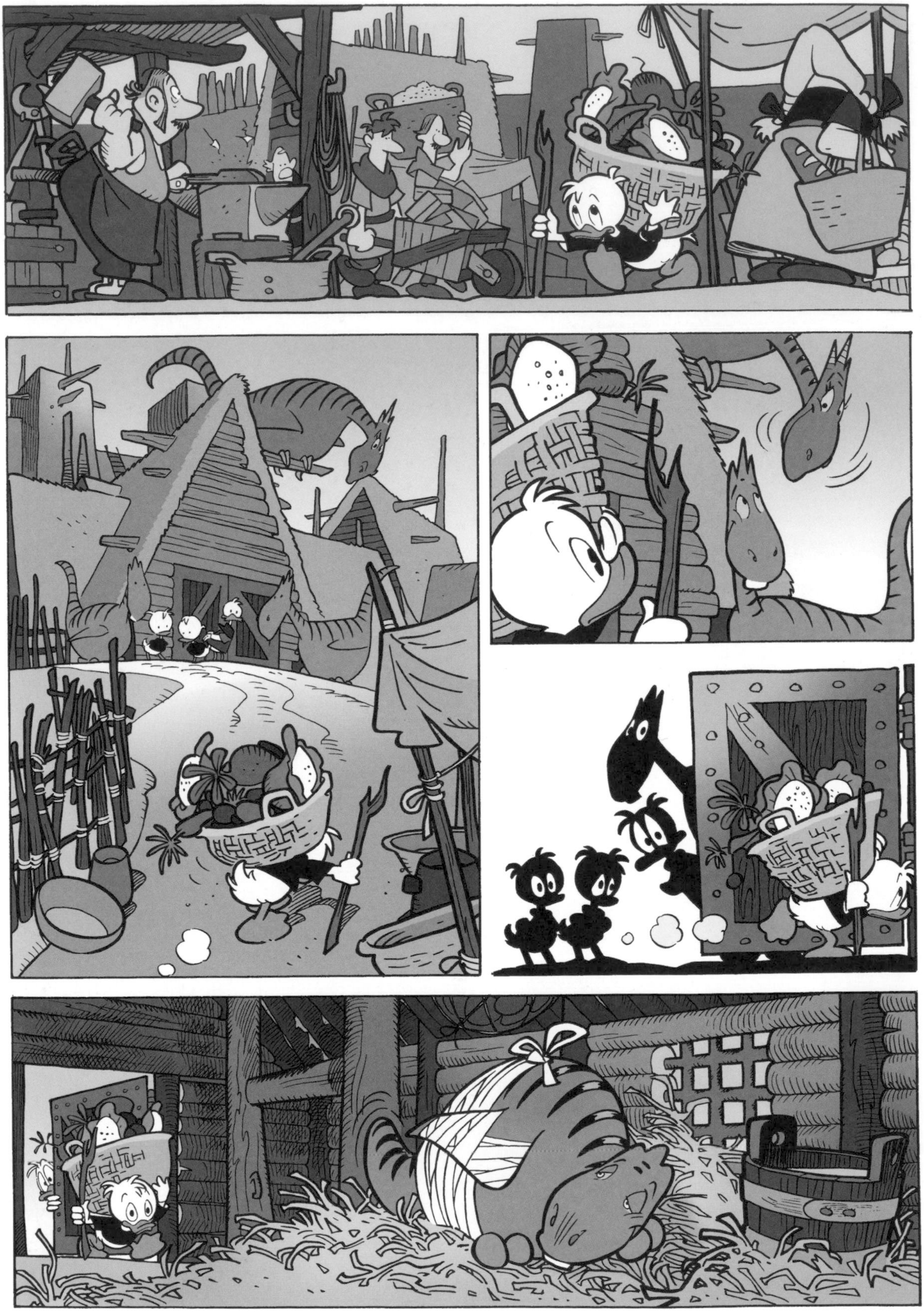

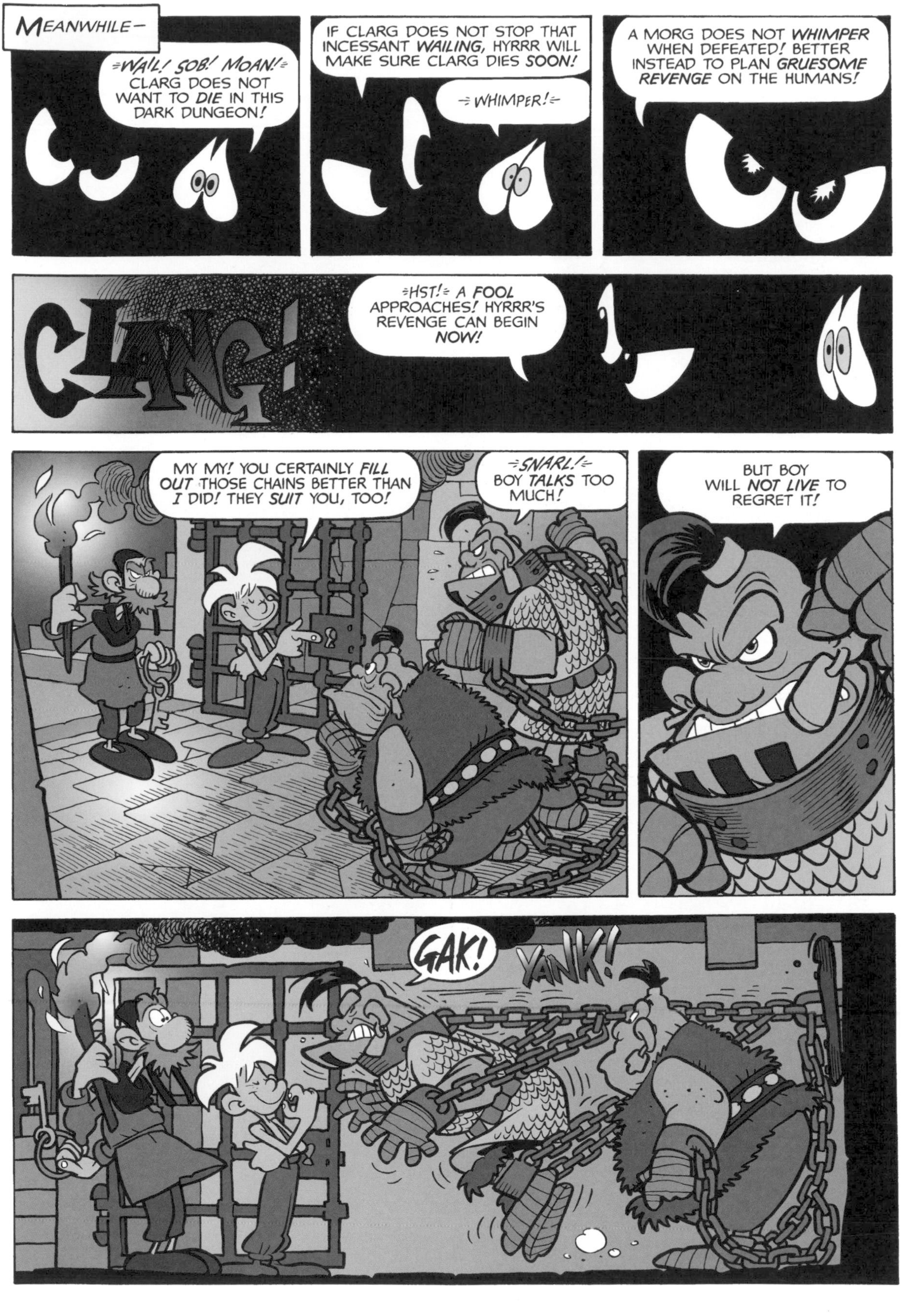
MEANWHILE–
WAIL! SOB! MOAN! CLARG DOES NOT WANT TO DIE IN THIS DARK DUNGEON!
IF CLARG DOES NOT STOP THAT INCESSANT WAILING, HYRRR WILL MAKE SURE CLARG DIES SOON!
WHIMPER!
A MORG DOES NOT WHIMPER WHEN DEFEATED! BETTER INSTEAD TO PLAN GRUESOME REVENGE ON THE HUMANS!
CLANG!
HST! A FOOL APPROACHES! HYRRR'S REVENGE CAN BEGIN NOW!
MY MY! YOU CERTAINLY FILL OUT THOSE CHAINS BETTER THAN I DID! THEY SUIT YOU, TOO!
SNARL! BOY TALKS TOO MUCH!
BUT BOY WILL NOT LIVE TO REGRET IT!
GAK!
YANK!

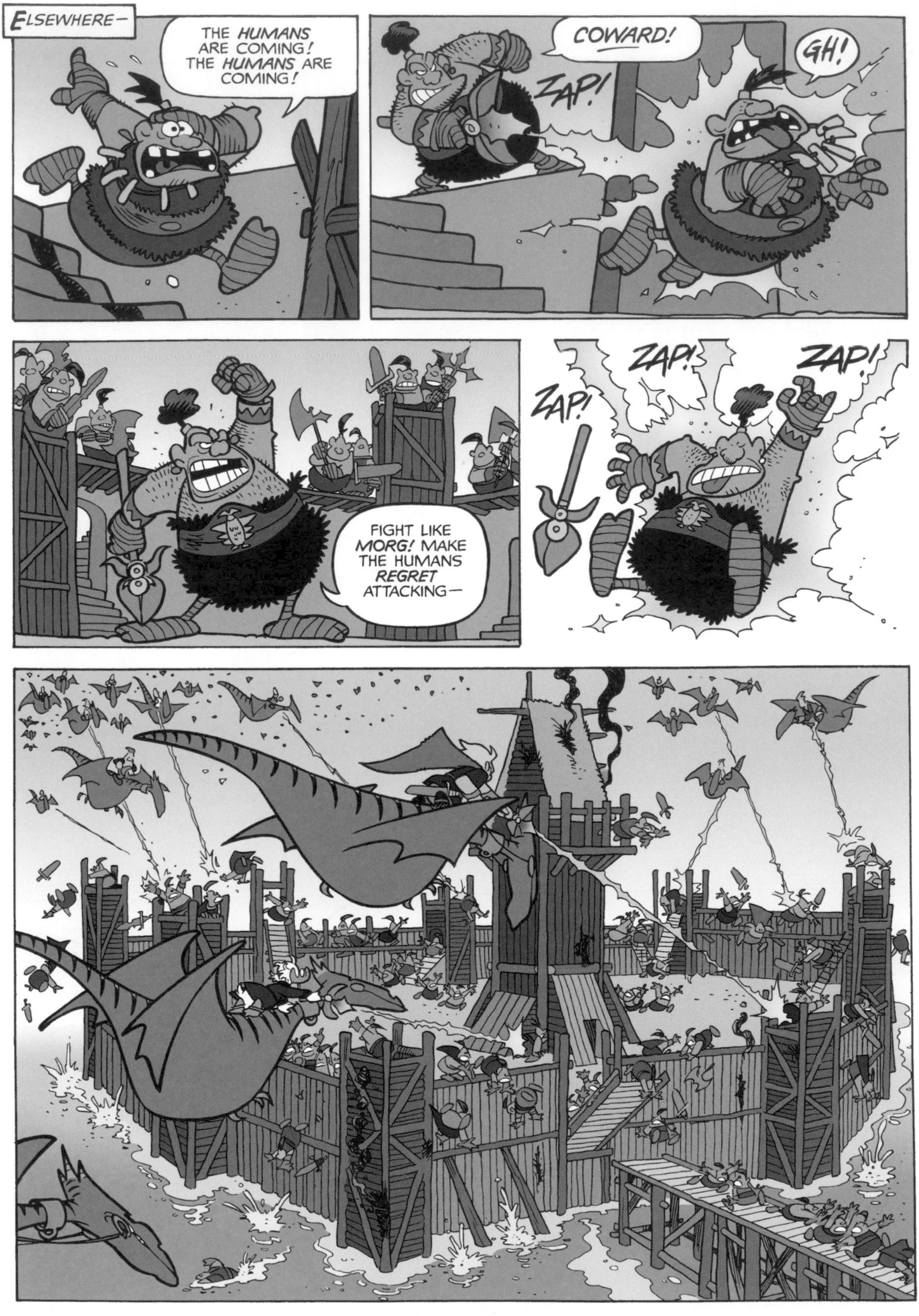

ELSEWHERE—
THE HUMANS ARE COMING! THE HUMANS ARE COMING!
COWARD!
ZAP!
GH!
FIGHT LIKE MORG! MAKE THE HUMANS REGRET ATTACKING—
ZAP!
ZAP!
ZAP!

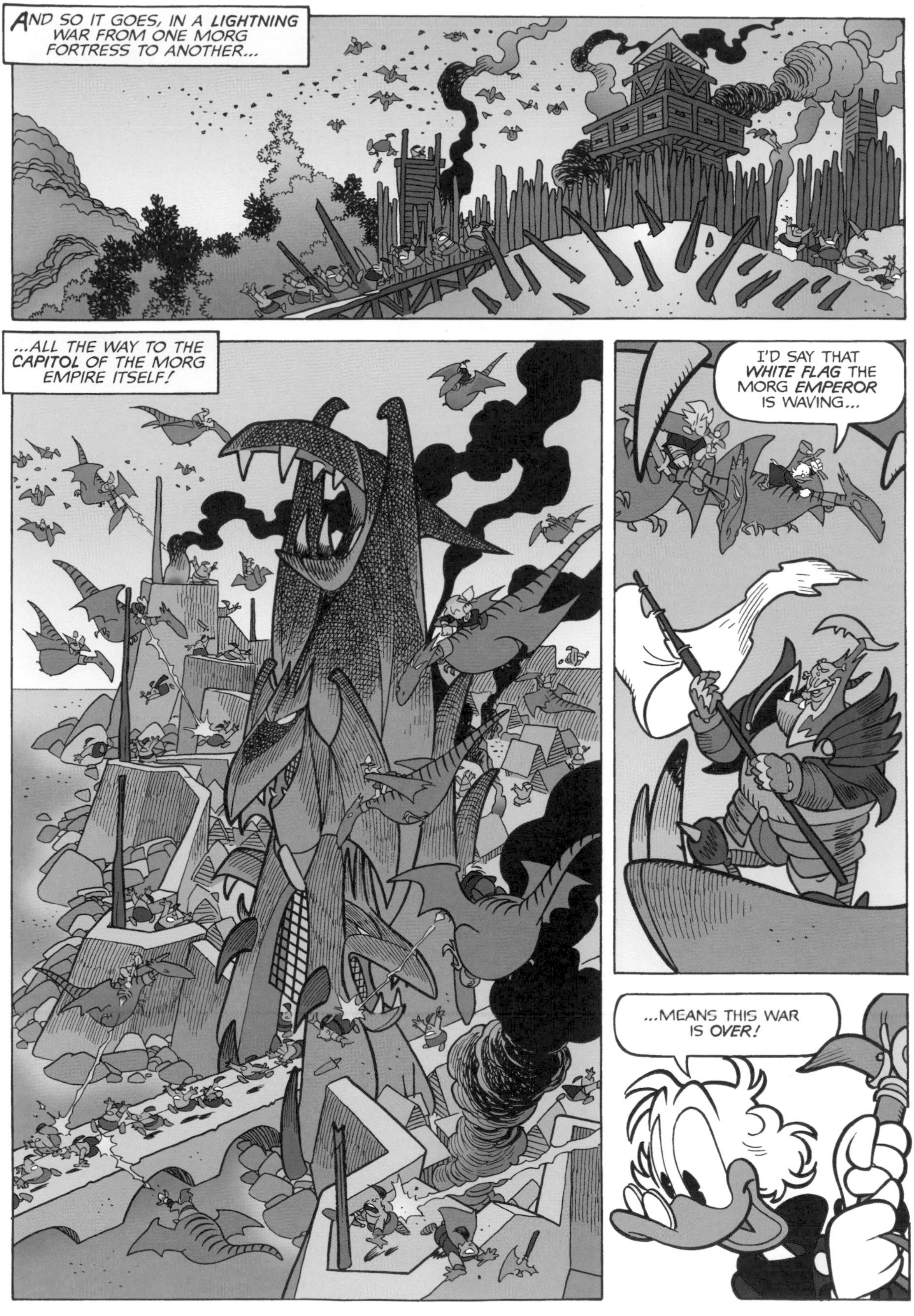
AND SO IT GOES, IN A LIGHTNING WAR FROM ONE MORG FORTRESS TO ANOTHER...
...ALL THE WAY TO THE CAPITOL OF THE MORG EMPIRE ITSELF!
I'D SAY THAT WHITE FLAG THE MORG EMPEROR IS WAVING...
...MEANS THIS WAR IS OVER!

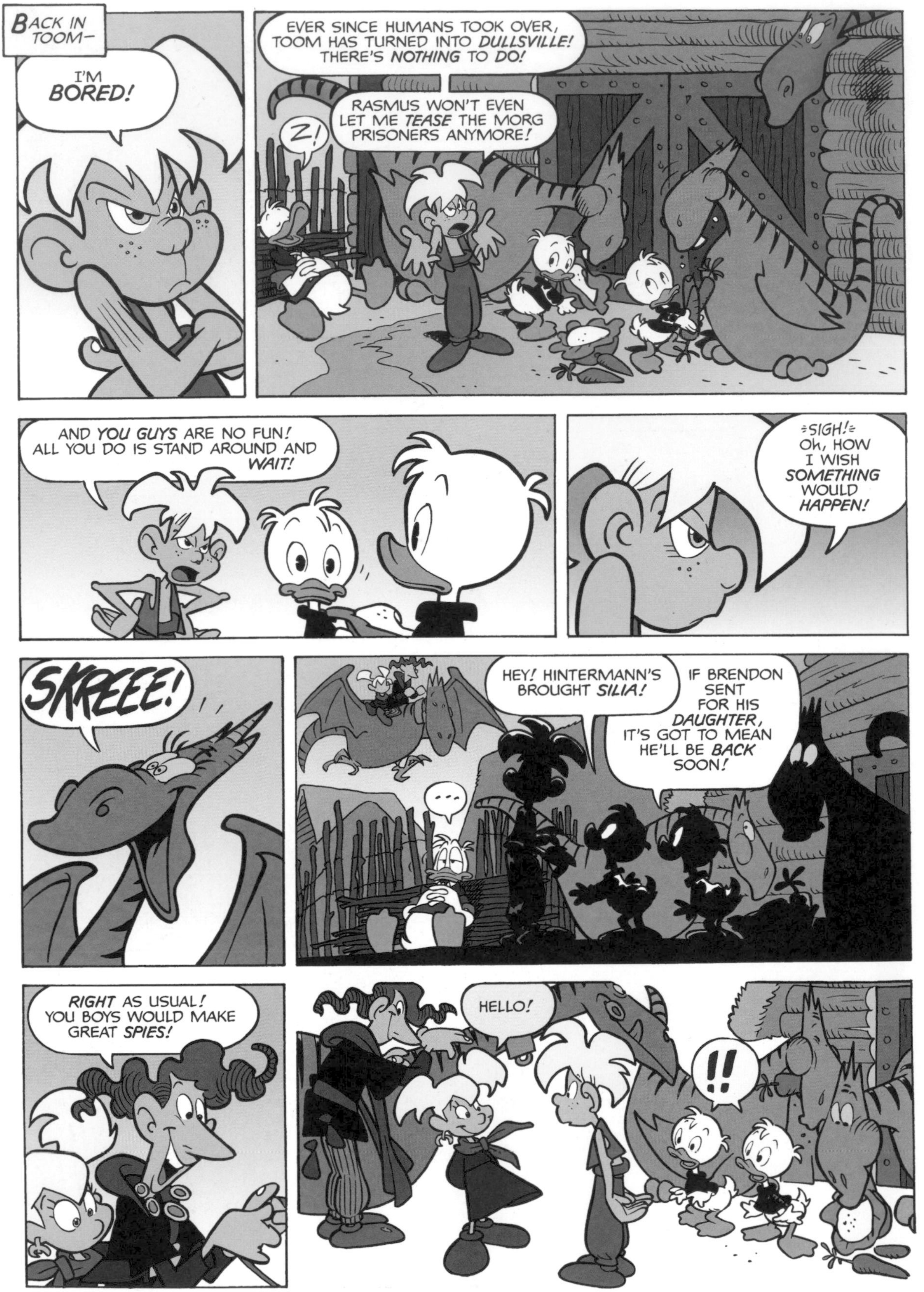

BACK IN TOOM—
I'M BORED!
EVER SINCE HUMANS TOOK OVER, TOOM HAS TURNED INTO DULLSVILLE! THERE'S NOTHING TO DO!
RASMUS WON'T EVEN LET ME TEASE THE MORG PRISONERS ANYMORE!
Z!
AND YOU GUYS ARE NO FUN! ALL YOU DO IS STAND AROUND AND WAIT!
SIGH! Oh, HOW I WISH SOMETHING WOULD HAPPEN!
SKREEE!
HEY! HINTERMANN'S BROUGHT SILIA!
IF BRENDON SENT FOR HIS DAUGHTER, IT'S GOT TO MEAN HE'LL BE BACK SOON!
...
RIGHT AS USUAL! YOU BOYS WOULD MAKE GREAT SPIES!
HELLO!
!!

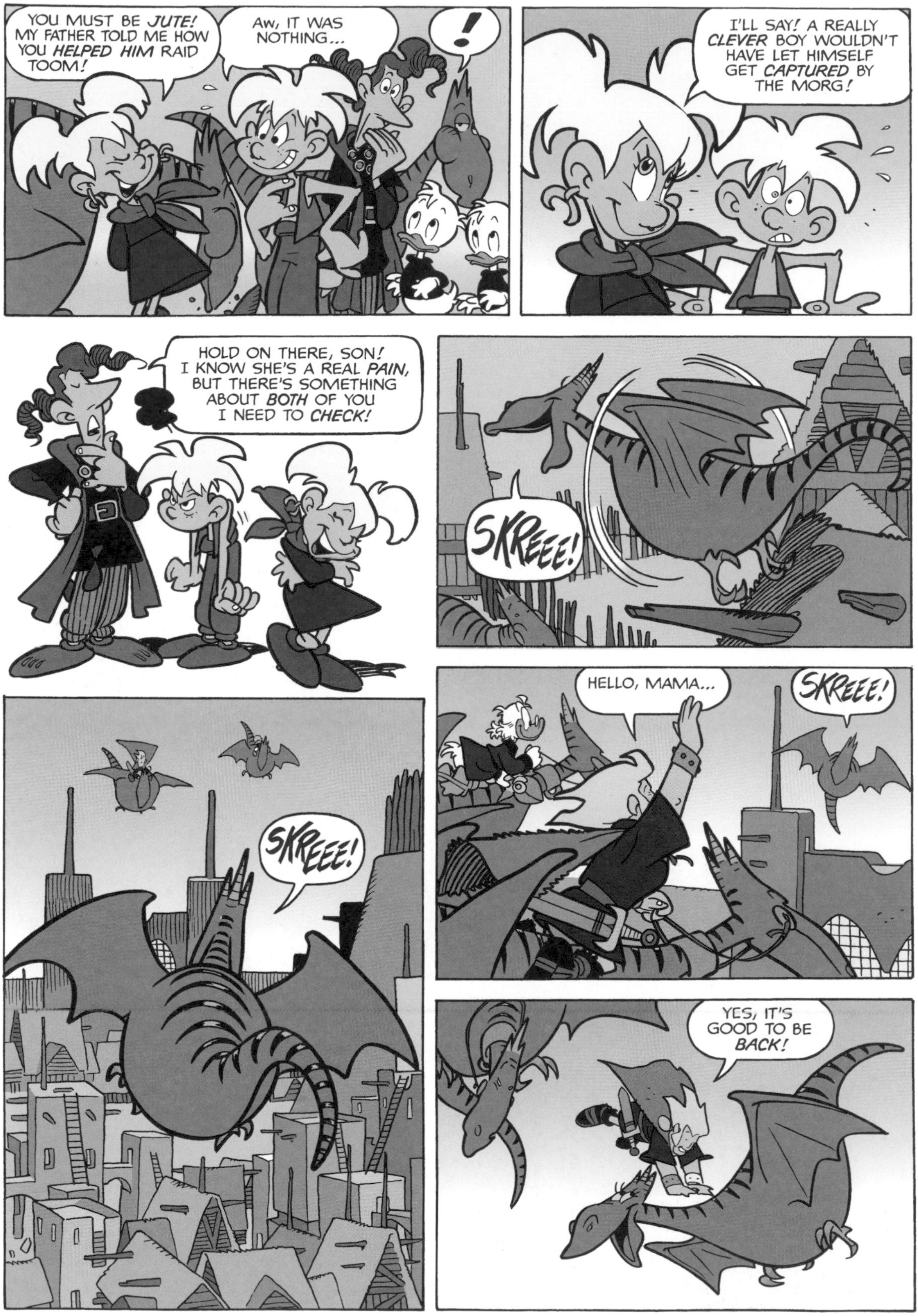

YOU MUST BE JUTE! MY FATHER TOLD ME HOW YOU HELPED HIM RAID TOOM!
AW, IT WAS NOTHING...
!
I'LL SAY! A REALLY CLEVER BOY WOULDN'T HAVE LET HIMSELF GET CAPTURED BY THE MORG!
HOLD ON THERE, SON! I KNOW SHE'S A REAL PAIN, BUT THERE'S SOMETHING ABOUT BOTH OF YOU I NEED TO CHECK!
SKREEE!
SKREEE!
HELLO, MAMA...
SKREEE!
YES, IT'S GOOD TO BE BACK!

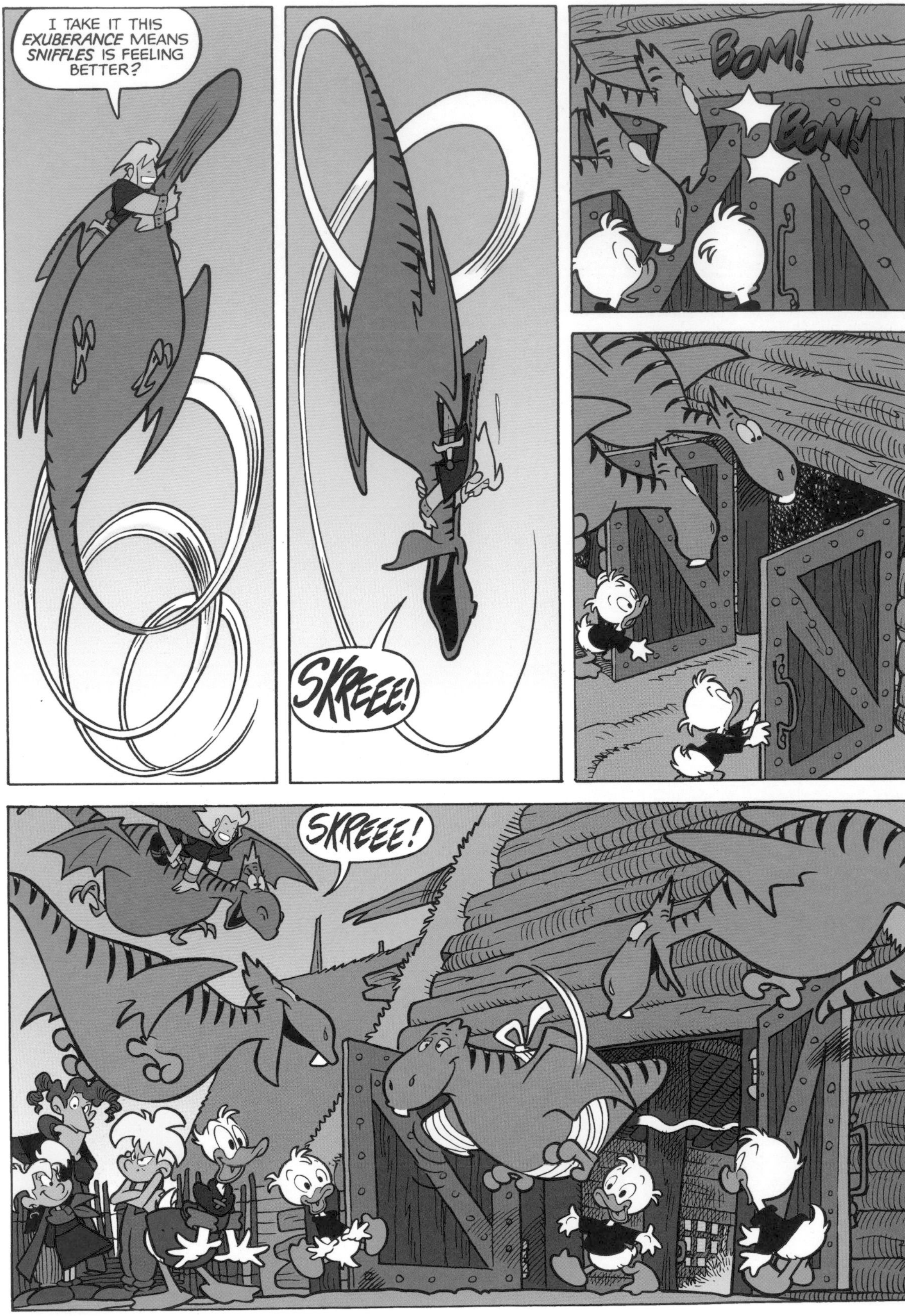
I TAKE IT THIS EXUBERANCE MEANS SNIFFLES IS FEELING BETTER?
SKREEE!
BOM!
BOM!
SKREEE!

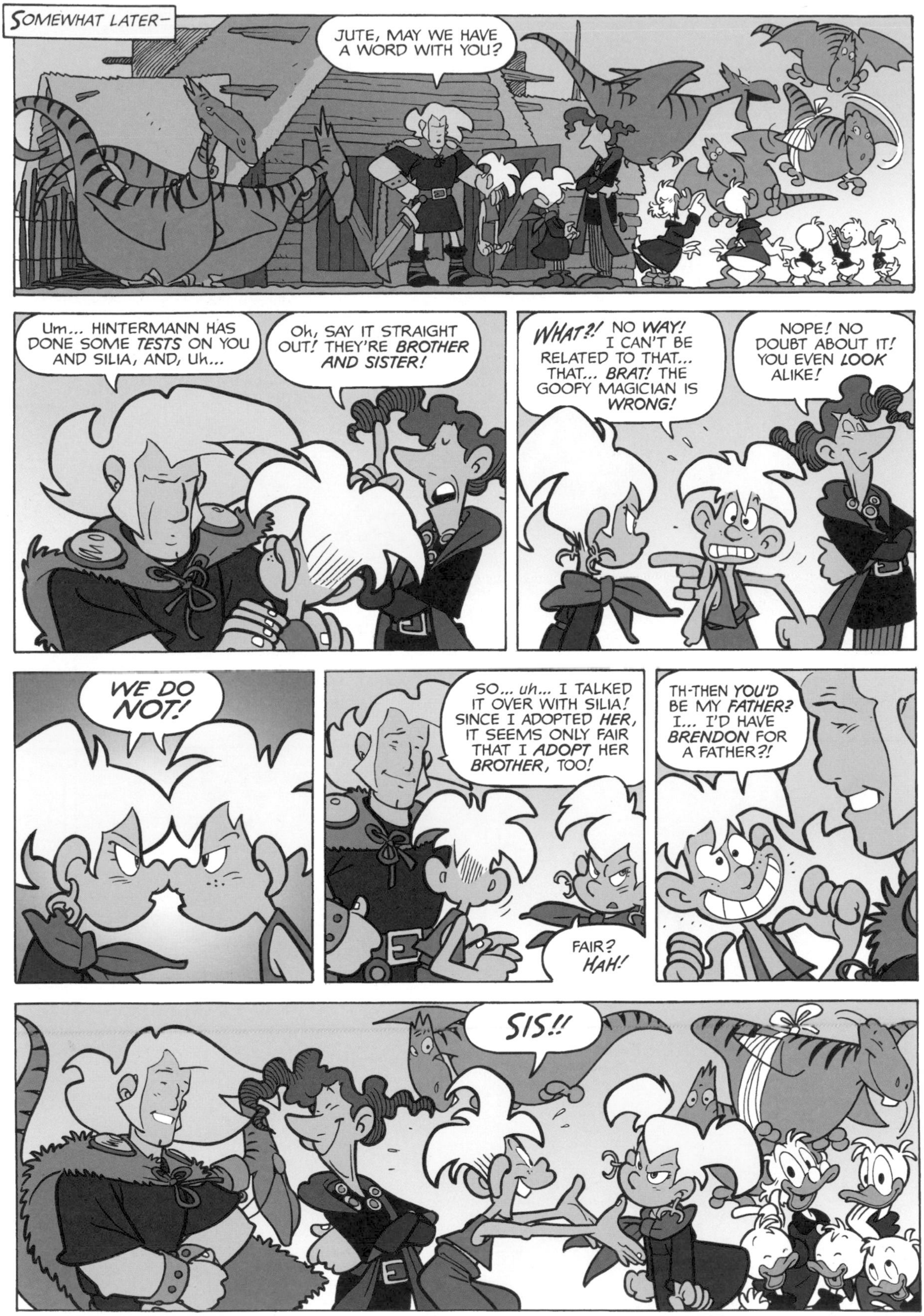
SOMEWHAT LATER—
JUTE, MAY WE HAVE A WORD WITH YOU?
Um... HINTERMANN HAS DONE SOME TESTS ON YOU AND SILIA, AND, Uh...
Oh, SAY IT STRAIGHT OUT! THEY'RE BROTHER AND SISTER!
WHAT?! NO WAY! I CAN'T BE RELATED TO THAT... THAT... BRAT! THE GOOFY MAGICIAN IS WRONG!
NOPE! NO DOUBT ABOUT IT! YOU EVEN LOOK ALIKE!
WE DO NOT!
SO... uh... I TALKED IT OVER WITH SILIA! SINCE I ADOPTED HER, IT SEEMS ONLY FAIR THAT I ADOPT HER BROTHER, TOO!
FAIR? HAH!
TH-THEN YOU'D BE MY FATHER? I... I'D HAVE BRENDON FOR A FATHER?!
SIS!!

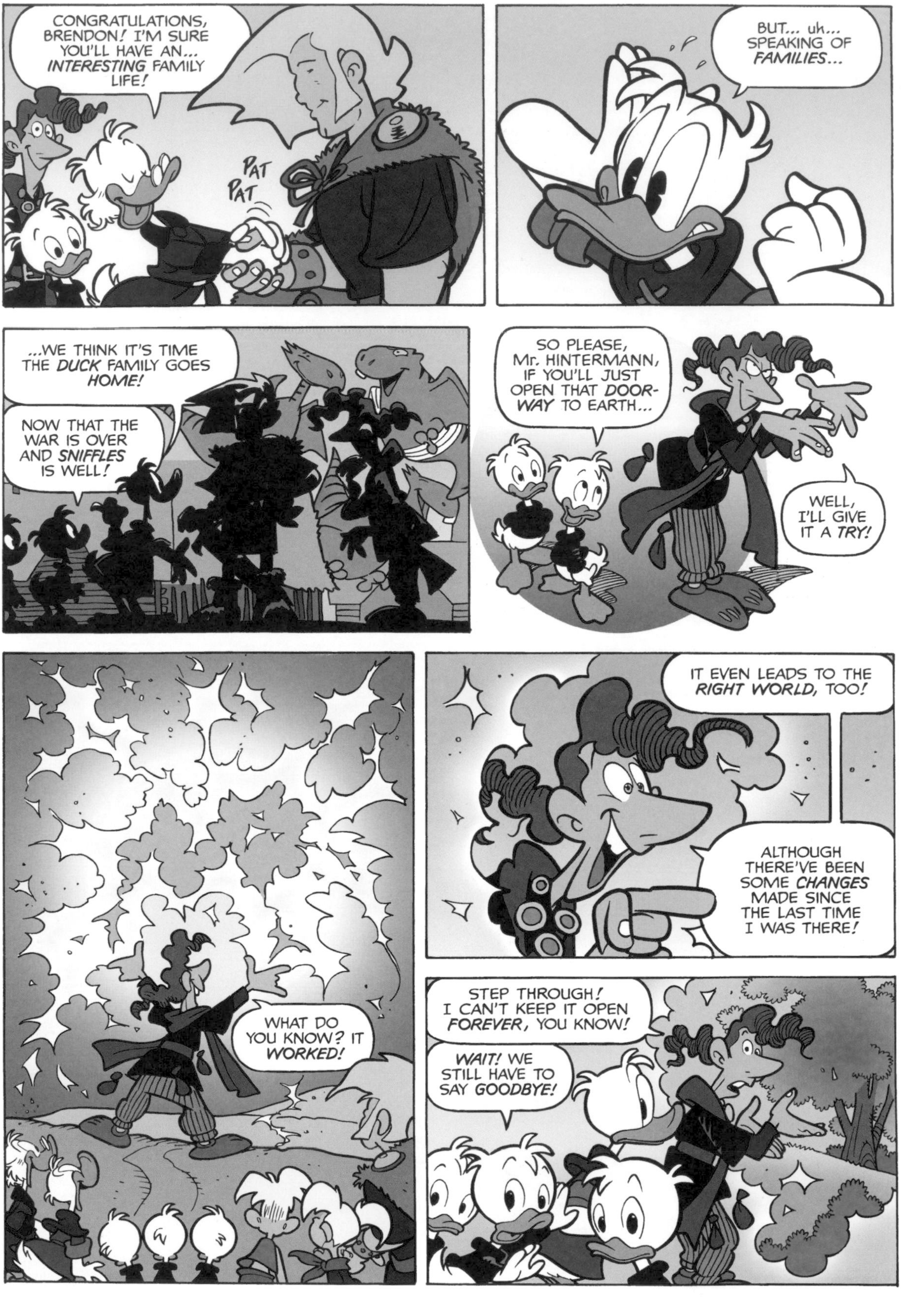

CONGRATULATIONS, BRENDON! I'M SURE YOU'LL HAVE AN... INTERESTING FAMILY LIFE!
PAT PAT
BUT... uh... SPEAKING OF FAMILIES...
...WE THINK IT'S TIME THE DUCK FAMILY GOES HOME!
NOW THAT THE WAR IS OVER AND SNIFFLES IS WELL!
SO PLEASE, Mr. HINTERMANN, IF YOU'LL JUST OPEN THAT DOORWAY TO EARTH...
WELL, I'LL GIVE IT A TRY!
WHAT DO YOU KNOW? IT WORKED!
IT EVEN LEADS TO THE RIGHT WORLD, TOO!
ALTHOUGH THERE'VE BEEN SOME CHANGES MADE SINCE THE LAST TIME I WAS THERE!
STEP THROUGH! I CAN'T KEEP IT OPEN FOREVER, YOU KNOW!
WAIT! WE STILL HAVE TO SAY GOODBYE!

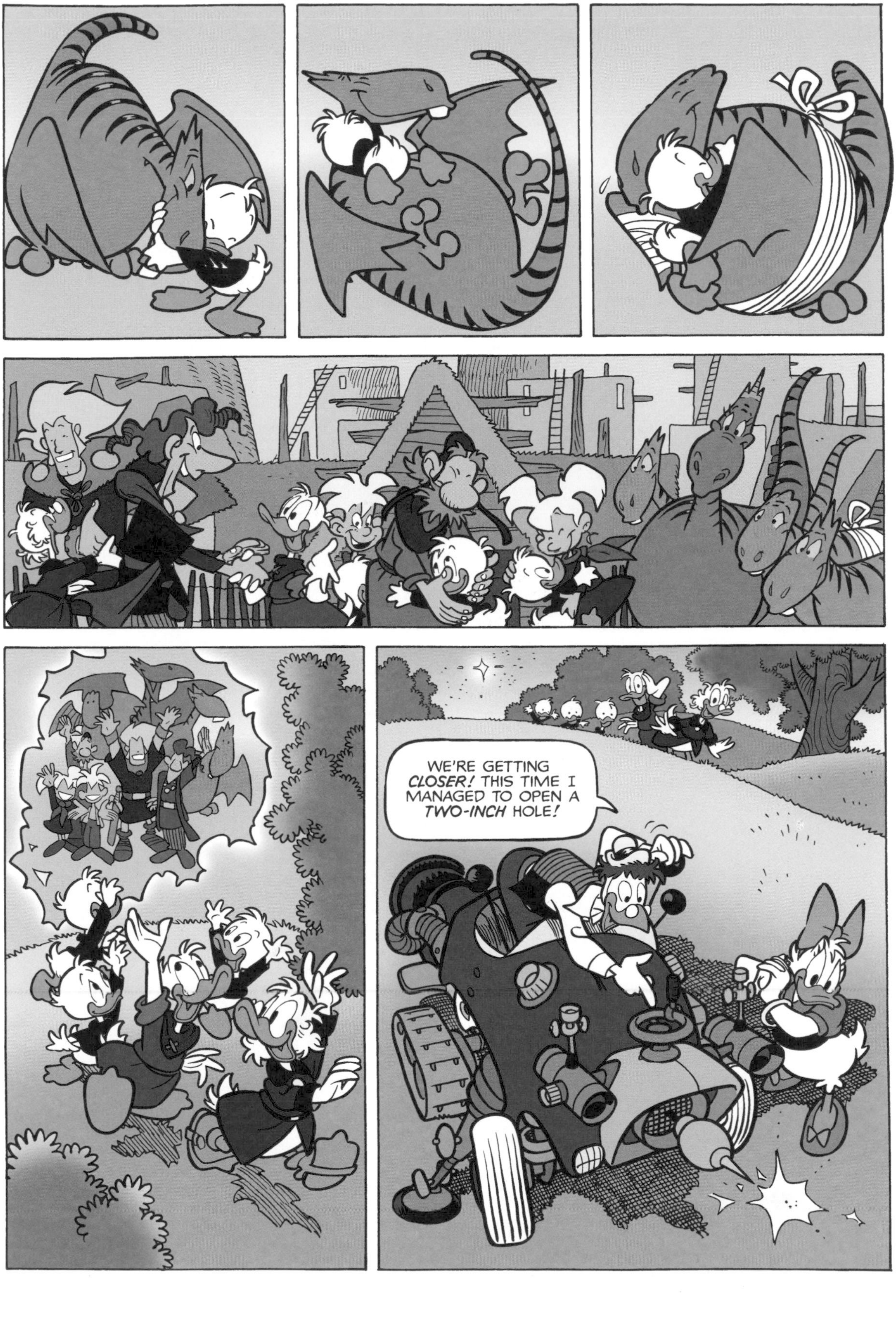
WE'RE GETTING CLOSER! THIS TIME I MANAGED TO OPEN A TWO-INCH HOLE!

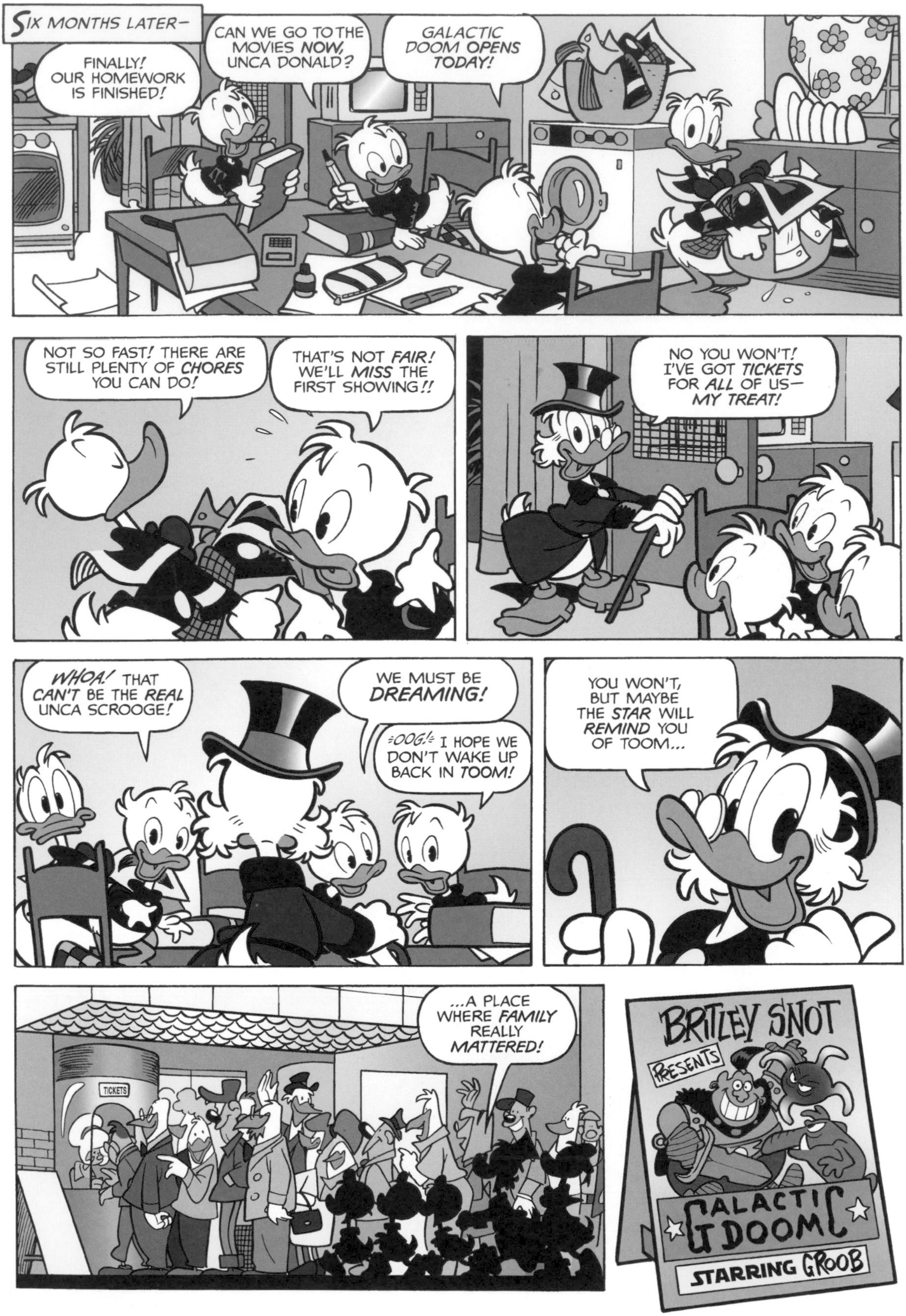
SIX MONTHS LATER—
FINALLY! OUR HOMEWORK IS FINISHED!
CAN WE GO TO THE MOVIES NOW, UNCA DONALD?
GALACTIC DOOM OPENS TODAY!
NOT SO FAST! THERE ARE STILL PLENTY OF CHORES YOU CAN DO!
THAT'S NOT FAIR! WE'LL MISS THE FIRST SHOWING!!
NO YOU WON'T! I'VE GOT TICKETS FOR ALL OF US— MY TREAT!
WHOA! THAT CAN'T BE THE REAL UNCA SCROOGE!
WE MUST BE DREAMING!
OOG! I HOPE WE DON'T WAKE UP BACK IN TOOM!
YOU WON'T, BUT MAYBE THE STAR WILL REMIND YOU OF TOOM...
...A PLACE WHERE FAMILY REALLY MATTERED!
TICKETS
BRITLEY SNOT
PRESENTS
GALACTIC DOOM
STARRING GROOB

Sketches

LORD MORAQ
A model study of the fearsome Morg commander.

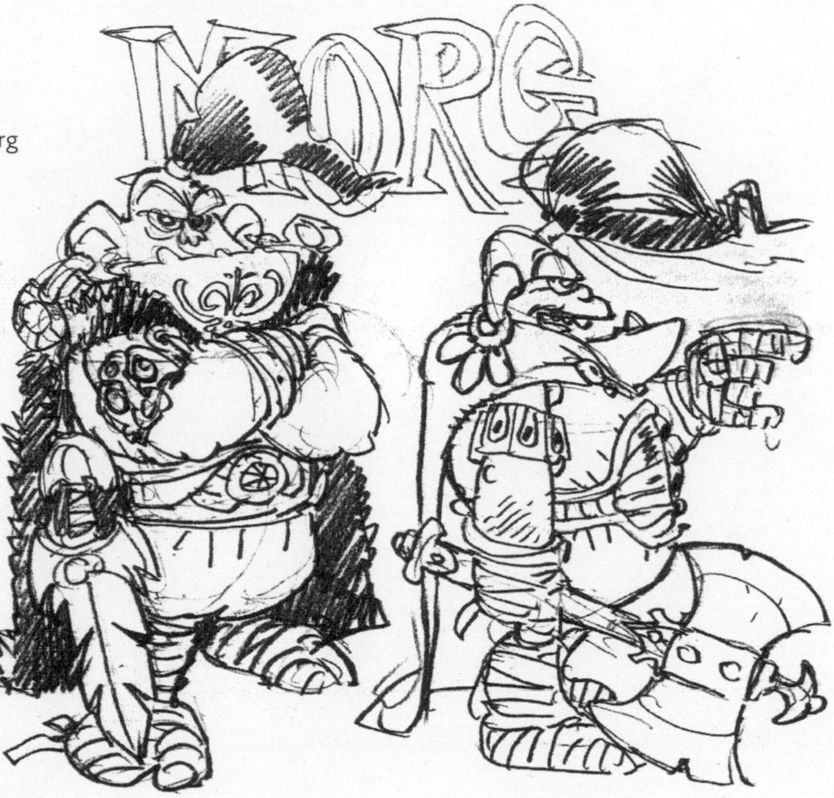
MORG

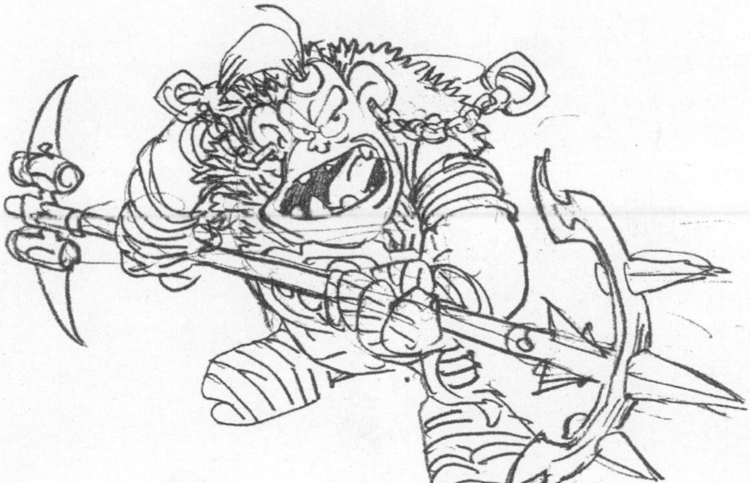

Sketches

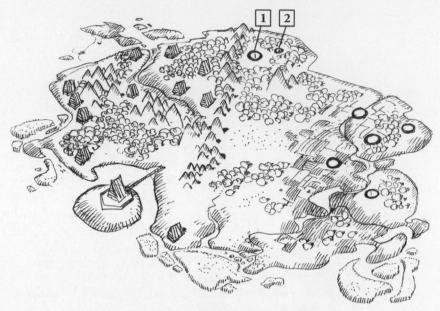

A map of Morgworld, as the Morgs call it. The action in our story takes place on the border between the Morg and human land, near the fortress city of Toom (#1) and Freedom Marsh (#2).

A rough overhead design of Toom, the Morg fortress city.

JOHN CLARK & DAVID GERSTEIN

Byron Erickson

BORN IN TUCSON, ARIZONA on February 3, 1951, Byron Erickson grew up reading far too many comic books, the best of which were the great American Disney comics of the 1950s. "It may be heresy to say so today," he comments, "but my favorite feature in *Walt Disney's Comics and Stories* was the continued Mickey Mouse adventures by Carl Fallberg and Paul Murry, not the classic Carl Barks Donald Duck ten-pagers."

After collecting more than 30,000 comic books, Erickson decided it was time to actually earn some money from that wasted youth. He accepted a job with Another Rainbow Publishing in 1983 to work on *The Carl Barks Library*, a compendium of all of Barks' Disney comics.

Another Rainbow was a small company founded and staffed by fans, and as it grew, Erickson's opportunities grew. As he puts it, "When Another Rainbow got a photostat camera, publisher Bruce Hamilton asked if anyone on the staff wanted to learn to run it. I said I would. Then a complex typesetting machine came along; I said I would learn that, too. Ditto negotiations and relations with printers and distributors. Finally, Another Rainbow got a license to publish the Disney comics in the United States under the Gladstone imprint, and when Bruce asked who wanted to be the editor, my hand went up."

Over the next three years, Erickson discovered and encouraged Don Rosa and William Van Horn, the first work of whom appeared in Gladstone comics. Erickson also printed high-quality Danish and Dutch productions for the first time in the United States.

In 1990, Disney decided to publish its own American comic books in-house, leading to Erickson's departure from Gladstone. The license would return to Gladstone in 1993, but long before that, Erickson had moved on to Chicago. There he worked at First Publishing as one of the editors of a diverse line of comics that included superheroes, action-adventure, manga, a new *Classics Illustrated* series, Eric Shanower's Oz graphic novels, and *Betty Boop's Big Break*.

Still, Erickson missed the Disney characters. So when Don Rosa prompted Nancy Dejgaard, the Editor-in-Chief of Gutenberghus Publishing Service (now called Story House Egmont), to offer Erickson a job in early 1991, Erickson accepted and moved to Denmark. He worked at Egmont for more than 25 years: first as Managing Editor, then Editor-in-Chief, then as Creative Director.

Beyond *World of the Dragonlords*, Erickson's legacy includes editing Don Rosa's *Life and Times of Scrooge McDuck*, scripting dozens of classic-style Mickey Mouse adventures, bringing Disney master Romano Scarpa to Egmont, and supervising hundreds of Duck and Mickey tales with as much wit and energy as Donald, Mickey, and Scrooge themselves. ₩

ABOVE: Byron Erickson (right) with another celebrated Italian Disney artist: Romano Scarpa, whose work Erickson edited later in his career. Photo courtesy Byron Erickson.

Giorgio Cavazzano

FRANCESCO STAJANO

UNQUESTIONABLY THE MOST innovative and dynamic of all the Italian Disney artists, Giorgio Cavazzano began his precocious Disney career as an adolescent. Although Cavazzano has written a few scripts himself, he is above all an outstanding graphic artist.

Born in Venice in 1947, Cavazzano was only 12 years old when he began inking the pencil art of his cartoonist cousin, Luciano Capitanio. Cavazzano's first Disney ink work came when he began several years' apprenticeship under the great Romano Scarpa. In time, he asked his master to let him have a go at the pencils. The first story Cavazzano both penciled and inked was "Donald Duck and the Sledgehammer Hiccups" (*Topolino* 611, 1967), scripted by Osvaldo Pavese. Cavazzano's creative curiosity got him interested early on in such great non-Disney artists as Albert Uderzo (*Asterix*), Andre Franquin (*Spirou, Gomer Goof*), and Benito Jacovitti (*Cocco Bill*)—all at the time unknown to his colleagues at Disney licensee Mondadori.

The 1970s saw the innovative Cavazzano experimenting with a vibrant new graphic style, in which the rubbery quality of traditional Disney characters merged with realistic rendering of machinery and hi-tech gadgets. Cavazzano's best stories from this "techno" phase, mostly written by the gifted Giorgio Pezzin, stood out so obviously from the rest that even very occasional readers recognized and appreciated his work at once. *Topolino* readers of the time fondly remember the submarine of "The Great Weight of Glory" (*Topolino* 1007, 1975) and the "Bristol Beaufighter" plane of "The Forgetful Hero" (*Topolino* 1059,

1976; American printing in Fantagraphics' *Disney Masters* 12). Cavazzano's subject matter alone shows that he had ventured far from Disney tradition; anyone of lesser talent might have strayed off course in so doing. But, as noted by comics scholar Tiziano Sclavi, "Over the years, Giorgio managed to be Cavazzano and Disney at once. Before him, this had only been achieved by people like Carl Barks."

Cavazzano's influence on other Disney artists has been enormous. Taken as an ideal of perfection by many—if not most—modern Italian Disney artists, Cavazzano was also inspirational to the evolution of his great contemporary Massimo De Vita: renowned, among other milestones, for his defining Duck Avenger and Arizona Goof stories and "The Ice Sword Saga" miniseries (see *Disney Masters* 9 and 11).

Over the course of his career, Cavazzanno has created an amazing array of comics characters outside the Disney universe, among them *Walkie & Talkie* (1974), *Oscar e Tango* (1974), *Altai & Jonson* (1975), *Smalto & Jonny* (1976), *Slim Norton* (1977), *I due colonnelli* (1977), *Silas Finn* (1979), *Capitan Rogers* (1981), *Big Bazoom* (1983), *Timothée Titan* (1987), and *Jungle Bungle* (1991), not to mention his work in advertising.

Cavazzano has also been the recipient of many comics awards. ⚥

ABOVE: A recent photo of Giorgio Cavazzano. Image courtesy The Walt Disney Company Italia.

LUCA BOSCHI

A Three-Year Dragon Quest: Giorgio Cavazzano Interviewed

A GENERATION HAS PASSED since Giorgio Cavazzano turned in the final pages of one of his most demanding and time-consuming works: *World of the Dragonlords*. Between interruptions and revisions, those detailed pages required three years of intense labor, however much readers appreciated the results.

Two decades later—over which time thousands of additional drawings have erupted from the Venetian cartoonist's volcanic mind and talented hand—we sit down with Cavazzano to take stock of this complex, 12-chapter fantasy epic.

***World of the Dragonlords* marked your second collaboration with Byron Erickson. The first was a story with Uncle Scrooge and Brigitta MacBridge set on the slopes of the Andes, "The Secret of the Incas" (*Uncle Scrooge Adventures* 53-54, 1997).**
That's right. It was a great adventure story, but still a traditional one. The more ambitious "Dragonlords" required a far greater commitment from the start. Once the plotline was decided, it still took me some time to comprehend the psychological aspects of the tale, and to find the visual inspiration I needed to help define the atmosphere of Morgworld. It wasn't easy; I wanted to study recent fantasy films, but I couldn't watch Peter Jackson's *Lord of the Rings* trilogy, as this was 1999 and it wouldn't start to be released until 2001.

What kind of script did Byron send you? Did he make a scribble-script with rough sketches to indicate staging?
No, I received no visual suggestions; the script was typed, told panel-by-panel, like "Secret of the Incas" before it. The plan to produce "Incas," by the way, had been hatched at the Bologna Children's Book Fair, where I first met Byron at the booth of Egmont, the Danish publishing house for which he worked.

Our Uncle Scrooge and Brigitta team-up turned out a happy experience, so in 1999, Byron came to visit me at my home in Venice. He had in mind his proposal for the *Dragonlords* fantasy saga, which he called "the dream of my life."

In a lull midway through the making of the saga, you drew the non-Disney comics *La città* and *Maledetta Galassia* for the publisher Sergio Bonelli Editore, both based on scripts by Franco "Bonvi" Bonvicini (*Sturmtruppen*). In one of those stories, there's a character who

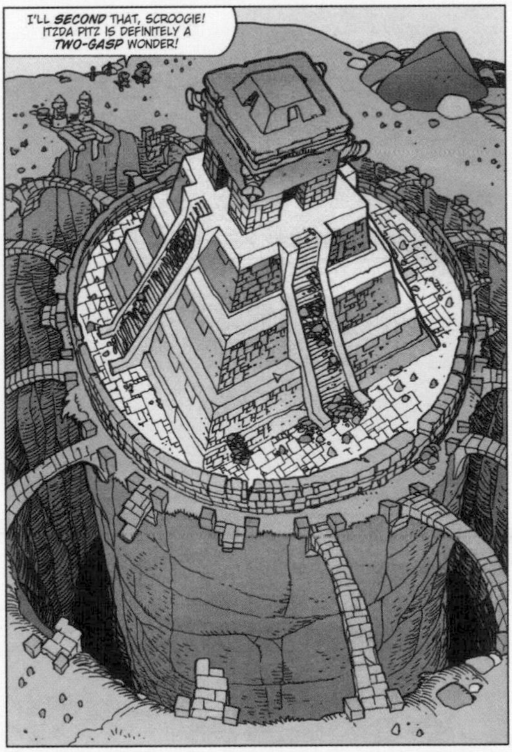
I'LL SECOND THAT, SCROOGIE! ITZDA PITZ IS DEFINITELY A TWO-GASP WONDER!

Scrooge and Brigitta MacBridge discover the lost city of Itzda Pitz in Erickson's and Cavazzano's first team-up, "Secret of the Incas" (*Uncle Scrooge Adventures* 53, 1997).

SNIFF!

looks a lot like Rasmus from *Dragonlords*, because both were inspired by your flesh-and-blood friend and colleague—

Yes! The character of Rasmus, kindly servant to the "bad guy" Clarg of the Morg, is a double for [longtime Italian Disney comics writer] Carlo Chendi, whom I also used as the model for a hobo in one of Bonvi's stories. I wanted to pay homage to a dear friend—as kind and caring as Rasmus himself—whom I have always considered a "second father" to the cartoonists of our generation.

In our Foreword, Byron Erickson writes that the *Dragonlords* saga was initially created to boost the sales of the German weekly *Micky Maus*, which was then going through a difficult period. By featuring a long, serialized adventure, the publisher hoped to bring loyal readers back very week to see the latest turns of events...

That must have been one of the first reasons for the saga's creation; but above all, Byron wanted to put to paper a story that he *cared* a lot about. He told me that this was why he wanted me to draw it; and he certainly didn't cut corners in constructing it! There were complex and challenging scenes on every page, and visualizing them kept me busy for months and months.

Dragonlords features an unusual amount of drama!

Without a doubt, the story pushes sentiment to the fore. The drama would have been even greater if, at a certain point, I hadn't revised a sequence that, in Byron's first draft, I considered too tragic: the death of the little dragon Sniffles. The kindest, the weakest...

I didn't think it was right. So I wrote to Byron: "Maybe he could be injured in such a way that he *looks* dead, but then let's have the nephews nurse him back to health. That would be ideal." Happily, Byron realized that his intent—to tug at readers' heartstrings—could be achieved less drastically.

From a graphic point of view, one notices that you tried to develop a consistent look for the story's many characters—including the newly-created human ones, who are stylistically as close as possible to the Disney Ducks.

One had to sense immediately that they all belong in the same story, even if they come from different worlds. So the humans had to share the Ducks' rounded and caricatured construction style. This is how I would always prefer to see human characters drawn in Duck stories; some of my colleagues tend to make them too "human"!

At first, when we were developing the new characters, I imagined them looking a little more realistic. In particular, I gave the heroic Brendon a mustache a la Albert Uderzo (*Asterix*), inspired by the Nordic warrior tradition. But Byron wanted Brendon younger,

Cavazzano's first color design for Brendon dates from an early period in which he still possessed a mustache and beard. Image courtesy The Walt Disney Company Italia.

without the facial hair. And Byron was right: my original Brendon looked too different from the other characters in the adventure.

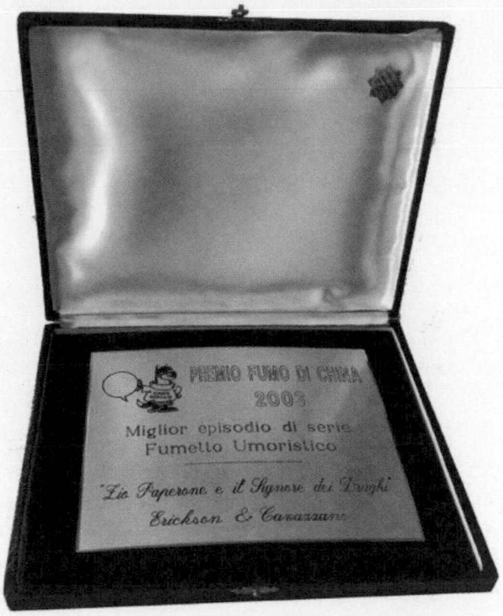
PREMIO FUMO DI CHINA
2003
Miglior episodio di serie
Fumetto Umoristico
Erickson and Cavazzano won the prestigious *Fumo di China* award—an annual prize given out by the eponymous Italian comics industry magazine—for *World of the Dragonlords* in 2003. Photo courtesy Byron Erickson.

As executed, Brendon looks like he might belong in *Thorgal*, the Viking comic by Grzegorz Rosinski, or in Hermann Huppen's series *The Towers of Bois-Maury*.
Huppen has indeed inspired some of my staging in the past, and the settings of a few *Dragonlords* sequences were also influenced by his works. Huppen is a "director" who has a lot to teach.

In the past, you've also cited Simon Bisley (*Heavy Metal*) as an inspiration...
Only a little: the power of Bisley's art inspired the fierce look of the dragons in the story-logo that opens each chapter. Of course, Bisley's graphic style is very different, much cruder than what you might think of using in a Disney comic.

The three fire-breathing dragons, Smoky, Spitfire, and Sniffles, are different from all previous Disney dragons—from *The Reluctant Dragon* (1941) to Maleficent's dragon form in *Sleeping Beauty* (1959).
It's true. Byron described fierce-looking, but still Disney-style dragons. I had to choose a middle ground between good-natured and more aggressive characters.

Oh! I forgot! Besides Carlo Chendi, the story also includes a caricature of *another* person who really exists.

To whom are you referring?
To a Swiss friend of mine who, by fate, was with us the day Byron came to visit me in Venice. He's the manager of a large computer company for which I'd drawn a book of humor cartoons at the turn of the century: *Year 2000 – Millennium Gags*. When Byron told me about a very kindly human character, to be introduced right at the start in Chapter 1, we thought he might have the features of this friend of mine. Byron even gave him his real name, Hintermann, which in German means "the man behind." It fit him perfectly.

Though *World of the Dragonlords* isn't a typical Duck story, it *does* feel a little like an extended-length Junior Woodchuck plot, even if Huey, Dewey, and Louie don't appear as Woodchucks.
It's an atypical story, isn't it? We don't usually see Uncle Scrooge acting like a con artist—but here he does. Donald is often relegated to the sidelines... Huey, Dewey, and Louie and the new characters emerge front and center.

There isn't a lot of comedy in the story; I added a gag at the end, when the Morg called Groob, instead of returning to his dimension, stays in the Ducks' world and makes ends meet as an actor.

In conclusion, are you satisfied with this effort of yours?
Yes, because I hope the strong commitment I put into it will show in the pages. Though some sequences were difficult to visualize, at the end of the day they were the most rewarding.

Do you think that you and Byron will collaborate again, even after the long break since *Dragonlords*?
In a letter, Byron once wrote to me that he hoped so, and so do I.

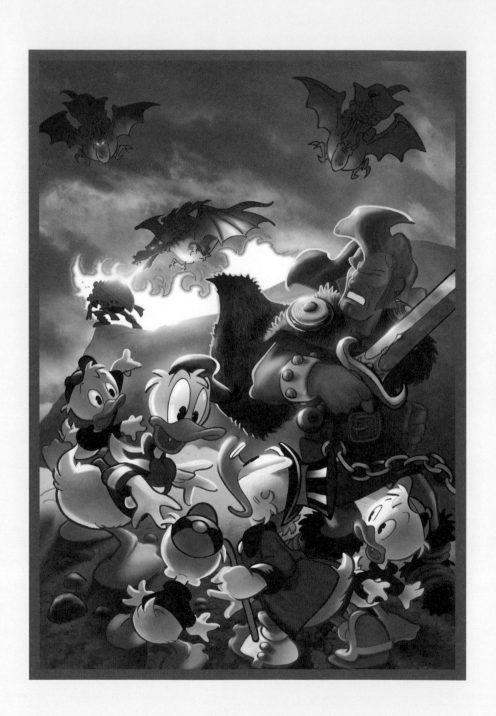